Transforming America

Transforming America

Barack Obama in the White House

Edited by
Steven E. Schier

ROWMAN & LITTLEFIELD PUBLISHERS, INC.
Lanham • Boulder • New York • Toronto • Plymouth, UK

Published by Rowman & Littlefield Publishers, Inc.
A wholly owned subsidiary of The Rowman & Littlefield Publishing Group, Inc.
4501 Forbes Boulevard, Suite 200, Lanham, Maryland 20706
http://www.rowmanlittlefield.com

Estover Road, Plymouth PL6 7PY, United Kingdom

British Library Cataloguing in Publication Information Available

Library of Congress Cataloging-in-Publication Data

Transforming America : Barack Obama in the White House / edited by Steven E. Schier.
   p. cm.
   Includes bibliographical references and index.
   ISBN 978-1-4422-0178-1 (cloth : alk. paper) — ISBN 978-1-4422-0179-8 (pbk. : alk. paper) — ISBN 978-1-4422-0180-4 (electronic)
   1. United States—Politics and government—2009– 2. Obama, Barack. I. Schier, Steven E.
   E907.T73 2011
   973.932092—dc22

2011013336

∞™ The paper used in this publication meets the minimum requirements of American National Standard for Information Sciences—Permanence of Paper for Printed Library Materials, ANSI/NISO Z39.48-1992.

Printed in the United States of America

To
Steven Poskanzer
President, Carleton College

Contents

Introduction

Obama's "Big Bang" Presidency

Steven E. Schier

In his 2010 State of the Union address, Barack Obama made clear the magnitude of his presidential ambitions: "From the day I took office, I've been told that addressing our larger challenges is too ambitious; such an effort would be too contentious. I've been told that our political system is too gridlocked, and that we should just put things on hold for a while. For those who make these claims, I have one simple question: How long should we wait? How long should America put its future on hold?" Obama's answer, fully evident in his approach to governance, was "no longer."

Many presidents initially enter office with grand ambitions, but no recent president has matched the scale of Obama's transformative plans. Domestically, they included a government restructuring of a health-care system comprising one-sixth of the nation's economy, the largest public investment program for economic stimulus in America's history, a far-reaching cap-and-trade system of emissions controls to combat climate change, a thorough reshaping of governmental regulation of the financial sector, comprehensive immigration reform, revoking the "Don't Ask, Don't Tell" policy for gays in the military, and a major revamping of the federal financial role in education policy. In foreign policy, Obama promised to "reset" America's relations with many nations and regions of the world. He favored greater accommodation with Russia and Europe, a new overture of friendship with the Muslim world, a stronger focus on nuclear proliferation, and a successful resolution of America's military involvement in Iraq and Afghanistan.

Obama's ambitions inevitably made him a highly polarizing figure for Americans, just as his predecessor George W. Bush, also a person of grand ambitions, had been. Like Bush, Obama led by acting as a national "clarifier" of differences between him and his partisan opponents. John F. Harris's description of Bush's leadership style fits Obama rather well: "rather than

1

blurring lines, illuminate and even exaggerate them. Rather than try to reassure opponents, antagonize them—at least on issues in which he believed he could excite his own supporters in even greater measure" (Harris 2009, 67–68).

A DIRECTIVE PRESIDENCY

This "clarifying" style is a characteristic of a "directive" presidency, defined by political scientists George C. Edwards III and Stephen Wayne: ". . . the president is the director of change, who creates opportunities to move in new directions and leads others where they otherwise would not go. In this view, the president is out front, establishing goals and encouraging others inside and outside of government to follow. Accordingly, the president is the moving force of the system and the initiator of change" (Edwards and Wayne 2009, 19). This approach, again similar to that of his immediate predecessor, holds the possibility of big changes, which Barack Obama has ardently pursued in the White House, but also entails large political risks.

A safer course, according to Edwards and Wayne, is for a president to act as a "facilitator" who builds coalitions, "exploiting opportunities to help others go where they want to go anyway or at least do not object to going" (2009, 20). Bill Clinton, who hugged the political center during much of his presidency and worked productively with Republican Congresses, was the archetypal facilitator, willing to settle for limited policy changes. A facilitator settles for narrower influence, but Obama, given his large Democratic majorities in Congress in 2009, had bigger goals in mind. No "small ball" for Obama. Nicol C. Rae argues in his chapter that Obama sought a political "reconstruction" that would create a lasting Democratic regime in the same fashion that Ronald Reagan revived GOP fortunes in the 1980s.

What led Obama to pursue a directive, clarifying presidency? The sweeping Democratic electoral victories in 2008 no doubt emboldened him, but certain personal qualities also fueled his big ambitions. Obama's public career consistently involved advocacy of strongly liberal principles, an approach that he carried with him into the White House. By 2010, the American public identified him as clearly on the left of the political spectrum. One 2010 survey by the Democracy Corps, a Democratic polling firm, found that 55 percent of registered voters thought the term "socialist" accurately described his ideological orientation (Greenberg Quinlan Rosner Research 2010).

Given his confident possession of liberal ideological convictions, a directive, clarifying leadership in their pursuit followed. Obama's academic background had given him a critical, analytic temperament, contributing to a policymaking style in which he worked from his ideological principles to a policy proposal. As journalist Jonathan Alter put it in his book on the Obama White House, "Obama was a deductive thinker with a vertical mind. He thought deeply about a subject, organized it lucidly into point-by-point arguments for a set of policies or a speech and then said, here are my principles and here are some suggestions for fleshing out the details" (Alter 2010, 212).

Obama's management style also encouraged dogged pursuit of his principle-based priorities. Obama's approach contrasted with that of Democratic predecessor Bill Clinton, whose more "horizontal" thinking contemplated a wide range of principles and alternatives and whose White House organization at times suffered from consequent disorganization. Barack Obama would have none of that. Early on in his presidency, he opted for a hierarchical White House organization with a strong chief of staff, a format usually favored by GOP presidents and by his predecessor George W. Bush. This style of organization facilitated the persistent pursuit of the president's goals.

BIG CHANGES

Working with a kindred congressional leadership and large Democratic majorities in Congress in 2009 and 2010, Obama's directive, clarifying leadership racked up a remarkable number of policy accomplishments during the early months of his presidency. PolitiFact.com, the award-winning research site of the *St. Petersburg Times*, charted Obama's success with 505 campaign promises. During his presidency's first 18 months, the president had only broken 3 of them, while keeping 119 and compromising on 35, with 245 "in the works" and only 45 stalled (PolitiFact 2010). Among those promises kept were major changes in public policy: the first comprehensive health-care reform since 1965, the largest public investment program ever, sweeping reform of financial regulation, a new federal "hate crimes" law, and a nuclear arms reduction pact with Russia.

The two landmark laws, discussed by several authors in this volume, were the health-care reform and the 2009 economic stimulus. On February 17, 2009, in his first month in office, Obama signed the American Recovery and Reinvestment Act of 2009, a $787 billion assemblage of spending increases and tax cuts designed to boost economic growth. Approximately 90 percent of its cost involved spending hikes in a wide variety of programs. Most notably among these were grants to state governments for their budget needs, temporary increases in Medicaid, emergency energy assistance and food stamp spending for low-income Americans, and the extension of unemployment insurance and highway and school construction (*Washington Post* 2009). The economy remained sluggish throughout 2009 and 2010, however, with unemployment rising from 7.7 percent in January 2009 to well above 9 percent by early 2011. Furious debate erupted about the effectiveness of the 2009 stimulus legislation (Biden 2009; Levy 2010). This prompted the administration to reach a bipartisan compromise with resurgent congressional Republicans in late 2010. The initiative included a two-year extension of personal income tax and estate (inheritance) tax cuts passed during the George W. Bush presidency, a 2 percent cut in Social Security taxes, a thirteen-month extension of unemployment benefits, and other tax cuts and spending measures. Like the 2009 stimulus, the plan involved more spending increases than tax cuts. Tax cuts constituted a little over a third of the total cost of the 2010 stimulus bill (Curry 2010). In April 2011, Obama also negotiated a bipartisan agreement to fund the government through September of that year.

On March 23, 2010, Obama signed into law the Patient Protection and Affordable Care Act, and later that month signed companion legislation, the Health Care and Education Reconciliation Act. Together they comprise the most sweeping change in health policy since the passage of Medicare in 1965. The legislation takes effect over a four-year period. It prohibits private insurers from denying coverage due to preexisting conditions, subsidizes insurance premiums, supports medical research, and expands eligibility for federal health care for low-income individuals through the Medicaid program. It also establishes health-insurance exchanges to facilitate more choice among insurance plans by consumers. The large cost of the program was offset by taxes on certain medical devices and a $500 billion cut in the Medicare Advantage, an optional program for higher-income seniors (Grier 2010). The administration argued it will reduce federal health-care spending, but opponents believe the expanded coverage will eventually bust the federal budget (Orszag 2010; Nix 2010). Richard E. Matland and Andrea L. Walker examine this big change in their chapter.

The 2009 stimulus and 2010 health-care laws were the product of a successful "elite governing strategy" employed by the president in the administration's first two years. Obama pursued his policy principles with fellow partisan power-holders, without much consideration for the popular politics of his actions (Alter 2010, 330). John J. Coleman notes in his chapter how Obama's initial approach relied on his congressional party as a resource for presidential leadership. Major domestic initiatives involved working with a heavily Democratic Congress to build partisan coalitions to pass the president's program. As Bertram Johnson puts it here, Obama played "small ball for the long game," cutting many particular deals to ensure passage of major legislation with long-lasting impact. Given the controversial and sweeping nature of Obama's main proposals, elite coalition building proved difficult, particularly regarding the health-care reform. Obama could usually rely on the House to take the initiative and help encourage the balkier Senate to pass similar legislation. This approach resembled that of the George W. Bush administration when it worked with a GOP-majority Congress from 2001 through 2006 (Johnson 2004). For the remainder of his first term, however, Obama's governing strategy may shift with the arrival of a Republican-controlled House and a more Republican Senate. A hint of a revised strategy—more facilitative and less directive than before—arrived with bipartisan budget agreements in December 2010 and April 2011.

The president was unable to extricate himself from the "rutted paths"—James L. Guth's phrase in his chapter—of other long-lasting policy controversies. On "culture war" issues such as abortion, gay rights, and the role of religion in public life, Obama held to culturally liberal positions but adopted a conciliatory tone toward conservatives. Despite this, the divisions persisted. Obama's successful 2010 repeal of the "Don't Ask, Don't Tell" policy concerning gays in the military received strong criticism from cultural conservatives. A similar split persisted regarding his federal court nominees. In her chapter, Nancy Maveety notes how Obama reinforced the partisan and ideological conflicts over the judiciary in his nominations. Liberals complained that his choices for the federal bench were not sufficiently activist while conservatives derided their approach to Constitutional interpretation. The culture and judicial wars showed no sign of receding.

Internationally, Obama sought to redirect American foreign policy. Obama's international outreach resulted in a warming of international opinion toward the United States and his receipt of the Nobel Peace Prize after only six months in office. He forged several diplomatic agreements with Russia in order to "reset" relations with that nation, most notably a new Strategic Arms Limitation Treaty. His war stewardship in Iraq and Afghanistan, however, varied little from the "surge" strategy pioneered by his predecessor, George W. Bush. In 2011, intervention in the Libyan civil war under NATO auspices and the death of Osama bin Laden represented a more aggressive international approach. Because of the many international challenges confronting the administration, Obama's foreign policy results were modest during his administration's early years, as James McCormick explains in his chapter.

PROBLEMS WITH THE PUBLIC

The key risk for a directive president lies in taking people "where they otherwise would not want to go." Obama's declining job approval resulted from public resistance to many aspects of Obama's policy leadership. Opinion polls in 2010 revealed public disapproval of many of his policy initiatives: the health-care reform, financial reform, Afghan war stewardship, and, most importantly, economic management (Pew Research Center 2010a; McCormick and Dodge 2010). Pursuit of an elite governing agenda without careful cultivation of mass support inevitably produces political problems for a president. During Obama's first two years in office, his job approval steadily declined as first Republicans and then political independents took exception to the major policy changes. This culminated in historically large Republican gains in the 2010 midterm elections.

The unprecedentedly mammoth deficits—totaling over $1 trillion a year for the first two years of his presidency and producing the largest ever peacetime increase in the national debt to Gross National Product ratio—received popular disapproval. The health-care reform, supported only by a minority of Americans at the time of its passage, has yet to garner majority support in the polls. The public also received the 2010 financial reform coolly (Associated Press 2010). Sixty-two percent of Americans believed by 2010 that the record $787 billion economic stimulus had been a failure (Pew Research Center 2010b).

What prompted this rapid rise in public disaffection? Many Obama supporters contended "it's the economy, stupid" that produced Obama's declining public approval (for example, see Krugman 2010a). Short-term outcomes of the administration's economic policies were important causes. As Raymond Tatalovich details in his chapter, economic growth remained sluggish. Unemployment, which Obama promised would not rise above 8 percent due to his stimulus spending, instead rose to 10 percent and then hovered above 9 percent through 2010. Many political science models have found that economic conditions strongly affect presidential job approval (for a summary, see Gronke and Newman 2000).

One can point to other contributing factors. As mentioned previously, many in the public came to view Obama as liberal in his political orientation, which inhibited his public support. This was evident in a series of Gallup polls. By late 2009, 54 percent of the public termed Obama's policies "mostly liberal" (Saad 2009). By the summer of 2010, 48 percent termed the Democratic Party "too liberal" (Saad 2010). The number of self-identified conservatives in the electorate had risen to 40 percent by mid-2010, the highest in six years, while the percentage identifying as liberal stood at 21 percent (Jones 2010). A big ideological distance from much of the public is seldom helpful to presidents. John J. Pitney Jr. notes here how it spawned a diffuse but effective grassroots opposition in the Tea Party movement of activists pressing for smaller government. Their enthusiastic activism helped propel the GOP to victory in the 2010 elections.

The sweeping Obama agenda proved difficult to explain to the public, and the president, focused on conceptualizing policy and pursuing his elite governing strategy, did not defend or explain his agenda well. As the president admitted to *ABC News* in 2010: "In this political environment, what I haven't always been successful at doing is breaking through the noise and speaking directly to the American people in a way that during the campaign you could do." One cost of an expansive agenda is its very complexity, which makes public comprehension difficult. The initial Obama agenda included increased deficit spending first, with a promise of later deficit reduction; an expansive stimulus, to produce both green jobs and economic recovery; sweeping financial reform; comprehensive immigration reform; cap-and-trade environmental legislation; and health-care reform, both to reduce health-care spending and to simultaneously broaden coverage.

It was not obvious how all these pieces related to each other or added up. Can health-care coverage expand while costs go down? Can the government encourage green jobs while reducing the deficit? Can increased regulation of carbon emissions coexist with an economic recovery? Even administration allies saw some contradictions in Obama's approach. Simon Rosenthal of the New Democratic Network "saw immediately that Obama's recipe for long-term economic growth by cutting health care costs and moving off foreign oil, though commendable, was at odds with the . . . recovery . . . that featured rising real estate prices and robust consumer sales. Reform, in that sense, was at odds with recovery" (Alter 2010, 270). By 2010, some economists argued that the many financial uncertainties for business resulting from the sweeping health-care and financial reforms had slowed investment and hiring and largely stalled economic recovery (Davis, Becker, and Murphy 2010; Seltzer 2010). Obama, however, argued that recovery and reform were simultaneously possible. The public was not reassured.

Shortly before the 2010 elections, Obama adviser David Axelrod spoke forebodingly about their likely outcome: "We have [Democrats] in office now whose elections were completely improbable. They got dragged in by a high tide. Now the tide is going out. I think structurally we're set up for a difficult election" (Wolffe 2010, 274). So it proved. The American electorate voiced their concerns over policy and the economy with a large GOP victory. Republicans took control of the House by winning 242 seats, a gain of 63—the largest for the opposition party, as John K. White notes in his chapter here—since the 1938 elections. Republicans won six Senate seats, reducing the Democratic majority in that chamber from 59 to 53. Pre-2008 divisions in the electorate reappeared to the GOP's advantage.

Are the 2010 elections a harbinger of America's electoral future? Authors here offer contrasting views about that. John K. White argues that demographic change favors long-term dominance by Obama's coalition of racial minorities and younger voters. Nicol C. Rae is less sure of this, pointing to Democrats' waning support with white voters, the poor economy, and the decline of the party's vote in many areas of the nation. These short-term trends may prove problematic for Obama's likely 2012 reelection campaign. John F. Harris and James Hohmann, like Rae, believe Obama at midterm faces important political difficulties. Perhaps, they argue, some lessons from Bill Clinton's more facilitative presidential style will prove helpful to the embattled president.

OBAMA AND THE DEMOCRATIC PARTY

American political parties have changed greatly over the last one hundred years. Formerly, they were pragmatic organizations including far-flung coalitions of disparate elements requiring issue compromises for their internal maintenance. At the turn of the twentieth century, parties also were "the primary connection between the average citizen and government" (Burbank, Hrebnar, and Benedict 2008, 20). Now, parties are just one of many players in our "candidate-centered politics," alongside interest groups, political action committees, and the campaign organizations of candidates themselves. The social ingredients of parties are different now, as well. As political scientist Morris Fiorina puts it, "Rather than broad coalitions deeply rooted in the American social structure, today's parties are coalitions of minorities who seek to impose their views on the broader public" (Fiorina 2009, 98).

Barack Obama's political career was shaped by these circumstances. His 2008 campaign, an impressive financial and grassroots exercise, was strongly candidate-centered. His consistent liberalism fit the ideological mainstream of his party activists. The Obama presidency has demonstrated greater fealty to liberalism's agenda, particularly in domestic policy, than any president since Lyndon Johnson. Yet Obama has not devoted attention to party building that might entrench his partisan regime as a dominant force in American politics.

The opportunity was there in early 2009. He ended his presidential campaign with a list of two million active volunteers and almost four million small donors, the makings of a grassroots partisan army geared to organize and agitate for liberal causes. But the White House balked at such a suggestion, instead creating an organization called "Organizing for America" (OFA) as a project of the Democratic Party. OFA was slow to organize, and then confined itself to community projects and occasional grassroots exercises in support of the administration's legislation, such as rallies and house parties.

The tepid pace of the organization drew criticism from veteran Democratic organizers Peter Dreier and Marshall Ganz: "Once in office, the president moved quickly, announcing one ambitious legislative objective after another. But instead of launching a parallel strategy to mobilize supporters, most progressive organizations and Organizing for America—the group created to organize Obama's former campaign volunteers—failed to keep up" (Dreier and Ganz 2009). The Obama administration limited Organizing for America to a grassroots-lobbying adjunct of marginal utility, instead of employing it to energize new partisan commitments. The president "failed to do what Reagan and Eisenhower did: he asked his supporters to rally around Democratic causes, but he has balked at asking them to become Democrats. He has asked his loyal enthusiasts to take ownership of a presidency, but not of a party" (Homans 2010).

Obama's approach to his party fits his times in some ways. The president has dutifully raised funds for his party and touted fellow Democratic candidates, as did his predecessors. Sticking to that traditional role means not devoting much effort to partisan regime building, as his predecessor George W. Bush and Karl Rove did to a much greater extent, but instead encouraging his grassroots arm to further his specific policy plans. Those plans during the administration's first two years were ideologically liberal, substantively in tune with the president's activist base. But Obama's party leadership ultimately serves the president's specific goals rather than aiming to reshape partisan allegiances in a lasting way. Obama's presidency, both directive and clarifying, is also a politically personal project.

Criticism from the president's activist base intensified in the wake of 2010 election reversals as critics accused the White House of poor "messaging" during the campaign (for example, see Rich 2010). Liberals also objected to the president's demonstrated willingness to abandon his directive approach by agreeing to a bipartisan compromise on tax cuts and spending increases (Walsh 2010, Krugman 2010b). Before the plan passed, the caucus of House Democrats voted against supporting it. Problems of party building, combined with increasing disaffection among his base, promised to complicate Obama's reelection efforts.

OBAMA AND THE INSTITUTIONAL PRESIDENCY

In recent decades, presidents have expanded their ability to act unilaterally to achieve their results. Recent presidents have found increased executive powers to their liking. This trend grows from long-standing presidential management and appointment powers and, more controversially, presidential use of several unilateral tools. One such tool is the use of the executive order, a legally binding document setting policy. To be constitutional, these orders must present an argument that the order derives from a congressional law. Given the broad language of many laws, this gives presidents a wide range of discretion. In recent decades, presidents have increasingly used these orders to impose their will—George W. Bush issued 290 and Bill Clinton issued 363 executive orders. As of May 2011, Barack Obama had issued 80 (Archives. gov 2011).

Given his directive approach to the presidency, Barack Obama issued a flurry of executive orders upon taking office. The purpose of many of them was to reverse politics of the previous Bush presidency. By March 2009, Obama had issued orders reversing Bush policies on the use of terrorist inter-rogation techniques, regarding union organizing, on access to the documents of former presidents, and concerning US governmental support for interna-tional family-planning organizations. His early executive order requiring the closing of the Guantanamo Bay detention facility by the end of 2009 eventu-ally was postponed indefinitely as problems with transferring the prisoners arose. An executive order proved vital to the passage of his landmark health-care reform legislation. In order to secure the support of a crucial bloc of anti-abortion Democrats, Obama issued an executive order "to ensure that Federal funds are not used for abortion services (except in cases of rape or incest, or when the life of the woman would be endangered)" (Executive Order 13535 2010, 1). Executive orders can be overturned at any time by a current presi-dent, causing anti-abortion groups to decry the order as inadequate protection for their cause. Obama's agreement to issue the order propelled the bill to passage in the House.

A more controversial tool of unilateral executive power is the signing statement, a public document issued by the White House when a president signs the bill. Traditionally, signing statements have been hortatory, but re-cent presidents, particularly George W. Bush, used them to impart extensive instructions to executive officials about how to interpret and implement new laws. Bush in signing statements challenged nearly twelve hundred provi-sions of bills over eight years, twice the number challenged by all of his White House predecessors. Most notably, Bush asserted that he could autho-rize officials to bypass a torture ban and oversight provisions of the antiter-rorist USA Patriot Act (Savage 2009). As a candidate, Obama voiced strong criticism of Bush's approach, asserting, "It is a clear abuse of power to use such statements as a license to evade laws that the president does not like or an end-run around provisions to foster accountability. I will not use signing statement to nullify or undermine congressional instructions as enacted into law" (Savage 2007).

But in 2009, Democrats and Republicans in Congress accused Obama of just that. In a March signing statement, he declared five provisions of a budget bill to be unconstitutional and non-binding, including one restricting US troop deployment under UN command overseas and another aimed at halting punishment of bureaucratic whistleblowers (Weisman 2009). In June, he issued a statement regarding a spending bill declaring that he would not comply with a spending bill putting conditions on aid to the World Bank and International Monetary Fund (Associated Press 2009). This prompted a bipartisan uproar in Congress, causing four senior House Democrats to draft a letter to the president expressing their disapproval: "During the previous administration, all of us were critical of the president's assertion that he could pick and choose which aspects of congressional statutes he was required to enforce. We were therefore chagrined to see you appear to express a similar attitude" (Savage 2009).

In the wake of the controversy, Obama stopped issuing signing statements. In early 2010, the administration revealed that the president would sign bills containing problematic provisions without issuing signing statements, but the administration would still disregard laws it found to be unconstitutional. This raised obvious questions of accountability. Democratic Representative Barney Frank objected: "Anyone who makes the argument that 'once we have told you we have constitutional concerns and then you pass it anyway, that justifies us ignoring it'—that is a constitutional violation" (Savage 2010). Jack Goldsmith, a Bush administration Justice Department official, argued, "It's a bad development if they are not going to highlight for the nation in all these new statutes where they think there are problems" (Savage 2010). The White House, however, claimed that its previous statements about problems in new laws would suffice as public notice in lieu of signing statements.

A third tool of unilateral power, the presidential memorandum, also can "specify how agencies should implement recently enacted laws" (Devins 2007). Like executive agreements and signing statements, memoranda must have some statutory basis but usually are narrower in scope and receive less public notice. This is because, unlike executive orders and signing statements, they do not have an established process for issuance of publication. During his first year, for example, Obama issued memoranda extending scientific reviews regarding possible endangered species, directing the secretary of transportation to formulate higher fuel-efficiency standards for cars and directing the secretary of energy to create new appliance-efficiency standards. In all, Barack Obama has found the use of unilateral powers more desirable than he did as a candidate. The tools of executive orders, signing statements, and presidential memoranda proved quite useful to his directive approach to the presidency.

Another important implement in a president's arsenal is presidential appointment. Federal law gives the chief executive the power to fill several thousand positions at the top levels of cabinet departments and federal agencies, boards, and commissions. By law, the Senate must approve 526 of these top-level appointments. Progress in securing appointments proved slow for the administration. Just over three hundred secured Senate confirmations during the administration's first twelve months. By January 2011, about one hundred positions remained open or unconfirmed (*Washington Post* 2011). The fractious politics of the highly partisan Senate combined with the administration's lengthy process for vetting appointees contributed to this slow pace. A similar slowdown beset Obama's judicial appointments, as detailed by Nancy Maveety in her chapter. By March 2010, Obama responded to the recalcitrant Senate by announcing fifteen people as his first-recess appointments. Federal law allows the president to make recess appointments—allowing those appointed when the Senate is in recess to serve until the end of the next Senate's term. Obama's fifteen thus could serve without Senate approval until the end of 2011. By the end of 2010, he had made twenty-eight recess appointments. Obama's predecessors had frequently employed recess appointments to circumvent Senate opposition. Bill Clinton made 95 such appointments and George W. Bush made 191 (Baker 2010).

Presidential management authority, granted through many federal laws, is another useful implement for chief executives. Obama's two immediate predecessors made management reform of the executive branch major initiatives of their presidencies. Both Bill Clinton's "Reinventing Government" initiative and George W. Bush's "President's Management Agenda" were announced with big plans and bold fanfare. Obama's management approach, though potentially far-reaching, has received much less public attention. Political scientist Donald Kettl described it as a "stealth revolution" with four main components. First, the administration increased usage of new media such as social networks to improve bureaucratic coordination and contact with citizens. Second, it created a group of "policy czars" in the White House—one each, for example, for auto-industry reorganization, banking reform, energy, environment, Afghanistan and the Middle East—to improve bureaucratic response in these areas. None of the "czars" is subject to Senate appointment, and they represent "a revolutionary-in-scale move to maneuver past the permanent bureaucracy" (Kettl 2009, 41). Third, the White House accepted the frustrations involved in accommodating congressional policy concerns, a challenge complicated by 2010 GOP gains on Capitol Hill. Fourth, it enhanced accountability by pushing out "enormous quantities of information about federal programs" and relying on interest groups and the public to digest the data, with information on the economic stimulus an initial example. For Kettl, this amounted to an overall strategy of "transparency and working organically from the bottom up. They want to test their ideas before they latch themselves to a loser" (Kettl 2009, 40).

The administration's experiments with czars and transparency constitute a departure from the management approaches of Obama's predecessors, who focused mainly on getting results without transforming executive bureaucratic operations. In contrast, the Obama approach is to try to shake up ongoing administrative processes with social networks, transparency, and czars in order to, perhaps, improve outcomes. The very complexity of "permanent Washington"—the networks of bureaucratic agencies, interest groups, and congressional committees who have their own, frequently consensual agendas that rival that of the president—makes enduring management transformations engineered by the White House a daunting task.

When a president's political clout is blunted both by the slow pace of appointments and by ongoing policy networks that predate a president and will persist after he loses office, presidents will seek ways to circumvent such impediments. Influence with the Washington establishment is hard for a president to maintain. So why not use unilateral powers like executive orders, signing statements, and memoranda? The risk, which I explore further in my conclusion, is that the exercise of unilateral powers courts political danger for a president and risks a lasting loss of political clout. George W. Bush encountered costly political opposition to his embrace of unilateral power in combating terrorism, drawing rebukes from the Supreme Court, Congress, and the public. Barack Obama must be on guard against similar risks should he succumb to the temptation to rely increasingly on unilateral powers because there are several similarities between his conduct of the presidency and that of his immediate successor.

BARACK AND GEORGE

Partisans on both sides of the fence will no doubt take offense at the suggestion that Barack Obama and George W. Bush have approached the presidency in similar ways. The two presidencies have vast policy differences, and Bush's agenda focused more on foreign policy, due to 9/11 and the Iraq war. Bush also had a more limited agenda, particularly concerning domestic issues, producing less domestic policy change than Obama but also less agenda congestion. Despite this, seven important similarities in governing approach characterize the two presidencies:

• First, "the decider," George W. Bush, also sought to direct national affairs from the White House, and this eventually resulted in his taking citizens where many of them "did not want to go"—into Iraq and toward private Social Security accounts, for example.

• Second, Bush's presidency also served to clarify political differences, inducing a political polarization that has grown even more pronounced during Obama's White House tenure.
• Third, Bush's governing style, like Obama's, was emphatically partisan as well, as he proceeded to pursue agenda specifics that usually met the approval only of fellow partisans.
• Fourth, particularly later in his presidency, Bush was willing to govern in defiance of popular opinion regarding the Iraq war, as Obama has done with health-care reform.
• Fifth, Obama has continued the Bush "surge" approach in both Iraq and Afghanistan, despite increasing public opposition to the Afghan policy.
• Sixth, Barack Obama has begun to employ several unilateral tools— executive orders, signing statements, and presidential memoranda—in ways practiced more extensively and controversially by George W. Bush.
• Seventh, Obama has continued several of the Bush administration's detention policies for suspected terrorists, most notably retaining the Guantanamo detention facility, to the chagrin of his liberal supporters.

Many of these similarities result from the political challenges presidents now face, which I have termed the "presidential power trap" (Schier 2010). Maintaining popular support is hard and frustrating work, and in seeking to maintain it, presidents encounter widespread constraints. The modern presidency grants an incumbent many formal powers over executive branch administration, as well as over foreign and security policy. So why not use the power while you have it, if popular support is so impermanent? The risk is that by using such powers, a president effectively destroys his popular support—the presidential power trap.

Richard Nixon's presidency, with its Constitutional violations, is the signal example of this, but one can find evidence of the power trap among other recent presidencies. Carter took his popular support for granted, ignoring the maintenance of its elite and mass aspects, and paid the price. Reagan gradually relied more on executive power as his domestic political opposition grew, leading to the Iran-Contra imbroglio. George Herbert Walker Bush exerted war powers but never found a stable basis in popular support. Clinton suffered early on from unpopularity and found his use of formal powers under steady political attack. George W. Bush's use of war powers destroyed his popular support during his second term.

Barack Obama thus faces a problem of popular support and a power trap. Only by solving the former is he likely to avoid the latter. It is the central political difficulty confronted by modern presidents. As Obama's first term concludes, securing popular support looms as his presidency's signal challenge.

NOTE

An earlier version of this chapter appeared in Schier, Steven E. 2010. "Obama's 'Big Bang' Presidency," *The Forum* 8 (3): Article 13.

REFERENCES

Alter, Jonathan. 2010. *The Promise: President Obama, Year One.* New York: Simon and Schuster.

Archives.gov. 2011. "Executive Orders Disposition Tables Index." http://www .archives.gov/federal-register/executive-orders/disposition.html. Accessed May 6, 2011.

Associated Press. 2009. "Obama's Signing Statements Draw Fire for Mimicking Bush." http://www.startribune.com/politics/51359172.html. Accessed December 9, 2010.

———. 2010. "Public Isn't Buying Wall Street Reform: AP Poll." June 21. http:// www.huffingtonpost.com/2010/06/21/wall-street-reform-poll-ap_n_620421.html. Accessed July 22, 2010.

Baker, Peter. 2010. "Obama Making Plans to Use Executive Power." *New York Times*, February 13.

Biden, Joe. 2009. "What You Might Not Know about the Recovery." *New York Times*, July 26.

Burbank, Matthew J., Ronald J. Hrebnar, and Robert C. Benedict. 2008. *Parties, Interest Groups and Political Campaigns.* Boulder, Colorado: Paradigm Publishers.

Curry, Tom. 2010. "Bush Tax Cuts Just 37 Percent of the Total Deal." Msnbc.com, December 10. http://firstread.msnbc.msn.com/_news/2010/12/07/5606406-bush -tax-cuts-just-37-percent-of-the-total-deal. Accessed December 16, 2010.

Davis, Steven J., Gary S. Becker, and Kevin M. Murphy. 2010. "Uncertainty and the Slow Recovery." *Wall Street Journal*, January 4. http://www.aei.org/article/ 101501. Accessed July 22, 2010.

Devins, Neal. 2007. "Signing Statements and Divided Government." *William and Mary Bill of Rights Journal* 16 (1): 63–79.

Dreier, Peter, and Marshall Ganz. 2009. "We Have the Hope. Now Where's the Audacity?" *Washington Post*, August 30. http://www.weeklystandard.com/blogs/ obama-rattles-business. Accessed July 22, 2010.

Edwards, George C. III, and Steven J. Wayne. 2009. *Presidential Leadership: Politics and Policymaking.* Florence, Kentucky: Wadsworth.

Executive Order 13535. 2010. March 24. http://www.presidency.ucsb.edu/ws/index .php?pid=87661. Accessed December 9, 2010.

Fiorina, Morris P. 2009. *Disconnect: the Breakdown of Representation in American Politics.* Norman, Oklahoma: University of Oklahoma Press.

Greenberg Quinlan Rosner Research. 2010. "Democracy Corps June Survey: Grim Stability Will Require Race-by-Race Fight." July 8. http://www.democracycorps .com/wpcontent/files/DC1006292010.political.FINAL_.pdf. Accessed July 22, 2010.

Grier, Peter. 2010. "Health Care Reform 101." *Christian Science Monitor.* http:// www.csmonitor.com/USA/Politics/2010/0322/Health-care-reform-bill-101-what -the-bill-means-to-you. Accessed December 16, 2010.

Gronke, Paul, and Brian Newman. 2000. "FDR to Clinton, Mueller to ??: A State of the Discipline Review of Presidential Approval." Annual Meetings of the American Political Science Association. http://people.reed.edu/~gronkep/docs/apsa2000 -gronkeandnewman.pdf. Accessed July 22, 2010.

Harris, John F. 2009. "Bush and Clinton: Contrasting Styles of Popular Leadership," in *Ambition and Division: Legacies of the George W. Bush Presidency*, edited by Steven E. Schier, 62–74. Pittsburgh: University of Pittsburgh Press.

Homans, Charles. 2010. "The Party of Obama: What Are the President's Grass Roots Good For?" *Washington Monthly.* January/February. http://www.washington monthly.com/features/2010/1001.homans.html. Accessed July 22, 2010.

Johnson, Bertram. 2004. "A Stake in the Sand: George W. Bush and Congress," in *High Risk and Big Ambition: The Presidency of George W. Bush*, edited by Steven E. Schier, 167–186. Pittsburgh: University of Pittsburgh Press, 2004.

Jones, Jeffrey M. 2010. "Near Record 49% Say Democratic Party Too Liberal." Gallup.com. June 14. http://www.gallup.com/poll/139877/near-record-say -democratic-party-liberal.aspx. Accessed July 22, 2010.

Kettl, Donald F. 2009. "Obama's Stealth Revolution: Quietly Reshaping the Way Government Works." *The Public Manager*, Winter 2009–2010: 39–42.

Krugman, Paul. 2010a. "Bleak Economy May Cost Obama." *New York Times*, July 19.

———. 2010b. "Let's Not Make a Deal." *New York Times*, December 5.

Levy, Phillip I. 2010. "The Straw Stimulus." *The American*, February 18. http://www .american.com/archive/2010/february/the-straw-stimulus. Accessed December 16, 2010.

McCormick, John, and Carol Dodge. 2010. "Americans Disapproving Obama May Enable Republican Gains." http://www.bloomberg.com/news/2010-07-14/ americans-disapproving-of-obama-policies-poised-to-enable-republican-gains .html. Accessed July 22, 2010.

Nix, Kathryn. 2010. "Obamacare Save Money? Not Likely." *The Foundry* blog, Heritage Foundation. http://blog.heritage.org/?p=46651. Accessed December 16, 2010.

Orszag, Peter. 2010. "To Save Money, Save the Health Care Act." *New York Times*, November 3.

Pew Research Center for the People and the Press. 2010a. "Obama's Ratings Little Affected by Recent Turmoil." Washington, DC: Pew Center. June 24. http://www .bloomberg.com/news/2010-07-14/americans-disappoving-of-obama-policies -poised-to-enable-republican-gains.html. Accessed July 22, 2010.

———. 2010b. "Pessimistic Public Doubts Effectiveness of Stimulus, TARP. Washington, DC: Pew Center. April 28. http://people-press.org/report/608/public-doubts-stimulus-tarp. Accessed July 22, 2010.

PolitiFact.com. 2010. The Obameter: Tracking Obama's Campaign Promises. http://www.politifact.com/truth-o-meter/promises/. Accessed July 22, 2010.

Rich, Frank. 2010. "Barack Obama, Phone Home." *New York Times*, November 7.

Saad, Lydia. 2009. "In U.S., Majority Now Says Obama's Policies Mostly Liberal." Gallup.com. November 7. http://www.gallup.com/poll/124094/Majority-Say-Obama-Policies-Mostly-Liberal.aspx. Accessed July 22, 2010.

———. 2010. "Conservatives Finish 2009 as No. 1 Ideological Group." Gallup.com. January 7. http://www.gallup.com/poll/124958/Conservatives-Finish-2009-No-1-Ideological-Group.aspx. Accessed July 22, 2010.

Savage, Charlie. 2007. "Barack Obama's Q and A." *Boston Globe*, December 20.

———. 2009. "Obama Says He Can Ignore Some Parts of Spending Bill." *New York Times*, March 12.

———. 2010. "Obama Takes New Route to Opposing Parts of Laws." *New York Times*, January 9.

Schier, Steven E. 2010. "The Presidential Authority Problem: Declining Political Capital 1937–2008." Annual Meetings of the Midwest Political Science Association. Chicago.

Seltzer, Irwin M. 2010. "Obama Rattles Business." *Weekly Standard*. June 26. http://www.weeklystandard.com/blogs/obama-rattles-business. Accessed July 22, 2010.

Walsh, Joan. 2010. "Party Time for Bush and Cheney!" Salon.com. http://www.salon.com/news/opinion/joan_walsh/politics/2010/12/06/bush_cheney_party. Accessed December 9, 2010.

Washington Post. 2009. "Taking Apart the $819 Billion Stimulus Package." http://www.washingtonpost.com/wpdyn/content/graphic/2009/02/01/GR2009020100154.html. Accessed May 6, 2011.

———. 2011. "Head Count: Tracking Obama's Appointments." http://projects.washingtonpost.com/2009/federal-appointments. Accessed January 21, 2011.

Weisman, Jonathan. 2009. "Signing Statements Reappear in Obama White House." *Wall Street Journal*, March 12.

Wolffe, Richard. 2010. *Revival: The Struggle for Survival inside the Obama White House*. New York: Crown Publishers.

HISTORICAL AND
ELECTORAL PERSPECTIVES

Chapter One

From Reconstruction to Recession

The First Phase of the Obama Presidency in Historical Context

Nicol C. Rae

Regardless of whether his presidency is perceived to be a success or failure, Barack Obama has already made history as the first African American (and "person of color") to reach the White House. Given that the normal pattern of white, Protestant males had only been broken once before by the Catholic John F. Kennedy in 1960, Obama's 2008 victory has been of immense symbolic importance in terms of the evolution of American society. Yet the first two years of Obama's presidency have also been shaped by longer-term historical forces that have constrained his political options. This chapter discusses the historical context of Obama's presidency and attempts to illustrate how this context has affected Obama's political decisions and influenced his political fate during the first phase of his administration—from inauguration day in January 2009 to the midterm elections of November 2010.

The modern American presidency is subject to recurrent rhythms that flow from the interaction between the federal elections cycle prescribed by the US constitution, the extended scope of presidential responsibilities since World War II, and the partisan context of contemporary American politics. Based on these rhythms, I argue that each post-1945 presidency has generally followed either a two-phase (for one-term presidents) or four-phase (for two-term presidents) pattern.

In the initial *honeymoon* phase, the new president converts his initial post-election popularity into the most significant legislative achievements of his presidency—particularly if his party has control of at least one house of Congress. Generally the presidential party suffers losses in the first midterm election—sometimes so severe as to lead to the other party gaining control of Congress (Truman, Eisenhower, Clinton).

This opens the *consolidation* phase, in which presidents try to build and maintain a reelection coalition. This phase is generally not characterized by any great legislative achievements; indeed legislative stalemates often occur, which a wily incumbent can turn to his advantage (Truman, Clinton).

Those who succeed in getting reelected—usually due to favorable economic circumstances—then enter the *hubris* phase, in which presidents invariably make serious political mistakes (Truman, Nixon, Reagan, Clinton, George W. Bush) that squander the political capital earned by their reelection victory and lead to a marked decline in popular approval, legislative stalemate, and further (and generally more severe) losses for the presidential party in the "second' or "sixth year" midterm election.

This ushers in the final *legacy* phase when presidents, constrained by the 22nd Amendment, can generally achieve little (they are often described as "lame ducks") in domestic policy but are increasingly mindful of their "legacy," particularly in foreign affairs. If the state of the national economy is good and America is at peace, two-term presidents tend to leave office with high approval ratings (Eisenhower, Reagan, Clinton). An unpopular war and an indifferent economy, however, will entail that two-term presidencies end with a public sense of failure and high incumbent unpopularity (Truman, George W. Bush).

We should also note that during the *consolidation, hubris,* and *legacy* phases, when domestic legislative achievements become progressively more difficult for presidents, the salience of foreign policy (over which presidents have more direct control due to their enumerated powers in Article II of the US constitution) tends to increase in almost every administration.

For the Obama presidency, we have only phase one to work with so far, but enough has occurred already to make some assessment of Obama's engagement with the historic context of his presidency. I will discuss the Obama administration in two aspects that I have previously utilized to discuss modern chief executives: (1) Obama's potential as a reconstructive president or creator of a new political "regime" and (2) his ability to function effectively as president in an era of intense partisan polarization (Rae 2004, 2009). For this chapter, I also add a discussion of another aspect that seems particularly apposite in addressing the central question of the Obama presidency—the fate of presidents in times of economic recession, and the political effectiveness of the measures that the Obama administration has taken to deal with the economic crisis. I conclude with some reflections on Obama's potential to manage the critical second (or *consolidation*) phase of his presidency successfully and his prospects of reelection in 2012.

OBAMA AS REGIME BUILDER

Post-presidential election media commentary habitually refers to the concept of realignment: a theory of political change in American politics that had its heyday among political scientists in the 1950s and 1960s. Advocates of realignment see American political history as characterized by a number of "critical elections"—1800, 1828, 1860, 1896, 1932, 1980—usually triggered by the rise of a new political issue or catastrophic event (Key 1955; Burnham 1970; Sundquist 1973). In these elections, the balance of electoral power between the major parties changed for a generation also enabling a change in the direction of American politics and public policy and thereby giving rise to a new political "regime."

Political scientist Steven Skowronek has argued that the cycle of political regimes—or what Skowronek refers to as "political time"—means that a certain rather small category of presidents—Jefferson, Jackson, Lincoln, Franklin Roosevelt, and Reagan—elected in the critical or realigning elections listed previously have been *reconstructive* presidents or founders of a political regime (Skowronek 1993, 2008). All other presidents, according to Skowronek, can be categorized according to their political relationship with the prevailing political regime of their time. *Orthodox innovators*—Truman, JFK, LBJ, the two presidents Bush—adhere to the fundamental political tenets of the regime and attempt to sustain and extend it during their presidencies. *Preemptors* are presidents from the regime's minority party—Wilson, Eisenhower, Nixon, and Clinton—who are generally torn between opposition and adherence to regime policies and are thus unable to use their presidencies to break the overall political configuration of the prevailing regime. *Disjunctive* presidents (Hoover, Carter) are adherents of a dying political regime who find themselves crushed electorally by rising reconstructive presidents.

Realignment theory rests on rather shaky historical foundations, and Skowronek's closely related concept of political time in effect deprives all but a half-dozen of the forty-four US presidents of effective control over their own political fates (Mayhew 2004). Another problem with realignment/political time is that both theories seem to work far better for past eras of American politics than for the contemporary—post 1960s—period (Ladd 1991). Nevertheless, realignment continues to exercise a powerful grip on the American political imagination, particularly in the aftermath of presidential elections. The dramatic rise in electoral support for the Democratic Party after George W. Bush's reelection in 2004, the Democrats' presidential nomination of the outsider Barack Obama, the financial crisis of the late summer and fall of 2008, and the atmosphere of excitement that greeted Obama's inauguration all gave rise to speculation that Obama might be a "realigner" or "reconstructive" president (Smith 2008).

On the face of it, the evidence appeared quite impressive. Democratic support did rise dramatically in the wake of the increasing unpopularity of the Iraq War and the onset of economic recession during the second term of the Republican George W. Bush administration. In 2006, the Democrats regained control of both houses of Congress. Democratic enthusiasm, energy, and party registration were all on the rise during the run up to the 2008 presidential election. Democratic-supporting political analysts appeared to detect a new Democratic majority coalition of African Americans, the growing Latino and Asian immigrant populations, and the socially liberal highly educated (Judis and Teixeira 2007). In other words, demographics and social change were finally turning George McGovern's minority 1972 Democratic coalition into a national majority.

The 2008 presidential election result appeared to confirm all of this and more. Obama's 53 percent of the national popular vote was the highest for a Democratic candidate since FDR in 1944—except for the freakish LBJ landslide of 1964. His winning coalition strongly resembled the New Democratic/Progressive majority outlined previously with large gains among Latino, Asian, and affluent, highly educated voters, added to an unprecedented mobilization of the already overwhelmingly Democratic African American vote (Pew Research Center 2008). Notoriously apathetic young and "first-time" voters—increasingly liberal on issues such as gay rights, marijuana use, and immigration—also flocked to Obama's banner. This combination enabled Obama to win states such as Virginia and Indiana that had not voted Democratic for president since 1964, and also North Carolina, which had not voted Democratic since Jimmy Carter's election in 1976. The fall 2008 banking crisis and the George W. Bush administration's massive federal rescue program or TARP (Troubled Asset Relief Program) appeared to undermine the fundamental tenets of the post-1980 "Reagan" political regime—limited government and deregulation. The severe economic recession that followed seemed to demand further new interventionist federal government policies. The Republican Party meanwhile had sunk to its lowest popularity ratings in decades and faced the danger of degenerating into a white, Christian, southern-dominated, elderly, angry, and intolerant rump (Abramowitz 2010, 111–38). As Obama's inauguration day approached, many on the liberal-left spectrum of American politics and their media allies anticipated a new Democratic-dominated political regime based on selective government interventionism, social liberalism, and a multilateralist foreign policy. Further Democratic gains in each house of Congress made implementation of this agenda even more likely.

The evidence for realignment from the 2008 campaign and election returns remained mixed at best, however. Republican John McCain still managed to secure 46 percent of the national popular vote despite the heavy unpopularity of his party, the near-collapse of the US banking system in late September 2008, an unimpressive general election campaign, and a heavy Democratic advantage in campaign funding. Exit-voter surveys demonstrated that the core Republican supporting groups in the electorate over the past quarter century or so—white men, older voters, conservatives, rural voters, and religious voters—stayed heavily Republican in 2008 (Pew Research Center 2008). General election turnout also did not rise dramatically from the 2004 level of 61 percent (Center for the Study of the American Electorate 2008). Obama owed his victory to the state of the national economy and the political fallout from the banking and financial crisis that hit in the middle of the general election campaign. Failure to remedy the economic situation once in office would almost certainly put great strain on his somewhat tenuous electoral coalition of younger voters, college-educated professionals, minorities, and public-sector union members.

In office, the Obama administration has indeed adopted further major legislative initiatives contrary to the "Reagan consensus." His first major success was the congressional passage in February 2009 of a $787 billion federal spending package—the American Recovery and Reinvestment Act of 2009 or "economic stimulus"—in an effort to regenerate the stagnant economy. The administration also had little hesitation in bailing out the troubled Chrysler and General Motors auto companies in the spring of 2009. As president, Obama fought hard for a major health-care reform package that promised to greatly reduce the number of Americans without health insurance and eventually passed it after a titanic congressional battle in March 2010. The new administration also secured a major Wall Street banking reform or "reregulation" in July 2010 and succeeded in gaining Senate confirmation for two liberal Democratic nominees to the US Supreme Court : Judge Sonia Sotomayor (August 2009) and Solicitor General Elena Kagan (August 2010).

Yet to many on the left of the Democratic Party, these measures seemed half-hearted at best and not characteristic of a reconstructive president. Progressive Democrats had wanted a "single-payer" health-care package and much tougher reregulation of Wall Street (Harris and Hohman 2010). They were also irked that Obama did not immediately deliver on standard Democratic social and cultural commitments including significant immigration reform and an end to the US military's "Don't Ask, Don't Tell" policy regarding gay servicemen and women. Even Obama's two Supreme Court appointments—Sonia Sotomayor (the first Hispanic Supreme Court Justice) and Elena Kagan—were hardly evidence of a reconstructive presidency, since they replaced two retiring members of the court's liberal wing rather than changing the ideological balance of power on the court.

So while President Obama, governing with a comfortably Democratic Congress, could claim significant legislative achievements during the first "honeymoon" phase of his administration, the continuing economic recession and the president's somewhat detached political style raised major doubts that this would actually be a reconstructive presidency (Bai 2010). The Democratic debacle in the 2010 midterm elections—with the loss of sixty-three seats and control of the House of Representatives and the loss of six Senate seats and the Democrats' filibuster-proof majority in that body—provided further evidence against reconstruction and a new Democratic majority. In his first midterm election in 1934, Franklin Roosevelt's Democratic Party actually gained seats in both houses of Congress. On the other hand, reconstructive presidents Lincoln (three seats) and Reagan (twenty-six seats) lost House seats in their first midterm elections, and both had the look of political failure about them at a similar stage in their presidencies (Lincoln had his worst year of the civil war in 1862, and Reagan's midterm, like Obama's, took place in the midst of a recession). If one holds to the standard formula regarding realignments and political regimes, then it is simply too soon to make a definitive judgment as to whether Obama will be a reconstructive president or a preemptor like Bill Clinton, making slight adjustments to the prevailing Republican-Conservative political regime founded by Ronald Reagan.

GOVERNING AS A PARTISAN PRESIDENT IN A PARTISAN ERA

We may glean more understanding of the early Obama presidency by focusing on the nature of American party politics over the past quarter century rather than attempting to place Obama in a political regime cycle. The election of Bill Clinton to the presidency in 1992 ushered in the most intensely partisan period in American politics since the late nineteenth century (Sinclair 2006). This development is a long-term consequence of the completion of the civil rights revolution in the mid-1960s, which initiated a gradual process of ideological "sorting" in the American electorate. The upshot is that the United States now has two ideologically consistent liberal and conservative major parties that seek to control the federal government to achieve policy objectives (Abramowitz 2010). This process of ideological sorting took some thirty years to complete at the sub-presidential electoral levels, and from the mid-1960s until 1994, the transition was masked by a two-tier "electoral order" (Shafer 1991). Republicans dominated presidential elections because most of the electorate generally favored Republican positions on national-security policy and cultural issues—the constitutional province of the presidency—during the Cold War, while Democrats continued to dominate US House elections due to the continuing electoral preference for New Deal economic and welfare policies—the constitutional province of the House. The Senate, with constitutional prerogatives in foreign, cultural, and domestic politics, was competitive between the parties after 1980.

President Bill Clinton's election with a Democratic Congress in 1992, however, precipitated the end of this electoral order. In 1994, the Republicans won the House for the first time since 1954 on a radically anti-government platform. Since that time, American federal elections have been extraordinarily competitive at all levels between the major parties. At the same time, the ideological divisions between the parties have calcified. Rates of partisan voting and polarization in Congress have risen sharply as partisan "message politics" (with an eye to the next election) has taken an increasing amount of time on both the House and Senate floor (Sinclair 2006). Congressional party leaderships have been empowered to a degree not seen in over a century, as more ideologically homogeneous party caucuses have delegated power to party leaders in order to implement a partisan policy agenda (Aldrich and Rohde 2000). Republican and Democratic members of Congress also have to pay more attention to their ideological base of party activists and fundraisers to get reelected. In the Senate, these effects are somewhat moderated by larger and more diverse statewide constituencies and Senate traditions of comity, but partisanship has risen precipitously in that body as well. Given the Senate rule that requires sixty votes to close debate on most legislation, however, the effect of increased partisanship has been to encourage legislative stalemate through increased use of the filibuster and other delaying tactics (Sinclair 2006).

The basis of this strong partisanship has been the subject of some dispute among political scientists. Much has been made of the so-called "culture war" which sees the axis of electoral and partisan divisions lying primarily around the intensity of religious affiliation (Layman 2001). The more religiously observant hold to more traditional views on issues of sexuality and reproductive rights—such as same-sex marriage and abortion—and increasingly vote Republican at all electoral levels (Guth 2011). More secular voters hold liberal positions on those issues and tend to vote Democratic. Geographically, the more culturally traditional "red" (the color labels originate from TV maps of the freakishly close 2000 election) states in the South, Midwest, and Rocky Mountains have tended to vote Republican in recent presidential elections, while the more secular "blue" states of the northeastern seaboard and the Pacific Coast have tended to vote Democratic.

Morris Fiorina considers the "culture war" greatly exaggerated and largely driven by party elites with most Americans—and a fair number of states—actually being "purple" rather than "red" or "blue" (Fiorina 2006, 2009). Alan Abramowitz, however, has demonstrated that elite polarization is now increasingly reflected among voters at the mass level, with the number of political independents having greatly diminished over the past twenty years and far greater levels of ideological consistency prevailing in the current US electorate (Abramowitz 2010). Polarization is further reinforced by the increasing tendency of like-minded Americans to self-segregate in conservative or progressive communities (Bishop 2008). Part of the key to the puzzle of partisan polarization and the culture war may lie in the continuing importance of party elites: the economic, ethnic, and cultural interests clustered around both major parties (Zaller et al. 2008). These elites—dubbed "policy demanders" by John Zaller and his co-authors—essentially control party nominations at all levels through their critical electoral resources: money, activists, and electoral constituencies. Only when voters are particularly aroused on some issue that does not fit the standard line of issue cleavages between major party elites are these Democratic and Republican policy demanders unlikely to prevail in nomination contests.

What has been the consequence of all of this increased partisanship for the presidency? In terms of nominations, the domination of each party by a coalition of ideological interests has forced the nomination of candidates who are acceptable to the policy demands of those interests, although they must still be electable (Zaller et al. 2008). Given that presidential general elections have the highest turnout with the largest number of independent voters participating, ideology needs to be tempered more at this level than in legislative contests. In order to get nominated, Obama had to be acceptable to the Democratic Party's economic and cultural policy demanders and he was, although there may have been some early doubts regarding his general-election viability compared with his rival, Hillary Rodham Clinton. Both candidates drew support from different sections of the Democratic interest group coalition: Obama from African Americans and the anti-Iraq War movement, and Clinton from organized labor, Latinos, and feminists. In the primaries, Obama actually positioned himself marginally to Clinton's right on the health-care issue but was clearly to her left on the Iraq War and foreign policy generally. In the general election, Obama's campaign emphasized national unity themes that resonated with the remarkable rise of an African American like Obama to a major party presidential nomination, and a more multilateralist foreign policy approach. Underneath the radar, like all recent presidential candidates, he aligned strongly with the major interests gathered under his party label.

Like all recently elected presidents, Obama has tried to deliver for his party's policy demanders in office. With a comfortably Democratic Congress including an apparent "filibuster proof" majority in the Senate, this should hardly have been a surprise. Regardless of the tenor of the presidential campaign, it is commonplace for newly elected presidents to claim a "mandate" for policy actions. In general, these claims are seen as legitimate by other significant political actors during the honeymoon phase of a presidency. Even George W. Bush, who reached the White House due to a highly controversial Supreme Court decision and lost the popular vote in the 2000 election, claimed a mandate for significant income-tax cuts on higher incomes early in his presidency and found his claims being taken sufficiently seriously for the essence of his proposal to be passed (Rae 2004). Obama came into office with an even greater display of public goodwill than most and was expected to get more or less what he wanted from the now comfortably Democratic Congress in policy terms.

The House of Representatives under Speaker Nancy Pelosi was generally to the left of the president and completely in accord with Democratic policy demanders on almost all issues that arose during the 111th Congress. Obama's problems in implementing his policy agenda occurred in the US Senate where his filibuster-proof majority was fragile at best (Johnson 2011). In both houses, he faced the unrelenting opposition of the Republican minority almost from the start of his presidency (Hulse and Nagourney 2010). In the House this mattered little, since the House minority these days functions identically to the opposition in a parliamentary system—its only possible political role is to oppose the majority and the majority's president. In the Senate, due to the possibility of a filibuster, a unified minority is much more of a problem for a president of the majority party and so it proved to be for Obama.

As Obama's legislative agenda for the 111th Congress reflected the interests that support the contemporary Democratic Party, there was obviously little incentive for the interests that support the GOP and its members of Congress to support him. After the defection of Pennsylvania Republican Arlen Specter in April 2009, Majority Leader Harry Reid theoretically had the sixty Democratic votes necessary to close debate in the Senate, but the Senate Republican minority held their forty members together well enough that with the addition of a red state Democrat, they could effectively impede the passage of Democratic measures (Hulse and Nagourney 2010). Even the popular stimulus package early in Obama's presidency was supported by only three of the forty Senate Republicans—one of them being Specter who changed parties in an (unsuccessful) attempt to hold his Pennsylvania Senate seat in 2002. Unified Republican opposition and the electoral vulnerability of red-state Senate Democrats (such as Senators Ben Nelson of Nebraska and Mary Landrieu of Louisiana) forced the White House to abandon a "public" option in the health-care bill, which opponents feared might be a "Trojan Horse" for the Canadian-style "single payer" health-care system favored by Democratic progressives (Pear 2009). After the election of Republican Scott Brown in the special election for the late Senator Edward Kennedy's Massachusetts Senate seat in January 2010, the Democrats lost their "filibuster proof" Senate majority. In effect, the Republican Senate minority forced Obama to water down his successful health care and financial reform initiatives, and with a handful of Democratic allies, the Senate Republicans also effectively blocked key initiatives sought by Democratic interests such as comprehensive immigration reform, "cap and trade," anti-global warming legislation, "card-check" legislation that would make it easier for unions to win certification elections, and (until the very last days of the 111th Congress) a repeal of the US military's "Don't Ask, Don't Tell" policy.

After the euphoria of his election and inauguration, Obama in his first two years was perforce another typically partisan president in a highly partisan era in American politics. The Democratic Party's major policy demanders expected President Obama to deliver, and his efforts to do so were bound to arouse the opposition of the congressional Republicans and their major policy demanders. Indeed, opposition to Obama's policies, specifically his adherence to TARP, the stimulus package, and the health-care bill, spawned a new mass movement—the "Tea Party"—on the right of American politics, in much the same manner as the Iraq War stimulated the "Netroots" movement on the Democratic left during the George W. Bush administration. Unlike his predecessor, Obama did not benefit politically from an unanticipated security crisis early in his presidency that might have rallied the country around his leadership and served—at least for a time—as a countervailing force to partisanship. Yet the example of the September 11, 2001, attacks also demonstrates that such "rally effects" are ephemeral and partisanship eventually tends to reassert itself as the chief executive's response to the crisis ultimately arouses a partisan group of policy demanders in opposition. Indeed the rally in public support that President Obama received in the polls following the successful military operation that killed the perpetrator of the September 11 attacks—Osama bin Laden—on May 1, 2011, appears likely to be of even shorter duration.

Partisanship has intensified the normal rhythms of the presidency and shortened the presidential honeymoon. Obama's presidential approval ratings have seen the routine drop-off that all presidents experience from post-inauguration highs to under 50 percent by the time of the first midterm election (Blake 2010). From being regarded with almost messianic fervor at his inauguration, Barack Obama inevitably morphed into a more divisive and partisan political leader during the first phase of his presidency. Yet Obama's reelection as president will not be determined by his abilities as a party leader but instead by the degree to which the United States recovers from its worst economic recession since the Great Depression.

OBAMA AS A "RECESSION" PRESIDENT

Presidents may endure terrible midterm election results but recover during the consolidation phase of their presidencies if the national economy is strong. Presidents Ronald Reagan and Bill Clinton are prime examples of this. Both suffered considerable losses for their party in midterm elections held in a recession atmosphere (1982 and 1994) but managed to recover politically in tandem with the economy to ensure easy reelection. Presidents whose reelection campaigns coincide with the depths of a recession—Hoover, Carter, and George H. W. Bush—tend to lose, badly. Yet for Democratic presidents, recessions also present an opportunity—or as President Obama's first White House chief of staff, Rahm Emanuel, put it, "never let a good crisis go to waste" (Cummings 2009). For the party of the New Deal and expansionist federal government, taking office during a recession should present an excellent opportunity to demonstrate the effectiveness of government management of the economy. For a generation, however, Democratic Party leaders, stung by the electoral success of Ronald Reagan and the small-government, anti-tax message of the Republican Party, had been learning the opposite lesson—that they could no longer afford to be depicted as the party of "big government." President Bill Clinton thus dramatically changed tack after the 1994 midterm election debacle, and in his 1996 State of the Union address proclaimed that the "era of big government is over." In his response to the economic crisis that greeted his presidency, would Obama decisively repudiate the "Reagan-Clinton consensus" and attempt to reconstruct the New Deal, or instead pursue an amalgam of traditional and "New Democratic" economic policies?

The economic recession has unquestionably been the predominant political issue of the Obama presidency. The US economy had already slowed significantly by the summer of 2008, but the near collapse of the banking system in late September greatly exacerbated the situation. Obama owed his decisive election victory in large part to the economic crisis (Pew Research Center 2008), but the economy continued to spiral downward in the weeks prior to his inauguration and for the first year of his presidency. Obama and congressional Democrats had largely supported Bush treasury secretary Henry Paulson's bailout of the banks via the TARP in October 2008 (most House Republicans actually opposed the legislation that enabled TARP), but many on the left of the Democratic Party felt that by adhering to TARP once in office, the Obama administration had missed an opportunity to bring about really significant reform of the financial system. There was also widespread outrage among Democratic progressives concerning the salaries and bonuses paid to financial executives through TARP, and they were further disappointed when Obama selected an economic team that had a distinctly Clintonian cast (Rich 2010). His Treasury secretary Timothy Geithner, a former Clinton administration Treasury under-secretary and president of the New York Fed, had close ties to Wall Street and former Clinton Treasury secretary Robert Rubin. Another former Clinton Treasury secretary, Larry Summers, was a senior economic adviser to the administration. This team was not likely to pursue any radically redistributive or interventionist economic policies—recession or no recession.

As Ray Tatalovich's chapter in this volume points out, the Obama administration did invest a great deal of early political capital in the economic stimulus package, which they hoped would give a jolt to the economy or at least staunch the bleeding (Tatalovich 2011). The results were mixed at best, as the unemployment rate stubbornly remained at 9 percent or above right up to the 2010 midterm elections. The stimulus package also contributed to escalating federal deficits, a matter of growing concern as the budget surplus left by the Clinton administration in 2001 had been progressively eroded after two rounds of tax cuts and the costs of fighting two wars simultaneously in Iraq and Afghanistan under George W. Bush. Public concern about the deficit placed constraints on the Obama administration's ability to extend government spending to counteract the recession. By the end of Obama's second year in office, there were some signs of economic recovery, but none of these were yet alleviating the economic stress on the American middle-class, which faced continued widespread home foreclosures, declining home prices and equity for those able to pay their mortgages, and the threat of unemployment. Many on the left of the Democratic political spectrum—such as Nobel prize-winning economist Paul Krugman (2010)—argued that Obama's stimulus had been too modest to boost an economy that was now facing the danger of deflation and the possibility of prolonged recession as Japan had experienced in the 1990s.

Given the overwhelming public concern regarding the economy, the political reasoning behind the Obama administration's decision to focus primarily on health-care reform as their legislative priority for the 111th Congress was not immediately obvious. There were a number of reasons underlying this decision that made perfect sense to the administration, however. The first was the Rahm Emanuel maxim regarding the exploitation of a political crisis. If traditional Democratic domestic policy interventionism had been relegitimated by the recession and the banking crisis, then Obama had been given an opportunity denied to his Democratic predecessors in the White House since FDR—to implement health-insurance coverage for all Americans (Cummings 2009). For the Democratic Party, health-care reform was unfinished business since the failure of the Clinton administration plan in 1994. Now with a Democratic president and congressional majorities in place, the party had been given a second chance to "do it right" (Bai 2010). For those concerned about the deficit, the administration argued that escalating health-care costs were a major contribution and that reform could be deficit neutral in the short term and actually contribute to deficit reduction in the long term. The 2008 exit polls also had indicated that health-care costs were a major public concern and that voters tended to trust the Democrats more on this issue (Pew Research Center 2008).

In truth, however, health-care reform seems to have been regarded by most of the public as a distraction from their major concern—the economy—and the more the public learned about the Obama administration's plan, the more skeptical they became (Pew Research Center 2010b; Rasmussen and Schoen 2010). One problem was that the Democrats were by no means united on the details of the reform plan. The Clintonians who dominated Obama-administration economic policy were more inclined to maintain a health-care system based on private insurance plans with some modifications, such as the elimination of preexisting medical conditions as a barrier to insurance and full coverage of all children and young adults. This would be done by a federal mandate on all individuals to purchase health insurance. More progressive Democratic voices wanted a Canadian style "single payer" system, which, they argued, was the only reform that would guarantee universal health-care coverage while containing costs. Realizing that this was not politically achievable, the Democratic left wanted at least a "public option" in the health-care plan to compete with the private health-care plans.

While the Obama administration played its cards close to its chest, the House passed a health-care reform plan in November 2009 along the lines previously noted with a public option. It was clear that such a proposal had no chance of beating the filibuster in the Senate due to unanimous Republican opposition plus a handful of red-state Democrats, and the Senate plan passed in late December 2009 had no public option. Meanwhile, public opposition to health-care reform began to mount as voters became concerned about the individual mandate, the implications for the federal deficit, and fears that, much as they might dislike their current health-insurance policies, the proposed reform might actually end up reducing their coverage and circumscribing their options (Rasmussen and Schoen 2010; Pew Research Center 2010b). Republican Scott Brown's victory in the January 2010 Massachusetts special election appeared to have ended health-care reform for good, as the

GOP now had forty-one Senate votes. Speaker Pelosi, sensing that another defeat for health-care reform would be even worse politically for the Democrats, stripped the House bill of the public option, inserted clauses to satisfy anti-abortion House Democrats, and proposed sending the bill to the Senate using the budget process's reconciliation procedure. That procedure was not susceptible to a filibuster and could thus be passed by a simple majority in the Senate (Bai 2010). By these means the Obama administration could claim to have achieved a long-term Democratic policy goal, but after passage, health-care reform proved to be no more popular with an American public that failed to see the relevance of health-care reform to economic recovery (Schoen 2010).

The persistence of the recession and the inability of the Obama administration to end it—at least in the perception of most Americans—led to a steady decline in the president's approval ratings and a potentially dire situation for his party in the 2010 midterm elections, as we shall see in the next section. Recessions tend to give rise to public despair and the rise of populist movements of the right and left in opposition to the status quo. The Obama administration's failure to end the recession coupled with its adoption of explicitly interventionist policies and an expansion of the federal government's role in health care was all fuel to the fire that produced the so-called "Tea Party" movement (Cannon 2010). For many fiscally conservative Republicans and Independents already disgusted with the profligacy of the George W. Bush administration and the (2001–2006) Republican Congress at home and abroad, Obama's early policy choices—adherence to the TARP, the economic stimulus package, and the bailout of the auto industry—served as a catalyst for grassroots mobilization against his presidency and Washington "politics as usual." The onset of health-care reform, dubbed "Obamacare," only intensified their efforts. The fact that the Tea Party movement had been created outside the still-discredited Republican Party apparatus gave greater credibility to its arguments and helped gain popular support.

Such "flash" protest movements are endemic to recessions, and their emergence says little about the future prospects of the incumbent president—FDR still managed to get overwhelmingly reelected in 1936 despite Huey Long, Father Coughlin, and the Townsend movement. President Obama's administration has been facing the twin problems of escalating budget deficits and economic stagnation, and while the administration's honeymoon phase allowed it to pass significant legislation to deal with the crisis, these measures were not seen as effective by the American public. The administration's substantial investment of political capital on health-care reform did not gain public popularity and helped regenerate American conservatism as a mass movement through the Tea Party. Finally, the administration was caught between the dilemma of trying to reduce the federal budget deficit while simultaneously stimulating the economy to create jobs—a very difficult political situation that was reflected in the continuing tensions between the deficit-conscious, Wall Street–oriented Clinton Democrats who dominated the Obama administration's economic policymaking apparatus and progressive Democrats in Congress and the media who were hoping for another New Deal.

THE 2010 ELECTION AND THE ROAD TO 2012

The failure of the Obama administration's economic policies to regenerate the economy and the schizophrenic nature of economic policymaking within the administration and between the administration and Congress contributed to the Democratic midterm election debacle of 2010. While it is normal for the president's party to lose seats in the first midterm election of a presidency, the sixty-three House seats lost by the Democrats in 2010 is the highest loss by a presidential party in any midterm election since 1938, outstripping the fifty-two seats lost in the 1994 debacle. The Senate loss of six seats was also higher than average, and the Democrats only held the chamber because (1) many of the eighteen Democratic Senate seats up for reelection were in "deep blue" states in the Northeast and Pacific Coast, and (2) the nomination (thanks largely to the Tea Party) of seriously flawed GOP candidates in four vulnerable Democrat-held Senate seats—Nevada, Colorado, Delaware, and Connecticut.

How did it come to this pass for the president of "hope and change"? The failure to regenerate the economy was critical, but the evidence from polling data says that the health-care bill did a significant amount of electoral damage to the Democrats and that the decision to persist with the legislation in the face of negative polling was a major political miscalculation—at least in the short term—by Speaker Pelosi and the Obama White House (Pew Research Center 2010a; Bowman 2010). The procedures used to pass the bill seemed all-too redolent of the type of Washington politics that the Obama 2008 campaign had appeared to repudiate, and the legislation aroused the vehement opposition of the Tea Party movement, undoubtedly motivated by the Republican electoral base to go to the polls, and swung Independent voters, who had decided the 2008 election for Obama, decisively to the GOP (Pew Research Center 2010a; Bowman 2010; White 2011).

The Democratic losses in a wide swath of northeastern and midwestern states stretching from upstate New York to Wisconsin reflected the effects of the recession and a serious weakness in Obama's appeal to the white middle- and working-class voters who predominate in much of the region (Thrush

2010; Bowman 2010; White 2011). This weakness had already been exposed by Hillary Clinton in the later primaries of the 2008 Democratic nominating campaign in many of the same states, and to some extent, even by John McCain in the 2008 general election, but it became dramatically evident in the 2010 results. The loss of Democratic governorships in four of the swing electoral college states of the same region—Pennsylvania, Ohio, Wisconsin, Iowa—was a severe blow to the White House with regard to the 2012 election. The Democrats' already weak position in the southern states became even weaker, and the number of southern Democratic congressmen elected beyond very heavily minority districts dropped to a handful. Republicans also swept the gubernatorial elections in the region, including the critical electoral college state of Florida.

Even the retention of the US Senate was something of a pyrrhic victory for Obama since (1) the GOP net gain of six seats made it much easier for the Republican minority to filibuster the administration's legislative proposals and appointments, and (2) with the Democrats still controlling one house of Congress, it would be more difficult for Obama to take the Bill Clinton/Harry Truman approach and try to blame a "do-nothing" Republican Congress for the country's problems. Moreover, unlike the voluble and polarizing Newt Gingrich in 1995, the new Republican house speaker, John Boehner of Ohio, is a genial House veteran with a very low public profile beyond the Capital Beltway. It is hard to imagine Speaker Boehner being as effectively demonized by the Democrats as Gingrich was by the Clinton administration from 1995 to 1996.

Obama's campaign appearances in 2010 were largely limited to safely blue states, as many Democratic senatorial and gubernatorial candidates in more competitive races strove to avoid campaigning with him (Thrush 2010). This was symptomatic of the president's declining approval ratings, which fell below 50 percent in the weeks leading up to the election. Again it should be emphasized, however, that the pattern of declining approval ratings is not untypical of contemporary presidents at the end of the honeymoon phase of their presidency. What is clear is that in contrast to the hope-and-unity candidate of the 2008 campaign, President Obama had become a much more polarizing political figure by the time of the 2010 election campaign, with particularly dramatic weaknesses among white middle- and working-class voters. Much of this can be attributed to the onset of the underlying partisan dynamics of modern American politics following the necessarily ephemeral euphoria around Obama's election and inauguration. Obama was now perceived as a partisan Democrat in the White House, and the grassroots of the Republican opposition turned out enthusiastically to repudiate him in the midterm election, as the Democratic grassroots had turned out to repudiate President George W. Bush in the 2006 midterm.

The 2010 midterm election indicated that Obama faced an uphill path to reelection in 2012. On the other hand, we should bear in mind that presidents who seek reelection to a second term generally get reelected. Of the ten presidents since FDR who have sought reelection, only Ford, Carter, and George H. W. Bush have failed—a 70 percent success rate. Carter and George H. W. Bush had to deal with major recessions that were still impacting voters during the reelection campaign and constituted a major factor in their losses. Ford also had to deal with a severe recession shortly after taking office from the disgraced Richard Nixon in 1974, which had not fully abated by the time of the 1976 presidential election.

Each of these three presidents was severely weakened by a renomination challenge from the ideologically purist wing of their party. Ronald Reagan almost robbed President Ford of the Republican nomination in 1976 by running a grassroots conservative campaign. Edward Kennedy's challenge severely undermined President Carter in 1980, and even the nuisance candidacy of media pundit Patrick J. Buchanan against the first President Bush in 1992 did real damage to Bush, even though Buchanan did not come close to winning a single primary. Such challenges indicate severe political weakness for incumbent presidents, and we should expect that the Obama White House will go to great lengths to preclude such a possibility. Midterm election exit-poll data indicated that the president was still polling relatively well among core Democratic constituencies such as minority voters, younger voters, and those with postgraduate degrees (Pew Research Center 2010a; White 2011). Obama's failure to advance major progressive goals on financial reregulation, immigration reform, union elections, and the environment, however, had already aroused disquiet among the Democratic grassroots and liberal punditocracy (Rich 2010). As of this writing, a protest challenge to Obama's 2012 renomination from the Democratic left is certainly not inconceivable.

Even if he avoids such a challenge, Obama's reelection remains contingent on an economic recovery that is sufficiently substantive to affect voters directly. This would probably require a sustained reduction in the unemployment rate and a tangible rise in voters' living standards by the fall of 2012. One advantage for Obama is the continuing public skepticism regarding the Republican opposition (Pew Research Center 2010a). Despite their 2010 electoral triumph, John K. White's chapter reminds us that the Republican "brand" remains unpopular with voters (White 2011), and the rise of the Tea Party movement has highlighted the tensions between the establishment wing of the GOP, as represented by the congressional leaders Boehner and Mc-Connell, and the Tea Party grassroots, which seeks real reductions in the size of the federal government and the federal budget. At the presidential level, this could be an even more severe problem should the Republicans nominate a polarizing Tea Party favorite—such as former Alaska governor and 2008 GOP vice-presidential nominee Sarah Palin—for president in 2012.

Obama might also gain from a strategy of "triangulation" similar to that adopted by President Clinton after 1994: co-opting the Republican opposition on some economic and foreign policy issues while keeping his Democratic congressional troops in line. Such a strategy might reduce the president's negative ratings among Independent voters, but the risk of further alienating the already restive Democratic base would be real. Clinton's triangulation succeeded in securing his own reelection as president in 1996, but it also ensured the reelection of a Republican Congress, as voters approved the bipartisan cooperation between the branches of the federal government. While the president has not yet demonstrated that he is as deft a politician as his Democratic predecessor, Obama's trifecta of legislative successes in the post-election "lame duck" session of the 111th Congress—a deal with the congressional Republicans to perpetuate the Bush administration's tax cuts on high incomes, the Senate ratification of the new Strategic Arms Reduction Treaty with Russia, and the final legislative repeal of "Don't Ask, Don't Tell"—demonstrated a Clinton-like capacity to combine effective bipartisanship with the fulfillment of a long-held goal of Democratic policy demanders. Similarly, the last-minute budget deal struck by President Obama with the new Republican House Leadership on April 8, 2011, to fund the federal government for the remaining six months of the fiscal year contained $38 billion in spending reductions (the House Republicans had sought more than $60 billion) but also averted a federal government shutdown that would have been highly risky politically for the administration.

President Clinton also had the benefit of an economic recovery, which helped sustain his Democratic base and thus preempt a primary challenge. For most Americans, the end of the recession is not yet on the horizon, however, and barring some further unanticipated external event (the elimination of bin Laden has likely come too early to have a decisive electoral impact), Obama's reelection prospects in 2012 will hinge on the degree of economic recovery from the severe downturn that elected him in the first place.

CONCLUSION

From examining the Obama presidency in various historical contexts, the evidence appears to indicate that as he approaches the "consolidation/reelection" phase of his presidency, President Obama's administration has followed many of the rhythms characteristic of American presidents since FDR: a honeymoon phase followed by a gradual erosion in presidential popularity; a reversion to partisan polarization after an initial brief period of bipartisan euphoria, as reflected in increasingly vehement opposition from the opposition party's grassroots and congressional leadership; a struggle with the problems of recovering economic prosperity; and substantial midterm-election losses for his party in Congress. In some ways Obama has dealt with these problems more effectively than most. He has substantive legislative achievements to his credit, having taken considerable political advantage of the Democratic congressional majorities during the honeymoon phase of his presidency. The problem is that these successes have as yet gained him nothing politically in the face of a continued economic recession, a resurgent grassroots conservative movement, and restive Democratic policy demanders and grassroots activists who expected more from a Democratic president with comfortable congressional majorities.

These actors hoped for a reconstructive progressive presidency—and the first phase of the Obama administration has not fulfilled their hopes. The American governmental system lends itself far more easily to incrementalism rather than reconstruction, and the events of 2008 in hindsight do not appear to have been sufficiently cataclysmic to create a reconstructive political opportunity. The resilience of the Reagan-Clinton "limited government" consensus has also been demonstrated by the return of Clinton White House personnel to occupy key economic policy positions in the Obama White House, the emergence of the anti-government Tea Party movement, the unpopularity of the Obama health-care reform (even six months after passage), and widespread public concern about the ballooning federal budget deficit (a severe constraint on the expansion of the domestic American state since the Reagan administration). The president's post-election decisions to strike a deal with congressional Republican leaders on perpetuating the substantial George W. Bush tax cuts (which contributed mightily to the resurgence of the deficit after the Clinton administration budget surpluses) and again on the 2011 budget provide further evidence of the durability of the Reagan-Clinton consensus on economic policy. The Obama administration will have to find its way to reelection and lasting political impact while working within the political parameters established by a severe economic recession, a world in which American global authority appears tenuous at best, a highly partisan political universe, and the political and economic legacy of a president who left the White House over twenty years ago.

REFERENCES

Abramowitz, Alan I. 2010. *The Disappearing Center: Engaged Citizens, Polarization and American Democracy*. New Haven: Yale University Press.

Aldrich, John H., and David W. Rohde. 2000. "The Consequences of Party Organization in the House: The Role of the Majority and Minority Parties in Conditional Party Government." In *Polarized Politics: Congress and the Presidency in a Partisan Era*, edited by Jon R. Bond and Richard Fleisher, 31–72. Washington, DC: CQ Press.

Bai, Matt. 2010. "Democrat in Chief." *New York Times Magazine*, June 8. http://www.nytimes.com/2010/06/13/magazine/13midterms-t.html. Accessed June 10, 2010.

Bishop, Bill. 2008. *The Big Sort: Why the Clustering of Like-Minded America is Tearing Us Apart*. Boston: Houghton Mifflin.

Blake, Aaron. 2010. "Obama and the Unpopularity Question." *Washington Post*, December 8. http://voices.washingtonpost.com/thefix/white-house/is-obama-really-unpopular.html. Accessed December 11, 2010.

Bowman, Karlyn. 2010. "What the Voters Actually Said on Election Day." *The American: The Journal of the American Enterprise Institute*, November 16. http://www.american.com/archive/2010/november/what-the-voters-actually-said-on-election-day. Accessed November 17, 2010.

Burnham, Walter Dean. 1970. *Critical Elections and the Mainsprings of American Politics*. New York: W. W. Norton & Co.

Cannon, Lou. 2010. "The Conservatives Come Back from the Dead." *Politics Daily*, October 31. http://www.politicsdaily.com/2010/10/31/the-conservatives-come-back-from-the-dead.

Center for the Study of the American Electorate. 2008. "African Americans, Anger, Fear and Youth Propel Turnout to Highest Level Since 1964." American University. http://domino.american.edu/AU/media/mediarel.nsf/1D265343BDC218978 5256B810071F238/EE414B16927D6C9E85257522004F109D?OpenDocument. Accessed December 17, 2008.

Cummings, Jeanie. 2009. "Obama Finds Opportunity in Crisis." *Politico*, January 8. http://www.politico.com/news/stories/0109/17244.html. Accessed December 11, 2010.

Fiorina, Morris P. 2006. *Culture War? The Myth of a Polarized America*, 2nd ed. New York: Pearson Longman.

———. 2009. *Disconnect: The Breakdown of Representation in American Politics*. Norman, Oklahoma: University of Oklahoma Press.

Guth, James L. 2011. "Obama, Religious Politics, and the Culture Wars." In *Transforming America: Barack Obama in the White House*, edited by Steven E. Schier. Lanham, MD: Rowman & Littlefield.

Harris, John F., and James Hohman. 2010. "Dems Urge Obama to Take a Stand." *POLITICO*, August 23. http://www.politico.com/news/stories/0810/41356.html. Accessed August 23, 2010.

Hulse, Carl, and Adam Nagourney. 2010. "Senate G.O.P. Leader Finds Weapon in Party Unity." *New York Times*, March 16. http://www.nytimes.com/2010/03/17/us/politics/17mcconnell.html. Accessed March 17, 2010.

Johnson, Bertram. 2011. "Small Ball in the Long Game: Barack Obama and Congress." In *Transforming America: Barack Obama in the White House*, edited by Steven E. Schier. Lanham, MD: Rowman & Littlefield.

Judis, John B., and Ruy Teixeira. 2007. "Back to the Future: The Re-emergence of the Emerging Democratic Majority." *The American Prospect*, June 19. http://www .prospect.org/cs/articles?article=back_to_the_future061807. Accessed December 11, 2010.

Key, V. O., Jr. 1955. "A Theory of Critical Elections." *Journal of Politics* 17 (1): 3–18.

Krugman, Paul. 2010. "Falling into the Chasm." *New York Times*, October 24. http:// www.nytimes.com/2010/10/25/opinion/25krugman.html. Accessed October 25, 2010.

Ladd, Everett Carll. 1991. "Like Waiting for Godot: The Uselessness of 'Realignment' for Understanding Change in Contemporary American Politics. In *The End of Realignment: Interpreting Electoral Eras*, edited by Byron E. Shafer, 24–36. Madison, WI: University of Wisconsin Press.

Layman, Geoffrey. 2001. *The Great Divide: Religious and Cultural Conflict in American Party Politics*. New York: Columbia University Press.

Mayhew, David R. 2004. *Electoral Realignments*. New Haven, CT: Yale University Press.

Pear, Robert. 2009. "Public Option Fades From Debate Over Health Care." *New York Times*, September 12. http://www.nytimes.com/2009/09/13/health/policy/13plan .html. Accessed September 13, 2010.

Pew Research Center. 2008. "Inside Obama's Sweeping Victory. Pew Research Center for the People and the Press." http://pewresearch.org/pubs/1023/exit-poll -analysis-2008. Accessed November 9, 2008.

———. 2010a. "A Clear Rejection of the Status Quo, No Consensus about Future Policies: GOP Wins Big Despite Party's Low Favorability." November 17. http:// pewresearch.org/pubs/1789/2010-midterm-elections-exit-poll-analysis. Accessed December 11, 2010.

———. 2010b. "Public's Priorities for 2010: Economy, Jobs, Terrorism: Energy Concerns Fall, Deficit Concerns Rise." January 25. http://people-press.org/report/584/ policy-priorities-2010. Accessed January 25, 2010.

Rae, Nicol C. 2004. "The George W. Bush Presidency in Historical Context." In *High Risk and Big Ambition: The Early Presidency of George W. Bush*, edited by Steven E. Schier, 17–36. Pittsburgh: University of Pittsburgh Press.

———. 2009. "The Bush Presidency in Historical Context: The Limits of the Partisan Presidency." In *Ambition and Division: Legacies of the George W. Bush Presidency*, edited by Steven E. Schier, 19–39. Pittsburgh: University of Pittsburgh Press.

Rasmussen, Scott, and Doug Schoen. 2010. "Why Obama Can't Move the Health Care Numbers." *Wall Street Journal*, March 9. http://online.wsj.com/article/SB10 0014240527487047849045751119935591742122.html. Accessed March 10, 2010.

Rich, Frank. 2010. "All the President's Captors." *New York Times*, December 4. http:// www.nytimes.com/2010/12/05/opinion/05rich.html. Accessed December 4, 2010.

Schoen, Douglas E. 2010. "The Stakes in the Health Care War." *POLITICO*, August 11. http://www.politico.com/news/stories/0810/40946.html. Accessed August 12, 2010.

Shafer, Byron E. 1991. "The Notion of an Electoral Order: The Structure of Electoral Politics at the Accession of George Bush." In *The End of Realignment: Interpreting*

Electoral Eras, edited by Byron E. Shafer, 37–84. Madison, WI: University of Wisconsin Press.

Sinclair, Barbara. 2006. *Party Wars: Polarization and the Politics of National Policy Making.* Norman, OK: University of Oklahoma Press.

Skowronek, Stephen. 1993. *The Politics Presidents Make: Leadership from John Adams to George Bush.* Cambridge, MA: Harvard-Belknap.

———. 2008. *Presidential Leadership in Political Time: Reprise and Reappraisal.* Washington, DC: CQ Press.

Smith, Richard Norton. 2008. "The Official End of the Reagan Era." *Time*, November 5. http://www.time.com/time/magazine/article/0,9171,1857001-1,00.html. Accessed November 30, 2008.

Sundquist, James L. 1973. *Dynamics of the Party System: Alignment and Realignment of Political Parties in the United States.* Washington, DC: Brookings Institution.

Tatalovich, Raymond. 2011. "The Obama Administration and the Great Recession." In *Transforming America: Barack Obama in the White House*, edited by Steven E. Schier. Lanham, MD: Rowman & Littlefield.

Thrush, Glenn. 2010. "Obama's White Working Class Problem." *POLITICO*, October 20. http://www.politico.com/news/stories/1010/43868.html. Accessed December 11, 2010.

White, John K. 2011. "Caught between Hope and History: Obama, Public Opinion, and the 2010 Elections." In *Transforming America: Barack Obama in the White House*, edited by Steven E. Schier. Lanham, MD: Rowman & Littlefield.

Zaller, John R., Marty Cohen, David Karol, and Hans Noel. 2008. *The Party Decides: Presidential Nominations Before and After Reform.* Chicago: University of Chicago Press.

Chapter Two

Caught between Hope and History

Obama, Public Opinion, and the 2010 Elections

John K. White

The president was extremely disappointed as he listened to the election returns. After a tumultuous twenty-four months punctuated with hopes of a long-lasting economic recovery and fears it would never come, the Democratic Party suffered its worst defeat in years. Everywhere one looked, the results were disheartening. In the congressional contests, nearly every candidate who received a once-coveted presidential endorsement lost. The president's wife was puzzled by the scale of the debacle, writing, "It is impossible to analyze or to understand the reason why one person was elected here and another defeated there." But the First Lady consoled her disappointed followers with these words: "On the whole, I think it is as easy to put through a well thought out program when the two major parties are more nearly equally represented in Congress" (Eleanor Roosevelt 1938).

The First Lady's hope for a renewed bipartisanship followed a bitter political season marked by a naysaying, pro-business-oriented Republican Party. Throughout the campaign, the president assailed the Republicans for their "merely negative purposes," telling voters: "Judge parties and candidates, not merely by what they promise, but by what they have done, by their records in office, by the kind of people they travel with, by the kind of people who finance and promote their campaigns. By their promoters ye shall know them" (Franklin D. Roosevelt 1938). Business executives were particularly vociferous in their opposition to the president's domestic reforms, labeling him a "socialist"—an inevitable result of a despondent Grand Old Party that the president claimed was "desperate in mood, angry at failure, and cunning in purpose" (Roosevelt 1936). After an election in which a resurgent Republican Party won nearly every close race, talk of a partisan realignment favoring the Democrats was silenced. Prospective presidential candidates rejoiced, bolstered by one poll showing 52 percent resolutely opposed to another term

43

for the president (Gallup Organization 1938d). Republicans began measuring the Oval Office drapes, certain that one of their own would occupy it two years hence. And that's the way it was—*in 1938*.

According to former FDR adviser Raymond Moley, the 1938 Republican triumph represented "a comeback of astounding proportions" (Busch 2006). Indeed it was. Republicans gained seventy-two House seats, seven Senate seats, and governorships in the key Electoral College states of Michigan, Pennsylvania, and Ohio. Taken together, these wins were astonishing, given that only two years before Republicans had 17 senators (out of a possible 96) and 88 House members (out of a possible 435). Led by Franklin D. Roosevelt, Democrats were at their zenith, and their political reign stretched as far as the eyes of forecasters could see.

Looking back, it is striking how similar the 2010 results were to those of 1938. In 2010, Democrats gave away sixty-three House seats, seven Senate seats, and the governorships of Michigan, Pennsylvania, and Ohio, although unlike 1938, Democrats lost control of the House. Obama political strategist David Plouffe was prescient when he predicted that 2010 would "not be a banner year" (Plouffe 2010). That forecast came to pass. After the 2010 ballots were counted, the Republicans had their largest House majority since 1946, and Democrats were mostly confined to the eastern and western coastlines. In fact, the percentage of Democrats representing New York and California soared to 28.1 percent of the House Democratic caucus, while in between these two deeply Democratic blue states lay a swath of red Republican congressional districts (Ostermeir 2010). One could drive from parts of New Jersey westward to California without entering a single Democratic district.

In one sense, the shellacking the Democratic Party suffered in 1938 and 2010 was hardly a surprise in either instance. Both contests provided the Democrats with a perfect storm: a tumbling economy and a double-digit (or close to double-digit) unemployment rate. In 1938, unemployment approached 20 percent, causing GOP critics to forget about Herbert Hoover and decry the new "Roosevelt Recession." Something similar happened in 2010: unemployment remained stubbornly stuck near 10 percent—something that had not occurred in a midterm election since 1982. The Gallup poll found economic confidence registered at a frigid minus 25 (Gallup Organization 2010).[1] Moreover, *90 percent* of voters rated the current economy as either "not good" or "poor," and *49 percent* said they were "very worried" about the nation's economic future (Edison Media Research and Mitofsky International 2010). For many, the American Dream was in jeopardy—if not for themselves, then for their children and grandchildren. Only 32 percent thought life for the next generation would be "better," 39 percent said it would be "worse," and 26 percent answered "the same" (Edison Media Research and Mitofsky International 2010).

The 1938 and 2010 elections were also eerily reminiscent insofar as they were preceded by Democratic landslides that resulted in victories where Republicans traditionally dominated. For example, in forty-nine House districts that Democrats lost in 2010, Republican presidential candidate John McCain beat Barack Obama in those same districts in 2008 (Fritze 2010). Given Obama's anemic job approval ratings, it was a foregone conclusion that most of these incumbent Democrats would surrender their seats. They did—and many more. The year 2010 marked the first time since 1938 that an incumbent party (the Democrats) would lose more than sixty congressional seats.

Another reason for the Democratic losses is that voters in both the 1938 and 2010 contests were telling the incumbent president to cool it. By 1938, the New Deal had worn out its welcome. A September 1938 Gallup poll found 59 percent of Americans saying that Franklin D. Roosevelt should pursue "more conservative" policies (Gallup Organization 1938c). Other polls showed voters wanted a more conservative approach to governance: 61 percent thought the federal government was spending too much (Gallup Organization 1938e); just 37 percent wanted more government spending to help businesses "out of the present slump" (Gallup Organization 1938a); and 63 percent favored reducing taxes on businesses (Gallup Organization 1938b). This reenergized conservative movement came despite FDR's warning that the popular progressive policies pursued by Theodore Roosevelt and Woodrow Wilson were reversed by conservative successors—something FDR feared would happen once more, telling his radio listeners: "We have to have reasonable continuity in liberal government in order to get permanent results. . . . The voters throughout the country should remember that need for continuous liberal government when they vote next Tuesday" (Franklin D. Roosevelt 1938). They didn't.

In 2010, voters likewise told Barack Obama to curtail his expansion of the federal government. Defending his efforts to combat the Great Recession, Obama told voters in effect, "We've done a lot, and it could be worse"— hardly a winning strategy. Asked after the midterm results were known, 35 percent said the Republican comeback occurred because voters rejected Democratic policies; another 44 percent said the cause was opposition to Obama (CNN/Opinion Research Corporation 2010a). The same poll found that of those who disapproved of Obama's performance, 76 percent said they were displeased because "his policies and actions since he became president were too liberal" (CNN/Opinion Research Corporation 2010a). Ron Fraatz, a sixty-one-year-old retired Pennsylvania school worker, was one of the disenchanted. Fraatz sided with the Republicans, saying of Obama and the Democrats, "They're moving too fast." Fraatz was particularly upset over passage of health-care reform: "I'm getting up to where in another couple of years I'll be in Medicare. So why are they messing around with it and how much is it going to cost?" (Fritze 2010). As House Republican Speaker-Elect John Boehner put it after the election, "The country is saying to all of us [in Washington, DC], 'Stop'" (quoted in Boyer 2010).

After 1938, no one would say that the Democratic defeat represented a vast transformation from the New Deal party system erected by Franklin D. Roosevelt six years earlier. In fact, Democrats went on to three more presidential victories. Just as the New Deal's run at the political box office wasn't over in 1938, it is equally true that the Barack Obama show is not over. In a 2010 post-election poll, 56 percent of voters said, "I'm still hopeful about Obama" (with 45 percent "strongly agreeing") (Greenberg Quinlan Rosner Research 2010). Moreover, 55 percent expressed confidence that Obama's policies would move the country in the right direction (CNN/Opinion Research Corporation 2010b). The morning after the 2010 election, Michelle Obama declared, "Let's get to work. There is a lot to do." Like Eleanor Roosevelt, the First Lady loyally defended her husband: "I think from a policy perspective he has done an outstanding job" (quoted in Diemer 2010).

One reason the Barack Obama era is not yet over is the disdain many Americans have toward the Republican Party. Although 52 percent of 2010 voters held an unfavorable view of the Democratic Party (an unsurprising number given the rebuke they were about to hand to the Democrats), an astonishing *53 percent* also disliked the Republican Party (Edison Media Research and Mitofsky International 2010). That a majority of voters had an unfavorable opinion of the party they were simultaneously endorsing is highly unusual. Most voters ordinarily resolve any negative views of a party they intend to support prior to the election. For example, in 2006 and 2008, the Democratic Party had favorable ratings of 49 percent and 56 percent, respectively. In these same contests, the Republican Party's favorable ratings fell to abysmally low figures of 36 percent each time (*CBS News/New York Times* 2006 and 2008). Psychologists refer to the condition whereby voters hold contrarian views as cognitive dissonance. Voters often hold some opposite facts in tension, but when the dissonance becomes untenable, they resolve their conflicts by changing their behavior. In 2010, voters could resolve their unfavorable views of the Republican Party by endorsing the so-called Tea Party. Exit polls found that 41 percent approved of the Tea Party, with 92 percent of Republicans saying they "strongly supported" it (Edison Media Research and Mitofsky International 2010).

In effect, the Tea Party became a stand-in for a discredited Republican Party still suffering from the after-effects of the George W. Bush presidency. As Republican House Speaker-Elect John Boehner wisely noted in claiming victory, "This is not a time for celebration" (Aigner-Trewory 2010), later adding, "What I got out of the election is not so much that we [the Republicans] won but they [the Democrats] lost" (Boyer 2010). Boehner and his colleagues sensed the obvious: Republicans were handed a second chance— and no more. One straw in the wind pointed to continued GOP difficulty in years to come. Instead of the broad-based victory the Republicans achieved in 1994—a year viewed by many as the capstone of a partisan realignment begun by Ronald Reagan fourteen years before—Republicans did *not* achieve a national victory in 2010. Republicans gained just one seat in the Pacific West—a sharp contrast with 1994 when the GOP picked up ten seats in California, Oregon, and Washington. The lone 2010 GOP gain was in Washington State, where a seat vacated by a Democrat turned to the Republicans (Farnam 2010, A-4). In 1994, Republicans won six House seats in Washington State, including beating incumbent House Speaker Tom Foley—the first time an incumbent speaker lost since 1862.

On the other hand, Republicans did much better in Dixie. The South had long been an area of Republican ascendancy—beginning with the wins amassed by GOP presidential candidates in the region since 1972. In 1994, for the first time since Reconstruction, a majority of House members from the Old Confederacy were Republicans. And in 2010, the southern Republican realignment reached new heights. Democrats lost state legislative seats throughout the region, and in 2011, the Democratic Party will control both state chambers in just two states: Arkansas and Mississippi. After 2010, Republicans will hold more state legislative seats in Dixie—the first time that has happened since the end of the Civil War (Storey 2010). Even in Alabama—a state that once symbolized the "yellow dog Democrat"—Republicans won control of both legislative chambers, the governorship, and a majority of its congressional delegation for the first time in history. One former Democratic governor surveyed the damage: "There's little reason to be optimistic in my region. We can opportunistically pick up statewides [*sic*] every now and then, but building a sustainable party program isn't in the cards" (Martin 2010).

The lopsided Republican majorities in selective areas of the country reflected a new political demography. Of the 63 House seats Republicans won in 2010, 47 have a higher *white* percentage of residents than the national average, 40 have a higher percentage of people *without college degrees*, and 39 have an *older* population than the national average (Farnam 2010, A-4).

Simply put, the demographic contours of the 2010 Republican victory spell trouble for the party's long-term future.

AN EMERGING POLITICAL DEMOGRAPHY

Barack Obama's 2008 victory was due to many things. Both Obama and the Democrats benefited from a severe economic downturn that became the Great Recession. A gyrating stock market, a collapsing housing market, and declining household assets set the country on edge. Adding to Obama's fortune was a Republican president in disrepute, and a country eager for a change in partisan control of the White House. The result was a comfortable Obama victory with 53 percent of the vote—the first time a Democrat captured a popular majority since Jimmy Carter beat Gerald Ford in 1976. Given these favorable conditions, had Obama lost the presidency, it would have been the result of political malpractice. Simply put, the 2008 election was Obama's to lose.

But behind Obama's victory was an emerging political demography that made the election of the first African American president not only possible but also likely (see White 2009). Obama's personal story is one with which most readers are familiar: he is the son of an African man from Kenya and a white woman from Kansas who was born in the most multiracial state in the United States, Hawaii. His parents' interracial marriage in 1960 was illegal in sixteen states on the mainland, and they divorced shortly after Obama's birth a year later. Obama was raised by his mother and maternal grandparents, even as his mother married an Indonesian man and divorced a second time. Obama's story resonated with many Americans in 2008, as he noted, "I think that if you can tell people, 'We have a president in the White House who still has a grandmother living in a hut on the shores of Lake Victoria and has a sister who's half-Indonesian, married to a Chinese-Canadian,' then they're going to think that he may have a better sense of what's going on in our lives and in our country. And they'd be right" (Traub 2007, 50).

The changing demography of the US electorate has manifested itself in two very important areas: (1) the altered complexion of the voter (i.e., more nonwhites), and (2) the fracturing and rebuilding of the once-traditional American family that consisted of a mom, dad, and kids.

The Racial Revolution

Speaking at the 1998 commencement exercises at Portland State University, President Bill Clinton told the student body that the nation was experiencing a "third great revolution"—one as powerful as the American Revolution, which gave birth to the democratic ideas of the eighteenth and nineteenth centuries, and as imposing as the civil rights and women's rights revolutions that broadened the definition of personal liberties in the late twentieth century. According to Clinton, this gathering revolution was being manned by an army of immigrants: "Today, largely because of immigration, there is no majority race in Hawaii or Houston or New York City. Within five years there will be no majority race in our largest state, California. In a little more than fifty years, there will be no majority race in the United States" (Clinton 1998).

The facts bear out Clinton's argument. Consider that when Richard M. Nixon took the presidential oath in 1969, there were approximately 9.6 million foreign-born residing in the United States. Forty years later, when Barack Obama raised his hand to repeat the same oath, the figure had grown to more than 38 million (Williams 2007, 37; Batalova and Terrazas, 2010). Today, there are more foreign-born living in California (9.9 million) than there are people residing in all of New Jersey, and there are more foreign-born in New York State than in the entire population of South Carolina (Buchanan 2002, 2; "Foreign Born Population Continues to Grow" 2010).

Everywhere one looks, the evidence is overwhelming that the United States is rapidly becoming a multiracial, multicultural, and multilingual polity. Los Angeles County, to cite one instance, provided special ballots in 2008 for its Latino, Chinese, Filipino, Japanese, Korean, and Vietnamese voters. But this new cultural diversity hardly signifies an ethnic "melting pot." In the twenty-first century, there are two distinct Americas coming into focus: one mostly white and English-speaking, and another mostly Hispanic and Spanish-speaking. In 2010, it was the mostly white, English-speaking America that dominated and handed the Republicans a sweeping victory.

But it is the Hispanic and Spanish-speaking portion of the populace that will dominate twenty-first-century politics. In 2000, for the first time in US history, Latinos outnumbered blacks (population 36.7 million) to become the nation's number one minority group (Younge 2004). As always, children are harbingers of the future. According to the Census Bureau, 70 percent of the population increase among children aged five and younger is Hispanic (Cohn and Bahrampour 2006, A-1). Should present trends continue, it is estimated that Hispanics will approach 29 percent of the total population in 2050 and could even reach 33 percent by 2100 (Passel and Cohn 2008, 1; Etzioni 2001, 37). In 2008, the Census Bureau issued a bulletin that by 2042 (eight years earlier than anticipated) whites will be the nation's new *minority* (see Passel and Cohn 2008, 2; Roberts 2008).

Today, the nation's skin complexion is rapidly changing from white to some form of beige. Peter Brimelow of *Forbes* magazine writes that by 2020, the proportion of whites nationwide could fall to an all-time low of 61 percent, while the number of nonwhites would constitute as much as one-third of all voters (Buchanan 2002, 129; Beam 2010). In some places, the decline of the white populace has been striking. California, for instance, saw its Anglo population fall below replacement levels, with just 57.6 percent of its population labeled white, while 37.6 percent are Hispanic (U.S. Census Bureau 2010c). As always, the nation's political future can be glimpsed in California. Remember that it was California that elected Ronald Reagan governor in the 1960s, experienced the tax revolution of the 1970s, and became a vanguard of the environmental movement by the end of the twentieth century. If the past is prologue, expect a nation that is multicultural, whose outlook is global, and whose citizens are environmentally friendly.

Newly Created Families

In the twenty-first century, Americans are taking the promises of "life, liberty, and the pursuit of happiness" contained in the Declaration of Independence and endowing them with heretofore unthinkable meaning. Political scientist Francis Fukuyama believes this hyper-individualism in the private realm has produced a profound shift in public values: "Traditional societies have few options and many ligatures (i.e., social bonds to others): people have little individual choice concerning a marriage partner, job, where to live, or what to believe, and are tied down by the often oppressive bonds of family, tribe, caste, religion, feudal obligation, and the like. In modern societies, options for individuals vastly increase, while the ligatures binding them in webs of social obligation are greatly loosened" (Fukuyama 1999, 47). Today, the sexual revolution of the 1960s and 1970s is no longer a revolution. Americans are making hyper-individualistic choices such as whom they should marry (often more than one person, and even members of the same sex) and when (often later in life). The result is a transformation of the American family. Consider the following:

- In 1960, 88 percent of children under eighteen years of age lived with a married parent. Fifty years later, that figure fell to 66 percent (Popenoe and Whitehead 2006, 30; US Census Bureau 2010b).
- In 1960, just 5.3 percent of newborns belonged to unmarried mothers. By 2008, that figure increased to 41 percent. Among whites, the share of single mothers stood at 29 percent; the share among Hispanics was 53 percent;

and the share among blacks registered at 72 percent (see Popenoe and Whitehead 2006, 3; Smith 1999, 3; Livingston and Cohn 2010, 3).

- Between 1960 and 2009, the number of single-parent families tripled from 9 percent to 26 percent of all households (See Popenoe and Whitehead 2006, 29–30; US Census Bureau 2009).
- The number of cohabiting couples grew from 439,000 in 1960 to 6.7 million in 2009 (Popenoe and Whitehead 2006, 24; US Census Bureau 2010a).
- In 2009, there were 581,300 same-sex couples in the US, and five states legalized gay marriage.[2] Of the households reporting same-sex couples, nearly one in five had a biological, step, or adopted child living there (National Center for Marriage and Family Research 2010).

Simply put, we are as far away from the 1950s (with that era's stay-at-home mom and working dad) as the 1900s (with its Model T Fords and urban tenements teeming with European immigrants) were from the mid-twentieth century. Reflecting on these transformations, the late Daniel Patrick Moynihan observed, "The biggest change, in my judgment, is that the family structure has come apart all over the North Atlantic world." Moynihan added that this phenomenon had happened in "an historical instant" (quoted in Bennett 2001, 1). Indeed, it seems so. Back in 1965, Moynihan, then the assistant secretary of labor in the Johnson administration, warned that black families were trapped in a "tangle of pathology," as fathers abandoned households, leaving bereft mothers to cope with raising children. Years later, sociologist Stephanie Coontz observed that this troubling phenomena was only "a rehearsal for something that was going to happen in the white community" (quoted in Cose 2005, 37). Today, white women under twenty-five years of age are just as likely to have a child out of wedlock as a black woman the same age. Among Hispanics, the unwed birth percentage has increased from 19 percent in 1980 to 48 percent in 2005 (Popenoe 2007, 10–11).

Initially, the destruction of the nuclear family provoked conservative outrage. In 1992, Vice President Dan Quayle won plaudits from the Religious Right when he criticized television's *Murphy Brown* for having an out-of-wedlock baby, saying Brown mocked "the importance of fathers by bearing a child alone, and calling it just another 'lifestyle choice'" (Quayle 1992). Quayle believed the program's subtext reflected a "poverty of values" among the nation's cultural elites who, he declared, "sneer at the simple but hard virtues—modesty, fidelity, integrity" (Quayle 1994, 318, 326). Yet just sixteen years later, the Republican Party nominated Sarah Palin for vice president even though her teenage daughter, Bristol, was pregnant and not married to the father of her child. The situation, once discovered, hardly caused a ripple. In fact, it *endeared* Palin to the party's conservative wing, as her daughter did not have an abortion. Following the 2008 election, Democratic Congress-woman Linda Sanchez also made history when she became the first House member to become pregnant without being married. Sanchez defended her pregnancy: "I'm not a high school kid, it wasn't an accident. I'm financially stable, in a committed relationship." At age thirty-eight, Sanchez told the *Washington Post* that she always wanted children and that the Bristol Palin pregnancy led her to conclude that her constituents would not object: "We've evolved as a society so much. The reality of single working moms is such a powerful reality" (Argetsinger and Roberts 2008, C-3). Sanchez did marry the father of her child in 2009, and she easily withstood the Republican wave a year later, having been reelected with 64 percent of the vote.

THE NEW DEMOGRAPHY TAKES A HIATUS IN 2010

In 2010, the political demography that elected Barack Obama in 2008 altered sharply. For example, whites, which were 74 percent of the 2008 electorate (only 43 percent of whom backed Obama) rose to 77 percent of the 2010 elec-torate. By contrast, nonwhites—including African Americans and Latinos (who gave Obama 95 percent and 67 percent of their votes, respectively)—had a smaller share of the electoral pie in 2010. Similarly, younger voters (66 percent of whom backed Obama), fell from 18 percent of the total electorate to just 12 percent. First-time voters fell from 11 percent to a mere 3 percent. On the other hand, the share of voters aged sixty-five and older rose from 16 percent to 21 percent—something that mirrored support for the Tea Party movement among older Americans (Edison Media Research and Mitofsky International 2008 and 2010).

Indeed, the 2010 outcome was pre-ordained when the two parties share of the electorate was tied at 35 percent apiece. By contrast, in 2008, Democrats outnumbered Republicans 39 percent to 32 percent. Similarly, the comfort-able 2008 Obama win was reduced to a tie: 45 percent of midterm voters said they supported Obama in 2008 and 45 percent backed McCain. Not surpris-ingly, an astonishing *42 percent* described themselves as conservatives; only 20 percent self-identified as liberals (see table 2.1).

The data depicted in table 2.1 has some troubling numbers for Obama and the Democrats. Independents shifted strongly to the Republicans in 2010, giv-ing the GOP 56 percent support for its House candidates—up twelve points from the backing John McCain received in 2008. In a press conference after the election, Obama went after his Democratic base, describing their opposi-tion to his post-election negotiations with Republicans as "sanctimonious"— a move sure to alienate liberal Democrats but designed to appeal to indepen-

Table 2.1.   The Shifting Demography of the 2008 and 2010 Electorates (in percentages)

Group	Percentage of Voters in 2008	Support for McCain in 2008	Percentage of Voters in 2010	Support for GOP Congressional Candidates in 2010
Race				
Whites	74	55	77	60
African American	13	4	11	9
Latino	9	31	8	38
Asian	2	35	2	40
Age				
18–29 years old	18	32	12	42
30–44 years old	29	46	24	50
45–64 years old	37	49	43	53
65 and older	16	53	21	59
Party				
Democrats	39	10	35	7
Republicans	32	90	35	94
Independents	29	44	29	56
Ideology				
Liberal	22	10	20	8
Moderate	44	39	38	42
Conservative	34	78	42	84
First-Time Voters				
Yes	11	30	3	43
No	89	48	97	53

Sources: Edison Media Research and Mitofsky International, exit polls, November 4, 2008, and November 2, 2010.

dents. At the same gathering, Obama described his job as "look[ing] out for middle-class families who are struggling right now to get by and Americans who are out of work through no fault of their own" (Obama 2010).

Accomplishing this task will not only help Obama with independents but with white blue-collar workers. In 2010, this group deserted the Democratic Party in droves: just 33 percent of whites without a college degree voted for Democratic House candidates (Edison Media Research and Mitofsky International 2010). Virginia Democratic Senator Jim Webb, whose 2012 reelection will depend on his (and Obama's) ability to garner support from the white working class, says, "Democrats have to reach out to the working class. Something has to change in the Democratic Senate." Webb has often scorned "the upper crust of academia and the pampered salons of Hollywood," telling Obama that he needs to let white non-college-educated workers know that he, too, is on their side (Chafets 2010). It is a sentiment other endangered 2012 Senate Democrats hope Obama will address.

Finally, 55 percent of 2010 midterm voters disapproved of Obama's performance in office, and 52 percent thought his policies hurt the country. Nevertheless, when asked who was to blame for the Great Recession, 35 percent chose Wall Street, 29 percent picked the still-unpopular George W. Bush, and only 24 percent named Obama (Edison Media Research and Mitofsky International 2010).

SIGNS OF THE FUTURE

There were places in 2010 where the political demography looked more like that of 2008, providing Democrats with morsels of good news. In Nevada, Senate Majority Leader Harry Reid was reelected despite long odds. The keys to Reid's five-point victory were his superb turnout operation, which drove Democrats to the polls, and a state Republican Party whose leaders could not deliver an endorsement to a viable candidate. Latinos constituted an astonishing *16 percent* of the Nevada electorate, and 69 percent of them backed Reid. Whites, on the other hand, were just 71 percent of the total voter pool, and only 42 percent of them supported Reid. (White men and older voters were especially critical of Reid, with only 39 percent and 45 percent respectively voting for the incumbent.) In addition to Hispanics, Reid won 91 percent backing from Democrats, 59 percent support from voters aged 18 to 29, and 52 percent from those with post-graduate degrees. In other words, Reid reassembled the coalition that gave Obama a victory in Nevada in 2008—the first time a Democratic presidential candidate carried the state since 1996.

Reid was also helped by the insurgent Tea Party movement that raised millions of dollars for Republican candidate Sharron Angle, whom the Senate majority leader repeatedly (to the point of exhaustion) labeled "extreme," and her bizarre statements calling for phasing out Social Security and Medicare "in favor of something privatized" (PolitiFact.com 2010). Angle further demanded that "Second Amendment remedies" be used by voters wanting change—a suggestion that was interpreted by some to mean a violent overthrow of the federal government—or, at the very least, the Obama presidency (Stein 2010).

Something similar happened in Colorado where Democratic Senator Michael Bennet emerged victorious over Republican Tea Party favorite Ken Buck. Bennet, who had never before held political office, was viewed by many as extremely vulnerable to defeat. But he was aided by a large Hispanic turnout (12 percent of the electorate) and by Colorado's emergence as an Information Age state. Two-thirds of Coloradans who voted in 2010 held a college degree, and these voters backed Bennet over Buck 53 percent to

43 percent (*ABC News* 2010). Colorado Democrats also rejoiced at the GOP bickering in the gubernatorial contest. In that race, Republican Dan Maes was so discredited that anti-immigrant and former Republican congressman Tom Tancredo stepped in as a third-party candidate. The GOP split enabled Denver mayor John Hickenlooper to win an easy victory, keeping the statehouse in Democratic hands.

But the twenty-first-century electorates that showed up in Nevada and Colorado were even more pronounced in California. There, Latinos constituted 22 percent of the total votes cast, resulting in twin Democratic victories in the state's senate and gubernatorial contests. Incumbent Senator Barbara Boxer easily beat Republican challenger Carly Fiorina, winning 52 percent of the vote to Fiorina's 43 percent. The key to Boxer's victory was the 65 percent backing she received from Hispanics, even as she lost support from whites (who were just 61 percent of the California electorate and cast 52 percent of their votes for Fiorina). Democratic gubernatorial candidate Jerry Brown also won strong support from nonwhites: 77 percent of blacks; 64 percent of Latinos; and 57 percent of Asians—giving Brown a comfortable 53 percent to 42 percent victory over his Republican opponent Meg Whitman. As in the Senate contest, Whitman won majority backing from the diminished white portion of the California electorate (50 percent) (Edison Media Research and Mitofsky International 2010). Had only whites voted, both Boxer and Brown would have been swept aside in the national Republican landslide (Schrag 2010).

Only in Florida did the new demography work for the GOP. There, Marco Rubio overcame the odds by first driving Governor Charlie Crist out of the Republican primary and into the Senate race as an independent, thereby enhancing his chances for victory. And Rubio's win was assured when he won pluralities from *both* whites and Latinos. Whites constituted 70 percent of Florida's votes, and Rubio won 48 percent. Latinos were a healthy 18 percent of the total vote and 45 percent backed Rubio (Edison Media Research and Mitofsky International 2010). Pundits heralded Rubio as a comer—some even comparing him to Ronald Reagan. Clearly, Rubio is a man on the make and a prospective candidate on a national Republican ticket in the coming decade.

CAUGHT BETWEEN HOPE AND HISTORY

The twin demographics of 2008 and 2010 are battling for the nation's future. The 2010 Republican victory was, in many respects, a resurgence of the old Reagan coalition. In the words of Richard Scammon and Ben Wattenberg,

Republicans owed their success to voters who were "un-young, un-poor, and un-black" (Scammon and Wattenberg 1970). It was these voters and their strong support for the Tea Party movement that created the "enthusiasm gap" between Republicans and Democrats. Of those who cast a 2010 ballot, 37 percent said their motivation was to oppose Obama; only 23 percent said it was to support him (Edison Media Research and Mitofsky International 2010).[3]

Moreover, the GOP House victory came at a propitious time because 2011 is a redistricting year, and Republicans won important governorships in places that are adding congressional seats (e.g., Florida and Texas) and also got control of governorships in places that are losing congressional seats (e.g., Pennsylvania and Ohio) (see Cohen 2010). Adding these governorships, along with control of the state legislatures in twenty-five states, means the Republicans will exert a mighty influence in mapping congressional districts designed to keep them in power and discourage defeated Democrats (especially former members of Congress) from making renewed attempts for lost seats (Storey 2010). In 195 districts, Republicans control the state's governorship and state legislature and have a congressional incumbent; Democrats will have the same advantage in just 49 districts (Electoralvote .com 2010). Divided government—the norm during the Eisenhower, Nixon, Reagan, George H. W. Bush, and Bill Clinton regimes—is likely to be the "new normal" once more.

At the same time, Barack Obama continues to benefit from a political demography where the numbers of nonwhites and non-traditional families increase with every passing year. As 2010 drew to a close, the nation was equally divided when asked whether it approved of Obama's job performance—46 percent approved and 46 percent disapproved—what is buoying Obama is the support he receives from nonwhites. Taken as a whole, 67 percent of nonwhites back Obama; only 37 percent of whites do. Specifically, 89 percent of African Americans and 58 percent of Hispanics like the job Obama is doing (Gallup Organization, November 29–December 5, 2010). David Plouffe explains the importance of these numbers: "Look at the growth areas of the electorate. Latino voters make up a larger and larger share of the electorate and are of special importance in key battleground states in the West like Nevada, New Mexico, and Arizona, which will be a new key battleground in 2012." Plouffe adds that if Obama can "show progress and leadership . . . we have the demographic strength to pull off victories for the foreseeable future, particularly in presidential election years when turnout is highest" (Plouffe 2010).

If 1938 is parallel to 2010, Republicans should worry. Since the George W. Bush presidency ended, Republicans have done little to reposition themselves for a twenty-first century electorate whose contours do not favor them. One attempt to do so was noticeably lackluster. In 2010, the GOP issued *A*

Pledge to America—a thinly veiled attempt to model the infamous *Contract with America* that meant so much to House Republicans in 1994. Notably, few minorities were depicted in the glossy pamphlet. A *Political Wire* reader noted that of the forty-two photographs included, *only two* featured African Americans—"and they're tiny specks in a much larger group, barely visible." Similarly, there were only "two identifiable people of Asian descent, and no one who might be considered Latino." Thus, while hundreds of whites were photographed, few minority faces (faces that are the hallmarks of the twenty-first century) were featured (*Political Wire* 2010). Moreover, the *Pledge* contained grandiose statements (e.g., "America is more than a country") but few specifics (Republican National Committee 2010, 1).

In the weeks after the election, Republicans have compounded their demographic challenges with their near-unanimous opposition to the DREAM Act, a bill sponsored by Senate Democratic Majority Leader Harry Reid. The DREAM Act would grant citizenship to minors illegally brought into the United States before the age of sixteen who have resided in the United States for five continuous years and either completed their high school education, had two successful college years, or joined the US military and were of good moral character. The Senate failed to muster the required sixty votes needed to pass the legislation, as only three Republicans joined fifty-two Democrats to support the legislation.[4] Alabama's Jeff Sessions, an ardent opponent of the bill, declared, "This bill is a law that at its fundamental core is a reward for illegal activity" (*USA Today* 2010).

Eventually, Republicans will have to accommodate themselves to new political realities—including specific and sustained appeals to minority groups they have long written off. Former Republican National Committee Chair Ken Mehlman rightly notes: "America is every day, less of a white country. We rely too hard on white guys for votes" (Silvia 2006). Ed Gillespie, another former Republican National Committee chair, agrees: "Our majority already rests too heavily on white voters, given that current demographic voting percentages will not allow us to hold our majority in the future" (Gillespie 2006).

But to date, virtually no thinking has been done to redefine conservatism for a post-Reagan period. Recently, Indiana Senator Dick Lugar admonished his fellow Republicans: "We must never be the party of no" (Lugar 2010). Meanwhile, conservative activist and Tea Party supporter Richard Viguerie warned that while the GOP and the Tea Party were "all on the same page until the polls close on November 2," what would follow would be "a massive, almost historic battle for the heart and soul of the Republican Party" (Rutenberg 2010, 1). That forthcoming battle pits an ensconced, yet fearful party establishment long-accustomed to designating presidential candidates against Tea Party-led insurgents who have already demonstrated their capacity to wrest control of state Republican parties from longtime leaders.

Rather than redefining what the GOP should be *for*, Republicans have adopted a "what-me-worry?" stance. And with reason: gaining 63 House seats, 7 Senators, 5 governorships, and 721 state legislative seats is a historic accomplishment. The latter number is important, as there have not been this many Republican state legislators since 1928 (Storey 2010). But the 2010 election is more likely to be viewed by history as an exception—an interesting interlude, not a prelude for coming attractions. Obama is sure to struggle with an anemic economic recovery and a recalcitrant Republican opposition between now and 2012, but he should not be counted out. As Republican pollster Glen Bolger cautions, "People still like Obama and want him to succeed" (quoted in Blake 2010). The 2008 electorate is poised to come to the polls once more, this time aided by four more years of ongoing demographic changes. In the meantime, Obama will remain caught between the hope he generated in 2008, and the history he hopes to achieve.

NOTES

The title for this chapter is adapted from a book written by President Bill Clinton in 1996. See President Bill Clinton, *Between Hope and History: Meeting America's Challenges for the Twenty-First Century* (New York: Times Books/Random House, 1996). Clinton had adopted the title from the Irish poet Seamus Heaney.

1. This measure is found by subtracting current economic conditions with prospects for the nation's economic future.
2. The five states are Iowa, New Hampshire, Connecticut, Massachusetts, and Vermont.
3. An additional 38 percent of respondents said Obama was not a factor.
4. The Republicans were Lisa Murkowski (who had won reelection in Alaska as a write-in candidate), Bob Bennett of Utah (who was defeated at the state Republican convention by Tea Party insurgents), and Dick Lugar.

REFERENCES

ABC News. 2010. "2010 Election Exit Poll Analysis: The Political Price of Economic Pain." November 3. http://abcnews.go.com/Politics/2010-midterms-political-price -economic-pain/story?id=12041739&page=2. Accessed December 10, 2010.

Aigner-Trewory, Adam. 2010. "GOP's Cantor: 'We Have to Deliver.'" CNN.com, November 3. http://www.cnn.com/2010/POLITICS/11/03/gop.tone/index.html. Accessed November 28, 2010.

Argetsinger, Amy, and Roxanne Roberts. 2008. "Oh, Baby! Big News for Sanchez." *Washington Post*, November 21.

Batalova, Jeanne, and Aaron Terrazas. 2010. "Frequently Requested Statistics on Immigrants and Immigration in the United States." Migration Policy Institute, December. http://www.migrationinformation.org/USfocus/display.cfm?id=818#1a. Accessed December 12, 2010.

Beam, Christopher. 2010. "Into the Blue: The New Census Data May Favor Republicans, but Long-Term Demographic Trends Favor Democrats." *Slate*, December 21. http://www.slate.com/id/2278861.

Bennett, William J. 2001. *The Broken Hearth: Reversing the Moral Collapse of the American Family*. New York: Doubleday.

Blake, Aaron. 2010. "Obama and the Unpopularity Question." *Washington Post*, December 8.

Boyer, Peter J. 2010. "House Rule: Will John Boehner Control the Tea Party Congress?" *The New Yorker*, December 13. http://www.newyorker.com/reporting/2010/12/13/101213fa_fact_boyer?printable=true. Accessed December 6, 2010.

Buchanan, Patrick J. 2002. *The Death of the West: How Dying Populations and Immigrant Invasions Imperil Our Country and Civilization*. New York: St. Martin's Press.

Busch, Andrew E. 2006. "The New Deal Comes to a Screeching Halt." Ashbrook Center, May editorial. http://www.ashbrook.org/publicat/oped/busch/06/1938.html. Accessed November 22, 2010.

CBS News/New York Times. 2006. Poll, October 27–31.

———. 2008. Poll, October 19–22.

Chafets, Zev. 2010. "The Next Fight: A Conservative Democrat Reassesses the Battlefield." *Newsweek*, November 19. http://www.newsweek.com/2010/11/19/the-new-calculus-for-conservative-democrats.html. Accessed December 8, 2010.

Clinton, Bill. 1998. "Remarks by the President at Portland State University Commencement." Portland, Oregon, June 13.

CNN/Opinion Research Corporation. 2010a. Poll, November 11–14.

———. 2010b. Poll, December 17–19.

Cohen, Richard E. 2010. "Report: Florida Adds Two Seats, New York Loses." *POLITICO*, September 26. http://dyn.politico.com/printstory.cfm?uuid=4FE67451-9F7A-0A87-808A44133C0FA28E. Accessed December 10, 2010.

Cohn, D'Vera, and Tara Bahrampour. 2006. "Of U.S. Children Under 5, Nearly Half Are Minorities." *Washington Post*, May 10.

Cose, Ellis. 2005. "Long After the Alarm Went Off." *Newsweek*, March 14.

Diemer, Tom. 2010. "On Bleak Election Night, Michelle Obama Tells President: Let's Go to Work." *Politics Daily*, November 26. http://www.politicsdaily.com/2010/11/26/on-bleak-election-night-michelle-obama-tells-president-lets-g. Accessed November 27, 2010.

Edison Media Research and Mitofsky International. 2008. Exit poll, November 4.

———. 2010. Exit poll, November 2.

Electoralvote.com. 2010. http://www.electoral-vote.com/evp2010/Senate/Maps/Dec08-s.html#8. Accessed December 10, 2010.

Etzioni, Amitai. 2001. *The Monochrome Society*. Princeton: Princeton University Press.

Farnam, T. W. 2010. "GOP's Midterm Gains Concentrated in Blue-Collar Areas." *Washington Post*, November 21.

"Foreign Born Population Continues to Grow." 2010. *Cincinnati.com*, October 12. http://cincinnati.com/blogs/economics/2010/10/12/foreign-born-population -continues-to-grow. Accessed December 11, 2010.

Fritze, John. 2010. "Obama Agenda in Jeopardy if GOP Hits Its Goal." *USA Today*, October 26. http://www.usatoday.com/printedition/news/20101026/1ahouse26 _cv.art.htm. Accessed December 6, 2010.

Fukuyama, Francis. 1999. *The Great Disruption: Human Nature and the Reconstitution of Social Order*. New York: Free Press.

Gallup Organization. 1938a. Poll, March 17–22.

———. 1938b. Poll, March 25–30.

———. 1938c. Poll, September 25–30.

———. 1938d. Poll, November 16–21.

———. 1938e. Poll, December 25–30.

———. 2010. Poll, November 2.

Gillespie, Edward. 2006. "Populists Beware: The GOP Must Not Become an Anti-Immigrant Party." *Wall Street Journal*, April 2.

Greenberg Quinlan Rosner Research. 2010. Poll, November 5, press release.

Livingston, Gretchen, and D'Vera Cohn. 2010. "The New Demography of American Motherhood." *Pew Research Center Report*, August 19.

Lugar, Dick. 2010. "CNN State of the Union." Broadcast, December 5.

Martin, Jonathan. 2010. "Democratic South Finally Falls." *Politico*, November 28. http://dyn.politico.com/printstory.cfm?uuid=9071B5F8-91E6-C69B -18EB312BE1C0D0C8. Accessed November 29, 2010.

National Center for Family and Marriage Research. 2010. "Same-Sex Households in the U.S., 2009," National Center for Family and Marriage Research, October. http:// ncfmr.bgsu.edu/pdf/family_profiles/file87414.pdf. Accessed December 12, 2010.

Obama, Barack. 2010. "Transcript: Obama Press Conference," Washington, DC, December 7.

Ostermeir, Eric. 2010. "Are Democrats Becoming a Two-State Party?" *Smart Politics Blog*, University of Minnesota Humphrey Institute, November 17. http://ms16 .lnh.mail.rcn.net/wm/eml/login.html?sessionid=60a55af0b730fdc8b37209552. Accessed November 17, 2010.

Passel, Jeffrey S., and D'Vera Cohn. 2008. *U.S. Population Projections: 2005–2050*. Pew Research Center, February 11.

Plouffe, David. 2010. *How Democrats Can Win by Leading America to a Better Future in 2010 and Beyond: An Update to the Audacity to Win*. New York: Penguin Books.

PolitiFact.com. 2010. "During the Primary, Angle Said Social Security Can't Be Fixed." http://www.politifact.com/truth-o-meter/statements/2010/jun/24/harry -reid/during-primary-angle-said-social-security-cant-be-fixed. Accessed December 10, 2010.

Political Wire. 2010. "A No Diversity Pledge." September 24.

Popenoe, David. 2007. *The Future of Marriage in America.* New Brunswick, New Jersey: Rutgers University National Marriage Project.

Popenoe, David, and Barbara Dafoe Whitehead. 2006. *The State of Our Unions, 2006.* New Brunswick, New Jersey: Rutgers University National Marriage Project.

Quayle, Dan. 1992. "Address to the Commonwealth Club of California." San Francisco, California, May 19.

———. 1994. *Standing Firm: A Vice Presidential Memoir.* New York: HarperCollins.

Republican National Committee. 2010. *A Pledge to America: A New Governing Agenda Built on the Priorities of Our Nation, the Principles We Stand for, and America's Founding Values.* Washington, DC, October.

Roberts, Sam. 2008. "A Generation Away, Minorities May Become the Majority in U.S." *New York Times,* August 14.

Roosevelt, Eleanor. 1938. "My Day." Newspaper column, November 10. http://www.gwu.edu/-erpapers/myday/displaydoc.cfm?_y=1938&_f=md055107. Accessed November 16, 2010.

Roosevelt, Franklin D. 1936. "Address at the Democratic State Convention." Syracuse, New York, September 29.

———. 1938. "Radio Address on the Election of Liberals." November 4. http://docs.fdrlibrary.marist.edu/php11438.html. Accessed November 16, 2010.

Rutenberg, Jim. 2010. "Rove Returns, With Team, Planning GOP Push." *New York Times,* September 25.

Scammon, Richard M., and Ben J. Wattenberg. 1970. *The Real Majority.* New York: Coward-McCann.

Schrag, Peter. 2010. "California Here We Come." *The New Republic,* December 6.

Silvia, Mark. 2006. "GOP Chairman: 'Message Received.'" *Washington Post,* November 9.

Smith, Tom W. 1999. "The Emerging 21st Century American Family." Paper presented at the National Opinion Research Center, University of Chicago, November 24.

Stein, Sam. 2010. "Sharron Angle Floated Second Amendment Remedies as 'Cure' for 'The Harry Reid Problems.'" *Huffington Post,* June 16. http://www.huffingtonpost.com/2010/06/16/sharron-angle-floated-2nd_n_614003.html. Accessed December 10, 2010.

Storey, Tim. 2010. "Legislative Landslide." *Crystal Ball,* December 10. http://www.democratunity.com/index.php?option=com_content&view=article&id=2206:legislature-landslide&catid=82:local. Accessed December 10, 2010.

Traub, James. 2007. "Is (His) Biography (Our) Destiny?" *New York Times Magazine,* November 4.

USA Today. 2010. "Senate Blocks Dream Act," December 18. http://content.usatoday.com/communities/onpolitics/post/2010/12/senate-dream-act-/1. Accessed December 27, 2010.

US Census Bureau. 2009. "Custodial Mothers and Their Child Support, 2007," released November. http://singleparents.about.com/gi/o.htm?zi=1/XJ&zTi=1&sdn=singleparents&cdn=parenting&tm=6&gps=324_432_1148_624&f=00&su=p284.9.336.ip_p504.1.336.ip_&tt=11&bt=1&bts=1&zu=http%3A//www.census.gov/prod/2009pubs/p60-237.pdf. Accessed December 11, 2009.

————. 2010a. "Census Bureau Reports Families with Children Increasingly Face Unemployment." Press release, January 15. http://www.census.gov/newsroom/ releases/archives/families_households/cb10-08.html. Accessed December 11, 2010.

————. 2010b. "U.S. Census Bureau Reports that Men and Women Wait Longer to Marry." Press release, November 10. http://www.census.gov/newsroom/releases/ archives/families_households/cb10-174.html. Accessed December 11, 2010.

————. 2010c. "2010 Census Data: California State Population by Race." http://2010 .census.gov/2010census/data. Accessed May 18, 2011.

White, John Kenneth. 2009. *Barack Obama's America: How New Conceptions of Race, Family, and Religion Ended the Reagan Era*. Ann Arbor: University of Michigan Press.

Williams, Kim M. 2007. *Race Counts: American Multiracism and Civil Rights Politics*. Ann Arbor: University of Michigan Press.

Younge, Gary. 2004. "Black Americans Move Back to Southern States. *The Guardian*, May 25.

Chapter Three

Parties as a Resource for Presidential Leadership

The Case of Barack Obama

John J. Coleman

Barack Obama entered office with the strongest partisan backing of any president in recent memory. Unlike George W. Bush, who was elected in 2000 under controversial circumstances with fewer popular votes than his opponent, or Bill Clinton, elected in 1992 with just 43 percent of the popular vote, Obama received 53 percent of the vote and brought large majorities with him to the US House and Senate. When Bush entered office, there were serious questions about how he would enact his legislative agenda and lead the government, given the raw emotions over the 2000 election and its resolution by the US Supreme Court. For Obama, these questions did not arise in the context of his electoral victory but instead in the frequently stated concerns about whether the new president had the requisite experience to make things happen.

What President Obama did have at his disposal, however, were the resources the American party system offers to presidents to exert leadership and tally legislative successes. Presidents seek to establish identities and political strengths independent of their parties, but they remain dependent on party members to achieve many of their goals. Presidential leadership is connected to the party system in two important ways. First, the historical trajectory of the party system may be more or less favorable for the establishment of presidential leadership. That is, presidents are in a better or worse position because of the strength or weakness of current party alignments. Second, a president whose victory was comfortable and whose party has large majorities in Congress has the potential for victories on a wide range of fronts that would be more difficult to achieve with narrow majorities or when the other party controls part of the legislative branch. I discuss each of these factors in turn.

OBAMA AND THE DYNAMICS
OF THE PARTY SYSTEM

President Obama was in a strong position regarding the first factor, the historical trajectory of the party system. Although the dynamics of the party system had pointed in a Republican direction for two decades, these began to slow and reverse during George W. Bush's presidency. Bush won a razor-thin victory in 2000 and then faced a Democratic Senate for most of his first two years. Bush won reelection in 2004 by very nearly duplicating the electoral map from 2000. He won a narrow majority and continued to enjoy Republican majorities in the House and Senate, but the president's approval ratings were drooping amidst economic problems, the war in Iraq, discontent in his own party about the growth of government, and the president's failure to gain much traction or get much of his party's support on ambitious plans to reform Social Security and immigration.

While one could certainly make a plausible argument that in many respects, life in the United States had never been better (Easterbrook 2008), the political reality was that vast swaths of the public felt uneasy and vulnerable to economic insecurity (Hacker 2006). The positive economic conditions of the late 1990s gave way to more troubled times. Unemployment, inflation, gasoline prices, mortgage foreclosures, and the federal budget deficit mushroomed. Trade deficits grew, while the relative value of the dollar fell. Health-care costs continued to climb, while the percentage of the workforce covered by company retirement pension plans continued its decline. Virtually none of these issues received a forceful or vocal response, whether market-oriented or otherwise, by the president and his fellow partisans.

Whether this failure to grasp the shifting landscape was due to preoccupation with the Iraq war, poor political calculations, or some other factor, it surely contributed to the overall public clamor for a change in direction in Washington and to nearly 80 percent of the population saying the country was on the wrong track in mid-2008. The Republican troubles were first clearly visible in the November 2006 elections, when Democrats gained majorities in both the US House and Senate. Although the situation in Iraq improved in Bush's final two years, economic conditions did not, culminating in the bursting of the housing bubble as well as the collapse or near collapse of major financial institutions. The November 2008 election results served up precisely what Republicans had feared: a victory by Barack Obama in many states won by Bush; a drop in the Republican percentage of the vote in nearly all states and among nearly all social groups compared to 2004; the first Democratic presidential candidate to finish with significantly more than 50 percent of the vote since Lyndon Johnson in 1964; and the loss of yet more seats in the House and

Senate. The hope for a Republican political era was over, and many analysts speculated the party would be in the political wilderness for some time.

Thus, President Obama took office in an electoral environment that had been friendly to Democrats in the preceding two elections and to some degree across the first decade of the twenty-first century, as they did not lose significant ground to Republicans in 2002 and 2004. The policy environment also was favorable toward presidential leadership. The conflict in Iraq was winding down and of diminished salience. Democrats could pin economic turbulence and insecurity at the feet of Republicans—as always, the blame game oversimplified political and economic reality, but presidents invite the public to give them credit and blame and the public obliges. Republicans themselves needed to determine how to overcome the wreckage of the 2006 and 2008 elections and the policy defeats of President Bush's second term. All of these factors provided a relatively favorable environment for Obama's leadership potential.

To some observers, Obama's victory was seen as possibly heralding in a new partisan realignment that would produce Democratic majorities for decades. The concept of *partisan realignment* is an umbrella term covering distinctive varieties of political change. These varieties include secular (or gradual) realignment and critical (or quick-moving) realignment. In effect, realignment theory takes "before and after" photographs of the party system. The "before and after" might be from a period in which one party is dominant to a period in which the other party dominates, or from a time when a party has a particular coalition to a time when that party has a different supporting coalition, or from a period in which one party dominates to a period in which neither party dominates. Whichever change it is, significant policy departures accompany the party realignment.

Our analytical eye is often drawn to the dramatic and disruptive, but V. O. Key (1959) alerted scholars to the fact that significant political change often occurs gradually, with the accumulation of small, incremental developments. This variety of realignment is known as secular (i.e., steady, gradual) realignment. As a social group becomes more affluent, for example, its members might find the policy appeals of a conservative political party more to their liking. As one particular social group becomes better represented within a political party, other groups might gradually pull out of that party. Scholars have suggested that both of these developments have occurred in the party system over the past few decades. For example, as Catholics moved steadily into the middle class, they became less reliably Democratic. As blacks gained a louder voice in the Democratic Party, whites, especially southern whites, increasingly supported Republicans. As religious and social conservatives played an increasing role in the Republican Party, Republican moderates found themselves increasingly likely to vote Democratic. Evangelical Christians moved from Democratic voting to Republican voting over time.

In the 1990s, secular realignment moved in a direction that tended to favor Republicans. Groups that were considered part of the Democratic New Deal coalition—organized labor, agricultural interests, urban ethnic groups, Catholics, Jews, the less educated, southerners, industrial blue collar workers—tended to support Democrats less strongly in the 1990s than in the 1940s (Mayer 1998). The New Deal coalition could no longer cement Democratic victories and that worked to the Republicans' advantage. Even a candidate who found that he or she did well with these traditional New Deal coalition groups—and most Democratic candidates did do reasonably well with them—would find that he or she needed to reach outside this cluster to ensure victory (Bartels 1998). This provided an opportunity for Republicans in general and George W. Bush in particular. Republicans were poised to strengthen their majority status when Bush entered office and his fellow partisans knew that. That gave them great incentive to cooperate with Bush, which they did at very high levels in roll call votes.

But there were also currents pointing in the Democrats' direction. Minority populations were growing as a share of the population, and minority groups voted more heavily Democratic than did white voters. The Democrats' share among the college educated was growing and was a majority among those with postgraduate education—both these groups were also gaining in size in the population. In some parts of the country—particularly the Northeast and the Pacific coast—high-income voters leaned Democratic, thus erasing the historical tie between income levels and support for Republicans. Democrats were doing better with young voters than they did with other age groups, and this advantage might persist in the future as this group aged, though perhaps not to the same extent as was evident in 2008. On party identification, Democrats gained nationally while Republican identifiers declined, and the Democratic gains among those aged eighteen to twenty-nine were especially dramatic. Given highly partisan voting—about 90 percent of party identifiers will tend to vote for their party's candidate—this created a stiff headwind against Republican victories. Finding a path to citizenship for "illegal immigrants" or "undocumented Americans" also would be likely to add to Democratic votes. Democrats were favored on virtually every issue by 2008. A survey by the Pew Research Center for the People and the Press in February 2008 showed Democrats were thought likely to do a better job on the environment, energy, health care, education, reforming government, the economy, taxes, morality, Iraq, foreign policy, and immigration. Republicans led only on handling terrorist threats. These trends continued throughout 2008. Overall, the issue landscape was growing bleaker for Republicans. Add to these trends the growing unpopularity of George W. Bush, and Democrats saw an opportunity. As did Bush and the Republicans previously, Democrats saw these trends and Obama's victory as potentially ushering in a new era, one they wished to assist by producing significant policy successes. In general, the new president would let Congress be Congress and do the legislating, while he provided the general outlines. This tactic, too, built support and loyalty among his fellow Democrats in Congress.

Another form of historical change is known as critical realignment. Elaborated most importantly by V. O. Key (1955) and Walter Dean Burnham (1970) and vigorously challenged by Mayhew (2002), realignment theory posits that some elections (either an individual election or a series of two elections in sequence) have enduring consequences for the party system. Rather than the gradual change at the heart of secular realignment, critical realignment focuses on sharp, quick transformations of the political landscape that have effects for a generation or longer. Typically, critical realignments bring a new majority party to power and have effects at the local, state, and national levels. To scholars, the 1800 (Jeffersonian Republicans), 1828 (Jackson and the Democrats), 1860 (Lincoln's Republicans), and 1932 (Roosevelt and the Democrats) elections fall into this category. Other realignments might keep the same majority party but create a new supporting coalition for that party, as in 1896 (McKinley and the Republicans). Scholars debate whether other years such as 1968, 1980, and 1994 qualify for the critical realignment label.

Claims that 2008 marked a critical election were occasionally seen in the blogosphere after 2008, but the more serious arguments that the historical position of the party system was advantageous for Barack Obama concerned secular realignment. Viewing the centrist "third-way" approach of Bill Clinton in the 1990s to have been a failure for building an enduring Democratic majority, the party was open to a different approach and somewhat different message, and its activist base was determined to push the party in a liberal, progressive direction. Obama capitalized on these openings and garnered tremendous loyalty from Democrats in Congress. Coming to office when he did, Obama was able to leverage his leadership opportunities to a great degree. His ability to exercise leadership, his Democratic colleagues reasoned, would enhance his public approval and help the party in upcoming elections. These expectations were dealt a severe blow in the November 2010 election.

One other feature of the historical dynamics of the party system contributed to Obama's ability to lead. Obama's leadership benefited among Democrats because of his place in political time. As explained elsewhere in this volume, Obama entered office as a potentially "reconstructive" president, in Stephen Skowronek's terms. These presidents take office in an environment that is hostile to the current dominant direction in public policy and that is poised to entertain presidential leadership and a new policy direction. Previous examples were Presidents Franklin Roosevelt and Ronald Reagan. In elections like those electing these two presidents in 1932 and 1980, respectively, all the wind appears to be at the back of the non-incumbent party. The economy, concerns over health care, and foreign policy troubles all intersected to provide a powerful push for the Obama candidacy. Once elected, expectations are high for this kind of president, as they certainly were for Obama, but these high expectations encourage fellow partisans to cooperate with him. President Obama was given substantial leeway to lead and shape the broad agenda among Democratic politicians and activists.

OBAMA AND PARTY CONTROL IN CONGRESS

The second major factor connecting the party system to presidential leadership success is the size of the president's victory and the strength of his or her party in Congress. In these respects, Obama was well situated. His own victory in 2008 was comfortable, registering gains among nearly every population group compared to Democratic nominee John Kerry in 2004 and winning nine states won by President Bush in that election. Obama's victory was not overwhelming, but it was solid and convincing. In Congress, Democrats increased their House majority. In the Senate, although this was not clear on election day, Democrats eventually obtained a supermajority of sixty meaning they could, if perfectly united, defeat any filibuster threat by Republicans. No president in five decades had such a favorable alignment in Congress. Intersecting this opportunity with the historical trajectory of the party system, as previously discussed, gave President Obama a rare ability to lead, an ability due not just to his own political skills but the resources provided him by the American party system. Knowing that the public's view of the party will depend heavily on its view about the president, and that their view about the president will depend on his policies and whether they are considered successful, members of the president's party have good reason to help him enact his agenda.

President Obama deployed his strong party advantage in Congress effectively. The president did not need to uncap his veto pen at any point in his first two years. Congress passed an ambitious agenda including an economic stimulus plan, health-care reform, and new regulations of the financial sector, among other items, with virtually no Republican support—Congress was more polarized along partisan lines in Obama's first two years than in any previous Congress since 1879—and in some cases against strong public opposition.

Democratic support for the president's position on roll call votes was extremely high. As a measure, roll call support has its weaknesses. For example, the votes in question might not be key items on the president's agenda. And items on that presidential agenda that never made it to a vote in both chambers, such as the president's "cap and trade" environmental plan or his attempt to revise immigration law to provide a pathway to citizenship for children whose parents brought them to the United States illegally, cannot be factored into the score. They did not come up for votes, but were in fact defeats. Still, the measure provides a reasonable signal that Congress was casting votes consistent with the president's wishes.

Whether unified party control, such as that during the first two years of the Obama administration makes a difference in legislative success, or whether divided control between the parties is just as productive, has been a simmering debate in political science. Research since David Mayhew's (1991) path-breaking contribution, which expressed skepticism that the enactment of major legislation differed much between eras of unified and divided party control, has produced a range of results. Some, consistent with Mayhew, stress that significant policy can be passed under a variety of partisan arrangements (Jones 1994, 1997; Skowronek 1993).

Overall, however, the findings in recent research strongly support the premise that party control matters for the passage of significant legislation. Howell, Adler, Cameron, and Riemann (2000) provide the most elaborate compilation of significant enactments and find that while enactment of what they categorize as major legislation does not appear to vary significantly between unified and divided government, enactment of landmark statues does so at a rate of about two or three statutes per congressional term. This is similar to the result—about two to three significant enactments per term—found by Coleman (1999). Certainly the president's passage of health-care reform and financial-industry reform would qualify for landmark status, and other legislation might arguably do so, as well. Other studies show that proposed significant legislation is more likely to fail in divided government (Edwards, Barrett, and Peake 1997; Binder 2003) and that when the president and Congress are more similar ideologically, Congress is more willing to delegate to the executive branch additional power and responsibility (Epstein and O'Halloran 1996, 2001). Health-care reform provides a classic example of the latter point. Although the legislation was detailed and two thousand pages long, most of the detail will be worked out by executive branch agencies. This delegation of decision was a remarkable legislative grant of authority to the executive branch. Although it cannot be said definitively that it would not have happened under divided government, research tells us it was far more likely to happen under the kind of unified party control enjoyed by President

Obama. In sum, the president's leadership benefited from the important partisan resource of having his party in control of both the House and Senate and from the fact that his own victory was comfortable and expanded the Democrats' vote share among almost every sector of the population.

ROCKY ROAD

President Obama inherited a party system that was well situated for his leadership efforts. He could make a reasonable claim to have an election mandate in 2008—if not for precise, specific policies, then for a change in direction and trying new ideas. In addition, many Democratic commentators were convinced that their party was on the verge of long-term dominance, freeing the president to enact bold, sweeping changes. Their confidence resulted from the size of the Democratic victories in 2006 and 2008, the strong support for Democrats among young voters and first-time voters, the improved turnout by minority voters, and the growing minority share of the American population. Despite this success, the president's public approval began drifting downward in his first two years, especially among Independents and Republicans.

Within twenty-four months, the president's party had gone from a rare position of historic strength to a midterm election repudiation that was itself historic in its breadth across the national and state levels and in its depth, with Republicans picking up over sixty seats in the House and another half dozen in the Senate. Unlike for President Bush, the increasing difficulties in a war—in Afghanistan, not Iraq—did not play a major role in President Obama's drooping approval ratings. The deterioration of the economy, particularly high unemployment, played a starring role in the president's reversal of fortune and the Democratic drubbing. Also playing a key role were highly energized conservative voters who were opposed to the policy direction being implemented by President Obama and the Democratic Congress and whose voice was expressed by the Tea Party movement. Whether inadvertent or anticipated, the president's agenda revived the debate over the proper role of the federal government, reminding many observers of the debates from 1995 to 1996, when the Republican Congress faced off against President Clinton, and from 1981 to 1982, when the Democratic House squared off against the Republican Senate and President Reagan. The 2009–2010 debate focused in particular on the federal government's proper role in the economy, the operation of private enterprise, the protection of property rights, and the government's fiscal and monetary management of the economy—precisely the kinds of issues identified by scholars of American political parties as central to political party competition over history and as essential catalysts to the resurgence of partisanship in the public (Aldrich 1995; Coleman 1996). The debate over the "fiscal state" from 2009 to 2010 was deep and passionate. This reversal of fortune in the 2010 election repeated a pattern seen frequently in US history. Democratic president Bill Clinton enjoyed unified government for two years before losing Democratic control of both the House and Senate in the 1994 election. President Jimmy Carter returned the White House to Democratic control following the 1976 election and inherited large majorities in Congress due to economic troubles from 1973 to 1976 during the Nixon and Ford administrations, as well as the lingering backlash against Republicans due to the Watergate scandal that drove President Nixon out of office. Nonetheless, Carter's disapproval was high by 1978, the Democratic majority thinned in that year's election, and the party was on the defensive electorally through 1979 and 1980. The unified Democratic Congress in 1965 and 1966 and Democratic president Lyndon Johnson had a large number of legislative victories but suffered massive electoral losses in the 1966 election. Republican president Dwight Eisenhower enjoyed two years of unified government in 1953 and 1954, but a weak economy flipped control to the Democrats after the 1954 election.

One thread connecting these examples is that partisan strength in Congress is a great resource for presidential leadership, but it does not guarantee subsequent high approval or electoral success, even when a party has full control of Congress and the presidency. There are at least three reasons why this might be so. First, parties can be thought of as coalitions or networks of interest and advocacy groups. The concerns of these groups might not necessarily align with the priorities of the public. When this is the case, the opposition party has a wide opening through which to begin a critique of the priorities of the president and his party. This is precisely what happened to President Obama. Democrats passed an economic stimulus plan with no Republican support in Congress, but the bill was characterized by opponents as primarily taking care of Democratic interest groups and constituencies and providing funding that would not be spent for well over a year despite the ongoing economic problems. The other key items on the Democratic agenda, such as health-care reform, financial reform, and new environmental regulation policies, could be cast by Republicans as distractions from the real national priority of revving up the economy and employment. Conservative talk show hosts delighted in presenting montages of the president saying at frequent intervals during his first two years that his intention *now* was to focus on the economy and jobs.

Second, a large win by the president's party exacerbates the problems just mentioned. With a supermajority in the Senate, a large majority in the House, and a president supportive of their positions, every significant interest group aligned with the Democrats wanted speedy action on items of interest to them. Better to have our interests addressed under these favorable conditions they calculate, than wait two years when the environment might be less accommodating. For a party that had not had unified control of government in fifteen years, there were many pent-up demands that rose to the top of the agenda. Surely some, maybe many, of these demands were important and deserved attention. However, amidst deteriorating economic conditions, they were easy to portray as a distraction.

Third, winning an election with large majorities, after a long period under divided government or government controlled by the other party, creates a risk of misreading the message from the election that swept you to office and overestimating Americans' appetite for change. This is not an inevitable feature of unified party control, but the risk rises when a party has been out of power for some time, when it wins at what appears to many of its supporters to be a historic turning point, and when a party has a high degree of internal ideological unity. Republicans and conservatives frequently reminded Americans, in the form of a warning, that the president promised to "fundamentally transform" the United States. The Tea Party movement arose in large part due to a conviction that Obama had improperly interpreted his election victory as a mandate to expand the size and scope of the federal government and change the nature of American society. Although not occurring under unified government, this assertion of over interpretation of a mandate was similar to the charge launched by Democrats against the Republican Congress of 1995 to 1996. That Congress was the first in forty years with Republicans in control of both chambers. It is perhaps not surprising that when a rare event happens, those applauding the event tend to read more into it than the political reality can sustain. Voters may be simply throwing out the previous bums who did a poor job, but victors often want to see their victory as a mandate for fundamental change. Not infrequently, they are rebuked by voters in a subsequent election.

Parties, as stated above, provide presidents with valuable leadership resources. They also, as networks of groups and activists, can produce legislative victories that may lead to electoral defeat. This pattern has been recurrent in US history. Presidents are in a difficult spot—their party network provides them leadership resources, but their dependence on their parties also means that it is difficult to discipline the party's multifaceted groups and maintain the public perception that the party is focused on the most important problems as identified by the public. Indeed, at times the Obama administration was criticized in strong terms by various components of the Democratic coalition—from environmentalists to gays and lesbians, labor union leaders, immigration reform advocates, antiwar activists, and advocates for a stronger government role in health care. All accused the president of caving in to opponents at key times or not giving their concerns the proper weight.

Party coalitions are dynamic, not static. Managing them is a difficult task and sometimes involves deprioritizing the interests of some coalition members and sometimes even supporting policies directly in opposition to the stated views of these members. In some extreme cases, such as the Democrats on civil rights in the 1960s or the Republicans and Democrats on trade policy after 1970, the parties flip their positions entirely as they try to mold a new coalition or respond to the changed viewpoint of another coalition member (Karol 2009). The savviest presidents learn how to use the party network to achieve their leadership goals while making sure the party does not appear to be veering too far outside the major concerns or the ideological boundaries shared by most Americans. Barack Obama succeeded on the first task, but struggled on the second.

THE PATH AHEAD

One does not have to look back far to find another president who had a rude awakening after electoral success. By the time of his second inauguration in 2005, George W. Bush could look back and see gains for Republicans in the House and Senate. He earned a reelection victory that was more comfortable than his initial victory, though thin by historical standards. Urged on by his chief strategist, Karl Rove, the president thought big, believing he could forge a durable Republican realignment. He unapologetically claimed a mandate and famously noted that he had earned "political capital, and now I intend to spend it" (Stevenson 2004). But midway through 2005, observers were already noting that the president seemed to be failing on several policy fronts and that Republicans were growing more restless. By 2006, Republicans had been booted out of their House and Senate majority.

After his election victory and two years of legislative accomplishment, President Obama now faces two years of divided government, with the Republicans in control of the House and in a stronger position in the US Senate. He also has fewer allies on the state level, where Republicans gained control of additional governorships and picked up the largest gains of either party in state legislatures in sixty years. Legislative successes will require the kinds of concessions to Republican positions that were unnecessary in his first two years. But Republicans themselves now face the challenge of being an opposition party with governing authority; a party that wants to stop the president's agenda but will need the president's help to advance any of its own initiatives. Republicans will have incentives at times not to cooperate with Democrats, and Democrats will have the same with Republicans—some issues, they will calculate, are best left to the next election rather than accepting a half-best solution now. Republicans will introduce bills in the House that they know Democrats in the Senate cannot support, and Democrats in the Senate will do the same to Republicans in the House. Party debate will flourish over many issues, but centrally it will revolve around the scope of government involvement in the economy, the issue around which party conflict has so often thrived, and what those beliefs demand of citizens and government. The parties will debate the appropriate balance between liberty, property, democracy, equality, opportunity, freedom, and other fundamental American beliefs. The president will, if history is a guide, try to portray himself as the reasonable leader above the squabbling parties.

This is the party politics to which we have become accustomed. Over the twenty years from Bill Clinton's election in 1992 through 2012, there have been eight years of unified control and twelve years of divided control. In the twenty years before that, there were only four years of unified control and sixteen years of divided control. So the country has been here before, and the business of government will go on. President Obama spent two years enjoying the fruits of his partisan advantages; the fruits of the Democrats' strong historical position in the dynamics of the party system, the size of the president's victory in 2008, and the victory of his fellow partisans in Congress. For the next two years, he would need to learn to lead without as strong a partisan base in Congress. Victories will be fewer, and more of the victories will not be ideal from the president's point of view. But his party still has some of the forces of secular realignment working in its favor, and with a growing economy, the president would position himself well for reelection in 2012.

REFERENCES

Aldrich, John H. 1995. *Why Parties? The Origin and Transformation of Political Parties in America.* Chicago: University of Chicago Press.

Bartels, Larry. 1998. "Where the Ducks Are: Voting Power in a Party System." In *Politicians and Party Politics,* edited by John Geer. Baltimore, MD: Johns Hopkins University Press.

Binder, Sarah A. 2003. *Stalemate.* Washington, DC: Brookings Institute Press.

Burnham, Walter Dean. 1970. *Critical Elections and the Mainsprings of American Politics.* New York: Norton.

Coleman, John J. 1996. *Party Decline in America: Policy, Politics, and the Fiscal State.* Princeton, NJ: Princeton University Press.

———. 1999. "Unified Government, Divided Government, and Party Responsiveness." *American Political Science Review* 93(4): 821–35.

Easterbrook, Gregg. 2008. "Life Is Good, So Why Do We Feel So Bad?" *Wall Street Journal,* June 13, A15.

Edwards, George C., III, Andrew Barrett, and Jeffrey Peake. 1997. "The Legislative Impact of Divided Government." *American Journal of Political Science* 41(2): 545–63.

Epstein, David F., and Sharyn O'Halloran. 1996. "Divided Government and the Design of Administrative Procedures: A Formal Model and Empirical Test." *Journal of Politics* 58 (3): 393–417.

———. 2001. "Legislative Organization under Separate Powers." *Journal of Law, Economics and Organization* 17(2): 373–96.

Hacker, Jacob S. 2006. *The Great Risk Shift: The Assault on American Jobs, Families, Health Care, and Retirement—And How You Can Fight Back*. New York: Oxford University Press.

Howell, William G., E. Scott Adler, Charles Cameron, and Charles Riemann. 2000. "Divided Government and the Legislative Productivity of Congress, 1945–1994." *Legislative Studies Quarterly* 25(2): 285–312.

Jones, Charles O. 1994. *The Presidency in a Separated System*. Washington: The Brookings Institute.

———. 1997. "Separating to Govern: The American Way." In *Present Discontents: American Politics in the Very Late Twentieth Century*, edited by Byron E. Shafer Chatham, NJ: Chatham House.

Karol, David. 2009. *Party Position Change in American Politics: Coalition Management*. New York: Cambridge University Press.

Key, V. O. 1955. "A Theory of Critical Elections." *Journal of Politics* 17: 3–18.

———. 1959. "Secular Realignment and the Party System." *Journal of Politics* 21: 198–210.

Mayer, William G. 1998. "Mass Partisanship, 1946–1996." In *Partisan Approaches to Postwar American Politics*, edited by Byron E. Shafer. Chatham, NJ: Chatham House.

Mayhew, David R. 1991. *Divided We Govern: Party Control, Lawmaking, and Investigations, 1946–1990*. New Haven, CT: Yale University Press.

———. 2002. *Electoral Realignments: A Critique of an American Genre*. New Haven, CT: Yale University Press.

Pew Research Center for the People. 2008. "Late February 2008 Political Survey." http://people-press.org/files/legacy-questionnaires/398.pdf. Accessed June 8, 2011.

Skowronek, Stephen. 1993. *The Politics Presidents Make*. Cambridge, MA: Harvard University Press.

Stevenson, Richard W. 2004. "Confident Bush Outlines Ambitious Plan for 2nd Term." *New York Times*, November 5.

Chapter Four

Obama, Religious Politics, and the Culture Wars

James L. Guth

Barack Obama's religious story is not only unique among American presidents but has also intersected repeatedly with his political career. His ties to religious communities frequently constituted a political advantage, but just as often presented obstacles to his success. Often a masterful orchestrator of religious interests and sentiments, he has sometimes been frustrated in building bridges across the theological, ideological, and partisan gulfs that divide America's religious faiths. This chapter will analyze President Obama's fortunes in executing an "ecumenical" political strategy in the context of conflicting preferences among religious groups.

RELIGIOUS GROUPS IN AMERICAN POLITICS

Any assessment of American politics must consider two competing interpretations of religious alignments. *Ethnoreligious theory* emphasizes the historic religious groups that migrated to America and often multiplied upon reaching its shores. Nineteenth-century party politics consisted largely of assembling winning coalitions of these groups (Kleppner 1979). Even into the twentieth century, the GOP represented historically dominant mainline Protestant churches, such as Episcopalians, Presbyterians, and Methodists, while Democrats spoke for religious minorities: Catholics, Jews, and evangelical Protestants (especially in the South). By the 1980s, these configurations had shifted, as mainline Protestants dwindled in number, evangelicals moved toward the GOP, the ancient Catholic-Democratic alliance frayed, and black Protestants became a critical Democratic bloc. Growing religious diversity added Muslims, Hindus, Buddhists, and others to the equation, usually on the Democratic side, along with increasing numbers of "unaffiliated" or "secular" voters. Still, even today many analysts think in ethnoreligious terms, referring to the "evangelical," "Catholic," "Jewish," or "Muslim" vote. An alternative view is the *culture wars* or *religious restructuring theory* introduced into political parlance by James Davison Hunter's *Culture Wars* (1991). Hunter saw critical theological differences emerging *within* the old traditions: "Orthodox" believers accept "an external, definable, and transcendent authority" and adhere to traditional doctrines, while "progressives" replace old religious tenets with new ones based on personal experience or scientific rationality (Hunter 1991, 44). The progressives are joined by secular Americans who ignore or reject religion but see morality in the same way. These new religious divisions quickly congealed around abortion, feminism, gay rights, and the role of faith in public life but infused other political attitudes, as well. Such factionalism was most evident in the historic mainline Protestant, evangelical Protestant, and Anglo-Catholic traditions but sometimes extended to other religious communities. As we shall see, Obama stands at the intersection of these perspectives; both ethnoreligious and culture war theories are useful in delineating his support and describing the battles over his policies.

BARACK OBAMA AND RELIGIOUS POLITICS

Learning from the two previous national campaigns, Democratic presidential candidates in 2008 sought to improve chances for victory by reducing the "God gap," the propensity of religious voters to favor the GOP (Guth 2009b). Barack Obama seemed ideally suited for this purpose, as he embodied several crucial Democratic ethnoreligious constituencies. As David Remnick has noted, Obama's own family was "multiconfessional." Raised by an agnostic anthropologist mother and her lapsed Methodist-Baptist-Unitarian parents, Obama nevertheless grew up in contact with several traditions: his (absent) father and Indonesian stepfather were Muslim (he himself was registered as "Muslim" in a school in Indonesia, where he also attended a Catholic school) (Remnick 2010, 60–69). He later encountered the black Protestant (and Catholic) traditions as a community organizer in Chicago and eventually joined the Trinity United Church of Christ, a large, politically potent congregation affiliated with the predominantly white United Church of Christ (UCC), the most theologically and politically liberal mainline Protestant denomination. To round out his ethnoreligious connections, Obama even had an in-law who was an African American rabbi in Chicago (Chafets 2009).

Obama's roots clearly situated him in the historic Democratic home of ethnoreligious minorities, but education and experience made him a "progressive" in the culture wars. Obama's theology is difficult to pin down but is clearly based more on rational commitment than emotive attachments or doctrinal affirmation. In college he read Christian theology and was especially impressed by Christian realist Reinhold Niebuhr, moved by "Social Gospel" thinkers of the early twentieth century, and was later impressed with the "black liberation" theology of his Trinity pastor, the Rev. Jeremiah Wright. Above all, his own organizing experience demonstrated the efficacy of religious institutions and people in social reform, leading him toward a nondogmatic, ecumenical religious liberalism that meshed well with a basic ideological "pragmatism" (Obama 1995, 2006; Kloppenberg 2010).

His presidential campaign drew astutely on his understanding of religious traditions. His famous speech to the 2004 Democratic National Convention asserted that "we worship an awesome God in the blue states," drawing on evangelical language to deny the Republicans a monopoly on religious conviction (Remnick 2010, 399). Against secularists in his own party, he welcomed "people of faith" to the public square and assiduously wooed religious leaders, including evangelicals often associated with conservative causes, such as megachurch pastors Rick Warren and Joel Hunter. He campaigned not only in black churches but also evangelical and mainline Protestant ones. (His speech at the June 2007 meeting of the UCC, his own denomination, actually triggered an IRS inquiry over possible improper political use of religious resources.) Obama's religious outreach staff was led by evangelicals but was quite ecumenical (Sullivan 2008).

During the early 2008 primaries, Democratic candidates regularly addressed faith-related issues. Although both Hillary Clinton and Obama cast an ecumenical net, the Democratic electorate quickly revealed worrisome religious cleavages. Obama steadily built support among black Protestants, obliterating Clinton's early lead among black clergy and churchgoers, and did increasingly well among Latinos, both Catholic and Protestant. But despite his early appeal to evangelical and mainline Protestants, who were key to his victory in Iowa, this support steadily diminished, as did that of working-class Catholics, Jews, and white churchgoers generally. Even campaign brochures with Obama standing behind a pulpit and overshadowed by a cross did not reverse the trend. At the same time, however, he dominated the secular Democratic vote, a source of consistent electoral strength.

Obama's "religious problem" was exacerbated by two crucial events in the spring of 2008. First, the media finally highlighted controversial statements of Obama's retired pastor and longtime ally, Jeremiah Wright, whose black liberation theology did not play well to white audiences. Obama quickly repudiated Wright's most provocative claims and reacted to further inflammatory statements by resigning his membership at Trinity (Remnick 2010, 517–38).

But Obama himself added fuel to the fire by telling Democratic donors in San Francisco that white working-class Pennsylvanians were "bitter" about their situation and, as a result, clung to guns and religion, setting off a firestorm of criticism from both Clinton Democrats and, of course, Republicans. By the end of the heated nominating contest, the Democratic constituency was deeply divided along ethnoreligious lines.

Obama quickly patched the holes in his coalition, meeting privately and repeatedly with ecumenical groups of religious leaders, establishing "Catholics for Obama," speaking to the African Methodist Episcopal Church convention, working with the "Matthew 25 Network" of religious liberals, and even advertising on Christian radio stations—usually the preserve of evangelical religion and Republican politicians. While remaining staunchly pro-choice, he emphasized a "common ground" objective of reducing the number of abortions. Most important, Obama endorsed a "faith-based initiative," not unlike the Bush administration's, appalling secular Democrats and liberal commentators, but pleasing many religious leaders, including some of the orthodox.

The Democratic National Convention provided additional opportunities for coalition building, oozing hospitality for the religious with an ecumenical prayer service, special sessions for faith groups, ample religious rhetoric, and a benediction by evangelical pastor Joel Hunter. Pro-life religious leaders on the Platform Committee, such as evangelical Tony Campolo, modified the usual pro-choice abortion plank with a pledge to support women taking a pregnancy to term, an achievement that did not prevent picketing by pro-life groups. Finally, Senator Joe Biden, an observant Catholic, was chosen as Obama's running mate in part to appeal to religiously orthodox Democrats, the very group most likely to defect to the GOP. Although Biden soon ran into his own "religious" problems, the nomination probably had the desired effect (Guth 2009b).

Obama's inaugural address may have quoted the Apostle Paul's admonition to "put away childish things," but his 2008 campaign exemplified that Christian missionary's determination to "be all things to all people." The campaign reached out not only to traditional Democratic religious constituencies, such as black Protestants, Hispanic Catholics, Jews, and secular Americans, but also to evangelical Protestants, traditionalist Catholics, and other groups more often thought part of the GOP's religious base. Although this approach did not shift large blocs of voters, it established Obama as a serious religious person and blunted the antipathy often directed at Democrats by religious conservatives. Although the "God gap" still appeared in November, Obama ran ahead of Kerry among frequent churchgoers and was actually seen by voters as more "religious" than McCain.

PRESIDENT OBAMA'S RELIGIOUS COALITION

Obama's decisive victory suggested to some the emergence of a "new Democratic majority." To consider possible religious aspects of such a majority, we draw on the National Survey of Religion and Politics, conducted by the University of Akron. In table 4.1, we have ordered ethnoreligious constituencies from most to least Democratic and divided the three largest Christian communities into theological or "culture war" factions. Obama clearly won strong backing from traditionally Democratic ethnoreligious minorities and secular voters, with large margins among black Protestants, agnostics and atheists, non-Christians, Jews, the religiously unaffiliated, and Latinos, both Catholic and Protestant. (The latter result reversed strong Latino Protestant preference for Bush in 2004.) Obama also benefited from enhanced turnout among his strongest supporters, especially African American Protestants. Indeed, as the fourth column shows, these ethnoreligious groups collectively made up over half the Democratic coalition.

Obama also broke even in two critical "swing" groups, Anglo-Catholics and mainline Protestants, but did poorly among Latter-day Saints and evangelical Protestants. As in previous elections, culture war divisions appeared in the large white Protestant and Anglo-Catholic camps, as Obama won over religious progressives but fared more poorly among the orthodox (and often worse than Democratic congressional candidates). Nevertheless, a good many centrist and orthodox voters felt close to Obama, even if they didn't vote for him.

On balance, then, Obama's arduous religious strategy was a modest plus for his masterfully executed campaign—or at the very least, prevented religious factors from being a negative. But although he improved on Kerry's 2004 performance in several ethnoreligious communities, the continuity of religious voting is quite impressive: evangelicals remained entrenched as the core of the reduced GOP, and Democrats depended on ethnoreligious minorities, as they have throughout history, and the growing secular contingent also enhanced its role. Mainline Protestant and Anglo-Catholic voters, on the other hand, remained divided, with the orthodox supporting the GOP and progressives supporting the Democrats.

The 2008 election produced a Democratic majority, but President Obama would have to consolidate this coalition by accommodating both the party's usual religious constituents and some new ones. As ever for Democrats, this would not be an easy task, as they would have to pick their way through their constituencies' preferences on social, economic, and even foreign policy. To illustrate the problem, table 4.2 reports religious voters' views on several representative issues. As we might expect, culture war questions such as

Table 4.1.   Religious Groups in the 2008 Presidential Election (in percentages)

Religious Groups	Obama Two-Party Vote	Close to Obama	US House Democratic Vote	Democratic Party Identification	Percentage of Democratic Coalition
Black Protestants	95	82	89	84	19.5
Agnostic/Atheists	81	68	80	79	4.1
Non-Christian	77	71	88	73	4.3
Jews	76	66	75	72	2.5
Latino Catholics	73	65	75	56	6.8
Unaffiliated (Secular)	68	63	67	59	12.6
Latino Protestants	66	51	75	71	3.2
Anglo-Catholics	49	51	52	46	18.6
Progressives	66	62	64	59	8.1
Centrists	40	45	47	41	7.6
Orthodox	41	47	45	38	2.9
Mainline Protestants	49	51	49	45	16.4
Progressives	59	59	56	54	6.8
Centrists	52	52	54	43	7.3
Orthodox	29	39	30	33	2.1
Latter-day Saints	28	33	23	22	1.6
Evangelical Protestants	24	31	24	25	10.6
Progressives	47	53	44	49	1.9
Centrists	41	40	43	38	4.4
Orthodox	14	25	18	17	4.3
Total	53	52	53	49	100.0

Source: National Survey of Religion and Politics, University of Akron, 2008.

abortion and gay rights certainly differentiated Democratic and Republican religious groups, but they also split the Democrats to an extent. A narrow majority of the electorate rejected substantial restrictions on abortion, but there were massive differences between agnostics, atheists, secular, non-Christian, and Jewish voters on one side, and Latino and black Protestants on the other. In the larger Christian communions, abortion divided progressives and the orthodox in stark fashion.

Although the same pattern appeared on removing Bush's limits on embryonic stem cell research, support was higher in almost every religious group, reflecting perhaps the scientific community's drumbeat on the research's potential benefits. Similar intraparty cleavages opened on gay rights. Although culture war patterns appeared on whether gays should have all the same rights as other citizens, overall public support was quite high, with only black Protestants and orthodox evangelicals dissenting in large numbers. On gay marriage, however, the gaps within the Democratic coalition were wider when respondents chose between same-sex marriage, civil unions, and traditional marriage.

Religious divisions also extended to government welfare policies. At the time of the election, support for a national health-care plan was one issue that clearly united the ethnoreligious core of Obama's coalition, while attracting substantial support from religious progressives and centrists in the large white Christian traditions. Nevertheless, evangelicals, Latter-day Saints, and orthodox believers were firmly opposed, leaving the electorate closely divided, portending a major battle. And although a majority of black Protestants favored more government services, even if this required higher taxes, this idea was not popular among other Democratic religious groups, although some were more likely to accept tax increases to reduce poverty. Even here, evangelicals, mainline Protestants, and Anglo-Catholics were less supportive, especially the orthodox and centrists. Responses to questions on tax cuts, aid to minorities, environmental protection, and global warming reveal similar lineups (data not shown).

Finally, religious divisions extended even to foreign policy. Despite considerable disagreement among Democratic religious groups over US military power, most gave it a lower priority than Anglo-Catholics, mainline Protestants, and especially evangelicals and Latter-day Saints. In the three large Christian communities, once again, the orthodox strongly backed military strength. On Iraq, Obama's ethnoreligious constituencies not only thought the war unjust (data not shown) but also strongly favored an immediate exit. In this preference, they were joined by many progressives from the larger traditions but opposed by centrists and the orthodox, who were willing to wait until Iraq was more stable. Finally, most Democratic ethnoreligious minorities favored an even-handed or even pro-Palestinian stance on the Middle East, while Jews, Latter-day Saints, and orthodox evangelicals tilted strongly toward Israel.

Of course, public opinion only sets the bounds within which a president strives to shape policy. Nevertheless, table 4.2 suggests that Obama would face religious obstacles in dealing with his agenda. In some instances, divisions within the Democratic coalition might prove troublesome. In others, the consistent conservatism of the orthodox on social, economic, and foreign policy would make his announced intention to construct new religious coalitions issue by issue more difficult. And these obstacles surfaced even as the new president began to build his administration and sought to set a new tone for public life through his inaugural activities.

RHETORIC, PERSONNEL, AND POLICY

During the transition, Obama and his aides held an unprecedented number of consultations with a broad spectrum of religious leaders, intensifying the

Table 4.2. Religious Groups and Policy Issues in 2009

	Pro-Choice	Lift Stem Cell Funding Limits	Back Equal Rights for Gays	Favor Gay Marriage	Favor National Health-Care Plan	More Public Services Even If More Taxes	Raise Taxes to Fight Poverty	Military Superiority a Top Priority	Bring Back Troops from Iraq	Favor Israel in Middle East
Black Protestant	52	66	51	18	63	53	57	50	85	37
Agnostic/Atheist	90	90	96	75	79	37	64	25	68	26
Non-Christian	87	70	80	58	71	44	75	23	63	25
Jews	91	86	88	55	78	46	68	44	55	81
Latino Catholics	58	45	59	32	55	17	49	56	54	35
Unaffiliated (Secular)	86	72	78	51	54	26	50	42	56	40
Latino Protestants	40	64	70	33	52	38	47	44	55	39
Anglo-Catholics	50	66	71	27	48	22	43	54	41	43
Progressives	79	78	82	45	66	24	52	44	52	39
Centrists	41	68	69	21	40	19	36	59	34	43
Orthodox	25	40	55	16	38	24	46	59	38	49
Mainline Protestants	67	77	70	30	44	20	46	47	38	44
Progressives	83	85	77	41	46	26	52	38	45	36
Centrists	70	78	73	32	47	16	44	49	40	41
Orthodox	37	61	53	11	34	17	40	59	26	61
Latter-day Saints	30	68	50	14	40	9	36	72	30	57
Evangelical Protestants	34	51	46	11	33	16	30	67	28	64
Progressives	87	72	62	35	47	13	32	56	42	42
Centrists	52	66	60	22	52	25	37	59	35	45
Orthodox	21	43	39	4	24	14	27	71	24	73
All Respondents	56	65	63	28	48	25	45	53	46	47

Source: National Survey of Religion and Politics, University of Akron, 2008.

ecumenical approach of his campaign. Religious historian Martin Marty argued cogently that Obama was trying to "enact the plurality that he embodies." Indeed, these contacts were obviously not for spiritual sustenance but to "mobilize faith-based communities behind his administration" (Saslow 2009). This ambitious effort continued with inaugural events suffused with religious observances and people.

For the inauguration itself, Obama chose the veteran United Methodist civil rights leader, Rev. Joseph Lowery, to give the benediction. But it was his choice for the invocation, Rev. Rick Warren, that immediately revealed the pitfalls in religious coalition building. Warren was not only an emerging evangelical leader, but had also engaged Obama in conversation for several years, had invited him to the massive Saddleback Community Church for events, and had hosted an Obama-McCain "forum" during the campaign. Warren was increasingly controversial among evangelicals for extending his concern beyond social issues to hunger and poverty, AIDs in the developing world, and the global environment. His selection was thus a symbolic bridge-building statement for Obama but aroused strong suspicion from some evangelicals. On the other side, Warren's traditionalism on abortion and homosexuality produced howls of protest from religious liberals. A prominent gay Episcopalian bishop, Eugene V. Robinson, an early supporter of Obama, said that the choice was "like a slap in the face" (Zeleny and Kirkpatrick 2008). Even some presidential aides were surprised and disappointed.

Obama adamantly resisted demands to "uninvite" Warren (but he did ask Bishop Robinson to pray at a pre-inaugural concert), and polls showed strong bipartisan public support for his choice (Cohen 2009). Inauguration Day began with the customary private services for the president-elect at St. John's Episcopal, just across from the White House, at which T. D. Jakes, the black pastor of a multiethnic Dallas megachurch, preached. At the inauguration itself, Warren's invocation reflected both the president's irenic objectives and Warren's own faith, as he emphasized compassion and love and used Jewish and Muslim formulations in referring to God. But he concluded "in Jesus' name" and segued into the Lord's Prayer, giving secular, non-Christian, and religiously liberal Democrats occasion for new complaints. After being sworn in with Abraham Lincoln's 1861 inaugural Bible, Obama's own address reflected a strong affirmation of civil religion, suitably modified for his own purposes. Although he quoted "the words of Scripture" in urging Americans to "put away childish things," he also affirmed the nation's religious "patchwork" as a strength: "We are a nation of Christians and Muslims, Jews and Hindus—and non-believers." And he pointedly invited the Muslim world to join in seeking "a new way forward, based on mutual interest and mutual respect." Lowery's closing prayer echoed these ecumenical themes, and in the evening, several religious communities staked their claim for inclusion by staging their own inaugural balls.

The traditional National Cathedral prayer service the next morning was primarily Christian, but included newly written prayers to reflect Obama's personal religious liberalism and to ease participation by an unprecedented array of clergy from almost every imaginable group: evangelicals and Catholics, Jews and Muslims, Hindus and Buddhists (but not Sikhs, who expressed strong disappointment). The service also featured the first woman to preach, the Rev. Dr. Sharon E. Watkins, president of the liberal mainline Disciples of Christ (Knowlton 2009).

Despite the impressive display of religious leadership and rhetoric during the Inauguration, Obama still lacked one element of a full religious strategy: a church home. The Obamas had never been regular churchgoers, but aides sensed that he wanted to connect to a religious community, and there was no dearth of congregations wooing the chief executive. Ultimately, after one Sunday venture to a black Protestant church, Obama decided not to join any, citing normal presidential concerns about security and the inconvenience for the host congregation. For spiritual sustenance, he relied instead on a daily devotional sent to his BlackBerry by Joshua DuBois, his religious outreach director, phone conversations with clergy friends, and occasional Camp David services conducted by a military chaplain. Although seemingly insignificant at the time, this decision denied Obama the weekly opportunity to visibly reaffirm his status as a Christian believer, one that would soon be questioned (Parsons 2010).

FAITH-BASED INITIATIVE, OBAMA STYLE

Obama's early reach across the political divisions among America's religious communities aroused some controversy but was generally a well-received attempt to reduce culture war hostilities. The strategy continued at the National Prayer Breakfast on February 5, when Obama announced creation of the White House Office of Faith-Based and Neighborhood Partnerships, a revision of the Bush administration's program that sought to enlist religious groups in the provision of social services. Bush had indeed expanded the access of religious groups to federal funds, but his broader objectives had been stymied by controversy over whether such groups could restrict staff to members of their own faith. Obama had endorsed faith-based programs during the campaign but had promised to ban restricted hiring. He also hoped to expand the initiative's constituency beyond religious groups and to encourage programs to strengthen family life and reduce abortion, attacking one source of the culture wars directly (Boorstein and Kindy 2009).

To oversee the new program, Obama appointed an advisory council of twenty-five, which compassed the religious waterfront. The council included several evangelicals, including Rev. Joel Hunter and Rev. Frank Page, past president of the Southern Baptist Convention (SBC), a bastion of the GOP religious coalition. In addition, Joel Stearns, president of World Vision, a major recipient of federal grants for overseas relief and development work, and Jim Wallis, a liberal evangelical and friend of the president, were also named to the council. Eventually the full membership included Catholic, mainline and black Protestant, Jewish, Muslim, Hindu, and gay rights leaders. The council was charged with finding ways to reduce poverty, minimize abortions, promote responsible fatherhood, and foster interfaith dialogue abroad—an ambitious agenda—and was headed by Obama's religious liaison, Joshua DuBois, a twenty-six-year-old black Pentecostal pastor (Parsons 2010).

Although Obama got considerable credit for bringing religious groups together to address a range of problems, he still received flack from adamant culture warriors. On the progressive side, secular and religious liberals joined separationist groups such as the American Civil Liberties Union (ACLU) and Americans United in condemning Obama's inclusion of "Religious Right" figures, such as Page and Stearns, and lamenting his failure to reverse immediately the Bush policy on religious hiring. Christian Right groups, for their part, saw the advisory council as a smokescreen for liberal policies on abortion, gay rights, and social welfare. Even some council members were skeptical of prospects for major achievements.

That skepticism seemed warranted. The administration soon took the abortion mandate away from the council and also restricted discussion of the divisive hiring issue. After a year of conference calls and meetings, the body presented the White House with a 168-page report full of vague and relatively innocuous recommendations on government policies under its purview. The advisory council expired with a White House ceremony, which, like the report, received little public or administration attention. Although separationist groups continued to press the White House for a clear ban on "religious" hiring, they were frustrated when the executive order finally issued in November 2010 left most of the Bush administration rules intact (Gilgoff 2010).

At the same time that the administration was wrestling with these regulations, it quietly directed substantial funds from the 2009 economic stimulus package into religious charities and other "faith-based" enterprises. Although conservative and Republican critics had complained that language in the stimulus bill seemed to preclude such spending, one early analysis showed that Obama easily matched the Bush program in totals expended. The largest amounts went to Catholic groups such as Catholic Charities (at the very time that the bishops and administration were locked in battle over abortion in the health-care bill—see the following section). Protestant and Jewish groups received considerably less, as did minority traditions such as Muslims (Smith and Tau 2010). And although the administration admitted to aggressive "marketing" of available funds to religious groups, the Faith-Based Office denied charges that such efforts were politically motivated to build support for Obama.

ADMINISTRATIVE APPOINTMENTS

Although Obama clearly had major hopes for his experiment in religious coalition building, the economic crisis turned his attention in other directions, and the personnel and policy decisions of his first months reveal little evidence of the strategy. Although the attentive press emphasized the ethnic and theological diversity of the religious leaders with some connection to the new administration, Obama's administrative and staff choices were generally confined to the core Democratic ethnoreligious, progressive, and secular constituencies. *National Journal* found that of the top 366 administration officials, only 31 percent were Protestant (even including black Protestants), 29 percent were Catholic (often Latino), 19 percent were Jewish, and 13 percent were unaffiliated (Barnes 2009). A perusal of the cabinet provides a more detailed religious assessment of top appointees, including three Methodists, one Chinese Baptist, one black Episcopalian, two Latino Catholics, one Lebanese Catholic, one Anglo-Catholic, and seven "secular" appointees. And even the nominees with religious affiliations had, for the most part, never been deeply engaged with religious institutions or even mildly observant. Similarly, Obama's Supreme Court nominees, Sonia Sotomayor and Elena Kagan, were raised in religious homes (Catholic and Jewish), but neither maintained regular religious practice. Both were warmly received by prochoice and church-state separationist groups but greeted warily by pro-lifers and Christian conservatives.

Even nominees with active religious attachments ran into the very culture war battles Obama was striving to avoid. The nomination of Kansas Governor Kathleen Sebelius, a Catholic, as secretary of health and human services elicited a heated struggle over her strong pro-choice stance. Although this did not prevent confirmation, it did result in criticism from the Vatican and a reminder from her bishop to refrain from participating in the Eucharist. (Later the appointment of a centrist pro-life Catholic to another HHS post evoked similar protests from pro-choice groups.) Obama's selection of Dr. Francis Collins as director of the National Institutes of Health aroused a different critique—from secular Democrats and scientists. Famous for his work decoding the human genome, Collins's evangelical faith led to fears that he would inject his religion into administrative decisions—such as funding for stem cell research—that should be made on scientific grounds. Collins was also confirmed (he actually favored such research), but this episode further illustrated the difficulty in surmounting the religious gulfs dividing Americans—or at least the American political elite (Boyer 2010).

INTO THE CULTURE WARS

Other confirmation skirmishes too numerous to mention almost invariably focused on abortion, gay rights, or related cultural issues, but these were merely a prelude for the inevitable confrontations on policy. On abortion-related issues, Obama played the role of "reverser" of GOP policies: lifting the "Mexico City" ban on federal funds for international organizations involved with abortion; modifying the Bush "conscience clause" protecting medical professionals who refused to perform procedures violating religious tenets; cutting funding for "abstinence-based" sex education; and, especially, removing limits on federal funding of embryonic stem cell research (Stein 2009).

Although Obama did not go as far as some supporters wanted on any of these decisions, all were applauded by secular Democrats and most religious liberals (the signing ceremony for the stem cell guidelines was witnessed by a bevy of mainline Protestant and Jewish leaders) but were deplored by Catholic officials and most evangelicals. Indeed, Catholic reaction was so strong that the University of Notre Dame's invitation to Obama to give the commencement address aroused a heated national debate that spread far beyond the Catholic community. Thus, although *New York Times* columnist Frank Rich (2009) exulted that "the culture warriors" had been "laid off," a wiser observer saw these decisions producing "a reassessment of Obama by some Christian conservative and other religious leaders, who now charge him with inflaming the very cultural divisions he once pledged to heal" (Brown 2009).

If the Notre Dame imbroglio was not enough to show that religious divisions over abortion could not be papered over, that fact became evident in the health-care battle. Obama hoped that his careful coalition building during the campaign and early months of his administration would create a powerful religious army behind his plan. At first, the prospects looked good: a broad phalanx of religious leaders from the left and center endorsed action, as did the US Conference of Catholic Bishops and Catholic Health Association, representing the large Catholic hospital sector. But the legislation still fell victim to the abortion issue. Pro-life Catholic Democrats in the House, led by Rep. Bart Stupak of Michigan, fought with pro-choice colleagues over inclusion of abortion services.

With Republican support, Stupak added an amendment prohibiting any possible funding of the procedure, a victory that later became the prime obstacle to House passage of a Senate bill with a weaker provision. In a serious intramural split, the Catholic bishops refused to accept anything except the Stupak amendment, but the Catholic Health Association and some religious orders supported the Senate bill. Under enormous party pressure to vote for the legislation, Stupak finally yielded, but only on the promise of an executive order implementing a restrictive interpretation (Alter 2010). Obama signed the order and the bill passed, but savaged by criticism from both pro-life and pro-choice groups, Stupak decided to retire. And the extent of permissible abortion funding quickly became a matter of administrative controversy, as did the Faith-Based Office's effort to use religious leaders to spread the word on the new health plan to their parishioners (Minnery 2010).

The president made even less progress resolving gay rights issues. During the campaign, Obama had strongly advocated repeal of the "Don't Ask, Don't Tell" (DADT) policy on gays in the military, equal treatment under federal employee health plans, and repeal of the Federal Defense of Marriage Act (DOMA), passed by a Republican Congress in 1996 and signed by President Clinton. Obama stopped short of supporting gay marriage, however, fearing that this might endanger his appeal to religious conservatives. Once in office, his focus on economic recovery and health-care legislation led to a "no distractions" policy on gay rights issues (Alter 2010, 79). Rather, Obama followed a low visibility, piecemeal strategy: appointing gays to important administrative posts, issuing an executive order providing some partner benefits for gay federal employees, preparing new rules to protect transgender federal employees, and formally inviting gay families to the White House Easter Egg Roll. But his continued verbal support for repeal of both DADT and DOMA, combined with the lack of action, only succeeded in frustrating both sides in the culture wars.

Events soon forced Obama's hand. As gay rights groups challenged DOMA in the federal courts, the Justice Department followed custom in defending the constitutionality of the statute. When the department's brief became public, gay rights leaders put enormous pressure on the White House to reverse this action. On June 29, 2009, at a White House gathering of gay rights leaders, the president reiterated his commitment to repeal DOMA, end DADT, and press for passage of hate crimes legislation. He lamented that congressional leaders saw little prospect for repeal of DOMA, but the Justice Department would amend its brief in defense of its constitutionality with a strong statement advocating repeal. Obama resisted suggestions to end DADT by executive order rather than statute (Hertzberg 2009), acceding to the wishes of Defense Secretary Gates and Joint Chiefs of Staff Chair Mullen to allow the military to ease into preparations for a change in policy with a comprehensive internal study.

These steps did not mollify gay rights leaders or religious progressives, but they did energize criticism from a coalition of religious conservatives, including some working with the administration on health care and other issues. The introduction of the Respect for Marriage Act by House Democratic liberals, continuing state battles over gay marriage, and a highly publicized same-sex marriage ordinance in Washington, DC, had activated conservative alliances comprising evangelicals, Catholics, black Protestants, and others. Now a national coalition was formalized by the "Manhattan Declaration," signed by a host of evangelical leaders, Catholic bishops and archbishops, Orthodox clergy, and black Protestant ministers. The tone of the document was strongly critical of administration actions on both abortion and gay rights (Goodstein 2009).

Although Obama was still hoping to avoid dramatic action, events—mostly court decisions—continued to force his hand. A federal district court in July declared DOMA unconstitutional, and a month later, another federal district judge ruled that Proposition 8, a California referendum passed in 2008 prohibiting same-sex marriage, was an unconstitutional denial of equal protection. And while the Senate was unable to act on a House bill repealing DADT, a California federal district judge held the 1993 statute unconstitutional, rejecting Justice Department arguments to the contrary. Although a Court of Appeals action stayed this ruling pending appeal (and was sustained by the Supreme Court), the combination of these and later court decisions put gay rights issues high on the political radar scope and presented the administration with a dilemma going into the 2010 elections: take a strong stand on both issues and risk losing some conservative or centrist religious voters, or delay action and further discourage gay rights and liberal religious groups in a year when Democratic enthusiasm was already lagging.

Although the repeal of DADT had broader public support and faced less resistance from conservative religious groups and Republicans, the prospects for repeal were still clouded. The Defense Department's elaborate review, released on November 30, after the congressional elections, recommended the repeal, as expected, but also noted strong objections to inclusion of openly gay military personnel on the part of a large section of the chaplaincy and soldiers in combat zones (Department of Defense 2010). Senate Republicans, led by John McCain, continued resistance during the lame duck session of Congress, but on December 18, the Senate passed the repeal, which the president signed on December 22 before a large and emotional crowd of invited gay rights advocates (Branigan, Wilgoren, and Bacon 2010). Although thorny administrative issues, especially involving the chaplaincy, remained to be settled, this action left DOMA front and center on the cultural battle lines carrying over into Obama's second two years as president. Vice President Biden argued that recognition of same-sex marriage was "inevitable," even as Obama admitted publicly to be "struggling" with the issue, despite his support for repeal of DOMA (Kellman 2010).

INTO THE WORLD: RELIGION AND FOREIGN POLICY

Although religious groups have always been interested in American foreign policy and religious beliefs influence citizens' views, the interaction between religion and American foreign policy has intensified in recent years (Guth 2009a; Rock 2011). Religious organizations are more involved in US government programs abroad, events overseas often impinge on domestic concerns, and above all, international terrorism problems often have a clear religious component, even evoking a "clash of civilizations." Obama's membership in a "cross-national, cross-confessional" family seemingly gave him an edge in dealing with international issues with a religious component, and he immediately charged his advisory council to seek out interfaith programs that would advance mutual interests with foreign countries. His secretary of state, Hillary Clinton, was also attuned to the religious resonances of foreign policy, especially in the Middle East. Yet here as well the president confronted high barriers to using religious values as diplomatic leverage.

A prime foreign policy objective was to restore warmer relations with the Muslim world, which were depleted by the Bush's administration war on terror and its failure to make any advances in Israeli-Palestinian reconciliation. Obama immediately began a public wooing of the Muslim world, using his inaugural address, giving his first official interview to an Arabic news agency, and visiting important Muslim countries. In April 2009, he told Turkey's Grand National Assembly that the United States "is not and never will be at war with Islam," noting his own part-Muslim family. In June, he reiterated these themes at Cairo University, asking for a "new beginning" in relations. While extending the rhetorical olive branch, the administration took quiet actions to reduce tensions, starting programs to encourage entrepreneurship, business development, science education, and health and intellectual exchanges in Muslim nations (Packer 2010).

This overture was complicated by other foreign policy objectives. Blue-ribbon reports from the Chicago Council on Global Affairs and the president's own Faith-Based Advisory Council had encouraged Obama to emphasize religious freedom in foreign policy, but he showed little inclination to do so. For many religious leaders, his attitude was epitomized by the delay in filling the post of ambassador-at-large for International Religious Freedom until June 2010, when he nominated a diplomatically inexperienced pastor but failed to press for quick Senate confirmation. Secretary Clinton's verbal shift from "religious freedom" to "freedom of worship" convinced advocacy groups that the administration was not only deemphasizing this policy objective, but narrowing it, as well (Farr 2010). Obama's evident reluctance to stress religious freedom in diplomacy with Muslim nations, China, and Vietnam raised serious concerns within the ecumenical alliance of evangelicals, Catholics, and Jews that had grown up around the issue (Hertzke 2004).

At least initially, Obama's Muslim outreach improved evaluations of the United States, but these gains were quickly limited by the continuing US role in Iraq and the decision to bolster military commitments in Afghanistan. These policies not only antagonized Muslims around the world but also divided Obama's ethnoreligious and progressive constituency at home. Most minority religious groups strongly opposed these ventures, as did religious liberals and seculars. But it was above all the administration's failure to make progress in settling the Palestinian-Israeli controversy that prevented much long-term improvement in relations with Muslim nations.

This continuing problem not only presented Obama with a diplomatic nightmare but threw him into a whirlpool of domestic religious conflicts, as well. The influential Jewish community was always sensitive to any hint that he was sacrificing Israel's safety or essential interests to achieve a "two-state" solution. Although Obama had old and close relations with Jewish Democrats (with many on his campaign and White House staffs), some Jewish groups had been suspicious of Obama's Muslim ties and had supported Hillary Clinton in the 2008 Democratic contest. And Jewish lobbies were credited with blocking Obama's nomination of Charles W. Freeman as chair of the National Intelligence Council on the grounds of his purported hostility to Israel (Smith 2009). While mainline Protestant officials, black Protestant leaders, and Catholic bishops favored an "even-handed" or even "pro-Palestinian" policy, evangelicals were, for the most part, vocally pro-Israeli. Thus, administration moves to prod Israel for concessions met strong resistance from Jewish groups and evangelicals, even as they were applauded by parts of Obama's core constituency. In the end, few religious groups were satisfied with US policy, even as negotiations remained stalemated (Lexington 2010).

Events at home further complicated relations with Muslims abroad and divided religious groups at home. Continued terrorist plots, the shooting of soldiers at Fort Hood by a Muslim officer, and above all, the proposed construction of an Islamic center a few blocks from the site of the 9/11 attacks in New York City revived anti-Muslim sentiments and hurt America's image in the Muslim world. Anti-mosque demonstrations in New York and well-publicized threats by a Florida preacher to burn the Quran threatened to undo the administration's work. When Obama commented that Muslims had a right to build the New York center but reserved judgment on the expediency of doing so, he angered both sides. By the end of 2010, international polls showed that America's image in Muslim countries (except in the president's boyhood home of Indonesia) had retraced 2008 levels (Pew Research Center 2010).

Ironically, Obama's Muslim initiative produced an undesired byproduct in domestic politics. By 2010, polls were showing increased public uncertainty about Obama's own religious identity, with large minorities, especially among Republicans, now seeing him as a Muslim. As surveys showed that Muslims were among the least-liked religious groups, such suspicions became a political albatross. Although nursed along by the conservative media and some Republicans, this perception also owed something to Obama's early decision not to attend a Washington church. Perhaps recognizing this mistake, soon after the release of one poll the Obamas attended Easter services at Allen Chapel AME in Washington with appropriate press coverage. Not only did the Obamas begin to attend religious services more regularly but also religious references began to reappear in presidential speeches with much greater frequency (Lee 2010).

RELIGIOUS GROUPS EVALUATE OBAMA

How did religious groups react to the Obama administration? Table 4.3 traces the trajectory of assessments, based on data from the Pew Research Center for the People & the Press. Although the Center's religious measures are not as detailed as those in tables 4.1 and 4.2, we can still get some purchase on trends. To produce sufficient numbers for smaller groups, we have combined two adjacent monthly surveys from the early administration, two from summer 2009, and three from February through April 2010, the latest available as of this writing.

The president began with almost two-thirds of the public approving his performance. Not surprisingly, his core ethnoreligious constituency gave him the highest marks, ranging from 90 percent among black Protestants to 65 percent among the unaffiliated. A solid majority of white mainline Protestants and Anglo-Catholics also approved, but evangelicals were more critical, with their average weighed down by very negative scores among their large orthodox contingent. By his second six months, Obama was slumping toward 50 percent overall, but religious patterns remained largely the same, with rock-hard support among black Protestants and significant declines among

Table 4.3.   Religious Groups and Support for President Obama, 2009–2010

	February/ March 2009	August/ September 2009	February/ March/April 2010	Change in Approval
Black Protestant	90	91	88	−2
Latino Catholic	85	53	68	−17
Jewish	79	68	54	−25
Agnostic/Atheist	76	70	60	−16
Latino Protestant	73	49	54	−19
Other Christians	71	57	59	−12
All Non-Christian	68	77	65	−3
Unaffiliated (Secular)	65	56	48	−17
Mainline Protestant	55	47	42	−13
Progressives	55	49	40	−15
Centrist	59	47	47	−12
Orthodox	50	43	34	−16
Anglo-Catholic	54	53	42	−12
Progressives	52	57	51	−1
Centrist	53	58	39	−14
Orthodox	55	48	41	−14
Latter-day Saints	56	27	24	−32
Evangelical Protestant	43	28	26	−17
Progressives	57	43	33	−14
Centrist	50	34	25	−25
Orthodox	38	23	24	−14
All Respondents	62	51	47	−15

Source: Pew Research Center for the People and the Press, 2010.

Latino Catholics and Protestants, Latter-day Saints, and evangelicals. And in the three large white Christian communities, the orthodox were clearly most negative. By the spring of 2010, his support had slipped a little more nationally, although black Protestants remained loyal and he had recovered some ground among Latinos. Ominously, Jewish evaluations had dropped substantially and Obama had also fallen well below 50 percent among mainline Protestants and Anglo-Catholics (groups he split evenly with McCain in 2008), and unaffiliated citizens were also turning against the president.

Although we cannot connect these ratings precisely with reaction to Obama policies, an April 2010 Pew Center survey asked respondents to score his performance on specific issues: handling the economy, health care, immigration, Afghanistan, Iran, and energy policy. Although these evaluations are naturally correlated with the president's overall rating, they do vary considerably. Looking at religious groups' deviations from national trends can give us some insight into their assessments. As one might expect, groups giving the president above-average ratings across the board were his strongest ethnoreligious constituencies: black Protestants, non-Christians, and agnostic/atheists. But the opposition varied. On economic management, for example, Latter-day Saints and evangelicals were far more critical than the national average, followed distantly by mainline Protestants. On health care, once again Latter-day Saints and evangelicals led the critics, followed more closely by mainline and Latino Protestants. On immigration, evangelicals were most critical, followed by mainline Protestants, Latino Protestants, and Anglo-Catholics. On Afghanistan, however, ethnoreligious differences were muted, with only black Protestants deviating much from the national average (in a positive direction). On Iran (and probably other Middle East issues), Jews were most critical, followed by Latter-day Saints, evangelicals, and Latino Protestants, all strong supporters of Israel (data not shown). Whatever the variations, however, traditional religious patterns appeared to be reasserting themselves.

RELIGIOUS CONSTITUENCIES IN THE 2010 ELECTIONS AND BEYOND

Although old religious alignments seemed to be reappearing as the 2010 campaign began, explicitly religious mobilization was remarkably modest. Although a few liberal Catholic groups fought (unsuccessfully) to protect several new Catholic House members who had backed the Obama agenda, Democratic religious leaders almost universally lamented the absence of the broad outreach that had worked so well in 2006 and 2008. The Democratic National Committee (and the "Hill" committees) left religious liaison posts unfilled and directed little money to religious appeals (Burke 2010). On the GOP side, conservative religious groups took a backseat to the Tea Party mobilization, which absorbed at least some religious activism, despite its libertarian bent. Pulpits were also relatively quiet, although 56 percent of Catholics and 31 percent of evangelicals did report clerical discussions on abortion, perhaps prompted by the health-care battle. Few other issues received much clerical attention (Jones and Cox 2010).

Despite the lack of religious activism and the campaign focus on economics, health care, and the role of government, religious alignments basically reverted to their pre-2008 form, with Obama's gains in most sectors rolled back. Combining reports from exit polls (conducted only in some states), a Public Religion Research Institute (PRRI) survey (Jones and Cox 2010), and a few other sources, we can get a reasonably detailed picture of religious voting. By various estimates, evangelicals gave 71 percent to 78 percent of the vote to Republicans, compared to 56 percent to 59 percent by mainline Protestants and white Catholics, up in both the latter communities from 2008 and 2006.

Unaffiliated voters favored the Democrats with 57 percent to 66 percent, down considerably from 2008 and 2006. Black Protestants and Latino Catholics remained Democratic bastions (although with lower turnout), but Latino Protestants inched back toward their 2004 Republican preferences. Overall, the "God Gap" persisted, as 60 percent of regular churchgoers voted Republican, compared with 44 percent of the less observant.

Thus, Obama's first two years not only failed to alter the basic religious configuration of American political parties, but the modest 2008 Democratic gains in some religious constituencies—especially among white Catholics, mainline and Latino Protestants, and the unaffiliated—were "given back." PRRI's survey (Jones and Cox 2010) also confirmed that the president's religious identity was problematic, as increasing numbers of Americans concluded that his religion was substantially different from their own, leading to more negative evaluations. This perception was most common among evangelicals (65 percent) but somewhat less prevalent among white Protestants and white Catholics (52 percent). Such assessments no doubt derived in part from the mistaken belief that Obama was Muslim. As a solid majority of evangelicals and white Catholics thought that Islam was incompatible with American values (57 and 53 percent, respectively), as did large numbers of mainline Protestants and minority Christians (47 and 45 percent, respectively), this misperception certainly contributed to poorer ratings. Indeed, two scholars argued that religious intolerance was now combining with racial prejudice to produce hostility toward Obama (Tesler and Sears 2010).

In the aftermath of the 2010 elections, Obama and the Democratic Party appeared uncertain about future religious strategies. The party's left renewed its call for a thoroughgoing liberalism on economic, social, and foreign policy, one that would appeal primarily to ethnoreligious minorities, religious progressives, and seculars. Indeed, Obama seemed to follow part of this strategy, meeting for the first time with officials of the National Council of Churches, representing the liberal mainline, and African American Protestant churches that had long constituted the religious partners favored by Democratic administrations (Dart 2010; Tipton 2007). And the revival of evangelical opposition and the drift to the right at the US Conference of Catholic Bishops might also seem to encourage reversion to old alliances.

Still, Obama's own convictions and instincts favor revival of his "ecumenical" strategy and a continuing reluctance to return to the rutted tracks of established religious politics. Perhaps, in the fashion of his post-election compromise with Republicans on tax policy (Bai 2010), Obama will renew his quest for a "grand religious coalition," chastened but not discouraged in his effort to tamp down the culture wars.

REFERENCES

Alter, Jonathan. 2010. *The Promise: President Obama. Year One.* New York: Simon and Schuster.

Bai, Matt. 2010. "Murmurs on Left of a Primary Challenge to Obama." *New York Times*, December 8, A20.

Barnes, James. 2009. "The Face of Diversity." *National Journal*, June 20, 21.

Boorstein, Michelle, and Kimberly Kindy. 2009. "Faith-Based Office to Extend Its Reach." *Washington Post*, February 6, 2.

Boyer, Peter J. 2010. "The Covenant." *New Yorker*, September 6, 60–67.

Branigan, William, Debbi Wilgoren, and Perry Bacon, Jr. 2010. "Obama Signs DADT Repeal Before Big, Emotional Crowd." *Washington Post*, December 22. http://www.washingtonpost.com/wp-dyn/content/article/2010/12/22/AR2010122201888.html. Accessed December 22, 2010.

Brown, Carrie B. 2009. "Stem Cell Decision Ignites Right's Ire." *Politico*, March 10. http://www.politico.com/news/stories/0309/19818.html. Accessed January 3, 2011.

Burke, Daniel. 2010. "Did the Democrats Forget Faith-Based Outreach?" *Christian Century* 127, November 30, 14–15.

Chafets, Zev. 2009. "Obama's Rabbi." *New York Times Magazine*, April 5, 34.

Cohen, Jon. 2009. "61% in Poll Back Rick Warren as Invocation Pick." *Washington Post*, January 20, A11.

Dart, John. 2010. "Obama Hears Concerns of NCC Leaders." *Christian Century* 127, November 30, 15.

Department of Defense. 2010. *Report of the Comprehensive Review of the Issues Associated with a Repeal of "Don't Ask, Don't Tell."* Washington, DC: Department of Defense.

Farr, Thomas F. 2010. "Obama Administration Sidelines Religious Freedom Policy." *Washington Post*, June 25, A17.

Gilgoff, Dan. 2010. "Obama Signs Order Clarifying Church-States Relationship." *CNN Belief Blog*, November 17.

Goodstein, Laurie. 2009. "Christian Leaders Unite on Political Issues." *New York Times*, November 20, A24.

Guth, James L. 2009a. "Religion and American Public Opinion: Foreign Policy Issues." In *The Oxford Handbook of Religion and American Politics*, edited by Corwin E. Smidt, Lyman A. Kellstedt, and James L. Guth. New York: Oxford University Press, 243–65.

———. 2009b. "Religion in the 2008 Election." In *The American Elections of 2008*, edited by Janet M. Box-Steffensmeier and Steven E. Schier. Lanham, MD: Rowman & Littlefield.

Hertzberg, Hendrick. 2009. "Stonewall Plus Forty." *New Yorker*, July 6–13, 23–24.

Hertzke, Allen D. 2004. *Freeing God's Children: The Unlikely Alliance for Global Human Rights.* Lanham, MD: Rowman & Littlefield.

Hunter, James D. 1991. *Culture Wars: The Struggle to Define America.* New York: Basic Books.

Jones, Robert P., and Daniel Cox. 2010. *Old Alignments, Emerging Fault Lines: Religion in the 2010 Election and Beyond.* Washington, DC: Public Religion Research Institute.

Kellman, Laurie. 2010. "Biden: Gay Marriage Is Inevitable." *Associated Press,* December 24.

Kleppner, Paul. 1979. *The Third Electoral System, 1853–1892: Parties, Voters, and Political Cultures.* Chapel Hill: University of North Carolina Press.

Kloppenberg, James T. 2010. *Reading Obama: Dreams, Hope, and the American Political Tradition.* Princeton, NJ: Princeton University Press.

Knowlton, Brian. 2009. "On His First Full Day." *New York Times,* January 22, A1.

Lee, Carol. 2010. "Obama Lets His Faith Show." *POLITICO,* December 28. http://www.politico.com/news/stories/1210/46841.html. Accessed December 28, 2010.

Lexington. 2010. "The President and the Peace Process." *The Economist,* August 28, 28

Minnery, Tom. 2010. "The Peril of Denying the Obvious." *Citizen* 24 (December), 30.

Obama, Barack. 1995. *Dreams from My Father.* New York: Three Rivers Press.

———. 2006. *The Audacity of Hope.* New York: Crown Publishers.

Packer, George. 2010. "Rights and Wrongs." *New Yorker,* May 17, 35–36.

Parsons, Christi. 2010. "Obama's Minister in Chief." *Washington Post,* July 31, p. B2.

Pew Research Center. 2010. "Obama More Popular Abroad Than at Home." *Pew Research Center for the People & the Press,* July 17.

Remnick, David. 2010. *The Bridge. The Life and Rise of Barack Obama.* New York: Alfred A. Knopf.

Rich, Frank. 2009. "The Culture Warriors Get Laid Off." *New York Times,* March 15, WK12.

Rock, Stephen R. 2011. *Faith and Foreign Policy: The Views and Influence of U.S. Christians and Christian Organizations.* New York: Continuum.

Saslow, Eli. 2009. "Obama's Path to Faith Was Eclectic." *Washington Post,* January 18, A18.

Smith, Ben. 2009. "Freeman Hits 'Israel Lobby' On Way Out." *Politico,* March 10. http://www.politico.com/news/stories/0309/19856.html. Accessed January 3, 2011.

Smith, Ben, and Byron Tau. 2010. "Obama's Stimulus Pours Millions into Faith-based Groups." *POLITICO,* December 3. http://www.politico.com/news/stories/1210/45897.html. Accessed January 3, 2011.

Stein, Rob. 2009. "Obama Plan Aims to Appease Both Sides of Abortion Issue." *Washington Post,* February 6, A5.

Sullivan, Amy. 2008. *The Party Faithful: How and Why Democrats Are Closing the God Gap.* New York: Scribner.

Tesler, Michael, and David O. Sears. 2010. *Obama's Race.* Chicago: University of Chicago Press.

Tipton, Steven M. 2007. *Public Pulpits: Methodists and Mainline Churches in the Moral Argument of Public Life.* Chicago: University of Chicago Press.

Zeleny, Jeff, and David D. Kirkpatrick. 2008. "Obama's Choice of Pastor Creates Furor." *New York Times,* December 20, A19.

WASHINGTON GOVERNANCE

Chapter Five

Accomplishments and Miscalculations in the Obama Presidency

John F. Harris and James Hohmann

The challenge in Barack Obama's gloomy, demoralized winter of 2011 was to somehow recall—like a bleary-eyed reveler with broken champagne glasses at his feet trying to summon details of the night before—the sunny exuberance of the winter of 2009.

"Now there are some who question the scale of our ambitions, who suggest that our system cannot tolerate too many big plans," Obama announced in his inaugural address. "What the cynics fail to understand is that the ground has shifted beneath them, that the stale political arguments that have consumed us for so long, no longer apply."

This chapter will explore the ways Obama must reckon with miscalculations of his first two years and with the new evidence—personified by the new Republican majority in the House of Representatives—that there was indeed a political limit to how many big plans the American electorate could tolerate without serious costs for Obama and the Democratic Party. Washington's great parlor game of the moment: Can Obama revive his presidency and win reelection in 2012? Our answer is of course he can—indeed in many ways it seems likely. But he can do so only by modifying some of the premises he carried with him into office and discarding some others. Obama must learn to practice a brand of defensive politics toward which he previously expressed disdain, and he must learn to be vastly more creative at using those powers of the presidency that go beyond simply pushing the Congress to pass legislation.

The inaugural address was the public face of Obama's extraordinary ambition as he roared into office as the forty-fourth president. For us, a revealing private glimpse into how these ambitions shaped the mood and political calculations of his West Wing in those early days comes courtesy of our *POLITICO* colleague Jonathan Martin. Several weeks into Obama's presidency, after

Obama had laid out his plans for bold government programs to overhaul the nation's health-care system, impose a new regulatory regime on the financial markets, and adapt a far-reaching "cap and trade" system to control carbon emissions into the environment, the moderate Evan Bayh, a veteran Democratic senator from Indiana, was quoted in the media sounding a bit squeamish. Perhaps, Bayh ventured, all this was too much, too fast. A senior White House aide irked at Bayh's timidity came to Martin with a story idea: do a piece on Democratic wimps. The subjects of the article, as the Obama aide contemptuously described it, would be people like Bayh who did not realize that history had passed them by. This was no longer the 1990s, the Obama team believed, and no longer Bill Clinton's Democratic Party. But there were people like Bayh who were still practicing a cautious, hide-covering brand of politics linked to the centrist Democratic Leadership Council (a group which both Bayh and Clinton once chaired). The political risk for Democrats, by these lights, was not in doing too much but in failing to recognize that the temper of the times had changed and doing too little.

The Democratic wimps piece, alas, never got written. But Martin's encounter does nicely capture the early spirit of the Obama team: impassioned, impatient, and more than a touch imperious. It is also a reminder of a political reality that occasionally sneaks partly into public view but usually stays cloaked in Washington background conversations. The core loyalists who populate Obama's West Wing perceived themselves as reversing the political and policy legacy not simply of George W. Bush and Dick Cheney, but also of Clinton.

Their problem is not personal animus toward Clinton (though there is some of that, particularly among the most unforgiving younger aides who joined the Obama fold during the bitter 2008 nomination battle against Hillary Rodham Clinton). The complaint is over what many Obama loyalists believe Clinton stood for: defensive-minded politics that during the 1990s forsook progressive ideals in exchange for "small-bore" policies that were oriented around protecting Clinton's personal political standing but in the end yielded only a marginally consequential presidency. Obama himself hinted at this view. During the primaries, Obama praised the leadership style (not the policies) of Ronald Reagan, whom he said made Republicans "the party of ideas." He explained that, "Reagan changed the trajectory of America in a way that Richard Nixon did not and in a way that Bill Clinton did not. We want clarity, we want optimism, we want a return to that sense of dynamism and entrepreneurship that had been missing" (Smith 2008). With the line, Obama unmistakably sought to tweak the Clintons and their brand of politics.

OBAMA'S EARLY MISCALCULATIONS

That was a preview of the Obama project: he saw his presidency as an opportunity to be a Democratic version of Reagan—passing bold policies that would move the nation's political center of gravity in ways that would make history and have impact even after his leaving office. The presidential version of the "big bang theory," the one that made Bayh so uneasy, was based precisely on this premise—that Obama would succeed in launching his term during the first year with a $787 billion stimulus package to revive a dangerously weakened economy *and* follow that with an explosive series of major policy initiatives on health care, energy, and financial regulatory reform.

The big bang theory rested on three assumptions that turned out to be hubris:

1. That Obama's 2008 victory—in which he carried such traditionally conservative states as Virginia (which had not voted Democratic at the presidential level since 1964), North Carolina, and Indiana—demonstrated that the country's ideological profile had shifted leftward in fundamental ways. Many inside and outside Obama's orbit prematurely announced a political realignment in 2008. As Nicol C. Rae argues convincingly at the start of this volume, "the events of 2008 in hindsight do not appear to have been sufficiently cataclysmic to create a reconstructive political opportunity" (chapter 1, this volume). Future elections might yet prove that Obama ushered in a long-term realignment, but the sharp setbacks in Virginia's 2009 off-year elections combined with the rout of Democrats everywhere but in the traditional strongholds of the northeast and West Coast in 2010, showed the near-term durability of the country's basic center-right orientation.

2. That early success would be self-reinforcing, and that each legislative gain would produce new momentum for the next one. This was not the case. The stimulus package passed, but House Republicans stood unanimously unified in opposition. The bill quickly became an unpopular lightning rod, even though on truth serum, many conservative business executives and Republican lawmakers could not claim that it did not help the economy. The cap-and-trade legislation that Obama and House Speaker Nancy Pelosi then pushed Democrats to vote for—despite scant prospects for passage in the Senate—in retrospect was a grievous, self-inflicted wound on Democrats. And the issue in the center ring, health-care reform, remained disliked after it was signed into law—exactly the opposite of what presidential adviser David Axelrod predicted.

3. That Obama, by virtue of his biography and special political gifts, had the unique ability to transcend the rising acrimony and partisan polarization that have defined American politics for the past generation. He arguably exacerbated it. Two Democratic pollsters who worked on presidential campaigns, Clinton's Doug Schoen and Jimmy Carter's Patrick Caddell, would complain in a *Washington Post* op-ed the weekend before the mid-terms that, "Obama is conducting himself in a way alarmingly reminiscent of (Richard) Nixon's role in the disastrous 1970 midterm campaign" (Schoen and Caddell 2010). Polls consistently showed that Obama and his views deeply divided the country, but he plodded ahead.

Even many sympathetic commentators were by the halfway point of his first term ruefully coming to the conclusion that perhaps he was not such a good communicator after all. Certainly Obama is a talented wordsmith, and has on occasion shown a flair for elegant speeches that inspire supporters and even send a thrill up the leg of such commentators as MSNBC's Chris Matthews. "Obama would sort of say, 'Look, I'm smart. I know what I'm doing. You'll just have to trust me. It was kind of beneath him to explain the reasons behind his actions to people—how TARP really worked, how the stimulus was helping," said Democrat James Carville (Harris and Thrush 2010). But effective presidential communication is not only, or perhaps not even mainly, about rhetorical acrobatics. It is about projecting a sustained, disciplined message that is harnessed to a clear policy agenda.

By this measure, Obama had not succeeded in his early outings. He veered, depending on mood or polls or the latest advice, between trying to confront Wall Street and the US Chamber of Commerce with a strongly populist message and trying to make amends with businesses and assure CEOs that they should consider him a pragmatic partner. He spent some days trying to send a message that he wanted to work constructively with congressional Republicans and other days dispatching his press secretary to send the message that the GOP lawmakers were little more than flying monkeys taking orders from Rush Limbaugh. At a time when the economy was the foremost domestic issue, Obama never fashioned a consistent economic message or employed surrogates who inspired widespread confidence among the general public.

Obama's articulate and cerebral style—the opposite in every way of George W. Bush's guttural certitudes—did not convey that he thought about the nation's travails as more than abstractions or that he understood the concrete human dimensions of public policy decision. By declining to speak clearly and often about his larger philosophy—and insisting that his actions were guided not by ideology but a results-oriented "pragmatism"—he bred confusion and disappointment among his allies and left his agenda and motives vulnerable to distortion by his enemies. In liberal intellectual circles, it was common by 2010 for Obama to be described as rudderless and politically expedient. Liberals said he retreated too early on a public option for health care, was too soft on big banks during financial reform, continued too many of George W. Bush's national security policies, and caved on the extension of the high-income tax cuts. In many precincts of the right, there seemed to be no uncertainty about who he really was: a would-be socialist, determined to dethrone private enterprise and individual liberty in favor of government power.

None of the White House's miscalculations seem fatal. The president and his team can plausibly argue that Obama presided over a series of highly consequential policy decisions on the economy and on health care that will be recognized in due course as major substantive and political triumphs. And there is no shortage of observers who project certainty in the wake of the disastrous midterms that Obama will rehabilitate his image. John Kenneth White, for instance, compares Obama favorably to Franklin Roosevelt in a separate chapter of this book. "Just as the New Deal's run at the political box office wasn't over in 1938, it is equally true that the Barack Obama show is not over," he argues (chapter 2, this volume). And, as Rae notes, Reagan and Lincoln suffered big setbacks in their first midterms yet still became reconstructive presidents. Time will tell, as will the perceived strength of economic recovery come November 2012. In the absence so far of promising new talent with national potential emerging among Republicans, Obama still seems easily the most formidable political figure of his generation.

Even so, it is hard to see Obama recovering from the Democrats' midterm disaster during the consolidation phase of his presidency without finding remedies to these early miscalculations. And here lies an irony: the most plausible model for Obama's rehabilitation is none other than Bill Clinton.

THE CLINTON MODEL

Clinton was a complicated man with a complicated presidency that left behind a complicated legacy. He has been termed "The Survivor" for his ability to persevere through continual cycles of triumph, setback, and recovery.

The essence of Clinton's success as an elected official was that he understood—early on in his Arkansas days—that to be a successful progressive politician in a center-right country means practicing the politics of reassurance. The politics of reassurance has two dimensions. There is ideological reassurance—convincing voters that a progressive agenda contains tangible benefits that will positively affect the lives of the swing voters on whom elections hinge. And there is personal reassurance—the ability of a politician to convey that he is sympathetic to the values of voters, that their likes and dislikes and preoccupations are the same as his own.

Obama, for all his gifts, did not in his first two years as president show much interest in the politics of reassurance or much skill at it. Then Clinton appeared at the White House press briefing room with Obama in December 2010, when the president invoked his predecessor's support in order to rally reluctant Democrats to support his bargain with Republicans that extended the 2001 Bush tax cuts. "Please go," Clinton told Obama, when the president said he was running behind (Lee 2010). Then he held forth with reporters as though he was still the commander in chief.

Clinton's reemergence raised suspicions that Obama might respond to the Republican gains through "triangulation," a naughty word that sounds like something which might still be illegal in some conservative locales, even if rarely prosecuted among consenting adults. Triangulation was consultant Dick Morris's advice for Clinton during his 1995–1996 comeback (Morris 1998, 80). As Morris explained in his memoir, the idea was to "create a third position: not just in between the old positions of the two parties but above them as well. Identify a new course that accommodates the needs the Republicans address but do it in a way that is uniquely yours."

CHANNELING THE SURVIVOR

Some people who advise a Clinton-like strategy for Obama make it seem like a simple thing, a matter of taking a few polls, making a few speeches, and *voila!*, reclaiming the center. In fact, the 1995–1996 comeback was an extended ordeal that fully taxed Clinton's own powers of resilience and relied also on a good measure of luck under circumstances of economic expansion that do not much resemble what Obama faces now with severe economic turmoil and two wars overseas. It is not clear that Obama, by virtue of his own temperament and ideological instincts, can easily replicate the Clinton recovery—even though it may be sensible to try.

There are five reasons why "pulling a Clinton" is a more formidable undertaking than most political analysts and strategists imagine:

1. Obama's left flank will object to any movement toward the center. Clinton now is generally recalled fondly among most Democrats and also regarded as a supremely effective politician. But in 1995, when he began the policy and messaging moves known as "triangulation," he faced a resentful and bitterly divided party. After he announced his support for a balanced bud-

get, it was easy for reporters to fill up a notebook on Capitol Hill with hostile quotes from Democrats calling Clinton a quisling, especially after they learned he was being advised by a Republican consultant. Rep. Patricia Schroeder of Colorado said Republicans were playing with the president "like a kitten with a string." Rep. Dave Obey of Wisconsin jeered, "I think most of us learned some time ago, if you don't like the president's position on a particular issue, you simply need to wait a few weeks" (Harris 2005, 185). During the midst of a troubled war in Afghanistan and more polarized politics generally, Obama has a tougher challenge keeping his party unified, and any moves that liberals interpreted as abandoning them for reasons of political expediency would probably earn a much harsher reaction than Clinton received.

2. Real change is really hard. Clinton's political reassessment was carried out in tandem with an exceptionally painful personal reappraisal by both him and First Lady Hillary Clinton. Days after the election, she broke down in tears in a conversation with Morris, confessing, "I don't know which direction is up or down. Everything I thought was right was wrong" (Harris 2005, 154). The president himself was so disoriented he looked everywhere for guidance. At Camp David, he played host to self-help gurus like Stephen Covey (*The Seven Habits of Highly Effective People*) or Anthony Robbins (*Awaken the Giant Within*), whose late-night infomercials advised that people could train themselves to walk across hot coals. But he also opened his West Wing operation to talented outsiders who were not intimates or veterans of his campaign, including then-Chief of Staff Leon Panetta. Some of Clinton's advice-seeking was eccentric, but it revealed his willingness to listen and an instinct for brutal self-critique that, at least to date, has hardly been Obama's signature.

3. Clinton shook up his staff in a way that would be hard for Obama. Like the current president, Clinton was initially surrounded with an exceptionally talented but sometimes brash group of advisers, who felt a sense of ownership of his presidency. They soon learned that they were tenants, not owners. Without explaining his actions even to the people affected, Clinton simply dropped many of his advisers, such as pollster Stan Greenberg. George Stephanopoulos for months found himself coldly on the outs, fighting to get into meetings. Onetime adviser Paul Begala left Washington for Texas rather than try to fight for influence with people he loathed like Morris. Clinton became weepy as he parted ways with people with whom he felt an early bond, like Press Secretary Dee Dee Myers. "We hired too many young people in this White House who are smart but not wise," Clinton told Stephanopoulos, as recounted in the latter's memoir (Stephanopoulos 1999, 254).

Some of the Washington operatives who are urging Obama to pattern his recovery after Clinton also rooted for a West Wing shake-up. In January 2011, Obama brought Bill Daley, Clinton's commerce secretary, on as White House chief of staff and Vice President Joe Biden chose Bruce Reed, Clinton's domestic policy architect, as his chief of staff. This was widely reported as a reunion of the "Clinton centrists" (Gerstein 2011). The result may or may not be effective. Almost certainly, the process of turnover among the lower ranks will be messy and full of Washington recriminations.

4. Obama did not articulate his underlying ideology during the campaign the way Clinton did. As bumpy as Clinton's recovery was, he had an advantage. For the most part, he was returning in 1995 to a core set of values that had become obscured amid the clamor of his first two years in office. Clinton was a centrist Democratic governor who learned in Arkansas how to navigate a conservative political environment. His speeches from the triangulation period may have seemed like lurches to the center compared with 1993, but for the most part, they were lurches back to the rhetoric he had used when he began his bid for the presidency in 1991. Some of Clinton's moves from his recovery period were easy to mock, such as allowing Morris to poll where to take the family vacation and giving speeches on such nontraditional presidential topics as support for school uniforms. But these seemingly trivial moves had a serious purpose. They were part of a sustained effort to reestablish Clinton's connection with middle-class values and concerns. Almost every day brought a new speech or new presidential directive designed to show that he could still be a robust leader even without a legislative majority behind him.

Obama, who ran for president mostly on the strength of his biography and personal qualities, does not have the same set of clear first principles to guide his political rehabilitation. And he and his aides have been vocally critical of what they regard as Clinton's instinct for "small-bore" politics. For the Obama team to embrace Clinton political techniques would require a radical shift in its own assumptions about how to use the power of the presidency.

This is consistent with Obama's aversion to being boxed in by philosophical labels during his 2008 campaign. Throughout the primaries, he steered clear of the familiar Democratic intraparty debate over whether he was a liberal or a "New Democrat" centrist. He avoided linking himself with the moderate Democratic Leadership Council, as Clinton did in the 1990s. He ran to the left of Hillary Clinton and other rivals (with his early opposition to the Iraq War) or slightly to the right of her (with a more incremental plan for health care), depending on the circumstances. In the general election, he easily united the disparate wings of his party and attracted a clear majority of Independents around disdain for the Bush years and the symbolic power of his personal story. In a *60 Minutes* interview after his election but before his inauguration, Obama spoke of his "pragmatism" and said he does not "get bottled up in a lot of ideology and 'Is this conservative or liberal?'" He said his interest is "finding something that works" (Kroft 2008). By some lights, however, he and his team became so enthralled with the idea of a personality-driven "Obama brand" that they neglected the need to explain—and in a modern media environment, to explain and explain again—the ideas behind the personality.

5. Clinton's comeback benefited immeasurably from some well-timed bounces that Obama cannot count on. Ghoulish as it is to contemplate, the reality is that Clinton and his political team took advantage of the horror of the 1995 bombing of a federal building in Oklahoma City to invite people to reassess him as commander in chief. The incident also put the most extreme anti-government rhetoric of Washington conservatives in a menacing light. In Obama's case, by contrast, no one during an age of terrorism is unaware that he is commander in chief, but issues of national security are much more contentious than in the 1990s. Obama's speech in Tucson after the shooting of Rep. Gabrielle Giffords (D-Ariz.) showcased his ability to stay above the fray and bring the country together, but the heated back-and-forth between pundits on the left and right before all the facts were known demonstrated how the political climate has changed since 1995.

Clinton was most fortunate of all that his main antagonist among the Republicans was a flamboyant and undisciplined figure like Newt Gingrich, who announced modestly, "I think I am a transformational figure." When Gingrich whined that Clinton had made him exit from the back of Air Force One rather than invite him upfront for budget negotiations, the *New York Daily News* depicted him on the cover as an infant in diapers holding a baby rattle. Obama has no reason to suppose that such stolid and conventional politicians as House Speaker John Boehner and Senate Minority Leader Mitch McConnell will present him with quite the same opportunities to draw politically winning contrasts in advance of his 2012 reelection campaign.

To this day, there is considerable debate even among Clinton aides themselves what the lessons of 1995 are, which makes them that much harder to apply. People like pollster Mark Penn, a centrist, believe the essential ingredient was Clinton reclaiming the center through such steps as endorsing a balanced budget and signing welfare reform—as a way of showing that he shared the values of swing voters. People like Paul Begala, James Carville, and George Stephanopoulos believe the more important element was Clinton's willingness to show spine during the budget showdown with Republicans, in which the GOP took the blame for two federal government shutdowns.

OBAMA'S EGO

No matter which lessons he takes away from the Clinton experiences, questions will persist about whether Obama himself is capable of adjusting. The 2010 election results also served as a reminder that Obama is not immune from a timeless truth: every president's defects are in part a magnification of his virtues.

As Obama walked toward the arena at the 2004 Democratic National Convention in Boston, where he gave an electrifying keynote address that jump-started the supernova phase of his political ascendency, a *Chicago Tribune* reporter noted that he seemed to be making a good impression. "I'm LeBron, baby," Obama told author David Mendell. "I can play on this level. I got some game" (Mendell 2007).

Self-regard can blur into self-delusion. Supporters and skeptics worry that Obama does not share with his most successful predecessors the capacity for self-critique and self-correction. After Democrats got trounced in 2009's off-year elections in New Jersey and Virginia—in large measure because of the same flight of Independents that helped the GOP triumph in the midterm elections—White House aides loudly and publicly stated that there were no lessons in the results that were relevant to Obama. And for most of the year that followed, they acted on that premise. This misplaced confidence, by some lights, did not merely lead to political miscalculations. It strained the emotional connection with voters on which the most successful presidents depend. Restoring that connection, and regaining the sympathy to be extended a second chance, would require a show of modesty.

It is the sort of complaint that comes to the fore in background conversations with lawmakers, lobbyists, and veterans of previous administrations who interact with Obama's West Wing staffers: that they have created a cult of personality around Obama, having followed their boss on his rapid and improbable ascent to the presidency. Many of these devotees do feel that he is the political equivalent of LeBron James, the NBA phenom. The view is based on a belief that Obama's outsize political skills and uncommon personal poise make him different than conventional politicians and immune to conventional political laws of gravity.

One Obama insider told us that it is a view that starts at the top. Having triumphed over an early perception by political insiders and many journalists that he could not defeat front-runner Hillary Clinton, Obama, this person said, frequently invokes the 2008 experience and what he believes was its lesson—always stay the course, do not be distracted by ephemeral controversies or smart-set importuning for a change of direction. Some believe this is an admirable instinct carried to a dangerous degree.

Obama's predicament at the end of 2010 suggested another refrain of the modern presidency: its occupants arrive in office shaped preeminently by experience, with character formed well before leaders reach the White House. A time traveler who went to Arkansas in 1977 would find plenty of people in Little Rock who would not be the least bit surprised that their newly elected attorney general would become president someday. And these same people would not be surprised to learn of the particular nature of the scandal that hobbled Clinton's presidency some twenty years later. Obama, however, burst on to the national scene with such speed and force in 2008 that he may have seemed sui generis, a man untouched by the normal cycles of success and setback. Instead, what became clear was that Obama is, like all presidents, a product of his past. Some believe his style is too cerebral. Was this a surprise from a former law professor? Some said he allowed himself to be defined too much by legislative victories and defeats, rather than sketching a higher vision of where he wanted to lead the country. Did people not recall that his most extensive government experience was as a state legislator?

Likewise, the contemporary argument about Obama's personal style has long antecedents. People have for decades regarded him as having special leadership traits. And some people have observed, for just as long, that Obama sometimes regarded himself as too special. In author David Remnick's Obama biography, *The Bridge*, he quotes White House adviser and longtime friend Valerie Jarrett:

> I think Barack knew that he had God-given talents that were extraordinary. He knows exactly how smart he is. . . . He knows how perceptive he is. He knows what a good reader of people he is. And he knows that he has the ability—the extraordinary, uncanny ability—to take a thousand different perspectives, digest them and make sense of them, and I think that he has never really been challenged intellectually. . . . So, what I sensed in him was not just a restless spirit but somebody with such extraordinary talents that had to be really taxed in order for him to be happy. . . . He's been bored to death his whole life. He's just too talented to do what ordinary people do." (Remnick 2010, 274)

Remnick also tells of how even Michelle Obama would sometimes bridle under "his ego and his self-involvement" (336).

A 2008 *New Yorker* article quoted Patrick Gaspard, now the White House political director, describing what Obama told him during the job interview: "I think that I'm a better speechwriter than my speechwriters. I know more about policies on any particular issue than my policy directors. And I'll tell you right now that I'm gonna think I'm a better political director than my political director" (Lizza 2008).

It was health care where the self-confidence of the Obama team had the most profound impact. The team produced landmark legislation, even after many pundits assumed that the Democratic reform package was dead. A preelection poll by *Politico* and George Washington University found that 62 percent of Independent voters held an unfavorable view of the health-care law (Hohmann and VandeHei 2010). Rep. Marion Berry, who retired from the House earlier this year, described a White House meeting between Obama and conservative Democrats, who warned the president that the measure was unpopular in their districts and asked him why he thought he could do better with health-care reform than Clinton had. "Well, the big difference here and in '94 was you've got me," Berry quoted Obama as saying (Thrush 2010).

Veterans of Illinois politics say Obama's Washington tenure reflects themes—great talent harnessed to great ego—that are familiar to them. During his first six years as a state senator, Republicans controlled the Senate and the governorship. So at the time, to get a bill out of committee, he needed Republican support. "I think he came into Springfield with an arrogance," said Dan Shomon, who was assigned by Democratic leaders to help Obama as an aide when he arrived. "He wanted to fix the process too quickly. . . . He didn't have 'time' to make nice with everybody. . . . I guess the word confidence and professorial-like is better than arrogance, occasionally a lecturing sort of nature—which I think he's toned [down]. Over time, he learned to get rid of that where he was, sort of, lecturing" (Shomon 2010). Others who knew Obama back then think he came in modest and became less so as he accumulated more power.

It may have been, however, that Obama felt more rebuked by the midterm results than he ever let on to outsiders. In his book *The Audacity of Hope*, he described his feelings of embarrassment and rejection after the 2000 loss in the Democratic primary against Rep. Bobby Rush (D-Ill.):

No matter how convincingly you attribute the loss to bad timing or bad luck or lack of money—it's impossible not to feel at some level as if you have been personally repudiated by the entire community, that you don't quite have what it takes, and that everywhere you go, the word "loser" is flashing through people's minds. They're the sorts of feelings that most people haven't experienced since high school, when the girl you'd been pining over dismissed you with a joke in front of her friends, or you missed a pair of free throws with the big game on the line—the kinds of feelings that most adults wisely organize their lives to avoid. (Obama 2006, 107)

A MORE CREATIVE PRESIDENCY

The "shellacking" in the midterms, as he called it, forced Obama to refashion his presidency at the start of 2011. He found himself confined on the right by the incoming Republican House majority and the reality of deep budget deficits. He was confined on the left by his own sullen Democrats, including many liberals eager to protest any signal that Obama was selling them out or cynically lurching to the center. Obama's cramped circumstances during the lame duck session at the end of 2010 highlighted the urgent need to reinvent his presidency—discarding the Congress-focused strategy of the first two years and coming up with new and more creative ways to exercise power and set the national agenda.

His allies pressed him to pursue a West Wing makeover. "He needs to be CEO of America," said former White House Chief of Staff John Podesta, an Obama sympathizer who ran his transition to power after the 2008 election. "It is a bully pulpit role as leader of the country to give people a sense of both the challenge of the project—and the opportunity of the project—of moving the country to a better place" (Podesta 2010). The way he saw it, Obama could no longer be "Velcroed to the Hill."

That involved paying more attention to aspects of the presidency that did not involve signing bills into law. Among those powers: executive orders that advance Obama's agenda without involving Congress, new policy ideas that transcend Washington's usual left and right divisions, and speeches that summon people to meet the long-term challenges facing the country, even, or especially, when the remedies involve more than actions by the federal government.

Even before the elections, many advisers around Obama essentially agreed with the critique that he needed to liberate himself from the "scrum of Capitol Hill," as Podesta put it. As a practical matter, however, many of the biggest items on Obama's agenda—from health-care reform to the stimulus—necessarily involved a legislative strategy. Republican gains in Congress made it essential for him to use new avenues of power.

Obama's West Wing was not especially well equipped for the challenge. Unlike his five immediate predecessors—everyone since Gerald Ford— Obama came to the office with no previous executive experience. A liberal with a background as a state and national legislator, he deplored and campaigned against what he called the abuses of executive power on national security and civil liberties policies under former president George W. Bush and former vice president Dick Cheney. And he had populated his West Wing with staffers who grew up on Capitol Hill as aides and legislative-minded strategists.

Finding more creative ways to use the presidency—and ensuring that Obama dominates the national agenda even if his party does not dominate Washington—would be an undeniable learning experience. Presidential scholars and veterans of previous administrations from both parties identified five strategies past presidents had used to confront such a challenge.

1. More effectively use the cabinet and executive agencies. Two million is the number of people working for the executive branch, not including the armed services or postal service. The most ambitious presidents find ways to make sure that all of them work for the West Wing in some way. There again, the Clinton experience offers a useful model.

    Clinton was the most creative president in the modern era at using the powers of the executive branch in legitimate ways that nonetheless expressly served his own political ends as he prepared for reelection in 1996. He issued an executive order to turn 1.7 million acres in Utah into the Grand Staircase Escalante-National Monument, a far-reaching move that thrilled environmentalists. He announced the move not in Utah, but in Arizona, a swing state.

    During his reelection campaign in his second term, Clinton set up a de facto think tank run by senior adviser Tom Freedman, who scoured the executive branch for ideas that the president could embrace and make his own. Many of these were ideas the government would do anyway, but they were fashioned to help the president. There were new Agriculture Department rules on meat inspection over the Fourth of July weekend, when voters were more apt to grill. There was also a new Department of Veterans Affairs initiative, which coincided with Memorial Day, to expand benefits to people who had been exposed to Agent Orange in Vietnam.

    Other presidents have also seen the government they oversaw at their personal disposal. In the 1960s, a young Air Force airman famously told President Lyndon B. Johnson, "This is your helicopter, sir." Johnson responded, "They're all my helicopters, son" (Halberstam 2001, 386).

2. Draw new ideological lines—with new ideas. The Congress-focused strategy of the first two years gave Obama some highly consequential victories, including the far-reaching overhaul of health care and the repeal of the Clinton-era "Don't Ask, Don't Tell" policy on gays in the military. For the most part, however, Obama's big ideas in the first twenty-four months served to spark arguments that divided Washington along the familiar left

and right lines that have existed for decades. "The Republicans are going to set the agenda in the House. That doesn't mean he can't influence it," said presidential scholar Charles O. Jones (Jones 2010). Two of the most promising issues on which policy experts say Obama could break free of stale ideological categories are energy (on which many conservatives support moving away from carbon-based power) and education (on which many liberals are wary of teachers' unions and support radical experimentation).

The Center for American Progress (CAP) issued a fifty-four-page report in the weeks after the midterm elections with dozens of steps Obama could take to advance progressive ideas via executive power, ranging from the big and substantive (slapping a fee on imported oil to discourage consumption) to the small and symbolic (revamping the recovery.gov website to better track public spending or appointing a special envoy for the Horn of Africa). The report urged protecting more federal land and generating solar energy on Air Force hangar roofs, as well as speeding up the implementation of an already-passed small-business jobs act that adds bigger incentives for hiring and purchasing and promoting automatic mediation to avoid more home foreclosures (Wartell 2010). Ideas from CAP and the more centrist Democratic group, Third Way, had a common theme: they showed Obama—not Boehner or Senate Majority Leader Harry Reid (D-Nev.), for that matter—as the dominant figure setting the national agenda.

3. Coopt the opposition's ideas. Republicans rode a huge wave of conservative anger and energy to power into the 2010 elections. Obama's continuing challenge is to make sure that wave is a spent force by 2012—in part by letting conservatives think they have achieved some of what they want. One way to do that, some presidential observers suggest, is by appointing a prominent Republican—ideally someone with high-level business experience—to a top position in his administration.

Another common way to do that is rhetorically. That was the idea behind Clinton's 1996 State of the Union announcement that, "The era of Big Government is over" (Harris 2005, 221). Liberals chafe at such steps. But the idea is to coopt the opposition—not to capitulate to it. Clinton made that statement as a tactical move to advance his larger strategy, which was to preserve Medicare and Social Security and expand government into new areas. "You stiff-arm your own party in both houses and cooperate with the other party. The American system calls for that," Yale political scientist David Mayhew, who wrote a landmark book on how divided government can be legislatively productive, told us. "There's a politically induced opening to try to get things done even if it requires inventive coalitions"

(Mayhew 2010). In Obama's case, he would be taking symbolic steps in order to preserve his substantive agenda.

4. Be leader of the country—not just the government. Many of the issues that average voters care about do not directly relate to federal government programs: Are children being corrupted by a coarse and degrading popular culture? Is the country too divided by race and class? Is the United States well positioned in the world or shadowed by the prospect of long-term decline? After the 1994 elections put his own relevance in doubt, Clinton spent much of the balance of his six years talking about things like school prayer, local education, and television sex and violence. All these things were—at least under conventional presidential powers—only tangentially within his purview. But nontraditional powers can have results. The Welfare to Work Foundation that Clinton started in 1996, at the recommendation of Freedman and the late Eli Segal, after signing welfare reform into law encouraged private corporations to hire millions of people off welfare rolls.

5. Increase focus on international issues. Foreign policy, including overseas travel, is the traditional refuge of presidents who have lost influence at home. Even Nixon in the weeks before his resignation could receive big crowds and deferential treatment on a trip to the Middle East. Obama's challenge is somewhat more complex, with a sullen and uncertain war in Afghanistan creating his most pressing policy and political burdens in advance of 2012.

Still, he too will likely come to appreciate the largely unchecked influence to set policy enjoyed by modern presidents—even ones who were badgered by adversaries on the home front. Beyond Obama's defensive agenda of winding down two wars inherited from his predecessor, he has a robust list of accomplishments he hopes to seek abroad on nuclear nonproliferation, climate change, and Middle East peace. Even in an era of partisanship, Americans of all stripes like to see their presidents respected and successful on the global stage—a fact that gives Obama wide latitude to be effective without a single bill-signing ceremony.

Obama's rehabilitation will require him to revise his notions of the presidency and how to be effective in it. It does not require him to surrender his ambitions, only to recast them into a new brand of leadership. "He needs to make his new efforts about a much bigger purpose than the way they appear right now, about more than just legislative wheeling and dealing," said Don Baer, a top adviser to Clinton during his period of recovery (Baer 2010). "It's not just about finding the middle ground. It's about finding the higher ground."

REFERENCES

Baer, Don. 2010. Personal interview with James Hohmann. Washington, DC. December 14.

Gerstein, Josh. 2011. "Joe Biden Picks Bill Clinton Aide as Chief of Staff." *Politico*, January 14. http://www.politico.com/news/stories/0111/47639.html. Accessed January 14, 2011.

Halberstam, David. 2001. *The Best and the Brightest.* New York: Random House.

Harris, John. 2005. *The Survivor: Bill Clinton in the White House.* New York: Random House.

Harris, John, and Glenn Thrush. 2010. "The Ego Factor: Can Barack Obama Change?" *Politico*, November 5. http://www.politico.com/news/stories/1110/44732.html. Accessed December 20, 2010.

Hohmann, James, and Jim VandeHei. 2010. "Poll: Independents Siding with GOP." *Politico*, October 24. http://www.politico.com/news/stories/1010/44092.html. Accessed December 20, 2010.

Jones, Charles O. 2010. Personal interview with James Hohmann. Washington, DC. December 10.

Kroft, Steve. 2008. "Obama On Economic Crisis, Transition; Also Discusses National Security, Iraq, And His Cabinet In *60 Minutes* Interview." *CBS News*, November 16. http://www.cbsnews.com/stories/2008/11/16/60minutes/main4607893_page5 .shtml. Accessed December 20, 2010.

Lee, Carol. 2010. "Obama Exits, Clinton Keeps Talking." *Politico*, December 10. http://www.politico.com/news/stories/1210/46256.html. Accessed December 20, 2010.

Lizza, Ryan. 2008. "Battle Plans: How Obama Won." *The New Yorker*, November 17. http://www.newyorker.com/reporting/2008/11/17/081117fa_fact_lizza. Accessed December 20, 2010.

Mayhew, David. 2010. Personal interview with James Hohmann. Washington, DC. December 10.

Mendell, David. 2007. *Obama: From Promise to Power.* New York: HarperCollins.

Morris, Dick. 1998. *Behind the Oval Office: Getting Reelected Against All Odds.* Milwaukee, Wisconsin: Renaissance Books.

Obama, Barack. 2006. *The Audacity of Hope: Thoughts on Reclaiming the American Dream.* New York: Crown Publishing.

Podesta, John. 2010. Personal interview with John F. Harris. Washington, DC. December 17.

Remnick, David. 2010. *The Bridge: The Life and Rise of Barack Obama.* New York: Alfred A. Knopf.

Schoen, Douglas, and Patrick Caddell. 2010. "Our Divisive President, Redux." *Washington Post*, October 30. http://www.washingtonpost.com/wp-dyn/content/ article/2010/10/29/AR2010102905966.html. Accessed December 20, 2010.

Shomon, Dan. 2010. Personal interview with James Hohmann. Washington, DC. November 3.

Smith, Ben. 2008. "Transformation, like Reagan." *Politico*, January 16. http://www.politico.com/blogs/bensmith/0108/Transformation_like_Reagan.html. Accessed December 20, 2010.

Stephanopoulos, George. 1999. *All Too Human: A Political Education.* New York: Little, Brown and Company.

Thrush, Glenn. 2010. "Berry: Obama said 'Big Difference' between '10 and '94 is 'Me.'" *Politico*, January 25. http://www.politico.com/blogs/glennthrush/0110/Berry_Obama_said_big_difference_between_10_and_94_is_me.html. Accessed December 20, 2010.

Wartell, Sarah Rosen, ed. 2010. "The Power of the President: Recommendations to Advance Progressive Change." Center for American Progress, November. http://www.americanprogress.org/issues/2010/11/pdf/executive_orders.pdf. Accessed December 20, 2010.

Chapter Six

Asymmetric Warfare

*Supporters and Opponents
of President Obama*

John J. Pitney Jr.

Asymmetric warfare is conflict between belligerents whose forces are not mirror images. One side is usually bigger and stronger than the other, but asymmetry involves more than size and power. The two sides also think, act, and organize differently (Metz and Johnson 2001). Historical examples range from the Indian Wars of the nineteenth century to guerrilla conflicts of recent decades.

Military concepts can help us understand politics, which draws much of its language from the world of combat. In this case, the idea of asymmetric warfare supplies a lens for early political battles between supporters and opponents of President Obama. These battles involved a sharp partisan divide, though they also included forces that were nominally nonpartisan. The most obvious source of asymmetry was that the Democrats held the presidency. As party leader, commander in chief, and head of state, a president has unique power to shape political life. There is no real counterpart on the other side. Unlike a parliamentary government, our system of federalism, bicameralism, and separated powers does not provide for a single leader of the opposition. Certain out-party figures may sometimes assume a high profile—think of Newt Gingrich in 1995—but cannot speak for their party as a whole.

This enduring feature of American political life periodically strikes the press as if it were a late-breaking story. In 2009, commentators called the Republican Party "leaderless." The news media had been saying such things about out-parties for more than a century. In 1898, in the middle of the first McKinley term, the *New York Times* declared, "Facing the greatest questions and the greatest opportunities that have presented themselves in a generation, the Democratic Party is without unity, without a policy, and without a leader." One can find similar statements about Republicans under Lyndon

Johnson and Democrats under George W. Bush. As we shall see, "leaderless-ness" is not only a passing phase, it may actually be a political asset. In the early days of Obama, the differences between the two sides extended well beyond the typical in-party/out-party distinction. As these differences played out, the asymmetric conflict moved in unexpected directions.

FEARFUL ASYMMETRY

Right after the 2004 election, a number of authors argued that Republicans had amassed advantages that would entrench their power for years. Some warned that GOP dominance threatened democracy itself (Hacker and Pierson 2005). When Democrats took control of Congress in the 2006 midterm election, these concerns seemed overblown. And when Barack Obama won the presidency and congressional Democrats enlarged their majorities in 2008, alarms about permanent Republican power looked downright quaint. Democrats and their allies commanded the political battlefield as no party had since the 1964 Johnson landslide.

President Obama was only the second non-Southern Democrat in American history to win more than 51 percent of the popular vote. The first was Franklin Roosevelt. Like FDR, Democrats hoped, the new president would realign the electorate, and the early signs heartened them. In the spring of 2009, Gallup found that 52 percent of Americans identified as Democrats or said they leaned to the party, compared with 39 percent who were Republican identifiers or leaners. Those figures marked the Democrats' best showing since Gallup started regularly tracking leaners in 1991 (Jones 2009). The party was adding the top of the economic and social structure to its base of poor people, ethnic minorities, and blue-collar union members. According to exit polls, Obama won a modest majority of those earning more than $200,000 a year and a big margin among those with postgraduate degrees. He took 68 percent in the Silicon Valley congressional district (California 15), 78 percent in Manhattan's Silk Stocking district (New York 14), and 84 percent in the Cambridge-centered district encompassing Harvard (Massachusetts 8). House Democrats now represented 57 percent of the 4.8 million households with incomes of $200,000. In 2005, Republicans represented 55 percent of those households (Cauchon 2009).

With such support, Democrats were pulling ahead of Republicans on the financial and organizational levels. The 2008 Obama campaign had built an unprecedented war chest, and now unified Democratic control of the government would draw the "access money" that had recently gone to the GOP. During the first six months of 2005, Republican committees filing federal disclosure reports had raised 64 percent more money than the Democratic ones. During the same period in 2009, Democratic committees raised 5 percent more (Federal Election Commission 2009). More good things seemed to lay ahead for the Democrats. Obama for America, the president's effective political committee, moved into the Democratic National Committee as a project named Organizing for America.

Out-party national committees are fundamentally different from their in-party counterparts (Klinkner 1994). Whereas the latter run under the direction of the White House—and in its shadow—the former have more leeway in setting their party's organizational course. Accordingly, the identity of the out-party chair has greater significance. In 2009, the Republican National Committee (RNC) chose former Maryland lieutenant governor Michael Steele as its first African American leader. Many Republicans were keen on Steele at first, but he soon proved a disappointment. Starting with his comment that the GOP needed a "hip-hop makeover," he became a human gaffe factory, making odd remarks about gay marriage, abortion, Rush Limbaugh, and the war in Afghanistan, among others. His managerial incompetence became the stuff of political legend when FEC filings showed that the committee had spent $2,000 at a lesbian-bondage strip club. Major donors fled the RNC, raising doubts about its ability to compete in the 2010 midterm.

On Capitol Hill, Democrats started 2009 with 257 House seats, about as many as they had before the GOP takeover in 1994. House procedures strongly advantage the majority party, and Democrats were already pressing this advantage. A Brookings study concluded, "The number and percentage of restrictive rules used by Democratic leaders to control debate and amending activity on the House floor exceeded the degree of control and departure from regular order exercised by their Republican predecessors" (Binder et al. 2009). The same level of control would persist throughout the 111th Congress. Democrats said that their approach was necessary because Republicans would abuse a more open process to score political points. When they were in the majority, Republicans offered similar rationales for restrictive procedures.

Because the filibuster allows minorities to stall action, the majority party typically does not have as much power in the Senate as in the House. But the Democrats came out of the 2008 election with fifty-eight senators. After Pennsylvania's Arlen Specter switched parties and Minnesota's Al Franken took his seat after a lengthy recount battle, Democrats crossed the sixty-seat threshold necessary to invoke cloture. Such strength was extraordinary. Democrats had last passed the sixty-vote line in the 95th Congress (1977–1979), and Republicans had not done so in more than a hundred years.

Some argued that the majority party's advantages were less decisive than they seemed because Democrats are more fractious than Republicans. The data suggest otherwise (Rubin 2010). In 2009, congressional Democrats had greater average party unity scores (91 percent in both chambers) than Republicans (87 percent in the House, 85 percent in the Senate). The high Democratic unity stemmed both from the majority's power to set the agenda and the long-term trend toward ideological polarization. Even the moderate "Blue Dog" Democrats voted with their party on most issues and were not nearly as conservative as the "Boll Weevil" Democrats of the twentieth century, much less the Republicans of the twenty-first.

Democrats had the upper hand in the mainstream mass media, in part because reporters give more coverage to the party in power. The president is always the focus of the Washington press corps, and congressional majorities are more newsworthy than minorities. One rough measure of media emphasis is the LexisNexis file of American newspapers and wire services. In the first three months of 2009, Speaker Pelosi got 1,682 mentions in headlines and lead paragraphs, compared with just 436 for House GOP Leader John Boehner (R-OH). The pattern was similar in the Senate: 1,047 for Majority Leader Harry Reid (D-NV) to 372 for Minority Leader Mitch McConnell (R-KY).

Although the network evening-news broadcasts have dropped in the ratings, they still draw larger audiences than conservative-leaning *Fox News*. In 2009, the lowest-rated evening broadcast news program (on CBS) had 79 percent more viewers than the highest-rated Fox program, *The O'Reilly Factor* (Pew Project for Excellence in Journalism 2010). There is little hard evidence of deliberate partisan bias in the mainstream media. Nevertheless, contribution data suggest that the press was at least open to the Democratic message. In the 2008 cycle, 1,160 employees of the Big Three networks gave just over $1 million to Democratic candidates and committees. Only 193 gave to Republican candidates and committees, for a total of $142,863 (Tapscott 2010).

Especially after the demise of Air America, major talk-radio programs continued to tilt to the right. Rush Limbaugh reached up to 25 million Americans, many more than other syndicated hosts. That number was large but it meant that at least 80 percent of voters were *not* listeners. And at the start of the new administration, liberals and Democrats seemed to dominate the Internet. The 2008 Obama campaign had mastered social networking, and now the White House and its political allies were planning to use online technologies to sustain support. Also in their corner was the most popular political blog, *The Huffington Post*. Along with *Talking Points Memo* and others, *The Huffington Post* conducted solid, original reporting that advanced liberal causes. Conservatives and Republicans lagged badly: their websites emphasized commentary over journalism. "It's something we have to get in gear on," said GOP operative Patrick Ruffini. "What drives discussion in the blogosphere is original information . . . Liberal media has traditionally been upstream media, generating information and putting it into circulation. Conservative media is downstream; it's the second bite at the apple" (Martin 2008). The line between news and entertainment was blurrier than ever, and the border region was a deep shade of blue. *The Daily Show* and *The Colbert Report* had become a regular feature of political conversation, and conservatives were usually the butt of the joke. Figures in popular culture remained firmly on the progressive side. Just before the inauguration, Demi Moore and Ashton Kutcher assembled celebrities to hail the Obama administration with a series of pledges, culminating with Ms. Moore's promise "to be a servant to our president" (Dreher 2009).

Finally, liberals and Democrats maintained their predominance in the intellectual community. According to surveys and voter-registration data, Democrats greatly outnumbered Republicans on American faculties (Klein and Stern 2005). In 2008, academics gave eight times more money to Barack Obama than to John McCain (Hebel and Wiedeman 2008). In 2009, they would support Democrats with favorable opinion pieces in the news media, as well as with policy advice. For instance, the "public option" for health care was the brainchild of a Yale political scientist (Hacker 2010).

BARACK OBAMA MEETS JAMES MADISON

Despite all the benefits that this asymmetry brought the Democrats, it came at a price. Unified control of government means unified responsibility for results, which can be quite a burden. Conversely, what an out-party loses in policymaking power, it may gain in political opportunity. To understand these paradoxes, consider some basic features of the American party system.

A party stands in one of four strategic postures, depending on whether it is the president's party or the out-party, and on whether it is the majority or minority in Congress. (For the moment, set aside the complication of different parties running the House and Senate). During the 110th Congress (2007–2009), Democrats were the party of government because of their majority status and the party of opposition because of a GOP White House. Majorities can force the administration to compromise or curtail its legislative agenda, and they can use hearings and investigations to throw the president on the defensive. As usual for this strategic posture, the Democratic majority's relationship with the president became a mix of conflict and cooperation during the last two Bush years. Together they kept the government running, but fought on major issues of foreign and domestic policy.

The Republicans of the 110th Congress were in the mirror-image stance: both opposition and government by virtue of minority status and the Bush presidency. The congressional minority/president's party combination is the *worst* of the four postures: a Dilbert Purgatory of responsibility without power. Senators in this posture have some blocking power but much less ability to advance their own priorities. A House minority party has a harder time, mostly unable to pass anything, stop anything, or do anything except complain. The administration must conduct its legislative bargaining with the majority, often leaving its partisans on the outside. Although congressional minorities have little influence, they take a full share of the blame when the White House gets into political trouble, as happened in 2007 and 2008 with the Iraq War and economic turmoil.

The 2008 election shifted the parties into new postures. Democrats were now primarily the party of government, and the Republicans were mainly in opposition. Qualifiers are necessary because no congressional party is ever *purely* government or opposition. On certain issues, a president may lose support from copartisans on Capitol Hill and need votes from the other side, as President Clinton did with NAFTA and as President Obama would with Afghanistan (Connelly 2010). On other issues, the minority gives at least a bit of support to presidents of the other party. In 2008, the average presidential support score for Democrats was 16 percent in the House, 34 percent in the Senate. The figures for 2009 were higher, with presidential support among Republicans averaging 26 percent in the House and 50 percent in the Senate (Zeller 2010).

In the past, presidential support from the out-party tended to be greater. The decline in these figures, of course, stems from increased partisan polarization. During the early Obama years, it also reflected the majority's working style. Presidents and majority leaders of the mid-twentieth century cultivated members of the minority party in order to take the edge off their opposition and keep their votes in reserve. Speaker Pelosi, by contrast, gave little emphasis to GOP outreach. In 2007, when reporters asked her if she was getting any Republican help with efforts to halt the Iraq War, she said, "I'm the last person to ask about Republican votes" (Levey 2008). Just as the tough procedural tactics of Speakers Gingrich and Hastert had unified Democrats, the Democratic majority was pushing Republicans together by pushing them away. "They are making it easier for us," said Pete Sessions (R-TX), a member of the Rules Committee and chair of the National Republican Congressional Committee (Dennis 2009).

Democrats said that the president tried to work with congressional Republicans from the start but met only relentless opposition. Republicans said that the president's gestures were empty. "A day doesn't go by where we don't hear one thing and see another. The outstretched hand by the left with the clenched clock across the face by the right," said Paul Ryan (R-WI), ranking Republican on the Budget Committee. "He would say nice things about me publicly, but there was never actual outreach" (Bendery 2010). They also noted that Obama's first one-on-one meeting with McConnell did not take place until August 2010 and that he never had one with Boehner before the 2010 election. In 2009, his limited contact with GOP congressional leaders took place in larger meetings. In one such meeting shortly after the inauguration, House Republican Whip Eric Cantor handed out copies of an alternative to the president's stimulus plan. According to Cantor, the president dismissed the GOP ideas, saying, "Elections have consequences . . . and, Eric, I won" (Boyer 2010).

Some journalistic accounts have said that Boehner had "instructed" rank and file members to oppose the stimulus bill—as if he could dictate their votes. Such descriptions overlook a key difference between the two sides of the aisle. Leaders of the majority party can sway votes because they can move bills and grant various perquisites that lawmakers prize. When they belong to the president's party, they can add White House favors to their arsenal. Minority out-party leaders lack such firepower and instead must rely more on appeals to principle and party unity.

Although the president came to the Capitol and spoke directly to Republicans in both chambers, the House GOP voted unanimously against the stimulus. On the Senate side, three Republicans—Olympia Snowe and Susan Collins of Maine, and Arlen Specter of Pennsylvania—provided the crucial votes for cloture, enabling the stimulus to pass. Despite this bit of GOP support, the Democrats owned the stimulus legislation, and thus assumed responsibility for the economy. Already, hints of political trouble were emerging. In a February CBS poll, a slight majority of Americans approved of the package, but support for the bill had dropped twelve points in just a few weeks, and nearly half the respondents voiced doubt that it would shorten the recession (CBS 2009).

Specter's vote was unpopular among Republican voters in his state, and polls soon showed him falling behind his challenger in the GOP primary. When it became clear that he would lose the nomination, he switched parties in a bid to save his seat. (The ploy would fail when Democratic primary voters rejected him, too.) The Specter story was a cautionary tale for congressional Republicans. The majority party was accountable for results, but the minority party was accountable for opposition.

TEA AND ANTIPATHY

Why did Republicans oppose the president so uniformly? And why did the opposition grow so hot? Here we should consider political calculation, ideological principle, and the perennial clash between insiders and outsiders.

Democrats voiced skepticism about the minority party's commitment to fiscal discipline. Just a few years earlier, they noted, federal expenditures and deficits had swollen under a GOP president and Congress. As author Jonathan Alter (2010, 117) wrote, they saw only cynical calculation on the minority side: "If Obama succeeded in stabilizing the economy with the support of Republicans, he would get all the credit. If he failed with their support, they would share the blame. But if he failed without their support, they could say 'We told you so' to voters before the 2010 midterms."

Republicans agreed that their own fiscal record was flawed. From their perspective, however, that record did not mean that they should yield to even more spending and bigger government. Rather, they thought that they should atone for their past sins by taking a hard line. In a 2010 campaign book titled *Young Guns*, Kevin McCarthy (R-CA) joined Cantor and Ryan to spell out what had become an article of Republican faith, that the party had *deserved* to lose its congressional majorities.

- Cantor: "[O]ur party has at times lost sight of the things we believe in, ideas like economic freedom, limited government, the sanctity of life, and putting families first . . . Republicans controlled Washington from 2001 to 2006. They did some good things but they also did a lot to give conservatism a bad name" (pp. 20–21).
- Ryan: "I admit that in recent years Republicans abandoned these principles. We lost the truth path and suffered electoral defeats" (p. 129).
- McCarthy: "Voters were deeply unhappy with Republicans. They weren't focused on the issues [they] assumed the [2006] election would be about. They were talking about the party's failures—our failures—from high-profile ethical lapses to the inability to rein in spending or even slow the growth of government" (p. 148).

In 2008, the trio had joined Boehner and eighty-seven other Republicans in voting for the Bush administration's Troubled Asset Relief Program (TARP), or "the bank bailout." That vote was perhaps their low point, with Boehner famously calling the bill "a crap sandwich." Now that they were in opposition, they were bent on putting the deviations and crap sandwiches behind them. They started to recover their esprit de corps with the stimulus vote. "That's where we got our mojo back," McCarthy told the *New Yorker*. "That's where we finally realized we did have ideas. We'd stand up to the President. And we stood up to him when he was at his strongest" (Boyer 2010).

They knew that it would take a long time to restore the tainted Republican image, but they could already start to attack Democratic issue positions. According to journalist Chad Pergram (2010), "It was this simple: who's the new sheriff in town? Barack Obama. Who's his partner in crime? Liberal Speaker of the House from San Francisco. The TARP 'bailout' was already on the books. But most voters don't pay close enough attention to track whose watch that came on."

The Democrats supplied their opponents with fresh ammunition. As was inevitable for such a huge measure, the stimulus spawned stories of inefficiency, and even the president eventually acknowledged that there were no "shovel-ready projects." Although the stimulus may have helped prevent a deeper slump, it failed to cut unemployment. The health-care bill was another major source of attack material. Its supporters asserted that it would be modest in comparison with health-insurance systems in Canada and other developed countries. Republicans thought that it conflicted with conservative principles of limited government, economic liberty, and federalism. Moreover, they saw it as the opening gambit for a much more extensive system in the future. They quoted the president's own words from his Senate race—"I happen to be a proponent of a single-payer universal health care program"—and his more recent comments that he would favor single-payer health care if he were designing the system from scratch (PolitiFact.com 2009).

Although the majority party got more coverage in the mainstream media, the alternative media of cable, talk radio, and the Internet enabled Republicans and conservatives to develop their critique and bring it to the attentive public. Liberals charged the Republican/conservative world with spreading misinformation, citing Sarah Palin's Facebook allegation about "death panels," as well as just about any allegation by Fox commentator Glenn Beck. Nevertheless, many of the conservative criticisms stuck, rousing the grassroots and in turn further hardening the resolve of Republican politicians. Representative Mark Kirk (R-IL), a moderate who would win a Senate seat in 2010, said, "I think the average Democrat who looks at the TV is happy and sitting on their sofa. The average Republican is getting angry and energized" (Dennis 2009).

The reaction gathered public momentum. Gallup noted a shift in the conservative-liberal balance from 37 percent and 22 percent in 2008 to 40 percent and 21 percent in 2009 (Saad 2010a). Andrew Kohut, president of the Pew Research Center, wrote in December 2009 of "a downward slope in support both for an activist government generally and for a strong safety net for the needy, in particular. Chalk up these trends to a backlash against Obama policies that have expanded the role of government" (Kohut 2009).

What riled a number of voters was not just the content of the policy but the character of the governing coalition. Since the Founding Era, a recurrent theme in United States politics has been resentment of "insiderism." From Anti-Federalist attacks against "monocrats," to Andrew Jackson's war against the Second Bank of the United States, to William Jennings Bryan's "Cross of Gold," to H. Ross Perot's jeremiads about "economic treason," Americans have heard warnings about unholy alliances of money and political power. Unfortunately for Democrats, the political base that had provided so many advantages also made them vulnerable to the stigma of insiderism. The new administration had close ties to economic elites. In the 2008 campaign, Obama received far more in contributions from the securities/ investment and hedge-fund/private-equity industries than any other candidate. Though he suggested that he would keep lobbyists out of the executive branch, he made no such promise about other corporate connections. Tom Daschle, the president's nominee for secretary of health and human services, had served as a business consultant since leaving the Senate. He had to withdraw when news emerged that he had failed to pay taxes on some of his consulting fees and a free limousine service that he had received. During the health-care debate, the president got support from insurers, hospital and physician groups, and pharmaceutical companies. Democrats saw the move as a shrewd maneuver to bring stakeholders on board and thus head off the business opposition that had doomed the Clinton health-care plan in 1994. Conservatives and Republicans saw the bonding of big business to big government to the detriment of free enterprise.

The president had the strong support of labor, especially public-employee unions. It may sound odd to depict organized labor as part of an elite, since the traditional image of the union member is a blue-collar factory worker. That image is obsolete: by the 1990s, blue collars were in the minority in union ranks, and in 2009, government employees outnumbered private-sector employees among union members (DiSalvo 2010). At a time of economic distress, federal employees' average compensation had grown to more than double what private-sector workers earned (Cauchon 2010). Union representatives said that the compensation gap reflected federal workers' skill and education—which, of course, made them an elite. A Pew survey (2010) found that 61 percent agreed that "labor unions have too much power," up from 52 percent in 1999.

The president and most of his circle belonged to a meritocracy with sterling academic credentials. Particularly since his campaign remarks about "bitter" Pennsylvanians clinging to guns and religion, he had suffered difficulty in connecting with blue-collar voters (Brownstein 2009). As John Harris and James Hohmann suggest in their chapter in this volume, the president's ego sometimes kept him from noticing his own mistakes in this regard. During a time of economic distress stemming from the Gulf oil spill, Democratic strategist Susan Estrich (2010) wrote that the president erred by vacationing in Martha's Vineyard. "[H]aving already spent time in Maine this summer, a second vacation to a place other than the hard-hit Gulf is an invitation for people to think what too many of them already think: The president just doesn't get it." Even when he was focusing on the blowout, he stumbled over the elitism issue. Eugene Robinson, a liberal *Washington Post* columnist, wrote with exasperation that the president kept citing Energy Secretary Steven Chu's Nobel Prize: "His Nobel was awarded for the work he did in trapping individual atoms with lasers . . . Chu surely knows less about blowout preventers than the average oil-rig worker and less about delicate coastal marshes than the average shrimp-boat captain" (Robinson 2010).

A number of Americans came to see the governing coalition as an elite clique intent on grabbing power and redistributing income at their expense. The president's supporters thought that this characterization was unfair, noting that the stimulus had cut taxes for most households. Opponents pointed to the rapidly mounting federal debt, which loomed over future generations, and to the health bill, which would affect medical care for everyone in the country. They drew analogies to the 1773 Tea Act, which did not raise taxes and actually aimed to reduce the price of tea (so the East India Company could unload its inventory). Americans objected to it because it aimed to benefit economic insiders and reaffirmed the power of a distant, unrepresentative government. The result was the Boston Tea Party.

THE STARFISH, THE SPIDER, AND SAUL ALINSKY

On February 19, 2009, CNBC editor Rick Santelli stood at the CME Group in Chicago and issued an on-air denunciation of President Obama's plan to help homeowners avoid foreclosure. Saying that the proposal would encourage "bad behavior," he made a broad attack on excessive government spending and called for a "Chicago Tea Party." A YouTube clip of his fiery remarks went viral. The next day, a network of conservative activists held a conference call to plan protests. Within a week, enthusiastic amateurs picked up the idea and staged rallies in dozens of cities. A second round of demonstrations on April 15—tax day—turned out half a million people at hundreds of events (Rauch 2010). The "Tea Party" movement had begun.

Survey data showed that most Tea Party supporters thought that the president did not share most Americans' values and that he did not understand the problems of people like themselves. When pollsters asked what angered them, Tea Party supporters most often mentioned the health bill, government spending, and a belief that their opinions went unrepresented in Washington (Zernike and Thee-Brenan 2010).

Two books are essential for understanding the movement. The first is *The Starfish and the Spider*, a business book by Ori Brafman and Rod A.

Beckstrom, which helps explain the movement's structure. The other is Saul Alinsky's *Rules for Radicals*, the activist manifesto that inspired Barack Obama's community-organizing mentors in Chicago. Much to the frustration of political progressives, their ideological opposites were now turning their own tactics against them, using Alinsky's teachings as their guide.

Brafman and Beckstrom (2006, 34–35) drew their book's title from a biological insight. If you chop off a spider's head, it dies. "But starfish are very different. The starfish doesn't have a head. Its central body isn't in charge. In fact, its major organs are replicated throughout each and every arm. If you cut the starfish in half, you'll be in for a surprise: the animal won't die, and pretty soon you'll have two starfish to start with."

By analogy, traditional, hierarchical organizations are like spiders: powerful but vulnerable to the loss of leadership. Decentralized organizations, or networks, are like starfish: they diffuse power and knowledge, and the loss of an individual unit is seldom fatal. The Tea Party movement was a starfish. It consisted of many informal groups whose active membership could wax or wane with circumstances. Although some news organizations spoke of the Tea Party as a unified organization, the movement had no chain of command. True, it received logistical support from organizations such as FreedomWorks, the Tea Party Express, and the Tea Party Patriots. But these groups were only part of the picture and often fought with one another. Tea Party activists took pride in their independence, frequently citing the Brafman-Beckstrom book to argue that their movement would grow and endure (Vogel 2010).

Because "membership" in such a starfish movement is amorphous, different surveys painted different pictures of Tea Party demographics (Newport 2010). One consistent finding was that people in the movement tended to be Republican identifiers or Republican-leaning Independents. They were not, however, acting at the behest of the GOP hierarchy: inept RNC chairman Michael Steele could not have pulled off such a feat of manipulation even if he had tried. Tea Party activists came into conflict with the party establishment, and in several Senate nomination contests, backed conservatives who won upset victories over more "mainstream" candidates. As Nicol C. Rae writes in this volume, the movement's independence from the party structure lent credibility to its arguments and helped build public support.

It is understandable that conservative activists would embrace a business book, but why would they also take up the writings of a leftist agitator? The answer is that Alinsky's work was less about pushing an ideological agenda than about teaching underdogs how to defeat the powerful. In other words, it was a field manual for asymmetric political warfare. Just as progressives of Alinsky's time saw themselves as a political resistance, so did Tea Party activists in the age of Obama. "As an organization, we have been very closely studying what the left has been doing," said FreedomWorks press secretary Adam Brandon, who received a copy of *Rules for Radicals* when he started work (Coller and Libit 2009).

"Whenever possible, go outside the experience of an opponent," said Alinsky (1989, 127). "Here you want to cause confusion, fear, and retreat." Rallies in the spring of 2009 got some press attention, but the real breakthrough came when House members and senators held town hall meetings. Until this point, they had seen these sessions as an advantage of incumbency. The lawmakers could show off their knowledge of Washington politics and local concerns while appearing to hear constituent views. Now, however, the Tea Party activists were asking tough questions about the stimulus and the health-care bill, and sometimes they turned raucous. Many Democratic lawmakers became nervous about the events, and not all of them responded skillfully. Republican-turned-Democrat Arlen Specter enraged an audience when he answered a hostile question about the health-care bill by saying, "we have to do this fast."

Specter's response highlights another Alinsky adage: "*The enemy properly goaded and guided in his reaction will be your major strength*" (Alinsky 1989, 136; emphasis in original). Tea Party activists liked to bait their targets in hopes of creating a YouTube moment. For instance, Rep. Phil Hare (D-IL) made himself a cyber-laughingstock when he botched a question about the constitutionality of a health-insurance mandate (Cannon 2010):

Rep. Hare I don't worry about the Constitution on this, to be honest.

Off-camera: [Laughter.] Jackpot, brother . . .

Rep. Hare: I believe that it says we have the right to life, liberty, and the pursuit of happiness. Now you tell me . . .

Off-camera: That's the Declaration of Independence.

Rep. Hare: It doesn't matter to me. Either one . . .

The "jackpot, brother" comment indicates that the Tea Party questioner got the kind of answer he was hoping for. Although this exchange was hardly the sole cause, Hare was defeated in 2010.

Alinsky (1989, 130) was blunt about the value of enemies: "Pick the target, freeze it, personalize it, and polarize it." Tea Party protesters, conservatives, and Republicans had a target-rich environment in 2009 and 2010. Activists and commentators hurled a variety of allegations against President Obama, ranging from the provocative (that he was a radical) to the ridiculous (that he was born in Kenya or secretly practiced Islam). Most mainstream politicians avoided the more flamboyant charges, but they did turn the president into a symbol of intrusive government. As Brafman and Beckstrom might put it, they were going after the spider's head.

Other administration figures drew fire, too. Treasury Secretary Timothy Geithner got off to a bad start when his confirmation process revealed that he failed to pay Social Security and Medicare taxes for several years. Republicans flayed him as a self-styled big shot who did not think that the rules applied to him. Months later, a pair of pollsters observed a protest march near the Treasury Building: "[A] woman turned to her young daughter and said: 'Look honey, that's where Tim Geithner lives . . . he doesn't pay his taxes!'" (Rasmussen and Schoen 2010, 127).

House Speaker Nancy Pelosi was a particular object of scorn. Her liberalism, her elite background (as the daughter and sister of Baltimore mayors and the spouse of a millionaire), and her dismissive attitude toward the GOP all combined to put her in the bull's-eye of attack ads. Republicans had complained that lawmakers passed bills that they had neither read nor understood, and Pelosi seemed to confirm their point when she said of the health legislation: "But we have to pass the bill so that you can find out what is in it, away from the fog of the controversy." By the fall of 2010, 56 percent of Americans had an unfavorable opinion of her—only slightly less than Newt Gingrich at his worst point (Saad, 2010b).

In asymmetric warfare, the less powerful side does not have to win all the battles, or even most of them. But it needs some victories to maintain its morale and unnerve its opposition. A triumph at Trenton kept the American Revolution alive and one at Yorktown persuaded the British to quit. On the night of the 2009 off-year election, these examples were much on the minds of the president's opponents when Republicans won the governorships of New Jersey and Virginia, two states that had gone for Obama just a year before. The Tea Party movement did not cause these victories, but it drew encouragement from them anyway. Early in 2010, Republican Scott Brown won a stunning upset victory in a special election to fill Edward Kennedy's Senate seat from Massachusetts. Tea Party activists played a visible role in the Brown campaign, which used his pickup truck as a symbol of his outsider status. Symbolism worked against the Democrats, who railed against the Tea Party (a foolish attack in the home state of the *original* Tea Party) and whose candidate blundered by openly sneering at the idea of shaking hands at Fenway Park.

Although Brown was a moderate who had backed his own state's healthcare reform law, he opposed the Obama plan. His election deprived Senate Democrats of their filibuster-proof majority. Bertram Johnson's chapter in this volume tells how this development forced the Democrats into intricate maneuvers to salvage the bill. They succeeded in passing the measure, but in doing so, they reinforced the idea that insider politics was thwarting the public will.

THE EMPIRE STRIKES BACK . . . INEFFECTUALLY

As often happens in asymmetric warfare, the initially dominant side went wobbly. An "enthusiasm gap" opened, with one March 2010 poll showing 67 percent of Republicans saying they were very interested in the midterm elections, compared with 46 percent of Democrats (Wallsten and Spencer 2010). At *Time*, Jay Newton-Small (2010) wrote that Organizing for America was a "ghost of its former self," with staffers, volunteers, and contributions at a small fraction of what they had been in 2008. "Virtually no one in politics believes it will turn many contests this fall. 'There's no chance that OFA is going to have the slightest impact on the midterms,' says Charlie Cook, who tracks congressional races."

Obama supporters had invested high hopes in their candidate during the 2008 campaign, and the reality of governance could not possibly match their aspirations. Some thought that the new president would transcend the politics of deal making—an expectation that he had encouraged during the campaign. After the media reported about backroom deals to move the health-care bill, White House aide David Axelrod just shrugged, "I think every senator uses whatever leverage they have to help their states. That's the way it has been. That's the way it will always be" (Amick 2009).

And then there was the economy. During a CNBC town hall in September 2010, Obama supporter Velma Hart told the president, "I'm exhausted of defending you, defending your administration, defending the mantle of change that I voted for and deeply disappointed with where we are right now. I have been told that I voted for a man who said he was going to change things in a meaningful way for the middle class. I'm one of those people, and I'm waiting, sir. I'm waiting. I don't feel it yet" (Stolberg 2010). Weeks later, she lost her job.

Faced with exhausted supporters, energized opponents, and a sputtering economy, Democrats turned to the Alinsky tactic of focusing on an enemy. With Bush and Cheney gone, they had difficulty finding foes who could not only fire up the base but scare Independent voters over to their side. There was some effort to discredit the Tea Party movement itself. Liberals and Democrats referred to the activists as "teabaggers." The term alluded to slang for an oral sex act, hence CNN anchor Anderson Cooper's smirking comment, "It's hard to talk when you're teabagging." Apart from the epithet's vulgarity, the attack on the Tea Party movement was doomed. After all, it was a starfish, not a spider. Alinsky (1989, 133) taught that the target "must be a personification, not something general and abstract such as a community's segregated practices or a major corporation or City Hall." And in the context of the 2010 election, it would backfire because Democrats needed to hold seats in moderate and conservative districts where the movement was popular.

Early in 2009, White House officials and their allies denounced Rush Limbaugh, dubbing him the leader of the Republican Party. The attacks only increased Limbaugh's listenership. "The administration is enabling me," Limbaugh boasted to *POLITICO* (Martin 2009). The gambit faded for lack of plausibility. A talk-show host who had never held office and often feuded with Republicans was not believable as the GOP's leader.

Chief Justice John Roberts was another possibility. Though not a party leader, he did have real power. And sure enough, during his 2010 State of the Union address, with Roberts sitting in front of him, the president took the unusual step of attacking the *Citizens United* decision on campaign finance. He kept it up, criticizing "the Roberts court" in press interviews. That tactic failed, too. With Roberts keeping a deliberately low public profile, only 28 percent of survey respondents could even identify him as a chief justice (Greenhouse 2010).

For a brief time, the president aimed at House GOP Leader John Boehner. The assault had little impact: polls showed that most Americans did not know Boehner or were neutral. In this case, asymmetry worked to the minority's advantage, since powerless politicians do not make good demons. The attack did leave the House Republicans even more wary. Paul Ryan, in whose district the president spoke, said, "The straw men arguments are intellectually hollow and disingenuous, and they send a clear signal that the president is more interested in combat than compromise" (Bendery 2010).

Toward the end of the midterm campaign, the president vented his frustration. In a Univision radio interview, he said the Democrats' task would be hard "if Latinos sit out the election instead of saying, we're gonna punish our enemies and we're gonna reward our friends who stand with us on issues that are important to us." The line about punishing enemies enabled Republicans to counterattack. "Sadly, we have a president who uses the word 'enemy' for fellow Americans, fellow citizens," said Boehner. "He used it for people who disagree with his agenda of bigger government" (Pace 2010). Obama then acknowledged that he should have said "opponents" instead of "enemies."

And so the old community organizer had to watch while his opponents were using Alinsky tactics against him, and he stumbled when he tried to use those tactics himself. Such things happen when insurgents become the establishment.

THE MIDTERM AND THE FUTURE

Citizens United, the Supreme Court decision that President Obama attacked in his State of the Union, held that the government could not bar corporations from financing independent political broadcasts in elections for office. (It did not affect existing limits on contributions to candidates and parties.) In the 2010 midterm, the first election after the decision, independent expenditures and electioneering communications by non-party groups more than doubled from 2008 levels, with most of the spending on the pro-Republican side (Glavin 2010). It is not clear that *Citizens United* was responsible for all of this increase, or that the outside money tipped the balance, but it probably helped Republicans offset a big Democratic advantage in party money.

Republicans had other things going for them as well. In a poll of Democratic consultants and operatives who worked on the 2010 campaign, 64 percent said the Tea Party "energized the Republican base and was one reason for Republican gains" (Martin 2010). Because of the Tea Party protests, many Democrats replaced in-person town hall meetings with mass teleconferences, which they could more easily control, but that included fewer participants. Republican challengers devised countermeasures by holding town halls of their own—with Tea Party supporters in attendance. "I just decided that if she's not going to throw the town hall meetings, then we'll do it," said Adam Kinzinger, Republican challenger to freshman Illinois Democrat Deborah Halvorson. "By the time this is said and done, my campaign will have provided close to 1,500 people the opportunity to speak out on health care" (Falcone 2009). He would go on to win.

As Election Day got closer, Republicans gained ground. At the start of the election cycle, Democrats had hoped that the economy would blunt their midterm losses. But as Raymond Tatalovich explains in this volume, the economic cavalry did not arrive. Contrary to Speaker Pelosi's confidence that the health-care bill would become more popular after it passed, it lost popularity as voters learned more about it. As the issue environment turned against them, Democrats deployed a massive amount of opposition research to depict their foes as corrupt or crazy, just as the Republicans had done four years before. The "crazy card" did work in a few Senate races where GOP candidates supplied Democrats with ammunition (Weigel 2010). But opposition research cannot reverse a national wave. "If you were in a red district, nothing worked," a veteran Democratic strategist told the *Rothenberg Political Report* (Gonzales 2010).

The election turned into a referendum on the party in power, which lost. In an exit poll, 37 percent of respondents said that their vote represented opposition to the president, and Republican House candidates got 92 percent of their vote. Democrats got 96 percent of those who were expressing support for Obama, but they made up only 23 percent of the electorate. Similarly, 41 percent of respondents called themselves supporters of the Tea Party movement, and Republicans got 86 percent of the vote. Democrats got 86 percent among Tea Party opponents, who were just 30 percent of the total. The midterm gave the GOP control of the House, with a net gain of sixty-three seats. In the Senate, they gained six—short of a majority, but enough to cause trouble for the Democrats.

And so the strategic postures shifted again. The Republicans came in from outside and would now have to share some responsibility for governing. "The price of a successful attack is a constructive alternative," wrote Alinsky (1989, 130). With a majority in the House, Republicans would have to place less emphasis on criticizing the Democrats and more emphasis on advancing their own proposals. Paul Ryan, who would now chair the House Budget Committee, did write a bold and comprehensive "roadmap" for reducing the deficit. House GOP leaders sidestepped his politically risky ideas about entitlement reform, instead issuing *A Pledge to America* with some specific proposals such as cancelling unspent stimulus funds. Making headway against mammoth deficits would require much bigger steps, creating danger for the House majority and potential opportunity for the minority.

Democrats retained control of the Senate, however, and that majority would face the same harsh budget decisions. Split-party control of Congress created a challenge for President Obama, who would have a hard time running for reelection by running against Congress. He would have to defend the record of the Senate majority while attacking the record of the House majority. While intellectually coherent, such a stance would be politically awkward. Moreover a campaign focus on Capitol Hill would draw attention to Democrats' congressional leaders, who remained unpopular.

What of the Tea Party movement? Its participants had to remember that what worked in the first two years of the Obama administration might not work in the next two. "Once a specific tactic is used, it ceases to be outside the experience of the enemy," said Alinsky (1989, 163). "Before long he devises countermeasures that void the previous effective tactic." And there was also the risk that success would spoil the movement. In the US House of Representatives and a number of statehouses, the outsiders had become insiders. "If the tea party starts bringing money and power into the equation, that makes some people more equal than others, and they will start losing the advantages of being adaptable and starfish-like," Ori Brafman told *Politico*. "That's the biggest challenge the tea party movement is facing" (Vogel 2010).

In the meantime, the movement could take heart from victories in the 2010 lame-duck congressional session. On December 16, the House gave final approval to a bill extending the Bush tax cuts, and on the same day, Senate Majority Leader Reid withdrew a pork-laden omnibus-spending bill. The date was the 237th anniversary of the Boston Tea Party.

REFERENCES

Alinsky, Saul. 1989. *Rules for Radicals*. New York: Vintage.

Alter, Jonathan. 2010. *The Promise: President Obama, Year One*. New York: Simon and Schuster.

Amick, John. 2009. "Axelrod Defends Merits of Senate Bill." *Washington Post*, December 20. http://voices.washingtonpost.com/44/2009/12/axelrod-defends-merits-of-sena.html. Accessed December 13, 2010.

Bendery, Jennifer. 2010. "GOP Calls Obama Approach Two-Faced." *Roll Call*, July 1. http://www.rollcall.com/issues/56_1/-48011-1.html. Accessed December 14, 2010.

Binder, Sarah, Thomas E. Mann, Norman J. Ornstein, and Molly Reynolds. 2009. "Mending the Broken Branch: Assessing the 110th Congress, Anticipating the 111th." Brookings Institution, January. http://www.brookings.edu/~/media/Files/rc/papers/2009/0108_broken_branch_binder_mann/0108_broken_branch_binder_mann.pdf. Accessed December 10, 2010.

Boyer, Peter J. 2010. "House Rule: Will John Boehner Control the Tea Party Congress?" *New Yorker*, December 13. http://www.newyorker.com/reporting/2010/12/13/101213fa_fact_boyer. Accessed December 12, 2010.

Brafman, Ori, and Rod A. Beckstrom. 2006. *The Starfish and the Spider*. New York: Portfolio.

Brownstein, Ronald. 2009. "Holding the Line with White Voters." *National Journal*, December 12. http://www.nationaljournal.com/njmagazine/nj_20091212_4622.php. Accessed December 13, 2010.

Cannon, Michael F. 2010. "Constitution, Schmonstitution—The Law Is What I Say It Is," Cato@Liberty, April 2. http://www.cato-at-liberty.org/constitution-schmonstitution-%E2%80%94-the-law-is-what-i-say-it-is. Accessed December 14, 2010.

Cauchon, Dennis. 2009. "In Major Flip, House Dems Now Represent Richest Regions." *USA Today*, October 14. http://www.usatoday.com/news/washington/2009-10-13-House-wealth-gap-Democrats-richest-districts_N.htm. Accessed December 13, 2010.

———. 2010. "Federal Workers Earning Double Their Private Counterparts." *USA Today*, August 13. http://www.usatoday.com/money/economy/income/2010-08-10-1Afedpay10_ST_N.htm. Accessed December 15, 2010.

CBS. 2009. "CBS Poll: Support for Stimulus Falls." February 9. http://www.cbsnews.com/stories/2009/02/05/opinion/polls/main4778192.shtml. Accessed December 13, 2010.

Coller, Andie, and Daniel Libit. 2009. "Conservatives Use Liberal Playbook." *Politico*, September 18. http://www.politico.com/news/stories/0909/27285.html. Accessed December 14, 2010.

Connelly, William F., Jr. 2010. *James Madison Rules America: The Constitutional Origins of Congressional Partisanship*. Lanham, Maryland: Rowman and Littlefield.

Dennis, Steven T. 2009. "GOP Unity Is Forcing Heavy Lifts for Democrats." *Roll Call*, June 16. http://www.rollcall.com/news/35922-1.html. Accessed December 10, 2010.

DiSalvo, Daniel. 2010. "The Trouble with Public Sector Unions." *National Affairs* 5 (Fall). http://www.nationalaffairs.com/publications/detail/the-trouble-with-public -sector-unions. Accessed December 15, 2010.

Dreher, Rod. 2009. "Hollywood's Creepy 'I Pledge' Video." *RealClearPolitics*, February 2. http://www.realclearpolitics.com/articles/2009/02/hollywoods_creepy_i _pledge_vid.html. Accessed May 23, 2011.

Estrich, Susan. 2010. "Does He Get It?" *RealClearPolitics*, August 5. http://www .realclearpolitics.com/articles/2010/08/05/does_he_get_it_106610.html. Accessed December 14, 2010.

Falcone, Michael. 2009. "New GOP Tactic: The Counter-Town Hall." *Politico*, August 30. http://www.politico.com/news/stories/0809/26491.html. Accessed December 13, 2010.

Federal Election Commission. 2009. "FEC Summarizes Political Party Activity for January 1–June 30, 2009," August 19. http://www.fec.gov/press/ press2009/20090819_6monthParty.shtml. Accessed December 10, 2010.

Glavin, Brendan. 2010. "Non-Party Spending Doubled in 2010 But Did Not Dictate the Results." Campaign Finance Institute, November 5.

Gonzales, Nathan. 2010. "Democratic Attacks Fell on Deaf Ears This Fall." *Rothenberg Political Report*, December 1. http://rothenbergpoliticalreport.com/news/ article/democratic-attacks-fell-on-deaf-ears-this-fall. Accessed December 13, 2010.

Greenhouse, Linda. 2010. "An Invisible Chief Justice. *New York Times*, September 9. http://opinionator.blogs.nytimes.com/2010/09/09/an-invisible-chief-justice. Accessed December 15, 2010.

Hacker, Jacob S. 2010. "The Road to Somewhere: Why Health Care Reform Happened." *Perspectives on Politics* 8 (September): 861–76.

Hacker, Jacob S., and Paul Pierson. 2005. *Off Center: The Republican Revolution and the Erosion of American Democracy*. New Haven, CT: Yale University Press.

Hebel, Sara, and Reeves Wiedeman. 2008. *Chronicle of Higher Education*, October 24. http://chronicle.com/article/Donors-From-Academe-Favor/32220. Accessed December 10, 2010.

Jones, Jeffrey M. 2009. "Democrats Maintain Seven-Point Advantage in Party ID." Gallup Poll, April 30. http://www.gallup.com/poll/118084/Democrats-Maintain -Seven-Point-Advantage-Party.aspx. Accessed December 15, 2010.

Klein, Daniel B., and Charlotte Stern. 2005. "Political Diversity in Six Disciplines." *Academic Questions* 18 (Winter): 40–52.

Klinkner, Philip A. 1994. *The Losing Parties: Out-Party National Committees, 1956–1993*. New Haven, CT: Yale University Press.

Kohut, Andrew. 2009. "Obama's 2010 Challenge: Wake Up Liberals, Calm Down Independents." Pew Research Center, December 17. http://pewresearch.org/pubs/

1444/obamas-challenge-december-approval-conservative-shift. Accessed December 11, 2010.

Levey, Noam. 2008. "Why Congress Didn't Get Troops Out." *Los Angeles Times*, January 27. http://articles.latimes.com/2008/jan/27/nation/na-wardebate27. Accessed December 10, 2010.

Martin, Jonathan. 2008. "GOP Losing the New Media War." *Politico*, July 24. http://www.politico.com/news/stories/0708/12008.html. Accessed May 23, 2011.

———. 2009. "Rush Job: Inside Dems' Limbaugh Plan." *Politico*, March 4. http://www.politico.com/news/stories/0309/19596.html. Accessed December 15, 2010.

———. 2010. "Democratic Operatives Credit Tea Party." *Politico*, November 17. http://www.politico.com/news/stories/1110/45274.html. Accessed December 13, 2010.

Metz, Steven, and Douglas V. Johnson, II. 2001. "Asymmetry and U.S. Military Strategy: Definition, Background, and Strategic Concepts." US Army War College Strategic Studies Institute, January. http://www.au.af.mil/au/awc/awcgate/ssi/asymetry.pdf. Accessed December 13, 2010.

New York Times. 1898. "The Leaderless Parties." December 12, p. 6.

Newport, Frank. 2010. "Polling Matters: More on the Tea Party Movement." Gallup Poll, April 7. http://pollingmatters.gallup.com/2010/04/more-on-tea-party-movement.html. Accessed December 14, 2010.

Newton-Small, Jay. 2010. "What Ever Happened to Obama's Army?" *Time*, September 9. http://www.time.com/time/politics/article/0,8599,2016973,00.html. Accessed December 15, 2010.

Pace, Julie. 2010. "Obama Pulls Back on 'Enemies' Remark to Latinos." *Associated Press*, November 1. http://news.yahoo.com/s/ap/20101101/ap_on_el_ge/us_obama_enemies. Accessed December 15, 2010.

Pergram, Chad. 2010. "The Echoes of TARP." http://politics.blogs.foxnews.com/2010/12/12/echoes-tarp-vote-tax-cuts-could-reverberate-through-next-election. Accessed December 12, 2010.

Pew Project for Excellence in Journalism. 2010. "The State of the News Media: An Annual Report on American Journalism." http://www.stateofthemedia.org/2010/index.php. Accessed December 10, 2010.

Pew Research Center for the People and the Press. 2010. "Favorability Ratings of Labor Unions Fall Sharply." February 23. http://people-press.org/report/591. Accessed December 13, 2010.

PolitiFact.com. 2009. "Obama Has Praised Single-Payer Plans in the Past." August 12. http://politifact.com/truth-o-meter/statements/2009/aug/12/barack-obama/obama-has-praised-single-payer-plans-past. Accessed December 15, 2010.

Rasmussen, Scott, and Douglas Schoen. 2010. *Mad as Hell*. New York: Harper.

Rauch, Jonathan. 2010. "Inside the Tea Party's Collective Brain." *National Journal*, September 11. http://www.jonathanrauch.com/jrauch_articles/2010/09/group-think-inside-the-tea-partys-collective-brain.html. Accessed December 13, 2010.

Robinson, Eugene. 2010. "Obama Disappoints from the Beginning of His Speech." *Washington Post*, June 16. http://voices.washingtonpost.com/postpartisan/2010/06/obama_disappoints_from_the_beg.html. Accessed December 14, 2010.

Rubin, Richard. 2010. "An Ever Thicker Dividing Line." *Congressional Quarterly Weekly Report*, January 11, 122.

Ryan, Paul, Eric Cantor, and Kevin McCarthy. 2010. *Young Guns*. New York: Threshold.

Saad, Lydia. 2010a. "Conservatives Finish 2009 as No. 1 Ideological Group." Gallup Poll, January 7. http://www.gallup.com/poll/124958/Conservatives-Finish -2009-No-1-Ideological-Group.aspx. Accessed December 15, 2010.

———. 2010b. "Pelosi's Favorable Rating as Speaker Drops to 29%, a New Low." Gallup Poll, October 20. http://www.gallup.com/poll/143885/pelosi-favorable -rating-speaker-drops-new-low.aspx. Accessed December 15, 2010.

Stolberg, Sheryl Gay. 2010. "Disappointed Supporters Question Obama." *New York Times*, September 20. http://www.nytimes.com/2010/09/21/us/politics/21obama .html. Accessed May 23, 2011.

Tapscott, Mark. 2010. "Television Networks' Employees Reward Democratic Candidates." *San Francisco Examiner*, August 30. http://www.sfexaminer.com/ node/221941. Accessed December 10, 2010.

Vogel, Kenneth P. 2010."The New Tea Party Bible." *Politico*, August 2. http://www .politico.com/news/stories/0710/40492.html. Accessed December 13, 2010.

Wallsten, Peter, and Jean Spencer. 2010. "Overhaul Splits Party Faithful." *Wall Street Journal*, March 16. http://online.wsj.com/article/SB10001424052748704686045 75125992538227492.html. Accessed December 15, 2010.

Weigel, David. 2010. "Upsetting." *Slate*, November 11. http://www.slate.com/ id/2274567. Accessed December 14, 2010.

Zeller, Shawn. 2010. "Historic Success, at No Small Cost." *Congressional Quarterly Weekly Report*, January 11, 112.

Zernike, Katie, and Megan Thee-Brenan. 2010. "Poll Finds Tea Party Backers Wealthier and More Educated." *New York Times*, April 14. http://www.nytimes .com/2010/04/15/us/politics/15poll.html. Accessed December 15, 2010.

Chapter Seven

Small Ball in the Long Game

Barack Obama and Congress

Bertram Johnson

> To my Democratic friends, what I'd suggest is, let's make sure we under-
> stand that this is a long game. This is not a short game.
>
> —Barack Obama, press conference, December 7, 2010

Barack Obama famously claimed that he was not interested in playing "small ball," and criticized people who did (Alter 2010, 90, 122). During the 2008 primary season, he upset some Democrats by praising Republican Ronald Reagan and appearing to disparage his Democratic Party predecessor Bill Clinton as a small-ball player. Reagan, said Obama "changed the trajectory of America in a way that Richard Nixon did not and in a way that Bill Clinton did not." Part of what made Reagan great, Obama implied, was his grand ambition. In accordance with this assessment, Obama set out a legislative agenda that sought to be transformative. At the beginning of his administration, he proposed bold changes in economic policy, health care, energy policy, and the education system. Allies on Capitol Hill were exhilarated. As Representative Barney Frank (D-MA) put it, "There's a very strong sense among those of us on the Democratic side that we are in a position now to do more for the national interest than almost any of us here have ever been able to do" (*NewsHour* 2009).

In the first two years of his term, however, Obama drew fire from both the left and the right for playing small ball—for compromising away key details of proposed laws, for making targeted concessions to particular members of Congress, and for not making a coherent argument to the country in support of his legislative agenda. As one frustrated columnist put it, "The delicate art of compromise has won Obama no Republican support. Instead, it has fueled the spread of a dangerous narrative that portrays him as a gutless wonder with no principles he will fight to defend" (Tucker 2010).

In this chapter, I argue that Obama's willingness to be flexible on the details of legislation was the result of a conscious strategy. The Obama team catered to the interests of individual members of Congress, playing small ball in the short run in the service of what they believed to be major legislative progress—and public support for reelection—in the long run. They played small ball with an eye to winning the long game.

Was this strategy a success? The answer to this question depends on one's perspective. On the one hand, Obama has been remarkably successful at moving legislation he supports through Congress. The 111th Congress (2009–2010) passed an unprecedented economic stimulus bill, a landmark health-care reform bill, and the most significant financial reform bill since the Great Depression. In its final "lame duck" days, it also enacted tax legislation that pumped nearly $1 billion into a sluggish economy, a major arms treaty with Russia, and an end to the military's "Don't Ask, Don't Tell" policy. The White House promoted and supported each of these laws as they moved through Congress. By a standard measure—*Congressional Quarterly*'s presidential support scores—in his first year in office, Obama received the most consistent support from Congress of any president since scoring began in 1953 (Zeller 2010). Obama's support rating fell slightly in 2010, but still ranked among the top ten ratings ever (Schatz 2011).

On the other hand, Obama's major legislative accomplishments remained controversial, even among his own core supporters. Liberals, who saw the 2010 tax deal as particularly revolting, applauded Senator Mary Landrieu's (D-LA) denunciation of it as being "morally corrupt" (Fabian 2010). By the starkest measure—the 2010 election results—Obama did poorly indeed, suffering the worst midterm "shellacking" (as the president put it) for a Democratic president since the 1930s. In the latter part of Obama's term, it will become more evident whether short-run small ball really did put the administration in a position to win the long game.

In the remainder of this chapter, I first outline some reasons that the Obama strategy is a plausible one in the context of the modern Congress. I next illustrate how the approach developed through two legislative initiatives: the economic stimulus package and the health-care reform bill. I conclude by discussing the prospects for the rest of Obama's presidency.

THE CONGRESSIONAL CONTEXT

The Obama administration was one of the most congressionally experienced new administrations in the modern era. The president and the vice president, Joe Biden, both served in the Senate—the latter for three dozen years. The president's chief of staff, Rahm Emanuel, had been chairman of the House Democratic Party Caucus under Speaker Nancy Pelosi. No fewer than four members of the Cabinet had served in Congress. And if that were not enough, the administration hired a crack legislative-affairs staff headed up by Phil Schiliro, a former staffer for House Commerce Committee Chair Henry Waxman (D-CA). Four out of the previous five presidents had served as governors and suffered in varying degrees from their inexperience with Congress. When Jimmy Carter and his staff first arrived in Washington, for example, then-Speaker of the House Tip O'Neill complained that "They failed to understand that the presidency didn't operate in a vacuum, that Congress was fundamentally different from the Georgia legislature, and that we [in Congress] intended to be full partners in the legislative process" (O'Neill 1987, 308). The Obama team cannot be similarly accused of being blind to the Washington ways of doing things.

To move legislation through Congress, one must first understand how Congress works. Political scientists have been studying this issue for as long as political science has existed as a discipline, so a lot could be said about this matter. Three key themes suffice to explain much of what Congress does and are therefore particularly relevant to a president working to move Congress in a particular direction.

First, members of Congress are interested in reelection. This is such an obvious point that it might strike the reader as a truism. But when David Mayhew developed this idea in his elegant essay "Congress: The Electoral Connection," he reached conclusions that are not as obvious as they might at first seem. The novelty of Mayhew's account rested on the suggestion that members of Congress are motivated by reelection *and nothing else.* Even those who are interested in promoting a particular ideological point of view must achieve reelection in order to do so. "Reelection," Mayhew wrote, "underlies everything else, as indeed it should if we are to expect that the relation between politicians and public will be one of accountability" (Mayhew 1974, 16–17).

The reelection-minded member of Congress will seek publicity in his or her district. Some of this publicity will be empty of issue content—hand shaking, yard signs, and appearances at fairs and sports events. A president can have some influence over this type of activity by holding an event in the district—if the presence of a popular president will raise the representative's profile. In most cases, however, the president has little effect on this basic "advertising" task (Mayhew 1974).

A second key theme regarding Congress, however, is that members of Congress seek to position-take—to state their views on issues of importance to the country or to the district (Mayhew 1974). They do this because they believe their positions have at least some influence on their reelection prospects. Positions that are most effective are those that are widely held in the district, those that are simple, and those that are easy to articulate. "I support the president" or "I oppose the president" on this or that issue are prime candidates for position taking. A poor position to take is "this issue is complex, and although I support some elements of it, others give me pause. On balance, I'd say this bill is better than no bill." Nuance does not translate well to sound bites.

Third, members of Congress are interested in taking credit for benefits that their constituents receive (Mayhew 1974). Credit claiming is more effective if it is plausible—that is, if it seems likely to voters that the member of Congress is responsible for the positive outcome. Voters will justifiably be skeptical if a member of Congress claims credit for a sweeping policy program, such as Social Security. In contrast to position taking, therefore, programs that are complex lend themselves better to credit claiming because members of Congress can tell a more plausible story about changing particular elements of the bill in such a way as to direct benefits to the district.

Voters' perceptions therefore affect the extent to which credit claiming is possible. Another particularly important way in which voter perceptions affect credit claiming is that voters often have clearer and more concrete opinions about policy outcomes than about policy proposals that have yet to be enacted (Arnold 1990, 17). This makes sense—after all, how sure can any of us be about the effects of policies that have not yet been put into place? Even if the national effects of a policy are predictable, the local consequences may be unclear. It is these local consequences that matter most to voters—not the broader picture. "One should never underestimate," wrote Richard Neustadt, "the public's power to ignore, to acquiesce, and to forget, especially when the proceedings seem incalculable or remote from private life" (Neustadt 1990, 82). Unemployment is personal and scarring; government-sponsored insurance exchanges are (for now) abstract and forgettable. Only when voters begin to participate in these exchanges will members of Congress get a clear sense of what they think of them.

A White House strategy predicated on the imperatives of members of Congress would recognize all of the issues previously noted. In doing so, it might follow several key guidelines:

Avoid publicized national debates on complex policy. Complex policy proposals (which social policy proposals often are) are unlikely to win enthusiastic support from members of the public. They are remote from voters' experiences, and they are difficult and costly to understand. Worse still, they are likely to incite debates about multiple dimensions of policy at once (Riker 1982, 128). The "No Child Left Behind" law proposed in the first Bush administration, for example, could be framed in terms of child welfare, in terms of local control versus national control, or even in terms of the role of government in religious education (Johnson 2004). Opposing members of Congress (and opposing interests) can pick and choose the terrain on which to fight their battles, position taking on issues that are most likely to win the support of their constituents. From the perspective of a president, this leads to unpredictable, unstable policy debates that are unlikely to be successful.

The 1993 through 1994 effort by President Bill Clinton to reform the health-care system could be interpreted as just such a failed national debate. The Clinton administration rolled out a health-care bill that would create an intricate system of health-insurance purchasing pools, regulate the health-insurance market, and guarantee all Americans "health care that's always there." President Clinton and his wife Hillary waged a national publicity campaign to try to build support for their ideas. The campaign backfired. The more aggressively the administration promoted its position, the more opponents gained the upper hand in the media and with the general public (Jacobs 2002).

Allow members of Congress to take the lead. Another aspect of the Clinton health-care plan that irked key senators and representatives was that the White House drafted the bill largely on its own, with little input from Capitol Hill. Pundits sometimes describe the problem here as a need for Congress to "take ownership" of legislation, but this formulation does not offer an account of what ownership is good for. The previous account of Congressional motivations indicates that it is good for credit claiming. As a complex bill works its way through Congressional subcommittees, committees, and even floor debates, members add subsections and tweak grant allocation formulas in such a way that allows them to take credit for particular provisions. The Clinton health-care bill, which was drafted by an ad-hoc task force, denied this opportunity to many members of Congress, thus making it difficult to assemble a supporting coalition. As one glum Clinton staffer put it, the bill "excites no one but our opposition" (Johnson and Broder 1996, 177).

Cut deals in the final stages. Once a bill nears passage, the White House can take a more active role in the process by dealing directly with pivotal legislators. Those who are on the fence can be cajoled, persuaded, and—more importantly—bought off with provisions that benefit them. Waiting until the end to make such bargains means the White House can reduce its uncertainty about what bargains are required. This tactic recalls Chicago Mayor Richard J. Daley's response to a reporter's accusation that he never made any commitment until the last possible moment: "That's a pretty good way to be, don't you think?" Daley said. "Pretty good way to run any business" (Banfield and Wilson 1963, 30).

In sum, the motives of Congress members make it attractive for an ambitious president to play a lot of small ball: be vague at first, allow members to take charge of the details, and make many small bargains in the final stages to assure passage of legislation. On the whole, the Obama administration sought to win the long game, gaining favorable outcomes for the voting public in the long run. I now turn to brief descriptions of the debates surrounding the fiscal stimulus bill and the health-care reform act to illustrate how this strategy worked in practice in the first two years of the Obama administration.

THE ECONOMIC STIMULUS BILL

Barack Obama won the White House in an election that also strengthened Democratic Party control of Congress. Democrats had already made big gains two years before, in 2006, when a thirty-one-seat pickup in the House and a six-seat pickup in the Senate gave the party control of both houses of Congress for the first time since the seminal 1994 election. Now the party won twenty-one more House seats and eight more Senate seats, giving Democrats the most commanding majority since the Lyndon Johnson years.

An atmosphere of crisis tempered the victory celebrations, however. Shocked by the near-collapse of the US financial system in the final months before the election, aides inside the president-elect's inner circle scrambled to develop a response. The previous fall, Bush Treasury Secretary Henry Paulson had spearheaded a massive rescue package for the financial industry that squeaked through Congress after briefly suffering defeat in the House, but most experts agreed that more needed to be done. As Obama economic adviser Austan Goolsbee put it just days after the election, "Unfortunately, the next president's number one priority is going to be preventing the biggest financial crisis in possibly the last century from turning into the next Great Depression" (Leonhardt 2008).

Some kind of fiscal policy was needed to jumpstart the economy. Nearly everyone agreed on that. The key questions were how big should the stimulus be, and of what should it consist? Obama advisers focused first on the amount. During the fall campaign, Obama had proposed $150 billion in stimulus funding. In the weeks following the election, economists and commentators floated figures in the range of $200 billion. The numbers rapidly ballooned. After canvassing economists and receiving recommendations from $400 billion to $1 trillion, Obama and his staff settled on recommending an amount around $800 billion (Alter 2010, 88–89; Kuhnhenn 2008). The content of the stimulus turned out to be much more flexible. Obama, buoyed by a productive early-December meeting with the governors of forty-eight states, leaned toward using most of the stimulus money for infrastructure projects. Governors assured the administration that this money could be put to rapid use. California Governor Arnold Schwarzenegger told the transition team that California highway workers could be "literally, putting shovels into the dirt within a few months after the administration starts" (Montgomery and Shear 2008). Republicans in Congress, on the other hand, recommended a package heavily weighted toward tax cuts.

Obama's team seemed to care less about the particular content of the stimulus than about the need for quick action. On December 17, Obama advisers contacted the office of Senate Majority Leader Harry Reid (D-NV) and provided a general outline for a stimulus bill, calling for the package to include, in the words of a Reid spokesperson, "Only those items that spend out quickly, create jobs, and constitute sound national policy" (Drucker 2008). Thus commenced a scramble to fill in the details.

The first shot at this task fell to a group on the House side that Minority Whip Eric Cantor (R-VA) scornfully called "the old bulls in the House majority" (Cantor 2009). House Speaker Nancy Pelosi (D-CA) worked closely with Appropriations Committee Chairman David Obey as that panel rushed to craft the bulk of the package, initially set to be about $550 billion of new appropriations for infrastructure programs, education, health-information technology, and unemployment benefits, among other purposes. Whether he was an "old bull" is debatable, but Obey was certainly an old-school Democrat in the tradition of Franklin Roosevelt. In his 2007 memoir, Obey wrote that "Unless government makes policy choices that provide a *New* New Deal to American workers, we will continue to erode our values and the quality of life that should be within the reach of every American" (Obey 2007, 400).

The administration discouraged congressional leaders from adding earmarks—the much-maligned "pork barrel spending"—to the stimulus, but members of Congress and interest groups had no trouble discerning which provisions would benefit their interests and then lobbying for their inclusion. Groups ranging from bike enthusiasts to the National Head Start Association to farm groups to the US Conference of Mayors all made their views known, and mostly came away satisfied (Clarke and Schatz 2009). Still, some grumbled that the package was too small to make enough of a difference in the economy. Obey wished he could go further. "I think you have to look at this bill not as a salvation to the economy by any means," he said. "It is simply the largest effort by any legislative body on the planet to try to take government action to prevent economic catastrophe" (Clarke 2009).

Obey's pessimism notwithstanding, the bill passed the House on January 28, eight days after Obama's inauguration. House rules that give the leadership the power to set the agenda and to structure debate over legislation made this easier—Republican amendments were swiftly dispatched on the House floor in mostly party-line votes. When the bill finally passed, not a single Republican voted for it.

The action now moved to the Senate, a slower, more ponderous body because of the power that each individual senator retains to slow down or block legislation. The Senate's filibuster rule also gives a minority of forty-one senators the power to block most bills by preventing an up-or-down vote on the floor. Hence, in a chamber with fifty-nine Democrats, it became necessary to persuade a handful of Republicans to fall in behind the president.

In contrast with the House debate, which it had left mostly to that chamber's leadership, the White House became more directly involved in the Senate negotiations. Three senators proved to be the most attractive potential supporters: Arlen Specter (R-PA) (who switched his party affiliation just a few months later), Olympia Snowe (R-ME), and Susan Collins (R-ME). At the same time, Obama had to keep the support of such moderate Democrats as Ben Nelson (D-NE). The president and his staff worked on these key senators in several ways. Some were invited to the White House Superbowl party; some attended the president's speech to congressional Democrats at Washington's "Newseum"; some got one-on-one Oval Office meetings with the commander in chief. Rahm Emanuel and Office of Management and Budget Director Peter Orszag (the former director of the Congressional Budget Office) set up a mini "war room" on Capitol Hill and fielded demands from individual senators (Alter 2010, 126–27).

In the end, Arlen Specter got a promise of $10 billion in funding for the National Institutes of Health. Ben Nelson got an extra $30 million for rural Nebraska hospitals (Alter 2010, 124, 129). And the Maine senators stressed their state's share of weatherization funds, transportation spending, state aid, and other measures. "I don't believe the people of Maine sent me to Washington to sit on the sidelines," Collins told her constituents. "I believe they want me to work across the aisle and try to solve problems" (Hewitt 2009).

President Obama traveled to Colorado, where newly appointed Senator Michael Bennet faced a tough 2010 reelection fight, to sign the $787 billion stimulus bill into law on February 17, 2009. Roughly one third of the amount of the bill was composed of tax cuts, one third was new direct federal spending, and one third represented aid to the states. As Obama described it, the bill "is the product of broad consultations—and the recipient of broad support—from business leaders, unions, and public interest groups, the Chamber of Commerce, the National Association of Manufacturers, Democrats and Republicans, mayors as well as governors." The claim of bipartisanship was an exaggeration. Republican House Leader John Boehner's initial reaction to the plan was a clipped: "Oh. My. God." After this point, he and most Republicans in Congress did all they could to stop the bill. No Republican House members and only three Republican senators supported it.

But in another sense, Obama was telling the truth about the breadth of the supporting coalition. Because he and his administration allowed Congress to take the lead, each friendly member of Congress built a small constituency of support. Local and national groups drew on their connections with members of key committees to make their interests heard. These representatives in turn shaped the bill in ways that responded to their constituency interests and, importantly, allowed them to take credit for doing so. When the outcome seemed to be in doubt, the administration homed in on key senators and made further concessions. By playing small ball with hospital funding, research grants, and construction projects, the Obama administration passed what was perhaps the most significant piece of economic legislation since the New Deal.

The day after Obama signed the measure, the *Portland Press Herald* of Maine ran a front-page analysis of the $1.13 billion that the state was about to receive from the stimulus. There was $470 million for Medicaid reimbursement, $262 million in education funds, $133 million for transportation, and so on. The *Portland Press Herald*'s correspondent concluded his article by pointing out that "Maine's Collins and Snowe both played major roles in negotiating a final agreement on the bill. . . . Without their support, it would not have passed" (Bradbury 2009). This kind of statement must be music to a senator's ears—and to a president's.

HEALTH-CARE REFORM

The stimulus was the easy part. Next, the Obama administration sought to reform the health-care system—a sector that makes up nearly one sixth of the US economy (Truffer et al. 2010). Obama moved forward on this issue against the advice of most of his staff, who argued that health care was too difficult and that energy policy or education might be better choices (Alter 2010, Wolffe 2010). But Obama was adamant, in part because of his commitment to the "long game." Health care had been a central campaign issue, and a national health-care policy had eluded each of his Democratic predecessors—and a few of his Republican ones—at least since the Harry S. Truman administration.

Working with Congress on health care was so important that one of the first things that Obama did on the issue was to choose a top ally with vast experience on Capitol Hill, Tom Daschle, to manage the effort. Daschle was set to simultaneously occupy posts on the White House staff and in the cabinet, as secretary of Health and Human Services (HHS). A former Senate majority leader, Daschle understood the legislative process as well as or better than anyone in Washington and would be a formidable inside-the-beltway negotiator. But Daschle's confirmation to HHS ran into trouble when journalists uncovered Daschle's failure to pay taxes on a limousine and chauffeur provided to him by a firm for which Daschle had consulted. The administration had just weathered a battle over unpaid taxes by one cabinet secretary, the Treasury's Tim Geithner, and had little stomach for another. In early February, Daschle withdrew.

Obama replaced Daschle at HHS with Kathleen Sebelius, the governor of Kansas and an able administrator. Without Hill experience, however, Sebelius did not take on the same role in negotiating the bill that Daschle might have. Instead, lead negotiators included Emanuel, Phil Schiliro of the White House Office of Legislative Liaison, and Nancy-Ann DeParle, a former Medicare administrator in the Clinton administration and the head of the newly created White House Office of Health Care Reform.

As in the case of the stimulus bill, the administration set out broad outlines and left it to Congress to fill in the details. In the campaign, Obama had pledged to lower health-care costs, guarantee coverage for all Americans, reorganize the insurance market into a "National Health Insurance Exchange," and provide a government-run plan as one insurance option (Obama for America 2008). Beyond that, the new president was vague. In his February 24 address to a joint session of Congress, Obama made the case for health-care reform by highlighting the "crushing cost of health care." "Health care reform," said Obama, "cannot wait, it must not wait, and it will not wait another year." The president left it to Congress to fill in the details of what health-care reform might specifically mean.

If the House Appropriations Committee set the agenda for the stimulus, the Senate Finance Committee set the agenda for health-care reform in the first months of Obama's term. That panel was chaired by Senator Max Baucus (D-MT), a key moderate player in the unsuccessful health-care reform effort of the mid-1990s. Back then, Baucus criticized Bill Clinton's top-down approach to legislating. "The more [a bill] is not the Clinton plan, the more it's someone else's plan, the more likely it is to pass," said Baucus at the time (Devroy and Priest 1994). Now the Obama administration gave Baucus leeway to negotiate a deal that could make it out of the Senate Finance Committee and be viable on the Senate floor. Baucus set to work negotiating with moderates on the Finance Committee, including Republican senators Charles Grassley (IA) and Mike Enzi (WY).

Meanwhile, the Obama team sought to ensure that the health-care reform effort would not turn into a publicized national debate in the same way that the Clinton reform effort had. A debate over health care in the public arena made success more uncertain. Polls showed public ambivalence about this confusing issue, and the many details of any health-care plan gave it a multidimensional nature that represented opportunities for opponents to attack the plan by focusing on particular provisions. Particularly on complex matters such as health care, an unstructured public debate allows opposing interests the opportunity to construct an ad-hoc coalition to block any proposal (Immergut 1992).

So the Obama administration cut deals with the key interests that had opposed health-care reform in the past: hospitals, doctors, insurance companies, and the pharmaceutical industry. In a series of agreements that emerged in spring and early summer 2009, administration officials—backed up by Baucus—agreed to limits on the amount each of these groups would be required to contribute to health-care cost savings. Pharmaceutical companies, for example, pledged $80 billion in cost reductions and hospitals pledged $155 billion in reduced Medicare expenses (Chaddock 2009). In exchange, these groups received assurances that the Obama team would not seek to extract more money from them. For its part, the White House won pledges that these groups would not engage in a public fight. On the contrary, the Pharmaceutical Research and Manufacturers of America (PhRMA) ran over $100 million worth of ads supporting reform. "I think the industry wanted to be at the table instead of being dictated to," one health-care executive explained (Thomaselli 2009).

This had the effect of taking some constituency pressure off members of Congress so that the administration's allies on the Hill had some room to negotiate. An unfortunate side effect of negotiation, however, was delay. Baucus continued his discussions on the finance committee well past the time that the White House had hoped he would be able to forward a bill to the full Senate. The summer drifted away, and members of Congress went home for the traditional August recess.

That was when the debate almost got away from them. Although the White House had avoided a high-profile national debate with the insurance companies, they got an unexpected challenge from a new force in US politics: the Tea Party. This grassroots conservative movement began sharply questioning members of Congress about the Obama administration's interventions in the economy. Chief among their concerns was the health-care proposal, which they saw as a "government takeover" of the industry. Some concerns, such as objections to requirements that businesses insure their employees, had a basis in the proposed legislation, while others, such as rumors that the plan would appoint government "death panels" that would ration care, did not.

Nevertheless, constituent anger was real enough to make pivotal members of Congress pause. At a Virginia forum, a middle-aged man in a polo shirt asked moderate Democratic senator Mark Warner, "Who are the people writing the language of these bills? Do they support the Constitution of the United States?" In fact, he suspected, they were people with "radical backgrounds [who are] communist-affiliated, and socialist" (C-SPAN 2009). At a meeting in Iowa, a soft-spoken woman wearing an American flag T-shirt told Grassley (to substantial applause), "I think we're leaning toward socialism and that scares me to death" (C-SPAN 2009).

These confrontations placed pressure on members of Congress to position-take, rather than to focus on the credit claiming that inside bargaining would allow. Voters were not sure about the details of the proposed bills—with legislative proposals totaling more than one thousand pages, how could they be? Instead, they wanted to know whether their representatives were for it or against it. And in a wide-open debate on a complex bill, being against it was in many cases politically safer than being for it.

Late to recognize the problem, Obama sought to refocus the debate on September 9 by delivering a speech to a joint session of Congress. But by that time, Grassley had hardened his position against the bill, and the prospects of bipartisan compromise, slim to begin with, had evaporated. Meanwhile, the administration faced a rebellion of its own on the left. Liberals who had heard that a government-run "public option" insurance plan might be dropped from the final proposal argued that it was vital to reform and must be maintained. In his September speech, Obama protested to "my progressive friends" that "the public option is only a means to [an] end—and we should remain open to other ideas that accomplish our ultimate goal."

Gradually, as fall turned to winter, the national debate cooled and attention turned back to internal bargaining. Three House committees had passed their versions of health-care legislation in July, and leadership negotiators combined these measures into a bill that would cover thirty-six million of the roughly forty-five million uninsured, would include a public option, and would be paid for through cost savings in Medicare and through a tax on high-income Americans. Speaker Pelosi's announcement of the final bill had the feel of a political rally, with a sign-waving crowd and U2 playing in the background. The following week, the bill passed the House with only one Republican vote: that of Anh Cao of New Orleans. (He later changed his mind.)

The Senate was tougher. Days after the House vote, Majority Leader Reid announced his version of the bill, which included a public option. This provision was not present in the Senate finance panel's version of the bill that had received one Republican vote in committee: that of Olympia Snowe. Although the public option pleased liberals, it threatened to alienate moderates. Baucus warned the White House that the sixty votes needed to pass the bill might be tough to get. "We'll just make deals," Chief of Staff Emanuel responded (Wolffe 2010, 71).

And deal they did. Undecided senators made out well in the negotiations leading up to the Senate vote. Nebraska (Senator Ben Nelson) got a higher Medicaid reimbursement rate. Louisiana (Senator Mary Landrieu) got more money for hurricane recovery. Vermont (Senator Bernie Sanders) got more money for community health centers. At last, an exhausted Senate passed its version of the health-care bill—without a public option—on December 24, and immediately headed home for the holiday break.

Still, the national political context threatened to make final passage impossible. In a January 19, 2010, special election to replace the late Senator Ted Kennedy, Massachusetts voters elected Republican Scott Brown, who had won the support of Tea Party activists with his vocal opposition to the health-care reform plan. Now Democrats lacked the sixty-vote supermajority they needed to make sure a House-Senate compromise bill could pass. What was more, House leaders demanded concessions from the Senate. They were upset by a Senate tax on large insurance plans, as well as the Senate bill's lack of a "public option." (Reid had vowed to include this provision in the Senate bill, but he eventually had to drop it.)

Pundits and politicians alike called the health-care bill dead, but the Obama administration did not stop bargaining. In mid-January, Obama hosted a meeting at the White House between House and Senate leaders to get them to reconcile their differences, theatrically walking out of the room in disgust in an effort to move the two sides closer to a deal (Wolffe 2010, 81). After Scott Brown's win, White House staffers continued to nudge the process onward. Eventually the House agreed to pass the Senate bill, and the Senate agreed to pass a package of revisions in response to House concerns. On March 21, the House passed the Senate bill by a vote of 219 to 212; both chambers passed the reconciliation package four days later.

The Obama White House got health-care reform through the Congress by playing small ball. Aides met regularly with key committee chairs and members of the leadership—White House health-care adviser Nancy-Ann DeParle met personally with over 170 members of Congress—many of them repeatedly, according to one report (Wolffe 2010, 66). The White House orchestrated the small adjustments in the bill that were necessary to satisfy particular members of Congress, allowing them opportunities to return to their constituencies and claim victory. When the debate became too public, as in late summer 2009, the administration lost ground. Members of Congress retreated to their respective bunkers, taking the stark positions on the "Obama plan" that their constituents demanded. The administration responded by getting back to the bargaining table, thinking small instead of responding with a high-profile national campaign of its own.

Small ball may have kept the process going, but the outcome was anything but minor. Out of the many White House–sanctioned concessions and changes and deals emerged a final product that represented an unprecedented change in the country's health-care system: a mandate that all Americans buy coverage. A system of health-insurance exchanges meant to rationalize the insurance market. New regulations that would prohibit insurance companies from denying coverage to those with a preexisting condition. And many other provisions that had far-reaching effects.

At the signing ceremony in the East Room of the White House, Obama explained the process that went into the reform.

> You know, there are few tougher jobs in politics or government than leading one of our legislative chambers. In each chamber, there are men and women who come from different places and face different pressures, who reach different conclusions about the same things and feel deeply concerned about different things.
>
> By necessity, leaders have to speak to those different concerns. It isn't always tidy; it is almost never easy. But perhaps the greatest—and most difficult—challenge is to cobble together out of those differences the sense of common interest and common purpose that's required to advance the dreams of all people—especially in a country as large and diverse as ours.

Vice President Joe Biden put it less elegantly in a private aside to the president that was captured by a nearby microphone: "This is a big f***in' deal" (Adams 2010).

SMALL BALL AND THE LONG GAME

The examples of the economic stimulus bill and the health-care reform bill illustrate what I argue has been the Obama administration's central strategy toward engaging with Congress. The White House played a patient insider's game of working with key members of Congress, allowing them to shape the contours of legislation. Obama shied away from settling issues by starting an unpredictable public debate, instead preferring negotiations to grandstanding. This strategy allowed members of Congress to claim credit for the bargains they struck. A national debate would force legislators into pure position taking, an activity that would be as likely—or more likely—to harm the administration as to help.

In this final section, I consider a central objection to this argument and conclude by outlining some of the possible perils of the "small ball-long game" approach.

One objection to my account might be to say, "This is not so unusual. Presidents always bargain and negotiate with Congress over key pieces of legislation, so the Obama approach should not be seen as distinctive." There is some truth to this assertion. Richard Neustadt's classic argument about the presidency rests on the central claim that it is an office whose fundamental task is to bargain (Neustadt 1990). To respond to this criticism requires me to propose a counterfactual hypothesis—to argue that Obama might have proceeded differently than he did. Fortunately, this is not very difficult.

Instead of pursuing an inside bargaining strategy, the president might have instead "gone public," widely publicizing his position on each key legislative measure, leveraging his own popularity, and urging voters to pressure their members of Congress to support health-care reform (Kernell 2007). Ronald Reagan used this strategy most effectively to pass the tax cuts that began his administration. In a nationally televised address, Reagan had urged voters to "join me in this dramatic but responsible plan to reduce the enormous burden of federal taxation on you and your family. . . . [C]ontact your senators and congressmen" (Kernell 2007, 157–58).

Obama might also have stuck with an insider's strategy but proposed his own far-reaching and detailed plan. He could have drummed up party support for it in the House, passed it there on a party-line vote, negotiated with enough senators to squeak it through that chamber, and threaten to veto any alternative proposal. This approximates the strategy George W. Bush used on his major tax-cut legislation (Johnson 2004). The historic level of party unity in the modern Congress might have made this strategy easier than it might have been a generation ago.

But Obama did neither of these things. The Clinton administration's health-care reform effort in the mid-1990s provided an important cautionary example against both. The public debate over health care simply allowed opponents to craft well-honed opposing arguments. Constituents pressured their members of Congress to take clear stands against the bill, which led to inflexibility when it came time to make bargains. Furthermore, the fact that the plan arrived at the Capitol fully formed from the White House gave members of Congress little opportunity to make the legislation palatable to their constituents by adding narrower provisions relevant to them. Clinton's threat to veto a bill without universal coverage fell flat in a Congress that couldn't even manage to bring a bill to the floor of either chamber for debate.

This discussion suggests that going public or drafting a White House bill may be more effective in situations in which proposed legislation is easily understood. Voters could readily comprehend Reagan and Bush's tax cuts, quickly arrive at a position, and call their representatives. With a complex issue such as health care or the stimulus bill, voters have no reference point in their own lives from which to draw, and as a result, a public debate can go off in unpredictable directions. In such an environment, opponents have the upper hand. Staffed with people who had experience in Congress and who witnessed the Clinton administration's health-care failures firsthand, the Obama White House consciously declined to take this chance.

The Obama approach to legislating has its drawbacks, however. Here I list several of the most evident.

First, placing so much weight on the negotiating process can lead to opportunistic behavior by legislators. During the health-care reform debate, for example, Independent Connecticut Senator Joe Lieberman said he would oppose a bill that contained a public option. Negotiators responded by dropping this provision and replacing it with an expansion of Medicaid, an idea Lieberman had supported in the past. Still, Lieberman objected. Frustrated Senate leaders had to rewrite the bill again to address Lieberman's complaints (Alter 2010, 414–15).

If members of Congress realize that they can profit by being obstinate, large numbers of obstinate legislators may swiftly emerge. The sheer quantity of private deals that had to be struck in the stimulus and health-care debates may owe something to this fact. The legislative process may be delayed and distorted as each member of Congress gets in line.

Second, even if the White House is careful not to stir up opposition by going public, opposition from voters can sink important legislation. In this case, it might be better for the White House to take its chances with a public campaign, thereby potentially giving members of Congress grassroots support for a compromise. In the case of climate-change legislation, for example, the key negotiators in the Senate—John Kerry (D-MA), Joe Lieberman, and Lindsey Graham (R-SC)—were well on their way to negotiating a bill with the White House when attacks on Graham began from the same groups of conservatives who had attacked the health-care plan. After issuing an escalating series of demands that frustrated Democrats, Graham finally walked out on the negotiations (Lizza 2010). No amount of special benefits for South Carolina was going to address the fact that a growing number of voters disagreed with Graham on climate change and that he needed their votes to win reelection.

A final potential problem concerns the fact that one argument in favor of a messy and confusing negotiation strategy is that voters will recognize how positive the policies are once they go into effect. In a speech on the eve of the House vote on health care, Obama reassured members of the House Democratic caucus that "after health reform passes and I sign that legislation into law, . . . it's going to be a little harder [for opponents] to mischaracterize what this effort has been all about." The long game rather than the short run is what really matters. This presumption is backed up by political scientists' observations that voters have much better formed views on policy outcomes than they do about policy proposals—especially complex ones.

But it is also possible that the negotiation process will result in policy that is incoherent and is therefore less likely to result in positive outcomes. When Obama aides first considered stimulus proposals, they thought of spending massive amounts of money on major development efforts: revitalizing the transportation and energy infrastructure and reforming the education system (Alter 2010, 90–91). These efforts got whittled down and the money redistributed to other programs, to the point where there are fewer visible effects of the stimulus. Nearly two years after its passage, according to an *ABC News/Washington Post* poll, more than two thirds of Americans thought federal money spent on the stimulus had been "mostly wasted."

Critics make similar arguments about other Obama legislative efforts, such as the reform of the financial industry enacted in mid-2010 and the tax package passed at the end of that year. Half a loaf, these critics argue, is sometimes worse than no loaf at all. The future of the Obama administration is likely to hinge on this last issue.

In the days after the 2010 Republican victories, pundits dredged up the term "triangulation" from the Clinton years. Obama, the argument went, would be forced to stake out a middle ground between congressional Democrats and Republicans, just as Clinton had in 1996 with that year's welfare-reform bill. A series of "triangulating" compromises might anger activists on both sides but (argued the pundits) would be the best way for the president to position himself for reelection. The difference between Obama's position and Clinton's, however, is that Obama's legislative achievements were more sweeping in his first two years than Clinton's were. While Clinton could pivot away from the health-care issue to other matters, the Obama administration is faced with shepherding its newly enacted programs through the implementation process. Some provisions of the health-care bill went into effect in 2010, but the most significant aspects of the legislation will not kick in until 2014. New regulations filling in the details of the 2010 financial reform bill will take many months to write and approve. And as of early 2011, nearly $200 billion of the 2009 stimulus money had not been paid out, according to the federal tracking figures available at recovery.gov.

Obama, far more than Clinton, faces the complicated task of managing the outcomes of major new policy. Although there may be times when compromises are available, as in the case of the 2010 tax-cut extension, defending and implementing past policy achievements will inevitably place the Obama White

House at odds with Republicans. As a result, there will likely be fewer major legislative achievements in the 112th Congress than there were in the 111th. In addition, the battle will shift from a debate over prospective policies to a debate over policy outcomes. No doubt, White House officials feel they are on firm ground here. The public will, they presume, soon warm to the economic growth and health-care security that the stimulus and health-reform bills sought to provide. Republicans—and even some Democrats—are not so sure.

The Obama administration did exceedingly well in playing small ball— well enough to pass major legislation that addresses important and pressing national problems. The question is, will these new laws solve these problems? Will Obama win the long game?

REFERENCES

Adams, Richard. 2010. "Bleeping Biden; Obama Health Reforms Marred by Gaffe." *The Guardian (London)*, March 24, 23.

Alter, Jonathan. 2010. *The Promise: President Obama, Year One.* New York: Simon & Schuster.

Arnold, R. Douglas. 1990. *The Logic of Congressional Action.* New Haven: Yale University Press.

Banfield, Edward C., and James Q. Wilson. 1963. *City Politics.* New York: Random House.

Bradbury, Dieter. 2009. "Maine's Stimulation? About $1.13 Billion." *Portland Press Herald*, February 18, A1.

Cantor, Eric. 2009. "What Should Be Done to Boost the Economy?" *Washington Times*, February 15, M12.

Chaddock, Gail Russell. 2009. "Healthcare Reform: Obama Cut Private Deals With Likely Foes." *Christian Science Monitor*, November 6. http://www.csmonitor.com/ USA/Politics/2009/1106/healthcare-reform-obama-cut-private-deals-with-likely -foes. Accessed December 12, 2010.

Clarke, David. 2009. "Democrats Roll Out Stimulus Plan." *CQ Weekly*, January 19, 126.

Clarke, David, and Joseph J. Schatz. 2009. "The Devil's in the Stimulus Plan Details." *CQ Weekly*, January 12, 77.

C-SPAN Video Library. 2009. Mark Warner Town Hall Meeting, September 3; Charles Grassley Town Hall Meeting, August 12. www.cspanvideo.org. Accessed December 15, 2010.

Devroy, Ann, and Dana Priest. 1994. "Clinton Plan Is Officially Laid to Rest; Announcement Signals New Effort to Salvage Some Health Care Reform." *Washington Post*, July 23, A1.

Drucker, David. 2008. "Obama Wants Stimulus to Sign January 20." *Roll Call*, December 18, 1.

Fabian, Jordan. 2010. "'Filibernie': Sanders Blasts Tax Deal for Four Hours and Counting." *The Hill*, December 10. http://thehill.com/blogs/blog-briefing-room/news/133089-sanders-begins-filibuster-of-tax-deal. Accessed December 10, 2010.

Hewitt, Rich. 2009. "Collins Defends Role in Stimulus; Senator: Plan is Part of the Solution." *Bangor Daily News*, February 20, B1.

Immergut, Ellen M. 1992. "The Rules of the Game: The Logic of Health Policy-Making in France, Switzerland, and Sweden." In *Structuring Politics: Historical Institutionalism in Comparative Analysis*, edited by Seven Steinmo, Kathleen Thelen, and Frank Longstreth, 57–89. New York: Cambridge University Press.

Jacobs, Lawrence R. 2002. "The Presidency and the Press: The Paradox of the White House 'Communications War.'" In *The Presidency and the Political System*, 7th Edition, edited by Michael Nelson. Washington, DC: Congressional Quarterly Press.

Johnson, Bertram. 2004. "A Stake in the Sand: George W. Bush and Congress." In *High Risk and Big Ambition: The Presidency of George W. Bush*, edited by Steven E. Schier. Pittsburgh, PA: University of Pittsburgh Press.

Johnson, Haynes, and David S. Broder. 1996. *The System: The American Way of Politics at the Breaking Point*. Boston, MA: Little, Brown and Company.

Kernell, Samuel. 2007. *Going Public: New Strategies of Presidential Leadership*, 4th Edition. Washington, DC: CQ Press.

Kuhnhenn, Jim. 2008. "Stimulus Price Tag Is Rapidly Growing; Obama Aides Leaning Toward $850 Billion Plan." *Associated Press*, December 18.

Leonhardt, David. 2008. "Top Priority is Stabilizing the Patient." *New York Times*, November 6, B1.

Lizza, Ryan. 2010. "As the World Burns: How the Senate and the White House Missed Their Best Chance to Deal with Climate Change." *New Yorker*, October 11. http://www.newyorker.com/reporting/2010/10/11/101011fa_fact_lizza. Accessed December 15, 2010.

Mayhew, David. 1974. *Congress: The Electoral Connection*. New Haven, CT: Yale University Press.

Montgomery, Lori, and Michael D. Shear. 2008. "Haste Could Make Waste on Stimulus, States Say." *Washington Post*, December 3, A1.

Neustadt, Richard E. 1990. *Presidential Power and the Modern Presidents: The Politics of Leadership from Roosevelt to Reagan*. New York: Free Press.

NewsHour. 2009. PBS, January 6. Transcript available at http://www.pbs.org/newshour/bb/politics/jan-june09/newcongress_01-06.html. Accessed December 13, 2010.

Obama for America. 2008. *Change We Can Believe In*. New York: Three Rivers Press.

Obey, David. 2007. *Raising Hell for Justice*. Madison: University of Wisconsin Press.

O'Neill, Tip, with William Novak. 1987. *Man of the House: The Life and Political Memoirs of Speaker Tip O'Neill*. New York: Random House.

Riker, William H. 1982. *Liberalism Against Populism: A Confrontation between the Theory of Democracy and the Theory of Social Choice*. Prospect Heights, IL: Waveland Press.

Schatz, Joseph J. 2011. "2010 Vote Studies: Presidential Support." *CQ Weekly*, January 3, 18.

Thomaselli, Rich. 2009. "Obama Health-Care Effort Gets $150 Million Boost From Unlikely Ally." *Advertising Age*, August 13. http://adage.com/article?article _id=138465. Accessed December 13, 2010.

Truffer, Christopher J., Sean Keehan, Sheila Smith, Jonathan Cylus, Andrea Sisko, John A. Poisal, Joseph Lizonitz, and M. Kent Clemons. 2010. "Health Spending Projections through 2019: The Recession's Impact Continues." *Health Affairs* 29: 3 (March), 522–29.

Tucker, Cynthia. 2010. "Compromises Don't Help Obama." *Atlanta Journal Constitution*, December 1, 16A.

Wolffe, Richard. 2010. *Revival: The Struggle for Survival Inside the Obama White House*. New York: Crown Publishers.

Zeller, Shawn. 2010. "Historic Success, at No Small Cost." *CQ Weekly Online*, January 11, 112–21. http://library.cqpress.com/cqweekly/weeklyreport111-000003276735. Accessed December 10, 2010.

Chapter Eight

A Transformative Politics of Judicial Selection?

President Obama and the Federal Judiciary

Nancy Maveety

In an era of partisan senatorial judicial confirmation politics, Barack Obama pursued a "clarifier" and "directive" presidential leadership style. As Steven E. Schier posits in his introduction to this volume, Obama by his policy initiatives and rhetorical actions sought to clarify the partisan differences between himself and his predecessor, Republican George W. Bush. Obama, too, characterized himself as a president directive of change and sought to use his institutional influence and political clout to produce reformative outcomes. But as presidential scholar George Edwards notes, Obama's successes were party-line pushes and not persuasive endeavors, and his campaign rhetoric about being "facilitative" was either disingenuous or forgotten after January 2009 (Edwards 2010). This contrast—between the clarifier and the facilitative president—is important for Edwards because "successful presidents *facilitate* change by recognizing opportunities in their environment and fashioning strategies and tactics to exploit them" (Edwards 2010; emphasis added). Obama neither facilitated the changes he oversaw in his first term, nor did he necessarily recognize and exploit available opportunities.

This diagnosis is nowhere more apparent than in Obama's federal judicial appointments. As this chapter will detail, the modern, polarized Senate's response to this directive president's judicial nominations was no different from any president's would probably be in the current confirmations era. Even so, Obama's two appointments to the Supreme Court certainly clarified his own partisanship and partisan difference from his opponents, serving one of his own presidential objectives. Yet despite this seeming accomplishment, his record of appointments to the lower federal courts—and even, to some extent, his two Supreme Court appointees—demonstrate missed or wasted opportunities in his political environment. This sense of opportunity passed up was only magnified by the "shellacking" Obama's Democratic Party suffered in the 2010 midterm elections, a phenomenon discussed and analyzed by other contributors to this volume. While Obama hung on to his party majority in the Senate, the narrowness of the Democrats' margin of control suggests that a partisan and directive approach to the judicial selection process would no longer yield "clarifying" appointments such as Sonia Sotomayor's or Elena Kagan's. Rather, the vastly more circumscribed ideological and agenda spaces within which Obama was forced to operate post-November 2010 necessitated ever-more diminished expectations for his staffing of the federal courts.

Obama has not evidenced a transformative politics of judicial selection, but to be fair, some of his failure to do so is not his fault. Rather, the politics of judicial selection have been transformed by events that predate the Obama presidency into a process that is deeply disabling of modern presidents, even in the best of circumstances. And in compromised circumstances—such as Obama faced in the second half of his 2008 to 2012 term—the optimal presidential strategy is far from clear, as many of the old rules—institutional, pragmatic—no longer apply.

THE POLITICAL FRAMEWORK OF
JUDICIAL APPOINTMENTS

There was once a well-known and time-honored matrix for predicting success in presidential judicial appointments—where success was understood as confirmation of a judicial nominee. That matrix observed that presidents seek the optimum of qualifications for their ideologically preferred judicial candidates and that presidential strength in light of senatorial party politics dictated the balance between the qualifications and the ideology of a nominee (e.g., Epstein and Segal 2005). Presidents were expected to prefer candidates who shared their policy views, political-party persuasion, or vision of the Constitution. Demographic considerations with an electoral connection for a president's party—candidates' geographic region, race, or gender—might be included in a nomination calculation. Senatorial deference to the presidential prerogative to nominate candidates of his choice was the senatorial default position, even for opposition-party senators. Still, a president could upset this dynamic with a poorly qualified or otherwise politically compromised selection, as President Richard Nixon discovered with his first two rejected Supreme Court nominees. Presidents also might run afoul of senatorial deference when their own political position was weakened, as unpopular or lame-duck figures lacking the political clout that inspires senatorial cowering, cowardice—or compliance. Weakened presidents, lagging in public opinion polls or suffering from a beating taken at midterm elections, might expect to have to offer ideologically compromised candidates as their judicial nominees—particularly at the more visible, more politically salient Supreme Court level—as the price of confirmation.

This matrix and this dynamic have all changed in the contemporary political era. Scholars differ as to the reasons why, but most agree that the watershed moment in judicial confirmation politics was President Ronald Reagan's nomination of Robert Bork in 1989. As a prospective Supreme Court justice, Bork was part of Reagan's agenda to "ideologize" the judicial selection process and make presidential appointment of federal judges a part of his administration's larger conservative political goals. Bork was also a well-known and well-published legal scholar with a long and visible track record on the hot-button constitutional issues of the day, including privacy rights and the abortion decision. What is important about the Bork nomination for the history of judicial appointment is that he galvanized an opposition to orchestrate a media campaign to defeat his candidacy, and this media campaign involved interest groups in the kind of advertising, pressure politics, and grassroots politicking usually reserved for electoral campaigns. Senate opponents, led by Democrat Edward Kennedy, argued that Reagan had gone outside the ideological mainstream in his choice and that disqualified Bork. After a lengthy and vituperative confirmation hearing televised in its entirety by the major networks, Bork was rejected in a party-line vote.

Post-Bork, judicial appointment politics became more partisan and more polarizing. The upshot has been that members of the Senate are increasingly driven by their own electoral fortunes and party constituency back home (Kastellec, Lax, and Phillips 2008) and do not defer but demur with respect to presidential choice. A recent study (Cottrill, Peretti, and Rozzi 2010) argues that, for modern Supreme Court appointments, neither nominee qualifications nor presidential strength plays the role it once did in moving opposing-party senators to support a president's candidates. Partisan opponents are more mobilized and unified in their voting opposition, particularly in those confirmations that have occurred since Bork, and even when they constitute a numerical minority. Partisanship is simply stronger and more polarizing for the modern Senate, with delaying tactics a prominent part of the modern confirmation process. Presidents have responded in kind—as have their respective political parties, in retaliation, when they control or can influence the Senate. GOP senatorial obstruction of Bill Clinton's courts of appeals appointments was met with Democratic stalling of George W. Bush's nominees, as well as an increasingly partisan confirmation-vote response to his Supreme Court candidates, especially Samuel Alito.

Interest groups figure importantly in two ways. First, they trigger obstructionist delay by sounding "fire alarms" to bring attention and scrutiny to otherwise low-salience or noncontroversial nominees (Scherer, Bartels, and Steigerwalt 2008). Second, they sustain ideological polarization by members of the Senate through "score carding" of senatorial confirmation votes for the consumption of senators' constituents—voting scores that become a litmus test of ideological purity for conservatives and liberals alike (Cohen Bell 2002).

In this context, a partisan clarifier and directive president like Obama has few choices. The ideological cast of his nominees is a given, even as the battle to frame these candidates in terms of their "judiciousness" versus their political ideology (Gibson and Caldeira 2010) is waged between the president, his party, and their special-interest supporters, and his political opponents. While presidential strength or political clout is of diminished importance in swaying senatorial votes, the president can assume the support of same-party senators and also count on the cohesion of the majority partisan coalition (Cottrill, Peretti, and Rozzi 2010). Thus, when that majority is of his own party, he can expect confirmation of his candidates, but not necessarily a smooth, speedy, or tranquil one. Nor can he expect—as was once the norm—near-unanimous confirmation votes for Supreme Court nominees or simple voice votes and otherwise expedited measures for confirming lower federal-court nominees. Instead, even when a president's party enjoys a majority in the Senate, the post-Bork-era president should expect filibustering, holds, lengthy and posturing questioning during Senate confirmation hearings, and whatever other parliamentary procedural tactics are at the disposal of opposing-party senators, as the senatorial "advise and consent" response to his judicial candidates.

For presidents outside the grace of a comfortable margin of same-party control of the Senate, the old tactics of "stealth" or even compromise candidates are no guarantee of successful confirmation. Stealthy candidates without a discernable and distillable track record are not only an unpredictable, double-edged sword (such as David Souter for George H. W. Bush), but minimal or opaque qualifications can serve as a reason for objection to a nominee—as George W. Bush discovered with respect to Harriet Miers, who would be forced to withdraw her nomination in the face of senatorial skepticism about her suitability (Maveety 2009). On the other hand, "compromise" is untested in the contemporary political climate. Bill Clinton approached his Senate adversaries with the ostensible olive branches of moderate, sitting federal judges Ruth Bader Ginsburg and Stephen Breyer, as opposed to the "big heart" politician-candidates that he initially seemed to prefer, who would have engendered more openly forceful opposition in a politically challenging environment. Clinton's "compromise" candidates were both confirmed by wide and bipartisan margins. George W. Bush, on the other hand, pursued the more high-risk and confrontational stratagem of patently conservative Supreme Court nominees who were nevertheless received as sufficiently within the "mainstream" to win Senate approval (see Gibson and Caldeira 2010)— albeit somewhat narrowly, in the case of Samuel Alito, who was confirmed by a margin of fifty-two to forty-eight.

The point is that the compromise-candidate option is almost two decades old, and its current utility is unknown—particularly in light of the heightened senatorial individualism and vigorous party-branding behaviors that characterize the 111th and 112th Congresses and in the face of an emboldened GOP delegation on Capitol Hill, post-2010 midterm elections. Speaking after Election Day results and preparing for the new 112th Congress, Senate Minority Leader Mitch McConnell sounded a rhetoric more consistent with vanquishing than cooperating with the president, whom he and his GOP allies boasted were dedicated to limiting to one term (*Politico* 2010). Even without such a gauntlet thrown down, the facilitative program of proposing judicial candidates who are a compromise, ideologically speaking, is hardly the tactic a directive president such as Obama would be expected to display—except of course if it became his only choice.

PRESIDENTIAL OPPORTUNITY AND THE PRESIDENTIAL AGENDA: OBAMA TAKES ADVANTAGE OF SOME AND SQUANDERS OTHERS

President Barack Obama entered office in January 2009 under very fortunate circumstances, to some degree. While his plate was full of serious economic policy challenges, he began his term with a sixty-seat, filibuster-proof majority in the Senate, a large electoral mandate for himself and his party, a Supreme Court peopled with aging justices ripe for retirement and replacement (most of whom were, of course, liberal and/or Democratic appointees), and a healthy but not crushing number of lower federal-court vacancies to fill. Obama was riding a wave of tremendous and seemingly momentous personal popularity. With respect to his judicial selection agenda, his prospects appeared fairly bright.

One year into his first term, such promise had not been realized. First, and by all accounts, Obama failed to act swiftly on lower federal-court nominations when political circumstances were very much in his favor. In 2009, Obama nominated thirty-three judges to the district and circuit courts and just twelve were confirmed. By February 2010, he had nominated only forty-two judges—a "pathetic" number by comparison with his predecessor's eighty-nine nominees by February 2002 (*Slate* 2010). In a study of federal judicial vacancies across time, Lanier and Hurwitz (2010) noted that Obama was laggard in a relative sense with respect to his judicial appointments. Certainly the mean time that judicial vacancies exist has increased across presidential administrations in the last several decades (Nixon and Goss 2001). Even so, Obama manifested a comparatively higher rate of *leaving vacancies without nominees*, suggesting that he "chose to deemphasize judicial selection and instead to focus his time and spend his political clout on other policy initiatives" (Lanier and Hurwitz 2010, 14).

Journalistic reports bear this out. While Senate Republicans tried unsuccessfully to filibuster the president's very first judicial nominee—David Hamilton, nominated for the Seventh Circuit Court of Appeals—Obama neither capitalized on nor learned from this example. The wave of press criticism of this case of GOP obstructionism did not spur a redoubled effort on the judicial selection front (*Slate* 2010). Further, the president failed to modify significantly his one-nominee-at-a-time approach to naming candidates for the federal bench—displaying a "strange lack of urgency" about the whole matter (*American Prospect* 2010). Such behavior was all the more strange given the large number of vacancies that had accrued, more than one hundred on the lower federal courts, with twenty-two district court vacancies classified as "judicial emergencies" according to a November 2010 Alliance for Justice study. Emergency vacancies or not, Obama's approach to the process of judicial staffing seems to have extended an already attenuated procedure. In addition to declining to present nominees in tidy, expedited "batches," Obama revived a more consultative and time-consuming method of conferring with home-state senators on prospective judicial nominees, as well as resuscitating lengthy ABA Standing Committee evaluation of potential candidates (*American Prospect* 2010). In retrospect, these actions look like dallying in the face of highly time-sensitive opportunities to shape the federal judiciary by filling vacancies early and often, while still in a presidential "honeymoon" period. Obama "neglect[ed]" an area in which a "president can create conditions for broad and long-lasting [policy] change" (*American Prospect* 2010)

As of January 2011, Obama's summary statistics on federal judges appointed had improved somewhat, with sixteen successfully confirmed to the US Courts of Appeals and forty-four to the US District Courts. Still, at the start of the new 112th Congress, he had to resubmit forty-two judicial candidates who had failed to clear the Senate confirmation process, including seven nominees for the circuit and thirty-five nominees for the district courts. Moreover, his appointee "score" compares rather unfavorably with George W. Bush's some one hundred federal judges seated during the first congressional session of his presidency. While Obama's are a more diverse group in terms of gender and ethnicity than those of his predecessor, most have not been in active service on the bench long enough to amass a clear aggregate picture of their cohorts' decision-making trends as of late 2010. Thus, although more than one third of his appellate court judges replaced GOP appointees and therefore stand to have comparatively greater influence on the outputs of their respective circuit courts, Obama's progress in infusing the federal courts with a new cadre of Democratic-leaning judges remains uncertain.

Of course, one could also counter by observing that Obama's 2009 to 2010 judicial selection agenda was quite full with Supreme Court vacancies. So, arguably, rather than frittering away Edwards's "opportunity in his political environment," President Obama was securing his party's legacy on the high court. By successfully appointing Sonia Sotomayor and Elena Kagan to replace retiring justices David Souter and John Paul Stevens, respectively, Obama maintained a liberal-progressive minority bloc with a chance to stand against the conservative wing led by Bush appointee, Chief Justice John Roberts. "Securing a legacy" this was—albeit in the form of holding the line, defensively, in the hopes of a subsequent balance-of-power-changing personnel opening. Nevertheless, Obama's sluggish staffing of the federal courts must be assessed in light of his considerable accomplishments at the Supreme Court level. His two Supreme Court appointees were bold gestures toward the court's demographic diversity, with each in her own way fulfilling Obama's campaign rhetoric about what kinds of people he wanted to see sit as justices.

Candidate Obama made several statements about federal judicial appointments during his 2008 presidential campaign, amounting to a promise to name justices who demonstrated "empathy" in approaching their judicial responsibilities. In remarks from the campaign trail on July 17, 2007, Obama opined that

> we need somebody who's got the heart to recognize—the empathy to recognize what it's like to be a young, teenaged mom; the empathy to understand what it's like to be poor or African-American or gay or disabled or old. And *that's the criteria by which I'm going to be selecting my judges.* (emphasis added)

Referencing his own behavior as a member of the US Senate, in voting against the confirmation of Bush's two Supreme Court nominees, Obama elaborated on the relevance of constitutional vision as a judicial qualification:

> I also think it's important to understand that there is nothing wrong in voting against nominees who don't appear to share a broader vision of what the [C]onstitution is about. I think the Constitution can be interpreted in so many ways. And one way is a cramped and narrow way in which the Constitution and the courts essentially become the rubber stamps of the powerful in society.

And then there's another vision of the court that says that the courts are the refuge of the powerless. . . .

With his "empathy" remarks, Obama seemingly aligned himself with the "living Constitution" position, which sees an elastic Constitution with the potential for progressive growth and one whose contours should be shaped by judicial interpretation. In so interpreting the Constitution, Obama was saying, judges should be able to see life through the eyes of those who come before the bench.

But for his party opponents, the "empathy test"—as some Senate Republicans would call it (Balz 2009)—was a prescription for jurists who "twist[ed] decisions to reach a desired outcome rather than the one mandated by the letter of the law" (Baker 2010). Democratic liberal allies, on the other hand, took the remarks at face value as a promise to place the most progressive jurists on the high court that Obama's sixty-seat, filibuster-proof party majority in the Senate would permit.

Obama and his Supreme Court appointments must be assessed in terms of how well he negotiated the party landscape with his selections and how the initial performance of his appointees reflected his administration's constitutional vision. On this second aspect of Obama's politics of federal judicial selection, his record is stronger than in the lower federal courts; however, the choices he made and the way those candidates were managed in the confirmation process suggest that any future high court vacancies may be much more complicated, if not problematic, to fill.

OBAMA'S JUSTICES, AND OBAMA'S DIRECTIVE AND CLARIFYING PARTISANSHIP

By the time Justice Souter announced his retirement at the end of the 2008–2009 term, the stage had been set for a partisan struggle over the judicial branch. As a May 2009 story in the *Los Angeles Times* ruminated, "fights over Supreme Court picks are nothing new, but this one is taking place with unusual specificity before a nominee has even been announced. That's because speculation about whom Obama will choose focused almost from the start on a small number of prospects. The battle," writer James Oliphant continued, "has been fueled by the Internet," with right-wing groups using Internet blogs to launch preemptive strikes against possible candidates and leftists in the president's party firing back (Oliphant 2009). Among the names already circulating in the information web-stream were the two that would eventually be confirmed as Obama's Supreme Court selections. One was a sitting federal judge, and the other his recently appointed solicitor general, both the products of elite legal education and denizens of the Northeast Corridor. Yet each passed what *ABC News* called "the diversity test" in terms of their backgrounds, but in different ways. Neither was, nor was presented as, a liberal activist in the classic model of the liberal legal agenda of the 1960s and 1970s; both were "pragmatists" who reflected their president's stated views of the limits of judicial liberalism (Toobin 2009). Despite the seeming effort at post-partisan judicial selection, Obama's candidates would find themselves framed ideologically by both his conservative GOP opponents and, at times and equally unsympathetically, by liberal detractors in his own party.

On May 26, 2009, President Obama announced his nominee for the first vacancy he would fill on the United States Supreme Court. His opening words in introducing the nomination of federal judge Sonia Sotomayor were grand: "Of the many responsibilities granted to a President by our Constitution, few are more serious or consequential than selecting a Supreme Court justice." The grand view reflected in Obama's words was reinforced by the political grandstanding on both sides that followed the announcement and continued until well after the confirmation vote itself.

Obama immediately set out to position his choice as eminently qualified but also historic. He outlined Sotomayor's professional credentials and judicial career, starting with her graduation from the elite universities Princeton and Yale, then her early legal practice as a federal prosecutor. Her first judicial office, as a federal judge presiding over trials in the US District Court for the Southern District of New York, was a position to which she was nominated by Republican President George H. W. Bush. Later appointed to the US Court of Appeals Second Circuit by Democratic President Bill Clinton, Sotomayor's bipartisan selection showed her to be, as Obama suggested, a nominee above partisanship. Her long and varied judicial experience as a trial and appellate judge also demonstrated the ability to be a fair and knowledgeable jurist. But Sotomayor was also the first Hispanic nominated to the Supreme Court, and Obama stressed her less-than-privileged upbringing as the child of Puerto Rican immigrants and as a person who had worked hard for every position and achievement and emblemized the American Dream. Her placement on the court would thus bring ethnic and gender diversity as the first Latina and the second woman among the current justices and only the third woman in the institution's history.

This diversity appointment's seeming connection to Obama's "empathy objective" for his high court judges became a major point of contention about Sotomayor, fueling the argument that she would weigh racial identity heavily in her decision-making process. Critics pointed to her lower federal-court opinions—most significantly to *Ricci v. DeStefano*, in which a group of white firefighters brought a discrimination suit against the city of New Haven when the results of a promotion exam were discarded, nullifying their own promotions. Because no African American candidates passed the exam, the city had determined that their advancement procedures were vulnerable to a civil rights action on race discrimination grounds and attempted to act correctively. Applying then-current Supreme Court precedent on civil rights law, employment discrimination, and racial classifications, Judge Sotomayor rejected the firefighters' reverse-discrimination claim. This decision garnered attention because she and her circuit court majority were later overturned by the Roberts Supreme Court (*Economist* 2009). Another aspect of Sotomayor's record that spawned critical notice was a speech she had made in 2001 to a Latino law-students' association, in which she said that "[She] would hope that a wise Latina woman with the richness of her experiences would more often than not reach a better conclusion than a white male who hasn't lived that life" (see Maveety 2010, 453). The "wise Latina" reference—in light of Obama's campaign statements about a vision of judicial empathy—became fodder for the president's GOP opponents, in the war of media sound bites about the nominee and, later, in the confirmation hearings themselves.

Still, that comment would not be the only crucial one for Obama's candidate to explain or defend. Another contentious, arguably less-than-judicious remark was her statement at an academic panel discussion that "the courts of appeals is where policy is made" (Stern 2009b). This statement—a seemingly unabashed embrace of judicial activism—fit easily into the Republicans' own party branding of themselves as the protectors of constitutional integrity, fidelity, and the appropriately restraintist role for judges. Here was a candidate who would willfully substitute her own policy preferences for the constitutional commands of the document's framers. Both the "wise Latina" and the judicial policymaking reference were potential points of attack, but even with these, most commentators agreed that, unless some major scandal emerged or she "melted down" under the pressure of the committee hearing, the mathematics of the Senate in that summer of 2009 indicated that she was likely to be confirmed (Stern 2009b). The "well qualified" rating that she received from the American Bar Association all but sealed the deal.

The Senate Judiciary Committee hearings proceeded fairly smoothly for Sotomayor, but they also proceeded according to a highly partisan script. Republicans tried to portray her as being outside mainstream views and judicial values, but were generally seen as having been unsuccessful (Stern 2009a). Her long judicial service and deep and varied judicial experience, combined with twice having been confirmed by the same body now evaluating her, made her difficult to undermine. Democrats were generally supportive of Sotomayor—although there remained voices of a liberal, dissenting minority within the party coalition that pined for a less conventional, less "safe" nominee from their liberal Democratic and ostensibly boundary-pushing president. From this perspective, Sotomayor's pedigree as a federal judge—selected to join a bench of all former federal judges—was unnecessarily narrow and unadventurous. Ultimately, of course, Sotomayor didn't require the Democrats' overwhelming or passionate support in or outside the hearing room, as she gave a "competent and cautious performance" before the committee (Stern and Perine 2009). In a style of answering questions that has become standard over recent confirmation hearings, she steadily and respectfully evaded questions about her views on salient issues and made generic, placating comments about respecting precedents and staying true to the law (Farganis and Wedeking 2010). For example, at one point Senator Lindsey Graham asked if she believed in the concept of a living constitution. She ducked in answering, saying, "I believe judges should follow the law"—the same answer she had given when asked to clarify the meaning of her statements about the relevance of life experience and personal background to judicial decision making. Even as Sotomayor was successful in placing her more controversial off-the-bench remarks in a suitable, palatable context, the Republicans' judicial-philosophy line of questioning successfully established the idea that their party's "brand" is one of thorough judicial examination (Driver 2010) and extensive scrutiny of nominees' constitutional jurisprudence.

In the end, the Judiciary Committee voted thirteen to six in her favor, with Senator Lindsey Graham of South Carolina as the only Republican who voted to recommend her confirmation to the Senate. Republicans were uneasy about the actual positions that Sotomayor would take on the court, given that her answers in front of the committee differed greatly from what she had said in previous speeches. Many Republicans cited these concerns as to why they opposed her confirmation. For instance, Senate Minority Leader Mitch McConnell said that "Judge Sotomayor's record of written statements suggest an alarming lack of respect for the notion of equal justice, and therefore, in my view, an insufficient willingness to abide by the judicial oath" (Stern 2009b). Such remarks served mainly to engage a party base in its opposition to the liberal policies of President Obama, and had no real effect on his judicial candidate. Craven compromise or not, judicial professional or activist crusader, Sonia Sotomayor was confirmed by a vote of sixty-eight to thirty-one, which included the support of nine Republican senators—neither a bipartisan landslide, nor a close call. In terms of negotiating the party landscape, Obama scored a victory with the Sotomayor nomination and succeeded in replacing a GOP appointee with a Democratic appointee. Of course, given Souter's voting alliance with the progressive wing of the court, Obama's presumably liberal replacement had little net impact on the direction of the court's decisions.

It was his second nomination to the Supreme Court that potentially constituted a game-changing appointment, with respect to the dynamics of court leadership on the Roberts bench. Before the end of the 2009 to 2010 term, Justice John Paul Stevens announced his retirement, after thirty-five years of service. Appointed by President Gerald Ford, Stevens had served through the tenure of three chief justices and acted as a moderate swing vote for much of his time on the high bench. However, in recent years and as new justices moved the court median toward the conservative end of the ideological spectrum, he became considered the senior member of the court's liberal wing. The public impression was that whoever was selected by President Obama would not shift the ideological balance of the court, in that the president was expected to fill the seat with another left-of-center jurist. Still, because of his coalitional and intellectual leadership role among the justices and his ability to attract the crucial moderate vote of Justice Anthony Kennedy, Stevens was pivotal to the balance of *power* on the court. To be effective in countering the conservative jurisprudence of agile minds like those of Chief Justice John Roberts and Associate Justice Antonin Scalia, Stevens's successor needed to be a rigorous and astute legal thinker.

On May 10, 2010, Obama announced his nominee as then-current Solicitor General Elena Kagan. Familiar to the punditry's short list of prospective Obama choices, Kagan was named for the court spot with an impressive legal pedigree. After graduating from Harvard Law School, she worked as a law clerk for US Court of Appeals Judge Abner Mikva and then Supreme Court Justice Thurgood Marshall. Following her clerkships, she went into private practice before becoming a law professor at University of Chicago Law School. During the Clinton administration, she served as associate White House counsel. Following the Clinton years, Kagan returned to academia at Harvard University before eventually becoming dean of Harvard Law School. This noteworthy career nevertheless left some senators muttering about her lack of actual judicial experience and the extensive political credentials on her resume.

The Kagan confirmation process was notably different from that of Sotomayor, in several ways. Sotomayor had relatively unassailable juridical qualifications. Elena Kagan was both the solicitor general as well as former dean of Harvard Law School, but she had no judicial experience and a limited amount of real courtroom experience, which opened her up to criticism of her qualifications *as a judge*. The very diversity component of her background—a professional background in policy and academia rather than in judgeships—became her weak spot. More significantly, she was appointed at a time when Obama's political strength had diminished from what it had been when Sotomayor was appointed. Ultimately, Kagan's confirmation was more contentious because the Republican Party was able to unify, to a greater extent, around a negative framing narrative of Obama's judicial candidate.

The public became aware of Kagan's lack of judicial experience, for she was the first nonjudge to be named for a seat on the US Supreme Court since William Rehnquist in 1971. Seemingly, the public had a relatively negative reaction to it. At the time of her appointment, Kagan's public approval rating was approximately 10 percent lower than Sotomayor's at the time of hers (see Gallup Organization 2009b and Gallup 2010). The Obama administration endeavored to give some context to Kagan's career, stating that, "Elena is widely regarded as one of the nation's foremost legal minds. She's an acclaimed legal scholar with a rich understanding of constitutional law" (*White House Press Release* 2010). Similarly, discourse about Kagan's position as the "Tenth Justice"—legal scholars' parlance for the solicitor general—began circulating as soon as she was nominated, with the professional symbolism afforded to her in that title and as "General Kagan" arguably as important as being referred to as "Judge."

In spite of these efforts, her credentials were a soft target to Republicans. Senator James Inhofe was indicative of conservative GOP thinking during the Kagan confirmation processes. He lambasted Kagan's judicial qualifications, noting "her lack of judicial experience . . . play[s] an important role in my decision to once again oppose her nomination. The position for which she has been nominated has lifetime tenure, and it is concerning that the President has placed such trust in a nominee that has not been properly vetted through a judicial career, having worked mostly in academia and never before as a judge" (*Senator Inhofe Press Release* 2010). Republicans also seized on some of Kagan's statements of admiration regarding Thurgood Marshall, a liberal member of the activist Warren Court. The argument didn't resonate as well as did those about the connection between Kagan's judicial experience and her putative "judiciousness." From the outset, the Republican Party cast Kagan not as an impartial, judicial figure, but as a political actor ready to defend her own policy positions rather than interpret the law and the Constitution. Republican opponents emphasized her liberal leanings in the context of the military recruitment ban at Harvard Law School that she had supported while dean. Even more than demonstrating the ideological distance between the Republican base and the nominee, the military recruitment example epitomized Kagan as a *policymaker*, an advocate, and not a jurist. Though only 50 percent of respondents rating her ideologically correct or "just right" in one public survey, her ideology was no more or less determinative for her confirmation than was Sotomayor's—who had been found the previous year to be ideologically "just about right" by 55 percent of respondents (see Pollster.com 2010 and *Washington Post* 2009). Despite a lack of substantive controversy or even real ideological taint, Kagan elicited less support from Democrats and greater resistance from Republicans than Sotomayor, across the board.

The real culprit was not the candidate's quality, but Obama's own weakening public approval rating at the time of Kagan's nomination. Obama's poll numbers dropped significantly between the confirmations: at the time Sotomayor was confirmed, Obama's approval rating hovered around 60 percent; after Kagan was confirmed, it had dropped to just under 45 percent. It is likely that more Republican senators felt comfortable defying Obama on Kagan due to his drop in popularity, feeling that to do so would not be a liability for them in their states. Obama's loss of presidential strength coincided with the decrease in senatorial support from Sotomayor to Kagan and, probably, with the lessened amount of bipartisan support Kagan received. Her confirmation, by a vote of sixty-three to thirty-seven and the votes of only five GOP senators (and the defection of one Democrat, Ben Nelson of Nebraska, who voted against her confirmation), suggested a more vulnerable president in the eyes of the Senate. As one source charged, criticism of Obama's presidency had created a wellspring of energy on the Republican side, so "despite the smoother reception, Kagan will probably garner fewer votes in the Senate than the 68 votes Sotomayor got. This is less a reflection on Kagan or Sotomayor than a marker of just how much Washington has changed since last August. The difference is the increased awareness among Republican senators of the energy and anger in the conservative base" (Green 2010). Cognizant of Obama's diminishing public support, Republicans hoped to tie Kagan's nomination to her president's larger agenda. The tactic was a direct result of a strategic GOP awareness of public disapproval of Obama's economic recovery and health-care agenda.

For Kagan, as with Sotomayor, presidential strength played a large role in the nomination and confirmation process. While some scholars describe presidential strength—defined as a function of partisan control of the Senate and year in office—as diminishing in importance when it comes to determining a senator's vote and "a significant factor only for same party senators" (Cottrill, Peretti, and Rozzi 2010, 16), Obama's two judicial confirmation votes point to something else. When Kagan was confirmed, the Senate Democrats were in a clearly weaker position. They had only one fewer seat in their majority, but the loss of that seat—the Massachusetts Senate seat of the late Edward Kennedy, which went to Republican Scott Brown—was and *was seen as* a very big blow to Democratic power in the body. A CNN report from January 19, 2010, was typical: "Brown's victory strips Democrats of the 60-seat Senate supermajority needed to overcome GOP filibusters against future Senate action on a broad range of White House priorities"—intimating that Obama had lost a significant source of presidential strength. Obama was also later in his term by the summer of 2010: when Sotomayor was confirmed, Obama's sizable electoral victory in 2008 was a recent event; when Kagan was confirmed, Obama was much closer to the critical 2010 midterm election. The loss of political clout showed. With the exception of Lindsey Graham, Kagan's Republican supporters tended to be the least conservative Republicans, while Sotomayor in contrast attracted senators who were more conservative, though still more liberal than most of their caucus. Impending electoral demographics in conjunction with Sotomayor's "famous first" appointment explain some of this, but Kagan was still confirmed with the support of only five members of the opposite party, a very small number even in the post-Bork era. The only other post-Bork nominee to have as little cross-party support as Kagan was George W. Bush's nominee Samuel Alito, who had only four Democrats voting for him. Arguably, Alito was the only one of the post-Bork nominees whose president had as little political strength as Obama had in late 2010, for Bush did not have an overwhelming majority in Congress and was late in his presidency at the time of the Alito appointment. While Obama had a much more favorably partisan Senate composition, the expanded use of the filibuster by a unified senatorial minority greatly reduced how effective that partisan composition was.

The Republican minority was noticeably more united against Kagan than they were against Sotomayor. RNC Chairman Michael Steele did not send out mixed messages of support and nonsupport, as he did for Sotomayor. There was no internal debate about whether Republicans should demur from fighting Kagan out of deference to a potentially significant segment of the electorate, as there was with respect to Sotomayor and Hispanic voters. Moreover, the narrative against Kagan was more unified. Rather than a diverse vocabulary of criticism such as "reverse racist," "radical liberal," "fiery Latina activist" and "judicial activist," criticisms of Kagan revolved around a vocabulary of "unqualified" due to judicial inexperience. The unified rhetoric was arguably telling in attacking Kagan as a candidate and challenging Obama's juridical frame for her professional record. While some prominent Republican senators agreed that she was qualified for a position on the Supreme Court—even though her dossier was less typical and more overtly political than those of recent appointees—they were a distinct minority of their coalition. Obama negotiated the party landscape with Kagan's appointment, but as a partisan clarifier who had extended the distance between himself and his agenda on the one hand, and the instrument and the goal of bipartisanship on the other.

Party polarization in the judicial-selection context is not only the doing of a president, however. Both the Senate's response to and a president's seizing of his political opportunities regarding judicial appointment are affected by the oppositional campaigns of interest groups. Their oppositional efforts communicate to a president's Senate opponents the importance of thwarting certain presidential choices. The interest groups' message for senators is both ideological *and* electoral. Therein lies their effectiveness, particularly when in opposition and to move senators off the default position of confirming an otherwise qualified candidate a "default" position now overtly espoused only by Senator Lindsey Graham, among Republican senators, suggesting the impact of oppositional, ideological framing of nominees by interest groups, at least at the Supreme Court level. For instance, the National Rifle Association's (NRA) stance and objective with respect to Obama's judicial nominees is clear:

> The dogmatically anti-2nd Amendment minority on the high court is within a heartbeat of reversing both *Heller* and *McDonald*, especially with an Obama rubber-stamp senate and a Judiciary Committee dominated by the likes of New York's Charles Schumer. The outcome of any future 2nd Amendment case before the high court would be disastrous if Pres. Obama and his senate ideological water carriers retain power to load the court. (See LaPierre 2010)

In this 2009 advocacy statement, the pro–gun rights organization, the NRA, made plain its intention to oppose candidates unsuitable because of their position on the right to bear firearms issue. The implicit electoral threat comes, of course, from senatorial fear of the NRA "score carding" that would include advertising to constituents a senator's confirmation vote adverse to gun rights.

Obama's Supreme Court nominees were also the first to sustain serious opposition campaigns from groups employing new social media tactics such as Facebook, Flickr, Twitter, and the like. The case of pro-life group Americans United for Life (AUL) is instructive. In its campaign to spread information about Sotomayor's "anti-life" and activist beliefs, AUL launched a website called Sotomayor411.com and created its AUL anti-Sotomayor Facebook page on the same day as her nomination was announced, May 26, 2009. Similarly, AUL's "Stop Kagan" Facebook page was used to reach youth— the heaviest users of this social media instrument—as well as to recruit new members for the organization's e-mail list, which would receive daily messages called "The Kagan File." Such efforts were directed at galvanizing public sentiment that would be expressed directly or "tweeted" to elected representatives.

Interest groups' capitalizing on the electoral connection between their sympathizers and those people's senators yielded polarization among the public itself. Opposition to both Obama selections was the highest recorded for successful Supreme Court nominees, with Kagan having less popular support than any other successful nominee. This may result from the public increasingly viewing the court in an ideological light and thus applying ideological standards to its prospective members. An August 2010 poll that asked, "Do you think the US Supreme Court justices usually decide their cases based on legal analysis without regard to partisan politics, or do you think they sometimes let their own partisan political views influence their decisions?" found 78 percent responding that the justices sometimes are influenced by political views. Another sign that the public is seeing potential justices in a political light was the response to a June 2009 poll that asked, "When the Senate votes on a Supreme Court nominee, should it consider only that person's legal qualifications and background, or along with legal background, should the Senate also consider that nominee's personal views on major issues the Supreme Court decides?" Sixty-two percent of respondents said issue positions should be taken into account, in contrast to the notion that being (or appearing?) judicious is sufficient. With respect to specific nominees, when asked, "Suppose the upcoming confirmation hearings indicate that Sonia Sotomayor is qualified and has no ethical problems. Do you think US senators would be justified or unjustified in voting against her if they disagree with her stance on current issues such as abortion or gun control?" respondents split almost evenly, with 49 percent saying this would be unjustified versus 47 percent saying it would be justified (see *Polling Report* 2011). Taken together, results like these seem to indicate that the public does not view the court as above politics. Instead, the public appears to expect the justices to inject ideology into the decision-making process, to some extent, and almost half the public thinks that a nominee's views on major issues are reason to reject him/her.

If the Supreme Court's supposed reservoir of goodwill, or diffuse support, is not infinite, that may be because of the stronger impact of negative over positive information. In one study, respondents asked about Supreme Court cases they remembered mentioned three times as many decisions that they disliked or disagreed with as those that they liked (Grosskopf and Mondak 1998). Scholars speculate, too, that recent, politically polarizing confirmations such as Samuel Alito's—with ads focusing on the ideology of the candidate—will be "sticky," in the sense that they will damage institutional support and cause the next judicial selection event to be viewed in even more political than legal terms (Gibson and Caldeira 2010, 118–19, 126).

If this is the case, it's hardly surprising that Obama was unsuccessful in framing his Supreme Court nominees as jurists without political preferences. Fortunately for his record of success in Supreme Court appointments, he did not need to. Neither persuasion about their judiciousness nor compromising in his ideologically preferred choice was required: his success in the Senate was directly and direc*tive*-ly partisan. Even so, he received no popularity boost from his new justices' publicity nor party-line congratulatory backslapping for their installment. The president, who made a low priority of and put little emphasis on judicial selection, found that he got little credit for his successful judicial selections—and not a little political grief.

TRANSFORMATIVE APPOINTMENTS, BUT NOT A TRANSFORMATIVE POLITICS?

Whatever they are at the time of confirmation, Supreme Court appointees are a presidential legacy. Successful appointments can effect a policy legacy that long outlives a president or his administration and its agenda. Obama's justices, therefore, should also be assessed in terms of what they have meant, to date, to the outputs of the Supreme Court. Yet Obama has also been described as a contemporary Democrat who "has nothing much he wants from the courts" (Toobin 2009). Empathy rhetoric notwithstanding, he did not select well-known political liberals or legal academics whose writings defend judicial activism, like Cass Sunstein or Pamela Karlan. Should he enjoy the opportunity to name no more justices, what do the voting records and opinion contributions of Sotomayor and Kagan reveal about the Obama legacy on the high court?

First and foremost, both his appointees were relatively young and stand to serve for decades on the high bench. This trend toward presidents naming Supreme Court justices who can contribute for many years to constitutional lawmaking began with Reagan's efforts to reshape the federal bench and came into full flower with George W. Bush's selections. Age was, arguably, one reason why a jurist such as Judge Diane Wood of the Seventh Circuit Court of Appeals was not named after being a finalist to fill Obama's first court vacancy. In terms of longevity, Obama's two appointments can keep pace with Bush's Roberts and, potentially, endure as forces on the court for as long as Reagan's Scalia and George H. W. Bush's Thomas have done.

Of course, contributing and being a force are also matters of substance and numbers. Complementing an existing bloc is not the same as completing or creating a voting majority. Both Sotomayor and Kagan can be expected to do the former, but for the moment, the latter depends on the ability to create a jurisprudential coalition that includes the most tractable of the GOP-appointees, Anthony Kennedy. While there are only early intimations thus far in this 2010–2011 term as to the impact of Elena Kagan on her judicial colleagues, Sonia Sotomayor has a full first term of decision making whose substance can be assessed.

The so-called freshman effect is of less moment with respect to a justice with the long years of federal appellate experience that Sotomayor possessed at the time she ascended to the high court. Growing into the role and learning on the job could be expected to proceed apace for such an appointee. Early assessments of her first term bear this out and present the unsurprising finding that she has thus far been a reliably liberal justice in ideologically divided cases (Barnes 2010). Statistically, the justice with whom she agreed most often was Clinton-appointee Ruth Bader Ginsburg (Leddy 2010). Additionally, her experience as a prosecutor does not seem to have made her more sympathetic to the government in criminal cases, as some expected (Adler 2010). Such support for the rights of criminal defendants was on display in her dissent from the Court's five to four ruling in *Berghuis v. Thompkins* (2010), a decision that limited the application of the *Miranda* privilege against self-incrimination. Predictably, too, she joined the dissenting positions in the Second Amendment rights case of *McDonald v. Chicago* and in the much-discussed *Citizens United v. FEC*, which extended an expanded First Amendment protection of campaign expenditures to corporations. A January 2010 portrait of Sotomayor for the *New Yorker* (Collins 2010) noted her as a vigorous and active questioner from the bench during oral arguments who had already begun to win allies among her colleagues (Collins 2010, 55). And while early indications regarding the engagement and impact of Justice Kagan are more impressionistic at this point, she too demonstrated an immediate comfort and involvement during oral arguments—frequently asking questions focused on the legal issue at hand but with a practical twist and, perhaps more significantly, collegially playing off her fellow justices' questions, as well (Biskupic 2010).

So in what sense are Obama's Supreme Court appointments *transformative*? There is, as yet, no "Obama Court" to rival the "Roosevelt Court" or the "Reagan Court" dominated by jurists in a president's own image or constitutional vision. There also remains some question as to whether "Obama's judges are really liberals" (Toobin 2009) who will see law as a liberal policy vehicle and marshal their colleagues to make majorities to do so. To the extent that Sotomayor and Kagan *are* legal liberals *and* become effective members of their collegial and coalitional decision-making body, their efficaciousness in embodying the legacy of their appointing president is constrained by the current alignment of justices. Still, their voices and votes ensure that a more progressively pragmatic jurisprudence remains strongly represented on the Roberts Court, albeit as a minority view. Of course, a court that regularly divides into five GOP appointees and four Democratic appointees may succeed only in transforming the image of the institution into something as partisan and as suspect as any political branch of the government.

CONCLUSION

A president's ultimate impact in staffing the federal courts is difficult to assess contemporaneously. Presidents who appear to be destructively confrontational or mismanage the nomination and confirmation process are sometimes judged later to have been highly influential in shaping federal judicial personnel and their decision making. Presidents Reagan and George W. Bush come to mind here, and their impact was largely due to an ideologically transformative politics of judicial selection that paid dividends in terms of sheer numbers of appointees and/or strategically situated appointees with judicial ideologies that furthered the presidential agenda in terms of legal policy.

Under the circumstances and given the way that President Obama exploited the judicial vacancy opportunities that came his way, he had not by the start of the 112th Congress and the mid-point of his presidential term secured either the numbers or the strategically situated appointments that ensure a legacy of success in this presidential endeavor. The best that his two appointees to a Roberts-led Supreme Court could be expected to do is to keep a liberal (dissenting) lamp burning in the window, perpetuate the protracted polarization and continued debate between left and right on the high court, and await a truly transformative change in personnel. Should that balance-of-power opening occur during the 2008 to 2012 Obama term, judicial staffing difficulties lie ahead for this "directive clarifier" who has been stripped of much of his political clout and, with it, any ability to effect a transformative politics of federal judicial selection.

With this and at this point in time, Obama's lower federal-court appointees are still more difficult to assess in terms of their impact—largely due to the fact that there are so few of them to make jurisprudential or decisional inroads on courts that are heavily populated by previous Republican presidents' appointees. While it is true that before adjourning from the lame-duck session of December 2010, Senate Republicans allowed action on nineteen of Obama's nominees, some of these had been left in limbo for nearly a year after clearing the Senate Judiciary Committee. Moreover, Republican senators declined to allow processing of the confirmation of fifteen other nominees who were considered noncontroversial and who were recommended unanimously by the committee after the November 2010 election. Those nominations returned to the president, ensuring further delays in filling federal judicial seats when those individuals are renominated and a newly reconstituted Judiciary Committee holds new hearings on them in 2011 (and beyond, presumably). In addition, four other nominees approved by the committee by a party-line vote were denied full-Senate consideration in the lame-duck session. That group of federal district court candidates included Ninth Circuit Court nominee Goodwin Liu, dean of Law at the University of California at Berkeley and a noted liberal legal scholar. His potential to fill a future Supreme Court vacancy had ignited early opposition from Republican senators—including Lindsey Graham, the only Republican on the Judiciary Committee to support Obama's nomination of Sotomayor. Commenting on Liu's critical remarks about Alito's nomination by George W. Bush, Graham ominously called Liu "a bridge too far for me" (Yost 2010).

This all suggests that a presidential record of successful and efficacious lower federal-court appointments will be compromised by partisan difficulties with appointment. Given the number of key issues that were working their way through the federal courts at the start of the decade—including the president's health-care law, Arizona's immigration reform measures, gay rights, and gun control policy—Democratic activists in 2010 to 2011 were prompted to categorize the Obama judicial selection record as a veritable crisis for the administration. A less alarmist—but no less discouraging—verdict might be that, taken together, Obama's management of the selection process and the legal policy impact of his judicial selections do not foretell an "Obama judiciary" as a significant policy arm of the president's political agenda.

REFERENCES

Adler, Jonathan. 2010. "Sotomayor's First Term." *Volokh Conspiracy*, July 11.
American Prospect. 2010. "The Vacancy Crisis," November 15.
Baker, Peter. 2010. "In Court Nominees, Is Obama Looking for Empathy by Another Name?" *New York Times*, April 26.
Balz, Dan. 2009. "Empathy and Judicial Picks Rarely Mix on Capitol Hill." *Washington Post*, May 3.
Barnes, Robert. 2010. "With Justice Sotomayor, a First Year That Stands Apart." *Washington Post*, July 11.
Biskupic, Joan. 2010. "Kagan Offers Practicality to Arguments, Settles in as New Justice." *USA Today*, November 16.
Cohen Bell, Laura. 2002. *Warring Factions*. Columbus: Ohio State University Press.
Collins, Lauren. 2010. "Number Nine." *New Yorker*, January 11.
Cottrill, James, Terri Peretti, and Alan Rozzi. 2010. "The Partisan Dynamics of Supreme Court Confirmation Voting." Paper presented at the annual meeting of the American Political Science Association, Washington, DC.
Driver, Justin. 2010. "It's Alive." *New Republic*, July 18.
The Economist. 2009. "Scrutinizing Sonia: Barack Obama's Supreme Court Choice." March 30.

Edwards, George. 2010. "Strategic Assessments: Evaluating Opportunities and Strategies in the Obama Presidency." Paper presented at the annual meeting of the American Political Science Association, Washington, DC.

Epstein, Lee, and Jeffrey Segal. 2005. *Advice and Consent: The Politics of Judicial Appointments.* New York: Oxford University Press.

Farganis, Dion, and Justin Wedeking. 2010. "No Hints, No Forecasts, No Previews: Analyzing Supreme Court Nominee Evasiveness, 1955–2009." Paper presented to the annual meeting of the American Political Science Association, Washington, DC.

Gallup Organization. 2009b. "Positive Initial Reaction to Sotomayor Nomination." Poll, May 28. http://www.gallup.com/poll/118886/Positive-Initial-Reaction-Sotomayor-Nomination.aspx.

———. 2010. "Initial Reaction: 40% Positive Toward Kagan Nomination." Poll, May 11. http://www.gallup.com/poll/127913/Initial-Reaction-Positive-Toward-Kagan-Nomination.aspx.

Gibson, James, and Gregory Caldeira. 2010. *Citizens, Courts and Confirmations.* Princeton, NJ: Princeton University Press.

Green, Joshua. 2010. "Kagan vs. Sotomayor." *Atlantic*, May 11.

Grosskopf, Anke, and Jeffrey Mondak. 1998. "Do Attitudes toward Specific Supreme Court Decisions Matter?" *Political Research Quarterly* 51:633–54.

Kastellec, Jonathan P., Jeffrey R. Lax, and Justin Phillips. 2008. "Public Opinion and Senate Confirmation of Supreme Court Nominees." Paper presented at the annual meeting of the American Political Science Association, Washington, DC.

Lanier, Drew Noble, and Mark Hurwitz. 2010. "Federal Judicial Vacancies across Time: A Study of Presidential Opportunities and Missed Opportunities." Paper presented at the annual meeting of the American Political Science Association, Washington, DC.

LaPierre, Wayne. 2010. "Democracy in Peril." NRA-ILA, September 10. http://www.nraila.org/Issues/Articles/Read.aspx?id=434&issue=010.

Leddy, Daniel. 2010. "Justice Sotomayor Shows Her True Colors." *Staten Island Advance*, August 3.

Maveety, Nancy. 2009. "Low Risk and Big Ambition: The Politics of George W. Bush's Judicial Appointments." In *Ambition and Division: the Presidency of George W. Bush*, 2nd Edition, edited by Steven E. Schier. Pittsburgh: University of Pittsburgh Press.

———. 2010. "Critical Perspectives on Gender and Politics." *Politics and Gender* 6:452–65.

Nixon, David, and David Goss. 2001. "Confirmations Delay for Vacancies on the Circuit Courts of Appeals." *American Politics Research* 29:246–74.

Oliphant, James. 2009. "Conservatives Take Aim at Supreme Court Candidates." *Los Angeles Times*, May 21.

Politico. 2010. "Mitch McConnell Doubles Down Against President Obama." November 4. http://www.politico.com/news/stories/1110/44688.html.

Polling Report. 2011. "Supreme Court/Judiciary." http://www.pollingreport.com/court.htm. Accessed January 3, 2011.

Pollster.com. 2010. "US: Elena Kagan: (CNN 5/21-23). June 1. http://www.pollster .com/blogs/us_elena_kagan_cnn_52123.php?nr=1. Accessed January 3, 2011.

Scherer, Nancy, Brandon Bartels, and Amy Steigerwalt. 2008. "Sounding the Fire Alarm: The Role of IGs in the Lower Federal Court Confirmation Process." *Journal of Politics* 70:1026–39.

Senator Inhofe Press Release. 2010. "Inhofe Opposes Kagan to Supreme Court." May 10. http://inhofe.senate.gov/public/index.cfm?ContentRecord_id=838a23c8-802a -23ad-4026-e0c7020cdff5&FuseAction=PressRoom.PressReleases.

Slate. 2010. "Fill the Bench Now." February 5.

Stern, Seth. 2009a. "Nominee Hardball: GOP's Turn at Bat." *Congressional Quarterly Weekly*, July 13, 1620–21.

———. 2009b. "Sotomayor Tapped for High Court." *Congressional Quarterly Weekly*, June 1, 1274–77.

Stern, Seth, and Keith Perine. 2009. "Sotomayor a Steady Hand at Hearings." *Congressional Quarterly Weekly*, July 20, 1712–13.

Toobin, Jeffrey. 2009. "Bench Press." *New Yorker*, September 21.

Washington Post. 2009. "Washington Post-ABC News Poll." June 18–23. http:// www.washingtonpost.com/wp-srv/politics/polls/postpoll_062209.html. Accessed January 3, 2011.

White House Press Release. 2010. "Nominating Kagan: 'Her Passion for the Law Is Anything but Academic.'" May 10. http://www.whitehouse.gov/blog/2010/05/10/ nominating-kagan-her-passion-law-anything-academic.

Yost, Pete. 2010. "Obama Admin Defends Use of Courts in Terror Cases." *Deseret News*, November 18. http://www.deseretnews.com/article/700083276/Obama -admin-defends-use-of-courts-in-terror-cases.html. Accessed June 8, 2011.

POLICY LEGACIES

Chapter Nine

Obama and Social Policy

Acclamation or Alienation among Women, Minorities, and Gays?

Richard E. Matland and Andrea L. Walker

Among Obama's staunchest supporters in the 2008 election were women, minorities, and gays. These groups provided large electoral margins for Obama. African Americans provided an eye popping 91 percent margin (95–4), while gays and Latinos provided lopsided margins of 43 percent (70–27) and 36 percent (67–31). Female voters gave Obama a more modest 13 percent (56–43) victory. It is important, however, to remember that while the other groups are small proportions of the electorate, a majority of voters are women. Obama's solid thirteen-point win among women was crucial to his victory.

As groups strongly supporting Obama and traditionally aligned with the Democratic Party, these interests approached the start of the Obama administration with great enthusiasm. Two years later, however, many disappointed liberals bemoaned the unwillingness of the Obama administration to be sufficiently bold and fight for the ideals he had espoused. These liberals claimed their concerns had been "sold out" by the Obama team and he had failed to achieve the goals he had promised. Is this characterization of the Obama administration fair? Did they fail to fight for the policies they had promised to pass, selling short their loyal friends? Alternatively, did they cleverly get the maximum out of a divided Congress and use their influence over executive branch agencies to move forward on the issues these interests were concerned about?

To answer definitively is impossible. We believe political science, however, provides insight on these questions. First, it is infinitely easier to make promises on the campaign trail than to enact them once in Washington. Conditions on the ground change, and problems turn out to be far more complex. What appeared feasible on the campaign trail turns out to be far less tractable once in office (closing the prison at Guantanamo Bay is a shining example). Presidential scholars emphasize the need to push hard at the start of a term and limit the agenda because everything takes more time than one expects, and initiatives quickly become bogged down.

Second, the American legislative process is one of the most convoluted in the world. Presidents find they do not have the power to implement plans by themselves. Instead, they must accommodate demands from Congress and other players. Political scientists refer to veto players as individuals or groups that can effectively stop policy from being changed. The leaders who put our system together were skeptical of power concentrated in the hands of a few. They developed a system with a plethora of veto points. In short, it may not be for lack of trying that policies are not changed, but because veto players effectively wield power to keep actions from happening. The increasing polarization within Congress exacerbates the situation, making it harder to forge compromises that can attract votes from both sides (McCarty, Poole, and Rosenthal 2006).

Third, policy change does not only happen in prime time. The media thrives on conflict and controversy. The changes that engender the greatest amount of conflict dominate the media. Certainly, in the first two years of the Obama administration there were many epic fights. In several of those fights, those who had been core pillars of the Obama Coalition saw themselves defeated. If these high-profile issues are the only ones on which Obama supporters evaluate the administration, then some disappointment is in order.

Public policy, however, is so much more than the pitched battles on TV and on the front pages of the newspapers. While dramatic battles unfold in Congress, it is possible that slow and steady progress on a whole set of issues may be occurring out of the limelight, within federal agencies that decide how to implement policy. Through agencies' rule-making authority, the decision making of regulatory agencies, the appointment of judges and independent commissioners, and the moving of resources to new policy initiatives, substantial changes in public policy occur. Furthermore, policies that at first glance may appear not to be relevant to these groups may be highly relevant when we look more carefully. This chapter provides an overview of some of the issues discussed prominently during the first two years of the Obama administration. We also wish to illuminate issues that received substantially less publicity but may have significant impacts.

THE OBAMA ADMINISTRATION
AGENDA AND WOMEN

The fierce battle between Hillary Clinton and Barack Obama for the 2008 Democratic Party presidential nomination left a number of pundits wondering if there would be a lasting schism between Obama and those women who felt cheated out of the chance to elect the first female president. After Obama received the nomination, however, Clinton encouraged support for his campaign, emphasizing unity within the Democratic Party. In the end, Obama's electoral gender gap was similar to John Kerry's in 2004. Pointing to their contributions to his successful election, women's groups expected to see a bevy of new policy initiatives spearheaded by the administration. These expectations were not unfounded. In the 2008 Democratic Party National Platform, the party pledged to work toward legislative goals on a number of women's issues. In a section titled "Opportunity for Women," the party pledged

> When women still earn 76 cents for every dollar that a man earns, it doesn't just hurt women; it hurts families and children. We will pass the "Lilly Ledbetter" Act, which will make it easier to combat pay discrimination; we will pass the Fair Pay Act; and we will modernize the Equal Pay Act. (Democratic National Committee Platform 2008, 16)

Lilly Ledbetter was a supervisor at Goodyear Tire in Alabama from 1979 until she retired in 1998. At that time, she was the only woman working as an area manager, and despite having considerable seniority, she discovered as she neared retirement that she had the lowest pay of any area manager. She filed suit alleging gender discrimination. The Supreme Court ruled against Lilly Ledbetter's claim because she had failed to file a complaint within the 180-day statutory limitations period set by Title VII of the Civil Rights Act. To protect her rights, the court said, she would have had to sue at the point her pay started to differ from those of the other managers, despite her being unaware of the salary discrepancy. Obama and the Democrats criticized the decision roundly, vowing to change the law. The administration and Democrats in Congress came through on the campaign promise, with passage of the Act occurring immediately after taking over in January 2009. The bill had failed in the 110th Congress (2007–2009) due to Republican opposition in the Senate; but with strengthened Democratic majorities in both Houses of Congress, the bill was introduced in early January and quickly passed both houses. The final version amended the 1964 Civil Rights Act by making discriminatory compensation practices unlawful each time an employee is paid, regardless of when the initial discriminatory decision was made. The Lilly Ledbetter Act was the very first bill that Obama signed into law on January 29, 2009. Women's groups, including the National Organization for Women (NOW) and the American Association of University Women (AAUW) responded positively to Obama's role in passing the law, lauding its passage in press releases. Their praise was tempered by calls for more legislation, including passage of the Paycheck Fairness Act.

The Economic Stimulus Package

Prior to taking office, the administration started preparing for what would become one of their signature issues, the American Recovery and Reinvestment Act of 2009, commonly referred to as the 2009 stimulus law. Early discussions emphasized the need for shovel-ready projects and substantial infrastructure investments. This emphasis concerned women's groups. A *New York Times* op-ed by Linda Hirshman criticized Obama's early plans for the stimulus bill, arguing that it increased jobs almost exclusively in traditionally male industries such as construction and energy production (Hirschman 2008). Women's groups lobbied both Congress and the administration to include a balance in the stimulus package, emphasizing health and education in addition to infrastructure and new energy. These efforts led to a number of provisions in the package providing funding for agencies and programs that benefited economic and civil equality for women.

As of 2008, 63.6 percent of women in the workforce have children below the age of six and 77.5 percent have children between the ages of six and seventeen (US Department of Labor 2009). The 2009 stimulus law provided an additional $2 billion toward the Child Care and Development Fund (CCDF) to fund childcare services for low-income families with children who require care while parents are working, looking for employment, or pursuing education. Additionally, the stimulus law provided over $2 billion dollars to expand Head Start and Early Head Start programs. All told, the economic stimulus package provided an additional $13.3 billion through the Department of Health and Human Services to childcare and community-support services including adoption and foster-care assistance and meals for the elderly and persons with disabilities. Overall, an estimated 42 percent of the jobs created by the stimulus law were expected to go to women (Romer and Berenstein 2009, 9).

In addition to job creation and programs that assist working women with families, the 2009 stimulus law aimed to improve civil and social equality for women. The stimulus package provided $225 million dollars to the Office on Violence Against Women to distribute to programs that help develop and fund state, local, tribal, and nonprofit entities that respond to violence against women (Justice.gov 2010). It provided funding to enforce worker-protection laws and regulations, including those banning discrimination and requiring federal contractors and subcontractors to take affirmative steps to ensure equal opportunities. Yet another provision increased the budget of the National Institutes of Health (NIH), helping to ensure women's health research initiatives.

After the adjustments, women's organizations gave their strong endorsement to the Obama administration. "Asked whether the Obama administration was more friendly to feminist advocacy groups than the last administration, Kim Gandy [President of the National Organization of Women] laughed and replied, 'Are you kidding? The difference is like night and day'" (Beyerstein 2009).

The Health-Care Reform Battle

Relationships with women's groups soon started to fray. The reality of limited political might and the need to make hard, even excruciating, compromises is seen in the debate around national health reform. Universal health coverage has been a goal of Democratic administrations for sixty years. With large majorities in both houses and universal health care as one of the cornerstones of Obama's presidential campaign, the administration vowed to take on the issue of health care.

While health care might not seem immediately to be a women's issue, when you evaluate the policy through a gendered lens, we see women are especially affected. Women are more likely than men to receive medical coverage through a federal program—approximately one in ten women are covered under Medicaid, and more than half of the Medicare recipients are women (Kaiser Family Foundation 2010b). As a group, women are more likely than men to have reduced access to medical care and prescription drugs due to the cost (CDC.gov 2009). Women as a group live longer than men (5.1 years) and have to deal with a series of serious health problems as they age. As one author notes, "Women get sicker, men die quicker" (Tolleson-Rinehart 2005). As such, access to health care matters to women. Additionally, women have primary responsibility for child and prenatal care and are affected uniquely by policies concerning birth control and abortion. Insurance coverage is of special concern because women are more likely to be covered under a spouse's insurance or employed in the types of positions and at small businesses that do not provide insurance.

The core of the health-care reform always was clear: extensive cost-control measures, a mandate requiring individuals to buy insurance, and a requirement that businesses provide either insurance or pay a tax to subsidize the purchase of individual health care. Much of the debate surrounded two issues: (1) Could a proposal for expanded coverage win bipartisan support? and (2) Would there be a public option, that is, the opportunity to buy health insurance from a government source? In the end, however, the abortion coverage debate almost derailed the bill.

In the early stages of the debate, both opponents and supporters of abortion rights agreed to maintain the status quo. At the time, the status quo was the Hyde Amendment, which prohibits federal money, provided through Medicaid or Medicare, from being spent on elective abortions. Federal money can be used only when the life of the woman is endangered or when the pregnancy results from rape or incest. The original House and Senate bills came out of committees applying the same restrictions to all insurance plans that received federal subsidies. Any insurance company providing abortion coverage would need to distinguish between the funds they got from the government and money paid in premiums. They could use premiums paid to cover abortions but not government money.

With no Republican support for the bill, those in the Democratic Party who were willing to oppose the bill, such as pro-life Democrats, became more powerful. In the House, the Stupak-Pitts Amendment replaced the original language. Sponsored by Bart Stupak (D-MI) and Joe Pitts (R-PA), the amendment extended the Hyde regulations by prohibiting the use of federal funds to pay for insurance plans that included coverage for elective abortions even if insurance premiums paid for the actual services. Although the House bill passed with the Stupak-Pitts Amendment, the Senate version allowed individuals to choose plans that included abortion coverage, as long as the costs were paid separately through private money. President Obama ultimately favored the Senate plan and released a similar proposal shortly before a bipartisan health summit with Congressional party leaders.

While there was a solid majority for the proposal in both houses, Senate rules allow any senator to filibuster a proposal they desire to stop. To shut down a filibuster and force a vote on a bill requires sixty votes for cloture. The initial proposal had passed by the thinnest of margins in the Senate, sixty to forty with no Republican votes. The Democratic intention in early January 2010 was to develop a joint proposal and pass it in both houses of Congress. In a stunning upset, however, in mid-January, Republican Scott Brown won the Massachusetts Senate seat formerly held by the recently deceased Edward Kennedy. The loss of the sixty-seat majority effectively derailed the Democrat's plans to put together a cross-house compromise. To avoid bringing the bill up in the Senate, Democrats developed an intricate plan. If the House passed the Senate's version of the health-care bill, it would go directly to the president for a signature and become law. The House would then immediately pass an additional bill with revisions to the Senate's proposal that would go to the Senate to ensure the most important adjustments demanded by the House were adopted. These revisions could only deal with financing and not change policies. This meant the bill could be taken up under "reconciliation" rules and passed with a simple majority of fifty-one votes.

A number of pro-life Democratic representatives, including Rep. Stupak, initially refused to vote for the Senate version of the bill, arguing that it did not include sufficiently strict language prohibiting the use of federal funds for abortions. As a concession to these Democrats, Obama agreed to sign an executive order assuring no federal funds would be used for elective abortions. With this guarantee, Stupak and nine of his Democratic colleagues switched and agreed to vote for the bill; it passed in the House 219 to 212. As promised, Obama signed the executive order the day after the health-care bill, officially titled the Patient Protection and Affordable Care Act, was signed into law on March 23, 2010.

Women's groups had widely varying reactions to the health-care law. Despite fighting the abortion restrictions at every opportunity, Planned Parenthood lobbied extensively for final passage of the bill and called it "the greatest single legislative advancement for women's health since Medicare and Medicaid were signed into law nearly 45 years ago" (Planned Parenthood Action Center 2010). The Commonwealth Fund estimated that 15 million uninsured women would receive federal or state subsidies toward coverage while an additional 14.5 million women would have improved coverage under the health-care law (Collins et al. 2010). On the other side, NOW went from commending the administration for bringing "real change for women" in its first one hundred days to condemning Obama for "negotiating health care reform on the backs of women" and describing "his commitment to reproductive health care shaky at best" (O'Neill 2010a, 2010b; Gandy 2009). NOW criticized the bill on a number of fronts including permitting gender-rating, which allows the imposition of higher premiums on women, and age-rating, which would disproportionately affect older women who have fewer savings and smaller pensions than older men (O'Neill 2010a).

Beyond the Economic Stimulus and Health Care

The ability of veto players to stymie legislation within the American system is seen starkly in the last-ditch attempt to pass the Paycheck Fairness Act at the end of the 111th Congress. NOW and AAUW described the bill as a crucial "next step" when Obama signed the Lilly Ledbetter Act. The Paycheck Fairness Act guaranteed that employers could not retaliate against workers who disclosed their wages to other employees; placed sex discrimination in pay on equal legal footing with racial discrimination in pay; and provided outreach and education by the Department of Labor. Supporters saw the bill as crucial to effectively implementing the Lilly Ledbetter law. The House of Representatives, where a simple majority is sufficient to push legislation through, passed the bill simultaneously with the Lilly Ledbetter Fair Pay Act on January 9, 2009, by a 256 to 163 vote. Over the next twenty-one months, however, the bill was not brought up in the Senate. Instead, the bill was brought up in the lame-duck session after the 2010 elections in the hopes that the Democrats would be able to muster the sixty votes needed to invoke cloture and pass the legislation. In the end, on November 17th, two weeks after the midterm elections, a cloture motion to allow a vote on the bill failed by two votes, fifty-eight to forty-one. Democrats (including Independents Lieberman and Sanders) voted fifty-eight to one for the bill, while Republicans voted unanimously against the bill, zero to forty (Alaska Senator Lisa Murkowski was not in DC and hence, did not vote on the bill). The bill had won ten Republican votes in the House, and the supporters of the bill had hoped they would be able to get at least two of the four female Republican senators (Murkowski, Collins, Snowe, and Hutchison) to vote for the bill. None voted for cloture, effectively dooming the bill.

Other policies were changed through actions that did not require legislative approval. In his first month in office, Obama rescinded the Global Gag Rule. The Global Gag Rule, instituted in 1984 by Ronald Reagan, prohibited family-planning assistance funding to any foreign nongovernmental organizations that provided abortion-related information or services, even when those services were legal in their own countries and were funded with their own money. This policy has been through several changes, as Democratic administrations rescind it when they come into office, and Republican administrations reestablish it when they come into office. Another international initiative spearheaded by Secretary of State Clinton emphasized the importance of women's rights. Clinton regularly set aside time to speak to women's groups when on official State Department visits and consistently highlighted the interest of the United States in seeing countries adopt programs to empower women.

The Obama administration has also brought a large number of women into high-level administrative positions. Obviously, the nominations of two women, Sonia Sotomayor and Elena Kagan, to the Supreme Court bench have been important advances. Beyond this, however, the Obama administration has brought a whole group of women into office. Women have been nominated to 145 of the 447 top administrative positions requiring Senate confirmation (excluding US attorneys, US marshals, and ambassadors) (*Washington Post* 2010). At 32.4 percent, this represents a high water mark for women in top federal administrative positions.

THE OBAMA ADMINISTRATION AND
THE LGBT COMMUNITY

On the day President Obama was sworn into office, the Human Rights Campaign (HRC)—the largest civil rights organization for lesbian, gay, bisexual, and transgendered (LGBT) equality in the country—announced, "Today's inauguration represents a paradigm shift. The pendulum has swung away from the anti-gay forces and toward a new president and vice president who acknowledge our equality" (Solmonese 2009a). Despite the HRC's initial endorsement of President Obama, the LGBT community has been frustrated at times with the administration. While seen as sympathetic, there was a perception of a lack of commitment. During the campaign, Obama specifically addressed six issues of concern to the LGBT community: (1) opposing a constitutional ban on same-sex marriages, (2) supporting federal rights for LGBT couples and supporting civil unions (but not gay marriage), (3) fighting AIDS worldwide, (4) expanding hate crimes statutes to include homophobic hate crimes, (5) fighting workplace discrimination, and (6) repealing "Don't Ask, Don't Tell" (DADT). Going into the final month of 2010, most gay activists characterized the administration's actions as too little, too slow, and mostly symbolic. Once the DADT repeal passed, however, support from the LBGT community picked up significantly.

The first of Obama's campaign promises was relatively easy to keep, as there has been no serious consideration of a Constitutional amendment banning same-sex marriage from Congress's side. The second pledge Obama gave to the LGBT community was to support federal rights for LGBT couples. He followed through via two initiatives. In April 2010, a presidential memo instructed the Department of Health and Human Services to create and implement rules requiring hospitals participating in Medicare or Medicaid (which is virtually all hospitals) to respect the rights of patients in designating visitors. Hospitals were not to deny visitation rights on the basis of race, color, national origin, religion, sex, sexual orientation, gender identity, or disability. The sentiment of Richard Socarides, adviser to President Clinton on gay rights issues, was typical: "While the memorandum on its own did not grant any new rights, it did draw attention to the very real and tragic situations many gays and lesbians face when a partner is hospitalized" (Stolberg 2010). Nevertheless, some gay rights advocates accused Obama of taking credit for a practice already implemented in most hospitals.

In June 2010, President Obama used a presidential memo to direct the heads of executive departments and federal agencies to extend a limited set of benefits to same-sex domestic couples. These benefits included guaranteeing the children of same-sex domestic couples the same federal childcare subsidies and services granted to children of married couples, naming the partner of a retiree as a person with an insurable interest, and expanding the family and medical leave policies to meet the needs of a domestic partner or their children. These benefits were extensions of existing laws, and Obama himself noted that "legislative action is necessary to provide full equality to LGBT Federal employees" (Federal Register 2010).

A commitment to fighting AIDS worldwide is the third promise and is of concern well beyond the LGBT community. The HIV/AIDS epidemic affects multiple populations both nationwide and internationally and is relevant to health policy, foreign policy, and development aid. Since taking office, Obama has taken several incremental steps. First, he removed the HIV entry ban for immigrants attempting to enter the United States. Under the ban, individuals with HIV were inadmissible to the United States. Second, the administration supported passage of the Ryan White HIV/AIDS Treatment Extension Act of 2009, which extends federal funding to state and local programs for health and support services for people with AIDS and HIV. Finally, the administration has consistently increased federal funding for AIDS treatment and prevention. The proposed budget for 2011 included an estimated $27.2 billion for combined domestic and global HIV/AIDS activities, a 5 percent increase from the previous year (Kaiser Family Foundation 2010c).

The fourth campaign promise was to support legislation that would include sexual orientation and gender identity under the federal hate crime laws. According to the FBI uniform crime statistics, 16.7 percent of the hate crimes reported stemmed from a sexual-orientation bias (Justice.gov 2009). Such legislation passed as an amendment to the Defense Reauthorization in the Senate in 2007 but was removed during conference committee negotiations when President Bush threatened to veto the bill if it included the hate crimes amendment. In 2009, with strengthened Democratic control of Congress and Obama in the White House, the legislation was approved. President Obama signed the Matthew Shepard and James Byrd, Jr. Act into law on October 28, 2009, as part of the National Defense Authorization Act for fiscal year 2010. The act provides funding for localities that do not have the money to cover the investigations of bias-motivated crimes, gives the attorney general's office greater jurisdiction in the investigation of hate crimes, and requires the FBI to record statistics about crimes against people based on their gender and gender identity. While the Obama administration did not initiate the legislation, his promise to sign it, as opposed to President Bush's threat to veto it, shows a distinctly different set of policy positions toward the LGBT community. Response to the passage of the hate crimes law was overwhelmingly positive—gay rights groups hailed it as a "victory," "a historic milestone in the inevitable march towards equality," and "a landmark step" (Keisling 2009; Solmonese 2009b; Barrios 2009).

The fifth promise was to fight workplace discrimination and ensure equal rights. In the 110th Congress (2007–2009), the Employment Non-Discrimination Act was sponsored by Barney Frank and passed the House but died in the Senate. In the 111th Congress, Frank reintroduced an expanded version of the Employment Non-Discrimination Act that included transgendered individuals in addition to the lesbian, gay, and bisexual community. While both the House and Senate introduced legislation to add sexual orientation and gender identity to employment non-discrimination statutes, and committees held hearings in both Houses, the bills never made it out of committee. Obama supported the bills, having his representatives strongly endorse them in committee hearings (Ishimaru 2009), but the bills did not move forward despite large numbers of sponsors (203 in the House and 45 in the Senate). In the end, the bill was killed both by the inclusion of transgendered individuals and by the rush at the end of the lame-duck session as Democrats worked to pass higher-priority legislation before relinquishing control to the Republicans.

An important reason the Employment Non-Discrimination Act did not come up for a vote was the decision by the House leadership to concentrate on ending the military's Don't Ask, Don't Tell (DADT) policy before taking up the employment legislation (Berman 2010). Established during the Clinton administration, DADT had three primary aspects: (1) limiting the armed services from asking or investigating the sexual orientation of those serving or applying to serve in the military; (2) prohibiting openly gay, lesbian, or bisexual individuals from serving in the military; and (3) discharging anyone who claims to be homosexual or anyone found engaging in or having the intent to engage in homosexual activities. Obama had endorsed the elimination of DADT during the campaign, but several groups in the LGBT community were dissatisfied with the pace of progress and accused the Obama administration of dragging its feet. This perception was exacerbated in September 2010 after a federal court judge ruled DADT unconstitutional, saying it violated individuals' First- and Fifth-Amendment rights. The Obama administration's Justice Department, however, asked the court's ruling not be enforced. Many gay activists felt the Obama administration's actions represented an attempt to backpedal on the promise to repeal DADT.

In January 2009, in his first state of the union address, Obama reiterated, "This year, I will work with Congress and our military to finally repeal the law that denies gay Americans the right to serve the country they love because of who they are. It is the right thing to do" (Obama 2010a). Despite his promises, work to repeal DADT moved slowly. The House voted to repeal the law pending a Department of Defense study on the potential effects of the repeal on the military when it included the Murphy Amendment to the 2011 National Defense Authorization Act in May 2010. The House vote was 234 to 194, largely along party lines. A similar amendment was held up in the Senate through a successful filibuster threat led by Senator John McCain (R-AZ). The Senate leadership agreed to wait until the Department of Defense released the findings of their report. That report, released on December 1, 2010, revealed overall support for eliminating DADT in the services and characterized the risk of repeal to military effectiveness as low. Senate Majority Leader Harry

Reid (D-NV) moved the Defense appropriation bill, including the repeal of DADT, to the floor; yet on December 9, a cloture vote failed by fifty-seven to forty along party lines with two exceptions (Collins of Maine [R] voted yes and Manchin of West Virginia [D] voted no).

Some Republicans claimed they were for repealing DADT and would vote for it if it was not tied to the appropriation bill. This assertion was met with great skepticism by forces that had fought for the repeal. Nevertheless, while it appeared the issue was dead, a stand-alone bill to repeal DADT was introduced in the House, in coordination with supporters in the Senate, by Representative Patrick Murphy (D-PA). Murphy was an Iraqi war veteran who had introduced the original amendment that had been voted down. He introduced the bill in the House and within a week it had passed 250 to 175, a noticeably bigger margin than previously, and was sent to the Senate. On the crucial procedural vote to allow the bill to come up for a final vote, the Senate voted sixty-three to thirty-three to proceed, three votes more than were needed. On December 18, on final passage the vote was sixty-five to thirty-one. In the end, eight Republicans voted for repeal—six moderates and, surprisingly, two conservatives who had been steadfast against it. Ultimately, the push from the LGBT community was important but having both Defense Secretary Robert Gates and the head of the Joint Chiefs of Staff Michael Mullen pushing for repeal was almost certainly crucial to successful passage. Furthermore, the aforementioned court case did have a political impact, as the military argued it was far better that Congress repeal DADT and allow the military to prepare an orderly change in the policy rather than allow a court to impose the change from outside. President Obama applauded the repeal stating, "By ending 'Don't Ask, Don't Tell,' no longer will our nation be denied the service of thousands of patriotic Americans forced to leave the military, despite years of exemplary performance, because they happen to be gay. . . . And no longer will many thousands more be asked to live a lie in order to serve the country they love (Obama 2010b)."

An issue over which the LGBT community had been considerably less happy with the Obama administration is the Defense of Marriage Act (DOMA). DOMA was passed in the mid-1990s; it strictly defined marriage as being between a man and a woman. It specifically noted that states were not required to recognize same-sex marriages performed in other states. The Obama administration has argued for repeal of the act, but there is limited support in Congress for such action. Nevertheless, the American system provides multiple access points for political interests. With legislative solutions unlikely, the LGBT community has turned to the courts.

Legal cases have questioned the constitutionality of DOMA. The Constitution states that "full faith and credit shall be given in each state to the public acts, records, and judicial proceedings of every other state." There is a question whether Congress can empower states to ignore legal (same-sex) marriages performed in another state. Furthermore, the act has been challenged as violating the equal-protection clause, as it identifies one class of citizens, homosexuals, and denies them an equal right to marry. In June 2009, the Justice Department presented a legal brief defending DOMA in a case challenging the law in California. The initial brief was met by an angry backlash from the gay community. The administration argued they had a constitutional obligation to defend the act even if they were actively urging its repeal. In a later case filed in Massachusetts, federal judge Joseph Tauro, a Nixon appointee, issued a ruling in July 2010 that the act violates the due-process clause, is an overextension of Congressional powers, and is therefore unconstitutional.

While the initial decision by the Obama administration was to appeal this ruling and keep fighting against the court's decision, the administration reversed itself in February 2011, when they announced they would no longer defend the Defense of Marriage Act in court. DOMA is presently being defended by a law firm hired by the Republican leadership in the House of Representatives. The final decision on the law's legality remains to be decided.

Until the repeal of DADT, activists within the LGBT community had a decidedly mixed view of the Obama administration. At a forum to discuss LGBT issues in DC in the summer of 2010, the gay activists on the panel primarily gave the administration grades of Cs or Ds (Jones 2010). On the one hand, the administration has provided support for several important policies. Obama could reasonably claim that of his six campaign pledges, he had achieved four. Furthermore, President Obama has appointed a record number of openly gay officials to his administration (Jones 2010). Critics, however, pointed out that most of the victories the Obama administration had scored were low-hanging fruit. While Obama failed to win on the Employment Non-Discrimination Act, with the repeal of DADT at the very end of the 111th Congress and dropping the administration's defense of DOMA, the Obama administration can legitimately claim to have delivered on a large number of issues of importance to the LGBT community. While the LGBT community did not reach all of its desired goals, it did win a large number of battles by taking advantage of the most gay-friendly political constellation in history that existed between 2009 and 2011.

THE OBAMA ADMINISTRATION AND RACE

President Obama's election was a momentous occasion for race relations in the United States. Yet one of the strategies Obama used to succeed was a conscious policy of downplaying race-related matters. As such, there were few policies in the campaign explicitly targeted to the black community. Policy messages, when delivered, often were intended for a broader audience than just the African American community, such as Obama's pronouncements concerning the importance of families and fathers in the black community, or the willingness to continue supporting faith-based initiatives. On the other side, Obama did make a clear promise to the Latino community that immigration would be taken up by his administration.

While there were a limited number of issues explicitly dealing with uniquely black concerns, civil-rights interest organizations have expanded the field of issues they are concerned about. The National Association for the Advancement of Colored People (NAACP) congressional scorecard for the first year of the 111th Congress includes a number of issues that could be seen as peripheral to their traditional interests in civil rights. Of the twenty-one votes the NAACP used to rate senators, four were on health care, four were on economic issues, five were appointment questions (including Sotomayor to the Supreme Court, Clinton as secretary of state, and Robert Groves as census director), three dealt with issues in the city of Washington, DC, two dealt with hate crimes, one dealt with education, one dealt with housing, and finally, one dealt with the Lilly Ledbetter anti-wage discrimination bill (NAACP 2010).

As with women, racially relevant policies are embedded in other legislation. Black and Latino communities were among the hardest hit by the economic recession. The unemployment rate as of November 2010 among whites was 8.9 percent compared to 16.0 percent for blacks and 13.2 percent for Hispanics (US Department of Labor 2010). The 2009 stimulus bill was strongly supported by minority groups hoping to escape the recession, and it did provide some services that went disproportionately to minority communities.

While the economic stimulus produced opportunities for minority businesses to increase their contracts, the impacts were limited. The Kirwan Institute for the Study of Race and Ethnicity at the Ohio State University tracked contracts for the first twenty months of the stimulus (February 2009 to September 2010) and found significant underrepresentation of minority businesses among those receiving contracts. Although black- and Latino-owned businesses make up 7.1 and 8.3 percent of US businesses respectively, of the stimulus law federal contract funds, only 2.6 percent have gone to black-owned businesses and 4.3 percent to Latino-owned businesses.

The 2009 stimulus law increased the budgets of a number of social services programs including the Temporary Assistance for Needy Families (TANF) program, the Supplemental Nutrition Assistance Program (SNAP), the Special Supplemental Nutrition Program for Women, Infants, and Children (WIC), and an increase to states for the CCDF program. As blacks and Latinos are more likely to live in poverty than whites, much of the additional funding to these programs would potentially aid minorities. In 2009, 25.8 percent of blacks and 25.3 percent of Latinos lived below the poverty line, while 9.4 percent of non-Hispanic whites lived in poverty (DeNavas-Walt et al. 2010).

Like the stimulus law, the health-care law also provided an opportunity for the administration to aid minority communities. Although people of color represent less than a third of the population, they make up over 50 percent of the uninsured (Kaiser Family Foundation 2010a). Many of the provisions in the bill should improve access to health care for minority populations. First, the bill expands Medicaid to everyone below 133 percent of the poverty line. Under the expanded criteria, nearly six out of every ten newly eligible, nonelderly, and previously uninsured individuals are minorities. Under the stimulus law, funding for community health centers in medically underserved areas was expanded by $2 billion. Over 50 percent of the people who receive medical services from community health centers are people of color. The health-care law expands this by increasing funding to community health centers and the National Health Service Corps by $11 billion. Second, the health-care program attempts to address explicit disparities between the health-care quality received by minorities compared to whites by establishing a national quality-improvement plan that tracks national indicators of quality health-care services by race and ethnicity. Additional features of the health-care law increase funding for medical research for a number of chronic illnesses, such as diabetes and heart disease, which affect Latino and African American communities at exceptionally high rates.

One of the central issues facing the administration was dealing with immigration. In their 2008 national platform, Democrats underscored their commitment "to pursuing tough, practical, and humane immigration reform in the first year of the next administration" (Democratic National Platform 2008, 45). Despite this promise, immigration was set aside to deal with health-care reform and efforts to reverse the deepening recession. While the administration consistently assured supporters it intended to deal with immigration, it was skeptical enough of the chance of success to continue delaying a push on the policy. Immigration also affected the debate over health-care reform, as controversy erupted over coverage for immigrants. Further complicating the immigration debate was Arizona's August 2009 passage of strict measures to enable local police to enforce immigration laws. This action drew national support and ire and ultimately led to federal involvement. The administration's condemnation of Arizona's law reflects their position that the law is counterproductive, impinges on federal perogative, and impedes true immigration reform.

In September 2010, the Comprehensive Immigration Reform Act of 2010 was finally introduced by Senator Menendez of New Jersey. While the comprehensive reform act never got serious consideration, the Democrats in

Congress and in the Obama administration continued to hope they would be able to get the Development, Relief, and Education for Alien Minors (DREAM) Act passed. This act dealt with one part of the immigration problem, namely children who came to the country illegally with their parents at a young age. The act proposed if someone came to the country before they were sixteen, presently are between the ages of twelve and thirty-four, have been here continuously for at least five years, and have graduated from high school or received a GED, they can obtain permanent residency status if they complete two years of college or two years of service in the military. The hope was these individuals, who were here through no fault of their own, would be a sympathetic group that could receive broad support. The groups traditionally on the side of providing the opportunity for illegal immigrants to earn citizenship supported the bill, but it also was supported by the military. They saw it as a chance to ensure they could meet their goals for recruitment and maintain an all-volunteer force during the war.

During the lame-duck session of Congress, the Obama administration pushed Congress to pass the DREAM Act. The bill passed in the House on December 8, 2010, by a vote of 216 to 198 with 8 Republicans, including 3 Cuban Americans from Florida, voting for the bill and 38 Democrats breaking party ranks and voting against the bill. The bill then moved over to the Senate, where once again the Democrats faced the dilemma of needing sixty votes to win a cloture vote. In theory, the votes should have been there, as several Republican members of the Senate had voted for the DREAM Act in the past, including former sponsors John McCain and Orrin Hatch, and there were still fifty-eight Democrats in the Senate. When the bill came up, however, the Republicans largely held firm against, and only three voted for the bill (Bennett, Lugar, and Murkowski). This was insufficient, when five Democrats (Baucus, Tester, Hagan, Nelson, and Pryor) failed to support the bill. The defeat of the DREAM Act, by fifty-five to forty-one, was an extremely bitter pill for the supporters of immigration reform. It will be interesting to see whether Latinos will view the last-minute push by the Democrats to try to pass the bill as a sincere effort and blame "obstructionist Republicans" in the Senate, or as a case of Obama and the Democrats letting the issue go far too long before taking action.

Other issues have stirred the interest of the black and Latino communities. Education is one of the primary areas of racial disparity in the country. The administration's efforts toward addressing this disparity have met significant criticism from African American organizations. The cornerstone of the administration's education policy has been the Race to the Top (RttT) program, under which states compete for part of $4.35 billion allotted by the Department of Education for comprehensive K–12 education reforms. RttT, as well as other education initiatives by the administration, has been criticized by multiple civil rights groups including the Urban League, the NAACP, and the Rainbow PUSH Coalition. The main objection to Race to the Top has been that the program only provides funding to states that win federal grants. In their criticism, they highlight the fact that only 3 percent of black students and less than 1 percent of Latino students would benefit from the first round of the competition (Lawyers Committee for Civil Rights under Law 2010). In addition to Race to the Top Obama expanded federal funding for Pell Grants. Pell Grants provide low-income undergraduate and graduate students with need-based grants to help pay for their education. African American and Hispanic students are among the largest beneficiaries of the Pell Grant Program. In 2004, 46.8 percent of African American and 36.9 percent of Latino undergraduate students were recipients of Pell Grants. The increased funding is a reflection of President Obama's campaign promise to provide opportunities for all students to afford college. In addition to increasing the number of grants to accommodate an additional 820,000 students, the program changed the repayment requirements to help increase the manageability of student-loan debt. Expansion of the Pell Grants was, however, short lived as there were significant cuts made to the Pell Grant program in conjunction with budget negotiations with the Republican House in the next year.

Another concern is the criminal justice system, which has long been criticized as biased in its treatment of minorities. The passage of the Fair Sentencing Act of 2010 noticeably reduced the sentencing disparities in drug-related convictions. Previously, there was a significant difference in the sentences received based on the type of cocaine an individual possessed. African American and Latino males are more likely to be arrested for possession of crack-cocaine, which entailed stiffer sentences, while whites are more likely to possess powder cocaine, which entailed lighter sentences. As Senator Durbin (D-IL), the bill's sponsor, argued, "The sentencing disparity between crack and powder cocaine has contributed to the imprisonment of African Americans at six times the rate of whites and to the United States' position as the world's leader in incarcerations." The new legislation eliminates the five-year mandatory minimum for possession and reduces the disparity in sentences between crack and powder cocaine.

In terms of administrative appointments, of the 447 positions tracked in the *Washington Post*'s (2010) evaluation of senior appointments requiring Senate approval, 55 positions (12 percent) have gone to African Americans and 40 positions (9 percent) have gone to Latinos. One of the most crucial boards dealing with issues of civil rights is the Equal Employment Opportunity Commission (EEOC). The EEOC hears workplace discrimination cases and rules on whether corporations have violated an individual's right to equal employment. The commission also does extensive work with companies working to assist firms in complying with equal-employment rules. Obama nominated three people to the EEOC, and while all were approved by the Senate committee with jurisdiction over them, they were held up by a single unidentified Republican senator (a senator can put a hold on any position he or she desires keeping it from coming to the floor). To get around this, President Obama made recess appointments. These are appointments the president makes when Congress is in recess. They allow the individuals to serve in their positions until the end of the next Congress. The appointments included Jacqueline Berrien, who left her position as the associate director of the NAACP legal defense and educational fund to become the EEOC chair; Chai Feldblum a lawyer and activist in the LGBT community who had previously worked for the American Civil Liberties Union and in Congress, where she helped draft the Americans with Disabilities Act and the Employment Non-Discrimination Act legislation Congress was considering; and Victoria Lipnic, who had worked as US assistant secretary of labor in the Bush administration. These recess appointments made it possible for the commission to reach the quorum needed to hold hearings and enact significant rule changes. In response to these appointments, several business blogs predicted a significantly more aggressive EEOC with tougher enforcement of existing laws and investigations of businesses.

CONCLUSION

The relationships between Obama and women, minorities, and gays have gone through several phases in a short time. The euphoria of the campaign victory was followed by strong support for Obama as initial victories were won after eight years of being stymied by the Bush administration. These were followed, however, by periods of frustration. The Obama administration succeeded in getting a series of significant bills adopted, with health-care being the most significant in terms of redefining the social contract in America. Putting together the votes to pass health care, however, often required painful compromises. Obama accepted restrictions on abortion that could not possibly have been imagined by women's groups when the process of health-care reform started. Furthermore, as Obama insisted on a congressionally led approach, the process of putting together proposals took an inordinate amount of time. With health care sucking all the oxygen out of the room, other issues never made it to the top of the pile.

As relationships between Democrats and Republicans grew increasingly tense, it became harder and harder to get policies passed. The House of Representatives has a strongly majoritarian set of rules allowing even narrow majorities to force issues to a vote and win; the Senate has very different procedures, where it is far harder to force issues through. Most prominent of these is the filibuster threat. The Republican minority in the Senate showed a greater willingness to use the threat in the 111th Congress than ever has been exhibited before. To overcome this threat required sixty votes, which was often difficult and sometimes impossible. If the Senate had the same rules as the House in the last two months of 2010, there is no question that there would have been an avalanche of bills passed, including many of the legislative desires of women, minorities, and gays. Nevertheless, there were gains, especially for gays. The repeal of DADT represents a sea change in policy and indicates that there has been a huge cultural change in America in the acceptance of gays.

With the Republican takeover of the House of Representatives and the smaller Democratic majority in the Senate, it is unlikely that the bills and issues that failed to make it through in the last weeks of the 111th Congress will reappear any time soon. When one looks at the Human Rights Campaign (HRC) ratings for the top three members of the Democratic House leadership for the 110th and 111th Congresses, they score an average of 95 percent on the HRC's "critical votes" scorecard. The three top members of the Republican leadership that took over at the start of the 112th Congress averaged 0 percent on the same votes. It does not take a crystal ball to predict that with that constellation, the Employment Non-Discrimination Act is effectively dead for the foreseeable future. It will be interesting to see whether women and Latinos will regard their near victories as proof that Obama sincerely tried to reward the groups who helped him win his presidency, or if they will feel disillusioned by the failure of the president and the Democratic Party to deliver when they had majorities. Certainly there is frustration, but not unlike the Clinton supporters who voted en masse for Obama after threatening to sit out the election, two years of seeing the Republican majority operate in the House is likely to be more than enough to get these forces solidly behind Obama's reelection campaign.

While there is unlikely to be significant legislative gains for these groups, there are still many avenues open to pursue their policy interests. Lower-level courts have declared DOMA unconstitutional. The LGBT interest organizations will continue to aggressively pursue this case, independent of the political constellation in Congress. Also note that those cases may be argued in front of judges newly appointed by Obama, probably increasing the likelihood of sympathetic rulings.

Furthermore, executive branch agencies will become points of increased attention. While women, minorities, and gays have not won all they had hoped for during the first two years of the Obama presidency, there have been significant victories. Now, given the central role of the bureaucracy in implementing policy, along with the inhospitable environment Congress currently provides, it is likely actions will switch over to lobbying the executive branch, as the bureaucracy must develop and implement programs in line with the policies Congress has adopted. As the Obama forces continue to control the executive branch agencies, and as representation of minorities, gays, and women are at or near record highs in most departments, the likelihood of having sympathetic allies on the inside seems high.

REFERENCES

Barrios, Jarrett. 2009. "Statement from Jarrett Barrios on Passage of the Matthew Shepard and James Byrd, Jr. Hate Crimes Prevention Act." October 28. http://www.glaad.org/Page.aspx?pid=1047. Accessed October 20, 2010.

Berman, Russell. 2010. "Gay Groups' Top Priority Crowded Off Schedule." *The Hill*, September 15. http://thehill.com/homenews/house/118811-gay-groups-top-priority-crowded-out. Accessed December 12, 2010.

Beyerstein, Linda. 2009. "Women's Groups See Success in Stimulus." *Washington Independent*, January 29. http://washingtonindependent.com/27846/women-and-the-stimulus. Accessed October 4, 2010.

CDC.gov. 2009. "Reduced Access to Medical Care Due to Cost." National Center for Health Statistics, CDC/NCHS, National Health Interview Survey. http://www.cdc.gov/nchs/health_policy/reduced_access_due_to_cost.htm. Accessed October 12, 2010.

Collins, Sara R., Sheila D. Rustgi, and Michelle M. Doty. 2010. "Realizing Health Reform's Potential." *The Commonwealth Fund*, July 2010. http://www.commonwealthfund.org/~/media/Files/Publications/Issue%20Brief/2010/Jul/1429_Collins_Women_ACA_brief.pdf. Accessed October 12, 2010.

Democratic National Committee Platform. 2008. "Renewing America's Promise," August 25. http://www.democrats.org/about/party_platform.

DeNavas-Walt, Carmen, Bernadette D. Proctor, and Jessica C. Smith. 2010. "Income, Poverty, and Health Insurance Coverage in the United States: 2009." *US Census Bureau, Current Population Reports, P60-238*. Washington, DC: US Government Printing Office.

Federal Register. 2010. "Extension of Benefits to Same-Sex Domestic Partners of Federal Employees." Memorandum of June 2, Federal Register 75 (109).

Gandy, Kim. 2009. "President Obama's First 100 Days Bring Real Change for Women." http://www.now.org/press/04-09/04-28.html. Accessed Oct. 4, 2010.

Hirschman, Linda. 2008. "Where Are the New Jobs for Women?" *New York Times*, December 9.

Ishimaru, Stuart J. 2009. "Statement of Stuart J. Ishimaru, Acting Chairman, US Equal Employment Opportunity Commission before the Committee on Education and Labor." Before the Committee on Education and Labor, US House of Representatives, September 23. http://edlabor.house.gov/documents/111/pdf/testimony/ 20090923StuartIshimaruTestimony.pdf. Accessed November 20, 2010.

Jones, Michael A. 2010. "President Obama Appoints a Record Number of Gay Officials." http://gayrights.change.org/blog/view/president_obama_appoints_a _record_number_of_gay_officials. Accessed December 4, 2010.

Justice.gov. 2009. "Hate Crime Statistics, 2008." US Department of Justice—Federal Bureau of Investigation, November, Table 1.

———. 2010. "Justice Recovery Act Programs." http://www.justice.gov/recovery/ rec-prog.html#ovw. Accessed September 15, 2010.

Kaiser Family Foundation. 2010a. "Health Reform and Communities of Color: Implications for Racial and Ethnic Health Disparities," September. http://www.kff.org/ healthreform/8016.cfm

———. 2010b. "Health Reform: Implications for Women's Access to Coverage and Care." Focus on Health Care Reform, December. http://www.kff.org/womens health/upload/7987.pdf. Accessed December 15, 2010.

———. 2010c. "HIV/AIDS Policy Fact Sheet," February. http://www.kff.org/ hivaids/3029.cfm

Keisling, Mara. 2009. "VICTORY: Hate Crimes Bill Signed into Law First Federal Law to Protect Transgender People." October 28. http://transequality.org/ hatecrimes.html. Accessed October 15, 2010.

Kirwan Institute. 2010. "Race Recovery Index." October. www.kirwaninstitute.org. Accessed November 23, 2010.

Lawyers Committee for Civil Rights under Law. 2010. "Framework for Providing All Students an Opportunity to Learn through Reauthorization of the Elementary and Secondary Education Act." https://docs.google.com/fileview?id=0B36JWPh1Vf r7OTc3ZWI0NDctODVlMC00N2I2LWExNmItZmIyZGEzY2E5Yzlm&hl=en& authkey=CNG2pP4E. Accessed December 7, 2010.

McCarty, Nolan, Keith T. Poole, and Howard Rosenthal. 2006. *Polarized America: The Dance of Ideology and Unequal Riches.* Cambridge, MA: MIT Press.

National Association for the Advancement of Colored People (NAACP). 2010. "How Congress Voted: 111th Congress, First Session, 2009." http://naacp.3cdn .net/9f85753565313cddc1_orm6vdkts.pdf. Accessed December 7, 2010.

Obama, Barack. 2010a. "State of the Union Address." January 27, 2010.

———. 2010b. "Statement by the President on the Senate Vote on the National Defense Authorization Act." The White House, Office of the Press Secretary, December 9. http://www.whitehouse.gov/the-press-office/2010/12/09/statement-president-senate -vote-national-defense-authorization-act. Accessed December 13, 2010.

O'Neill, Terry. 2010a. "Health Care Reform Victory Comes with Tragic Setback for Women's Rights." NOW Press Release, March 21. http://www.now.org/press/03 -10/03-21b.html. Accessed October 9, 2010.

———. 2010b. "President Obama Breaks Faith with Women." NOW Press Release, March 21. http://www.now.org/press/03-10/03-21a.html. Accessed October 7, 2010.

Planned Parenthood Action Center. 2010. "Health Care Reform and Women." http://www.plannedparenthoodaction.org/positions/health-care-reform-76.htm. Accessed October 8, 2010.

Romer, Christina, and Jared Berenstein, 2009. "The Job Impact of the American Recovery and Reinvestment Plan." January 9. http://www.politico.com/pdf/PPM116_obamadoc.pdf. Accessed October 20, 2010.

Solmonese, Joe. 2009a. "Human Rights Campaign Statement on Inauguration of Barack Obama and Joe Biden." HRC Press Statement, January 20. http://www.hrc.org/news/11949.htm. Accessed October 12, 2010.

———. 2009b. "President Barack Obama Signs Hate Crimes Legislation Into Law." October 28. http://www.hrc.org/issues/hate_crimes/13699.htm. Accessed October 15, 2010.

Stolberg, Sheryl Gay. 2010. "Obama Widens Medical Rights for Gay Partners." *New York Times*, April 15.

Tolleson-Rinehart, Sue. 2005. "'Women Get Sicker; Men Die Quicker': Gender, Health Politics, and Health Policy." In *Gender and American Politics: Women, Men, and the Political Process*, edited by Sue Tolleson-Rinehart and Jyl J. Josephson. Armonk, NY: M. E. Sharpe.

US Department of Labor, Bureau of Labor Statistics. 2009. "Quick Stats on Women Workers, 2009." *Employment and Earnings, 2009 Annual Averages and the Monthly Labor Review*, November 2009. http://www.dol.gov/wb/stats/main.htm. Accessed September 25, 2010.

———. 2010. "The Employment Situation—November 2010." News Release, December 3. http://www.bls.gov/news.release/pdf/empsit.pdf. Accessed November 25, 2010.

Washington Post. 2010. "Head Count: Tracking Obama's Appointments." http://projects.washingtonpost.com/2009/federal-appointments. Accessed December 15, 2010.

Chapter Ten

The Obama Administration and the Great Recession

Relief, Recovery, and Reform Revisited

Raymond Tatalovich

President Obama inherited the Great Recession, which began in December of 2007, but the economy was further devastated by the financial "crisis" that began in September 2008 when the Wall Street firm Lehman Brothers went bankrupt. In October 2007, the Dow Jones Industrial Average (DJIA) peaked at 14,164.53, but after Lehman's bankruptcy on September 15, 2008, the DJIA closed below 11,000. Two years later, the DJIA was still struggling to reach 11,000. This chapter discusses the economic policies adopted by the Obama administration to cope with the worst economic downturn since the Great Depression.

The National Bureau of Economic Research (NBER) tracks the ups and downs of the business cycle. One indicator of recession is when the gross domestic product (GDP), which measures the value of the total output of goods and services for the American economy, declines for two consecutive quarters. The Great Recession "technically" ended in June 2009 and, according to the NBER, its 18-month duration surpassed all previous post-War recessions: 2001 (8 months); 1990–1991 (8 months); 1981–1982 (16 months); 1980 (6 months); 1973–1975 (16 months); 1969–1970 (11 months); 1960–1961 (10 months); 1957–1958 (8 months); 1953–1954 (10 months); 1948–1949 (11 months); 1945 (8 months). For all 12 post-War recessions, the average duration was 10.8 months, so the Great Recession deserves its name.

But length does not indicate its full impact on the American economy. More important is the fact that unemployment has remained very high despite our moving into the expansionary phase of the business cycle. In January 2009, the unemployment rate stood at 7.7 percent, but it increased to 9.4 percent in May 2009 and stayed above 9 percent through the end of 2010. During October through December 2009, the unemployment rate hit 10 percent. The unemployment rate is a "lagging" indicator of the macro-economy, meaning that the jobless rate will not fall immediately after the recovery phase begins but will only improve gradually. One year after the Great Recession ended, the unemployment rate was 9.5 percent, as compared to the lower rates one year following the recessions of 2001 through 2002 (6.0 percent), 1990 through 1991 (7.4 percent), and 1981 through 1982 (8.3 percent). Although the 1981 through 1982 recession was the worst since the 1930s, with unemployment above 10 percent from September 1981 through June 1982, eventually the jobless rate fell to 8.3 percent by December 1983 and to 7.3 percent one year later. The problem is that the 9-percent-plus jobless rates have now lasted twenty months, the worst performance in the post-War era.

To combat the Great Depression, President Franklin D. Roosevelt promised Americans a New Deal. The three building blocks of the New Deal were *relief* for the unemployed, *recovery* from the economic downturn, and *reform* of capitalism to prevent the abuses that aggravated the economic crisis. One way to understand the economic challenges that President Obama faced is to analyze his policies in terms of FDR's three New Deal planks: relief, recovery, and reform.

RELIEF

When President Roosevelt assumed office, there were no federal welfare programs, and a program of "unemployment compensation" had to await the enactment of the Social Security Act of 1935. One provision established a federal-state program jointly financed through federal and state employer payroll taxes by which the unemployed receive federal funds temporarily until the economic downturn ends and jobs become more plentiful. With "unemployment compensation" now established in every state, the only debate in Congress involves how long these "temporary" grants to unemployed individuals should last. In most states, the unemployed receive benefits for twenty-six weeks.

During periods of high unemployment, an extended benefits program continues jobless benefits for up to thirteen additional weeks after the regular unemployment insurance benefits are exhausted. But that still may not be enough, so Congress often enacts "temporary" programs to extend unemployment benefits during economic recessions. Emergency Unemployment Compensation (EUC) is a fully federal-funded program that provides benefits to individuals who have exhausted their regular state benefits. Created on June 30, 2008, it has been modified several times, most recently when President Obama signed the Unemployment Compensation Extension Act of 2010. The 2010 act extended the expiration date of EUC until November 30, 2010.

Since the Great Recession began, total jobless benefits were calculated to be $319 billion, of which $109 billion was the federal share, but the economic downturn forced thirty-one states to borrow $41 billion in loans in order to finance their unemployment compensation systems (Luhby 2010).

But the "relief" given to financial institutions and the "bailouts" of banks and the auto industry cost much more. In September 2008, the Bush administration and the Federal Reserve Board asked Congress to establish a $700 billion fund to purchase "toxic" (or risky) mortgage loans and hopefully stabilize the financial industry. At first, Congress resisted but on October 3, 2008, it established the Troubled Asset Relief Program (TARP). Most TARP funds were allocated through the Capital Purchase Program to directly strengthen the capital reserves of banks. The problem is that a huge number of home mortgages, many sound but too many held by people with dubious credit ratings who could not really afford them, were "packaged" with credit-worthy mortgages and sold through a variety of ingenious investment vehicles. Nobody really knew the true market value of those bundled financial securities, so banks were worried about their own capital reserves and therefore became unwilling to issue loans. The entire credit market began to seize up, so the federal government intervened with infusions of capital for those struggling banks and financial institutions.

By all accounts, TARP was a success story, and ultimately taxpayers would only lose a fraction of the original $700 billion (Gross 2010). But more controversial was the use of TARP funds by the Obama administration to "bail out" General Motors (GM), General Motors Acceptance Corporation (or GMAC, which provides auto loans, mortgages, and insurance), the Chrysler Corporation, and various auto-parts suppliers that got $80 billion, probably half of which (if not more) will be a loss to the taxpayers. But the bailout of GM hardly inspired confidence among investors. The Obama administration favored the pro-Democratic United Auto Workers (UAW) at the expense of GM bondholders who had loaned GM $27 billion but received only 10 percent of the company. For its $50 billion bailout, the federal government got 61 percent of GM, and for the $20 billion that GM owed the employee health trust, the UAW got 17.5 percent of the GM stock plus $2.5 billion in cash and $6.5 billion in preferred stock with a 9 percent dividend. The Obama administration also forced the closure of 1,650 GM dealerships (Modica and John 2010).

In April 2010, the CEO of GM wrote a column declaring, "We're paying back—in full, with interest, years ahead of schedule—loans made to help fund the new GM" (Whitacre 2010). What he did not say but what came to light later was that GM repaid the $5.8 billion loan using a TARP-funded escrow account and not its own revenues. GM owed $4.7 billion to the United

States and $1.1 billion to the governments of Ontario and Canada. But Neil Barofsky, the special inspector general for TARP, reported to Congress that GM paid its government loan mostly with TARP funds because, in fact, the automaker lost $3.4 billion in the fourth quarter of 2009 and has yet to earn a profit. The Obama administration took issue with this revelation, but it was reported that the Special Inspector General's Office had "a letter from General Motors requesting that they take the money out of escrow and pay the other debt down. And the money in the escrow was clearly TARP funding" (*Washington Times* 2010).

The next GM success story that came under intense scrutiny was its November 2010 initial public offering (IPO) of GM stock at a price of $33 per share. President Obama called it "a major milestone" since it occurred so soon after GM's forced restructuring. But the Treasury Department paid about $40 billion for its 61 percent ownership in GM (or 912 million shares of GM stock), and since its IPO sale of 358.5 million shares produced $11.8 billion of revenue, the taxpayers already lost about $10 billion on the initial sale of GM stock. To recover its entire investment, the remaining 554 shares would have to be sold for nearly $51 per share. It was reported that the Obama administration sold the GM stock at below the break-even price so that the US government could quickly exit the automobile business (Mitchell 2010). Obviously the jury is out in terms of GM's ability to survive and whether the US government will recover its investments in GM. One certain thing is that the public was opposed to the GM bailout. A March 2009 Gallup poll found 59 percent opposed the federal loans to bailout GM and Chrysler (Gallup 2009), and in May 2009, Rasmussen reported that 67 percent were opposed to the GM bailout (Rasmussen Reports 2009).

RECOVERY

The Obama administration fully embraced Keynesian economics to shape policies aimed at ending the Great Recession. Keynesians are disciples of John Maynard Keynes, the British economist who advocated a revolutionary new theory in 1936 to combat the Great Depression. During an economic downturn, consumers will inherently spend less (because many are unemployed) and businesses will cease investing (because consumer spending is down), so the only way to reignite economic growth is for the government to increase its spending. Keynes preferred massive government spending and defended deficits as essential during an economic downturn (though he anticipated budgetary surpluses would result when economic recovery took hold). There have been serious challenges to the precepts of Keynesian economics by "monetarists" who believe that a stable money supply is more important and by "supply-side" economists who favor using tax cuts as incentives for work, investment, and savings.

But there were no monetarists or supply-siders in the Obama administration. Nor were there appointees with substantial corporate-executive experience. "Obviously, the Obama administration doesn't stack up with previous Republican administrations but they don't even stack up with previous Democratic administrations," observed Stephen Hess of the Brookings Institution (Kuhn 2010). Moreover, the anti-business rhetoric of the Obama administration was arguably the worst since the early days of the New Deal (Langley 2009; Dorning 2010).

Keynesian Advisers

The chief economic spokesman for the Obama administration was Lawrence H. Summers, director of the National Economic Council (NEC), who had been the president of Harvard University. The NEC was established by President Bill Clinton to coordinate economic policy, and its director was supposed to be an "honest broker" of contending ideas. But observers questioned whether Summers could act in that role given his intellect and energy (Heilemann 2009). Summers also had been treasury secretary during the last years of the Clinton administration, and he got involved with the Obama campaign when the financial "crisis" hit in September 2008. Summers wanted to be treasury secretary but settled for the NEC, though from the very start his "prickly personality" clashed with other economic advisers (Calmes 2009).

Besides Summers, four other economic advisers met daily with President Obama (Lizza 2009). Christina D. Romer was appointed chairwoman of the Council of Economic Advisers (CEA). An economic historian at the University of California at Berkeley, Romer concluded that Franklin D. Roosevelt had not pulled the nation out of the Great Depression because FDR spent too little (Lizza 2009). The constraint of budgeting usually makes the director of the Office of Management and Budget (OMB) more tightfisted, and that attitude has characterized Obama's appointee, Peter R. Orszag. Orszag urged the appointment of the eighteen-member National Commission on Fiscal Responsibility and Reform (to reduce the debt) and gradually shifted more budgetary responsibility from Congress to the executive branch (Bai 2010). Probably the most liberal member of this economic team is Jared Bernstein, chief economist and economic policy adviser to Vice President Joe Biden. Bernstein is a critic of free-trade agreements and growing income inequality who worked at the Economic Policy Institute (EPI), a think tank with ties to organized labor.

For treasury secretary, Obama nominated Timothy F. Geithner, onetime protégé of Lawrence Summers, who spent two years with the International Monetary Fund and became president of the Federal Reserve Bank of New York in 2003. His reputation as a "consensus-builder" appealed to Obama, as did his hands-on experience working with former treasury secretary Henry Paulson during the financial "crisis" of 2008 (Heilemann 2009). But Wall Street became alarmed when Geithner delayed in announcing his plans to rescue failing banks, and the lack of specifics in his speech of February 2009 caused the DJIA to drop almost 20 percent. Economists surveyed by the *Wall Street Journal* gave Geithner lower marks compared to Paulson (Izzo 2009). But despite the barrage of criticism, Geithner had the unflinching support of President Obama, and Geithner continues to head the Treasury.

President Obama also named a Presidential Economic Recovery Advisory Board (PERAB) of outside economists, corporate CEOs, and labor officials chaired by former Fed chairman Paul Volcker. Volcker is highly respected. As Fed chairman under President Reagan, Volcker brought down the rate of inflation and paved the way for long-term price stability. But it was reported that Volcker had reservations about Obama's economic team and that NEC director Summers had frustrated his desire to be more involved (Heileman 2009).

Just before the disastrous midterm elections, CEA chair Romer and OMB director Orszag resigned, then Summers departed at the end of the year, and Bernstein resigned in April 2011. Romer was succeeded by Austan D. Goolsbee, another decidedly liberal economist from the University of Chicago who was a member of Obama's CEA, and Orszag's successor was Jack Lew, who had been OMB director under President Clinton. In January 2011, the president named Gene B. Sperling to succeed Summers as head of the NEC. Like Lew, Sperling had occupied the same position in the Clinton administration.

Economic Stimulus

At a December 2009 meeting of his economic advisers, Romer bluntly declared, "Well, Mr. President, this is your 'holy-shit moment.' It's worse than we thought" (Lizza 2009). The consensus among Obama's economic advisers was that a stimulus package was needed; the only debate was on its size. Romer ran computer simulations of the probable impact of different-sized stimulus packages, and her analysis indicated that the optimal fiscal stimulus should be more than $1.2 trillion (Lizza 2009). "The Job Impact of the American Recovery and Reinvestment Plan" was a report drafted by Romer in collaboration with Jared Bernstein. It argued that a massive economic stimulus package would keep unemployment under 8 percent, but without it, unemployment would rise to 9 percent in 2010. But unemployment almost reached 10 percent during 2009 and 2010, and during the lead-up to the 2010 congressional elections, Republicans repeatedly pointed to that memo as conclusive evidence that the stimulus package was a complete failure.

The collective feeling among Obama's economic advisers was that Congress would resist a $1.2 trillion price tag, so Summers only presented two economic scenarios to President Obama, one based on a $550 billion stimulus versus an $890 billion stimulus. NEC director Summers was pivotal in these Obama administration deliberations, and he persuaded his colleagues that a larger stimulus was needed (Heilemann 2009). Ultimately, Congress approved $787 billion (the congressional struggle is discussed by Bertram Johnson in this volume). "People can quibble on the details," said CEA member Austan Goolsbee. "Republicans say that it should have had even more tax cuts. Others say that it should have had more infrastructure spending. But what's not under dispute is that in the first four weeks of the presidency, we passed the biggest stimulus package in American history" (Heilemann 2009).

The 1,073-page American Recovery and Reinvestment Act of 2009 (ARRA) is commonly known as the economic stimulus package. It passed the House of Representatives on a 246 to 183 vote, with not one Republican voting yes; it was approved by the Senate on a 61 to 37 vote with only three Republicans voting with the majority. The final bill included $507 billion in spending programs and $282 billion in tax relief, including tax credits of $400 per individual and $800 per family (within specified income limits), and a one-time payment of $250 to recipients of Social Security and federal disability payments. But congressional Republicans charged that the stimulus package was badly designed to fuel economic recovery, was a spending bonanza by Democrats on their favorite constituencies, and would saddle future generations with massive debt. "Yesterday the Senate cast one of the most expensive votes in history," said Senator Mitch McConnell (R-KY), the Senate minority leader. "Americans are wondering how we're going to pay for all this" (Herszenhorn and Hulse 2009).

The outrage among Republicans, conservative pundits, and the public at large might never have materialized had the expenditure of $787 billion for a stimulus package helped bring down the unemployment rate. It did not. President Obama signed the stimulus legislation in February, but four months later, unemployment was 9.4 percent, a twenty-five-year high, when the economic models derived by White House economists had promised an 8 percent unemployment rate. "At the time, our forecast seemed reasonable," observed Jared Bernstein. "Now, looking back, it was clearly too optimistic" (Blackledge and Apuzzo 2009). What followed was a highly publicized debate in the mass media, with Democratic-aligned economists defending the stimulus and Republican-leaning economists on the offensive. The Democratic argument was that the stimulus prevented the Great Recession from deteriorating into another depression, and the Obama administration alleged that the $787 billion "saved" jobs that otherwise would have been lost to the economic downturn. The credibility of that assertion was quickly demolished because the Bureau of Labor Statistics (BLS), which collects monthly data on unemployment, does not monitor the number of jobs "saved" in calculating the overall jobless rate or the growth in total employment.

Princeton economist Alan S. Blinder, a committed Keynesian whom President Clinton appointed vice chairman of the Federal Reserve Board, and Mark Zandi, chief economist with Moody's Analytics, authored a highly publicized study defending the Obama administration (Blinder and Zandi 2010). Based on their economic simulation of the total macroeconomic effects of the government's entire policy response, they concluded that "its effects on real GDP, jobs, and inflation are huge, and probably averted what could have been called Great Depression 2.0. For example, we estimate that, without the government's response, GDP in 2010 would be about 11.5% lower, payroll employment would be less by some 8½ million jobs, and the nation would now be experiencing deflation." The simulation models they employed looked at "two components—one attributable to the fiscal stimulus and the other attributable to financial-market policies such as TARP, the bank stress tests and the Fed's quantitative easing—we estimate that the latter was substantially more powerful than the former. Nonetheless, the effects of the fiscal stimulus alone appear very substantial, raising 2010 real GDP by about 3.4%, holding the unemployment rate about 1½ percentage points lower, and adding almost 2.7 million jobs to U.S. payrolls" (Blinder and Zandi 2010).

Their assertions did not go unchallenged. A strong dissent was penned by Lawrence B. Lindsey, who was director of the NEC for President George W. Bush. Lindsey wrote the Blinder/Zandi simulation model was similar to the economic model generated by Romer/Bernstein in early 2009 when they advocated a massive stimulus package (Lindsey 2010). Although the Romer/Bernstein model was criticized because it predicted that unemployment would peak below 8 percent in the middle of 2009 and decline to 7.5 percent by the end of 2010, their defenders rebutted that Romer and Bernstein had underestimated the severity of the Great Recession. That is true, admits Lindsey, who then compared the actual unemployment rate against three variations of the Romer/Bernstein economic simulation model: their original 2009 forecast beginning with a 7.5 percent unemployment rate; a second forecast beginning with a higher 8.2 percent unemployment rate (the actual rate in February 2009); and a third forecast beginning with a much higher 9.3 percent unemployment rate. Long-term, the predicted unemployment rates based on the 7.5 percent and 8.2 percent jobless rates were lower than the actual unemployment rate, whereas the forecast based on the 9.3 percent unemployment rate showed "the actual performance of the economy is almost exactly what Romer and Bernstein said would happen if we had done nothing, rather than passing the $800 billion package." In other words, the stimulus had no effect on joblessness.

Lindsey was not alone in his criticism that public works projects, though entirely defensible because they are permanent infrastructure improvements, cannot be implemented in the short term. The claim by the Obama administration that a multitude of "shovel-ready" projects could be launched was pure propaganda. "I think we can get a lot of work done fast," said president-elect Obama in December 2008 after meeting with governors. "All of them have projects that are shovel ready, that are going to require us to get the money out the door." But that was not exactly true, as President Obama admitted in an ill-timed interview two weeks before the disastrous midterm elections. "But the problem is," said President Obama, "that spending it out takes a long time, because there's really nothing—there's no such thing as shovel-ready projects" (Shear 2010). As soon as the stimulus package was enacted, economic columnist Robert Samuelson favored a huge stimulus but called this legislation "a colossal waste" because "partisan politics ran rough-shod over pragmatic economic policy." His primary concern is that too little money is spent in the short term, particularly on infrastructure. "Big projects take time. They're included in the stimulus because Obama and Democratic congressional leaders are using the legislation to advance many political priorities instead of just spurring the economy" (Samuelson 2009). Nearly two years later in October 2010, the *Economist* editorialized that "infrastructure may have been doomed to mediocrity from the start" because "even on the broadest definition of the term, infrastructure got $150 billion, under a fifth of the total" and moreover, "hopes for an immediate jolt of activity were misplaced" since by October 2009 "even the fastest [highway and transit] programmes . . . had seen work begin on just $14.3 billion-worth of projects" (*The Economist* 2010).

The other big point of contention about the $787 billion stimulus (which actually grew to $862 billion) focused on the Keynesian "multiplier" effect. In his October 2010 interview, President Obama said that for every dollar spent on infrastructure "you get a dollar and a half in stimulus because there are ripple effects from building roads or bridges or sewer lines" (Shear 2010). What President Obama said was precisely what the original Romer/Bernstein economic simulation model had assumed, namely that the "multiplier" was 1.5 insofar as each $1.00 in federal spending would yield an additional $1.50 in private spending. Hard to believe, argued Harvard economist Robert J.

Barro, who studied the "multiplier" effects that resulted from the massive defense spending (which equaled 44 percent of GDP) from 1943 to 1944 at the height of World War II. He found the wartime "multiplier" to be 0.8, and the addition of huge federal expenditures during World War I, the Korean War, and the Vietnam War only confirms its validity. If anything, Barro believes that "the war-based multiplier of 0.8 substantially overstates the multiplier that applies to peacetime government purchases" (Barro 2009).

Apparently Blinder, Zandi, and Lindsey all agree that two small stimulus programs actually worked as intended. One was the "Cash for Clunkers" program, which ran from July 1 to November 1, 2009, and allowed consumers to trade in their older-model vehicles for $4,500 in rebates toward more fuel-efficient new cars. Under President Bush, the Housing and Economic Recovery Act of 2008 established a $7,500 tax credit for first-time home-buyers, and that program was expanded by ARRA during 2009 and further extended to apply to home purchases made before May 2010 by the Worker, Homeownership, and Business Assistance Act of 2009. Both put cash directly into the hands of consumers who had to spend it in a limited time period.

In his February 2010 budget message to Congress, President Obama requested $266 billion in "temporary recovery measures," but Congress failed to act, unable to block a GOP filibuster in the Senate. But now there were growing concerns about deficit spending, given the $1.4 trillion budget deficit for FY09, and polls also showed that the public did not think the first $787 billion stimulus package worked. To encourage Congress to act, Vice President Joe Biden and President Obama kicked off a six-week campaign in June (the so-called "Recovery Summer") to defend the stimulus and publicize the "shovel-ready" construction jobs. In Columbus, Ohio, President Obama reminded the crowd that a year ago "America was losing 700,000 jobs per month" and "we knew if we failed to act, then things were only going to get much worse" (Montgomery 2010). Republicans were not convinced, and House Minority Leader John A. Boehner (R-OH) sent President Obama a letter signed by one hundred economists explaining that 95 percent of the jobs created in May were temporary employees hired by the US Census (Montgomery 2010).

The proclaimed "Recovery Summer" never materialized. Instead, some economists warned that the United States could fall into a "double-dip" recession given the multitude of nagging economic problems. Putting aside the arcane debates among economists, it will take months if not years to assess the true impact of the stimulus on the economy. In the short term, however, what matters politically is public opinion, and politically the stimulus was a disaster. The $862 billion coupled with the $700 billion in financial bailouts (not to mention the $1 trillion health-care legislation) yielded deficits of unprecedented size. The FY09 federal budget was 12 percent of GDP, whereas the previous post-war high was President Reagan's 1983 budget deficit that equaled 6 percent of GDP. And for the first time in the post-war era, deficits and the national debt became salient important issues in the public mind. By mid-2010, there was a global debate over whether governments should continue with fiscal stimulus or begin budgetary retrenchments. The Obama administration continued to argue for stimulus, but Great Britain, Germany, and Europe have generally shifted their priorities to deficit reduction. Europe was shocked by a "sovereign debt crisis" that threatened bankruptcy for Greece, Ireland, Portugal, and Spain. Here, a June *Wall Street Journal/NBC News* survey asked people which statement reflected their views: (1) The president and Congress should worry more about boosting the economy even if it means bigger deficits; or (2) The president and Congress should worry more about keeping the deficit down even if it means the economy will take longer to recover. The latter was chosen by 63 percent of respondents (Hilsenrath 2010).

The midterm congressional elections were a massive repudiation of Obama. The Republicans won control of the House of Representatives with the largest pickup of seats (63) since 1938 and added 6 more senators, in addition to winning 6 more governorships and a total of 720 more state legislative seats since the start of 2009. Exit polls showed that the economy was the most important issue on Election Day. The 62 percent citing the economy was twice as large as the percentages of respondents who mentioned three other issues (health care, Afghanistan, and immigration). Only 14 percent said their family's financial situation was better than two years ago, the lowest response since 1984. Looking ahead, however, more voters told exit pollsters that the highest priority should be reducing the deficit (39 percent), compared to the 37 percent who favored spending more to create jobs or the 18 percent who wanted to cut taxes (Bowman 2010).

The Democratic leadership of the 111th Congress reconvened a lame-duck session in November and December 2010 to address much unfinished business. One immediate problem was that the tax cuts enacted under President George W. Bush in 2001 and 2003 were scheduled to expire on January 1, 2011. Not only would that raise taxes on the middle class and on upper-income individuals, but this deadline forced legislators on the horns of a dilemma: raising taxes is not an appropriate Keynesian remedy in the midst of a recession, but on the other hand, cutting taxes would also worsen the already bad forecasts of future annual deficits of over \$1 trillion. The Democratic congressional leadership deliberately refused to allow a vote on the politically perilous question of extending the Bush tax cuts before the midterm election, but immediately thereafter, the GOP went on the offensive. Republicans were united in supporting an extension for all taxpayers, whereas the Democratic leadership favored middle-class cuts but would let the tax rates rise for individuals making more than $200,000 a year and married couples making more than $250,000 a year. Republicans countered that many high-income taxpayers were small businesses and farmers, and taxing them would hurt job creation and economic recovery.

For his part, President Obama began by sending mixed signals, being opposed to upper-income tax cuts but willing to compromise. One compromise would be to temporarily extend all the Bush tax cuts rather than make them permanent, as demanded by many Republicans (Ohlemacher 2010). In early December, the Senate failed to obtain the necessary sixty votes (for cloture) to prevent a filibuster on two Democratic-sponsored bills, one to extend the Bush tax cuts for households earning less than $250,000 and another to extend those tax cuts for incomes under $1 million. Then President Obama signaled his readiness to accept a temporary extension for the entire package of Bush tax cuts, so long as the congressional Republicans agreed to another extension of unemployment benefits for two million chronically jobless Americans (the last temporary extension ended on November 30, 2010). In a deal negotiated between President Obama and Mitch McConnell (the GOP Senate minority leader), they agreed to extend all Bush tax cuts for two years, fix the estate tax at 35 percent after exempting estates under $5 million (or $10 million for a couple), reduce the employees portion of the Social Security payroll tax from 6.2 percent to 4.2 percent for one year, continue tax breaks designed to encourage business investment, and extend unemployment benefits for another thirteen months. The Congressional Budget Office estimated its total cost to be $858 billion over the next ten years, of which $675.2 billion was the price tag for extending all the Bush tax cuts (Yadron and O'Connor 2010). Liberal Democrats believed that Obama capitulated to Republican demands, but former president Bill Clinton publicly endorsed the deal and urged its enactment. It was, passing the Senate on an 81 to 19 vote and then the House by a 277 to 148 vote.

Another item of unfinished business was the failure of the 111th Congress to pass a budget for FY11, which began October 1, 2010. With the preliminary estimate of the FY11 budget deficit at $1.416 trillion, the Democrats did not want to give the Republicans a powerful campaign issue to exploit. And this deficit follows the record-high deficits of $1.416 trillion in FY09 and $1.294 trillion in FY10 (Bater 2010). The lame-duck House of Representatives approved a "CR" (continuing resolution, a temporary extension of current funding levels) to spend during FY11 at the same rate as FY10. But the Senate unveiled a 1,924-page, $1.108 trillion omnibus spending bill (consisting of twelve appropriations bills) that included $8 billion of "earmarks" (projects targeted to specific states) and funding to implement Obama's health-care reforms. Minority Leader Mitch McConnell (R-KY), who recently announced his support for a GOP-proposed two-year ban on all earmarks, was opposed and, given the reality of a GOP filibuster, Majority Leader Harry Reid (D-NV) pulled this bill from the Senate floor. Then Reid and McConnell agreed on a continuing resolution to fund the federal government only into early March, which was enacted, meaning that the 112th Congress had to revisit the FY11 budget battles.

Backed by a unified GOP majority in the House of Representatives, Speaker John Boehner (R-OH) forced the Senate Democrats and the White House into an agreement that cut $33.8 billion from the budget submitted by President Obama to fund FY11. Since Obama had proposed to increase FY11 spending by $40 billion, total outlays were actually reduced by $78.5 billion.

REFORM

On July 21, 2010, President Obama signed a 2,323-page Wall Street Reform and Consumer Protection Act, the largest financial overhaul since the New Deal reforms of the Great Depression. Although the cornerstone of efforts to reform the Wall Street abuses that precipitated the financial crisis of 2008, it did not receive bipartisan support in Congress. It passed the Senate on a sixty to thirty-nine vote, with only three Republicans in favor. It grants new regulatory authority to the Securities and Exchange Commission, creates a Financial Services Oversight Council and a new Consumer Financial Protection Bureau, and vastly augments the authority of the Federal Reserve Board.

The "Volcker Rule" (named for the former Fed chairman who served under President Reagan) sought to limit speculative investments by commercial banks. Previous legislation enacted during the New Deal prohibited commercial banks (with conventional savings and checking accounts) from engaging in risky investments, but that law was repealed. Critics argued that repeal of the Glass-Steagall Act of 1933, which separated commercial and investment banking, under President Clinton was a major cause of the financial meltdown. Thus, some legislators advocated a strict separation, but this legislation grants the Fed wide discretion in determining whether or not investments are too speculative and risky. What precipitated the financial "crisis" of 2008 were the bankruptcy of Lehman Brothers and the threatened bankruptcy of Bear Stearns, Merrill Lynch, Goldman Sachs, and Morgan Stanley, all huge investment banks. Except for Lehman, the federal government intervened with funds to bail out those financial institutions, fearing their bankruptcy would destabilize the entire financial industry and lead to smaller bank failures across the country and a complete breakdown in consumer confidence.

The phrase "too-big-to-fail" meant that, unlike small businesses that face bankruptcy if they undertake risky investments, the failure of mega-banks would have such a disruptive impact on the national economy that the federal government would have to intervene to prevent that from happening. This double standard of bankruptcies for small business but bailouts for big banks was very unpopular with the American people, and political leaders drew a sharp distinction between the integrity of Main Street and the sleazy practices on Wall Street. Some members of Congress opposed to bailouts wanted any failing business to go into the normal bankruptcy proceedings. One provision would have levied a fee on mega-banks to create a $150 billion fund to dismantle a failing mega-bank, but it was stripped from the compromise bill. The final law allows regulators to use public funds for bailouts and then seek to recover those funds afterward. This provision was attacked by Republicans. "Instead of enacting real reform to modernize our financial regulatory structure and protect taxpayers, the Democrats have delivered a bill that enshrines 'too big to fail,' hurts our Main Street companies, kills jobs, and places taxpayers at risk for trillions of dollars in bailouts authorized under this bill," said Congressman Spencer Bachus (R-AL), the ranking GOP member of the House Financial Services Committee (Orol 2010).

The financial "crisis" worsened because the housing "bubble" burst after interest rates began to rise and millions of individuals quickly learned that they could not afford their mortgage loans, which brought about a huge increase in home foreclosures. The new law requires lenders to verify that borrowers can afford their mortgage payment; otherwise, the lender can be penalized for "irresponsible lending." But another big loophole is that the law does not apply to Fannie Mae and Freddie Mac (which were primarily responsible for the spread of "subprime" mortgages that banks awarded to people with bad credit ratings). These two government-backed private lending companies that tolerated, or even encouraged, bad lending practices were not included in this legislation. Thus, it is unclear whether this financial reform law will work as intended. Because members of Congress are not experts in finance, they drafted this law in very general language. Its policy impact, therefore, will depend on how this legislation is interpreted by the Federal Reserve Board and other regulatory agencies.

MONETARY EASING AND THE FED

The turnover in Obama's economic team did not extend to Fed chairman Ben S. Bernanke, but he was scarred by the Great Recession. In February 2006, President George W. Bush appointed Bernanke to a fourteen-year term on the Federal Reserve Board of Governors and to a four-year term as its Chairman. When the financial "crisis" hit in October 2008, Bernanke and Treasury Secretary Henry Paulson engineered the infusion of $700 billion and the bailout of failing mega-banks (Frendreis and Tatalovich 2009). Although economists and pundits generally praised Bernanke's intervention in the financial crisis, public opinion was less convinced of his success given the stalled economic growth and excessively high levels of unemployment. By the time Bernanke had to be reappointed to a second four-year term as chairman, there was substantial opposition from conservative and liberal members of Congress. President Obama believed that Bernanke helped prevent the Great Recession from becoming another Great Depression and that keeping Bernanke would reassure the financial and business communities (who viewed Obama as hostile to their interests), just as both presidents Ronald Reagan and Bill Clinton had retained Fed chairmen who were appointed by their predecessors in the other party. In August 2009, Obama did renominate Bernanke, and he was confirmed by the Senate on a seventy to thirty vote but with the largest margin in opposition to an incumbent Fed chairman since the Fed was created in 1913.

The financial crisis that began in 2008 forced the Federal Reserve Board to engage in very creative arrangements to infuse many billions of dollars of credit into troubled financial institutions. But Fed policy was not applauded by all observers. One powerful dissent was authored by Stanford economics professor John B. Taylor, whose "Taylor Rule" for guiding monetary policy to achieve price stability and full employment seemingly described Fed policy under chairmen Paul Volcker and Alan Greenspan (Clarida, Gali, and Gertler 2000). Taylor argued that the Fed policy of keeping interest rates too low for too long from 2002 to 2005 was the fundamental cause of the housing bubble that burst, and moreover, that the accompanying financial crisis resulted less from a shortage of liquidity (credit) than the fact that banks held toxic (high-risk) assets like mortgages whose true value could not be determined (Taylor 2009).

But the Fed and the Treasury Department believed that a shortage of liquidity was the root cause of the financial crisis, so both agreed to stimulate the economy using both fiscal policy and monetary policy. Monetary policy means the money supply, and more money and credit in circulation means that consumers can borrow to augment their income and businesses can borrow in order to build plants and other investments. The Fed can expand or contract the money supply by using three conventional policies, but the Great Recession prompted Fed chairman Ben Bernanke to utilize many unorthodox and creative tools. First, the "discount" rate is the interest rate that the Fed charges for lending money to its most credit-worthy banks and financial institutions, who would then increase that rate of interest (in order to make a profit) on the funds they lend to consumers and businesses. A higher "discount" rate causes all interest rates to increase, thus discouraging borrowing and thereby "tightening" the money supply, whereas a lower "discount" rate means that banks can offer cheaper loans. In January 2008, the "discount rate" was 4 percent, but by late October, the Fed lowered it to 1.25 percent, and then to 0.50 percent in December 2008, where it remained until being raised to 0.75 percent in February 2010.

Second, the "federal funds rate" is essentially the interest rate that banks charge other banks for short-term loans because law requires all banks to maintain certain "reserves" either with the Fed or as vault cash. In other words, no bank can lend all its deposits as loans, and the federal funds rate is set by the Fed. Raising the federal funds rate discourages banks from making so many loans that threaten to breach their "reserve" requirements, since to maintain the required reserves, they would have to pay higher charges to other banks for a short-term loan. But since December 2008, the federal funds rate ranged between 0.0 percent and 0.25 percent, meaning that it was virtually costless for banks to borrow money from each other.

Third, the Federal Open Market Committee (FOMC) buys and sells federal government securities (like Treasury bonds). When the FOMC sells government securities, banks, pension plans, and other investors pay for them in currency and receive interest payments until those Treasury bonds mature. But when the FOMC buys them back, those banks, pension plans, and other investors are paid for the market value of those securities, which means that currency is pumped back into the economy. In sum, not only do FOMC purchases of government securities from bond holders increase the money supply, but they also hold down long-term interest rates since there is more liquidity available in the credit markets to finance loans to consumers and businesses. From December 2008 to March 2010, the FOMC purchased $1.75 trillion in Treasury bonds to help fuel economic recovery, but with unemployment stuck at close to 10 percent, the Fed announced in November 2010 new plans to purchase $600 billion more in US government debt over the next eight months (Di Leo and Barkley 2010).

But where the first massive purchase by the FOMC was widely applauded as necessary to end the Great Recession, this new round of Treasury purchases (called "quantitative easing" or QE2) was criticized here and abroad. An open letter to Bernanke signed mainly by economists, most of whom served in previous Republican administrations or with conservative think tanks, said that QE2 would "risk currency debasement and inflation, and we do not think they will achieve the Fed's objective of promoting employment" (*Wall Street Journal* 2010). To this, a Fed spokeswoman replied that "the Federal Reserve has Congressional-mandated objectives to help promote both increased employment and price stability" (*Wall Street Journal* 2010). That is true, since Democrats in Congress added the statutory obligation to reduce unemployment in the 1970s, although since World War II the Fed had been an inflation "hawk," and even former Fed chairmen Paul Volcker and Alan Greenspan accepted inflation fighting as their primary responsibility. The problem for Bernanke was that, with the failure of the stimulus package to bring about economic recovery, monetary policy was pretty much the only weapon available.

Yet as those dissenting economists argued, massive increases in the money supply could hasten new inflationary pressures by cheapening the value of the US dollar. This charge was leveled against the United States by our allies when President Obama met with other leaders of the G-20 nations in South Korea. The G-20 replaced the G-8 group of industrialized nations (United States, Canada, Great Britain, France, Germany, Russia, Italy, and Japan) and includes those eight countries, the European Union, and the fast-developing nations of China and India, as well as Australia, Argentina, Brazil, Indonesia, Mexico, Saudi Arabia, South Africa, South Korea, and Turkey. The G-20 nations met in South Korea to discuss trade "imbalances," but the meeting was not successful, and Bernanke's QE2 decision did not help. The problem is that the United States has long had an "imbalance" of trade, with Americans buying many more imports compared to the US exports purchased by foreigners. The trade imbalance is especially pronounced with China, and the Obama administration believed that China was deliberately holding down the value of its currency (renminbi) relative to the US dollar (the "exchange rate" for international transactions). If the US dollar is stronger than the renminbi, then Chinese goods are less expensive for Americans to purchase, but US goods are more expensive in China. Because of the huge trade imbalance between the United States and China, China accumulated billions upon billions of US dollars, which China used to purchase US government securities. In other words, China (a Communist country with a nonsocialist economy) is the largest creditor for the United States.

The Obama administration urged China to "re-evaluate" its currency upward so that Chinese goods would become more expensive in the United States, thereby hopefully reducing the imbalance of trade between the two countries. China resisted and was supported by US allies who charged that the weak US dollar was caused by deficit spending and by the monetary policies of the Fed. They pointed specifically to QE2. In doing so, our allies supported the viewpoint of former Fed chairman Alan Greenspan, who wrote that the United States was "pursuing a policy of currency weakening." Both UK prime minister David Cameron and German chancellor Angela Merkel agreed (Chan, Stolberg, and Sanger 2010).

Not until late 2010 did the Fed, under orders from Congress, report the full extent of its intervention during the financial crisis. From December 2007 to July 2010, the Fed made more than twenty-one thousand transactions (emergency loans and other credit arrangements) to financial institutions, corporations like

General Electric and Harley-Davidson, and even foreign banks including the European Central Bank as well as the central banks of Australia, Denmark, England, Japan, Mexico, Norway, South Korea, Sweden, and Switzerland. Previously the Fed had only revealed that four unnamed financial firms had utilized its special lending programs, but this report showed that the Fed extended nearly $9 trillion in short-term loans to eighteen financial institutions from March 2008 to May 2009. Against congressional critics, the Fed defended its role. "I think our action prevented an even more disastrous outcome," said Fed vice chairman Donald L. Kohn. Without Fed intervention, "liquidity would have dried up even more than it did, asset prices would have fallen even more than they did, and economic activity and employment would have fallen further and faster than they did" (Chan and McGinty 2010).

OTHER ECONOMIC POLICIES

Economists uniformly agree that the "protectionist" trade policies of the United States (notably the Smoot-Hawley Tariff of 1930) and European countries worsened the global impact of the Great Depression. That lesson was learned by FDR, who persuaded Congress to enact the Reciprocal Trade Agreements Act of 1938, which authorized the president to negotiate a lowering of tariffs with other countries. That began the modern era of "free trade," which was fully embraced by presidents George H. W. Bush, Bill Clinton, and George W. Bush. Although the first president Bush signed the North American Free Trade Agreement (NAFTA) with the prime minister of Canada and the president of Mexico, it was President Bill Clinton who persuaded Congress to approve the pact. But unions representing the manufacturing sector were always skeptical if not opposed, believing that free-trade policies "shipped jobs" overseas to low-wage paying nations. The second Bush administration had negotiated several trade agreements, and the 2008 GOP presidential contender, Senator John McCain (R-AZ), fully embraced those policies.

But candidate Obama voiced concern about free-trade agreements, including NAFTA, and argued that he would renegotiate them toward upgrading environmental protections and labor rights. Soon after taking office, the Obama administration was embroiled with Mexico in a long-standing dispute over NAFTA. In March 2009, President Obama signed an appropriations bill that included a prohibition of any funds from continuing a two-year-old pilot program that allowed some Mexican trucks to operate in the United States. The Teamsters Union had that provision included, arguing that Mexican trucks do not meet US safety standards. NAFTA mandated that Mexican truckers could begin operating near the US-Mexican border in 1995 and throughout the United States by 2000, but this dispute continued for sixteen years until both countries agreed to the pilot program in 2007. After Congress ended the pilot program, Mexico began slapping tariffs on US agricultural and manufactured goods. Although the 2010 appropriations bill was enacted without any prohibition on the pilot-trucking program, this trade dispute remains deadlocked (Mitchell and Kiernan 2010).

Having expressed protectionist views during the campaign, President Obama took no initiatives on the free-trade front until he visited Seoul, South Korea, for the G-20 summit immediately after the midterm elections of 2010. The G-20 summit was convened to address a multitude of problems, including trade. In 2007, the Bush administration negotiated trade agreements with Peru, Panama, Colombia, and Korea, but only the Peru deal was approved by Congress whereas congressional Democrats reneged on the other three. President Obama had promised to renegotiate the free-trade agreement with South Korea and sign it at the G-20 summit. But negotiations for the United States failed to get concessions on automobiles, although President Obama expressed hope that an agreement could be submitted to Congress. The South Korean deal "largely replicates" previous trade pacts "which cost the U.S. more than one million jobs," alleged the AFL-CIO (Youngman 2010). Soon after his return home, however, President Obama announced success in finalizing that trade pact, the largest since NAFTA, and presumably it will be easier to gain approval from the 112th Congress with its larger numbers of sympathetic Republicans.

Another item on organized labor's policy agenda that was not enacted, despite the Democrats' control of the 111th Congress and the White House, was "card check" legislation to facilitate union organizing. The National Labor Relations Board (NLRB) now allows workers who want to organize a union to sign a card to that effect, but if less than a majority, then the NLRB requires an election with a secret ballot to determine the wishes of the majority of workers. The proposed Employee Free Choice Act (EFCA) was introduced in Congress in 2005, 2007, and 2009 but never passed. It would allow union organizers to collect card checks and require the NLRB to certify the union without the requirement of election with secret ballot. Many businesses, including the US Chamber of Commerce, argue that card check without a secret ballot invites intimidation by union organizers and, more fundamentally, denies workers the democratic right to vote.

TRIANGULATION OR INTRANSIGENCE

The failed summit of world leaders at the G-20 meeting symbolized the stark policy choices that face the United States. The "sovereign debt crisis" that is sweeping over Europe, as illustrated by the threatened bankruptcies of the PIIGS nations (Portugal, Ireland, Italy, Greece, and Spain) has prompted Europe, led by the United Kingdom and Germany, to advocate budget frugality and an end to deficit spending. President Obama was the only voice championing more stimulus to fuel economic recovery, but the results of the 2010 election pretty much ended any chance of more massive federal spending like the 2009 stimulus. When President Clinton's health-care reforms were repudiated in the 1994 midterm elections, he survived politically by devising a "triangulation" strategy (see discussion by Harris and Hohmann in this volume). Clinton articulated a "new" moderate approach to public policy that was more conservative than the congressional Democrats but more liberal than the GOP majority in the House of Representatives (Tatalovich and Frendreis 2000). One result of his triangulation strategy was that President Clinton came into agreement with congressional Republicans on a blueprint to balance the budget, which resulted in budgetary surpluses at the end of his term.

The question now is whether President Obama will "triangulate" with the Republican House majority in the 112th Congress or govern as an ideologically intransigent liberal (also see discussion by Nicol C. Rae in this volume). And will Obama begin by confronting the fiscal crisis of the national debt? In mid-2010, the Congressional Budget Office reported that the federal debt rose from 36 percent of GDP in 2007 to 62 percent in 2010 and could reach 90 percent of GDP by 2020 (Congressional Budget Office 2010). Moreover, in early December 2010, the bipartisan National Commission on Fiscal Responsibility issued its final report, but only eleven of its eighteen members endorsed its plan to slash deficits by nearly $4 trillion over the next decade, reduce the national debt to 41 percent of GDP in twenty-five years, and balance the budget by 2035 (Dennis and Montgomery 2010). Its report had to be endorsed by fourteen members to force Congress to consider its recommendations, but its highly publicized findings served as an early warning alert about the imminent fiscal crisis. Other warning signs came when two bond-rating agencies, Moody's as well as Standard and Poor's, made announcements that the US top-rating of Aaa for its government securities might be cut unless our growing debt burden eases. There were some early post-election signs that President Obama might accommodate the new political reality: his free-trade agreement with South Korea; his decision to freeze federal salaries for two years; his capitulation to GOP demands that all Bush tax cuts be continued for two years. But only time will tell whether President Obama takes decisive steps to address the sovereign debt crisis, or what his ultimate economic legacy will be. But President Obama did not show much leadership with respect to fiscal policy.

When the 112th Congress convened, President Obama's $3.7 trillion FY12 budget (with a $1.1 trillion deficit) was dead on arrival. A study by the Congressional Budget Office showed that Obama underestimated its forecast of deficits by $9.5 trillion over ten years. Then House Republicans in April passed a budget under the leadership of Budget Committee chairman Paul D. Ryan (R-WI) that would cut $6.2 trillion over ten years and limit the growth of "entitlements" under Medicare and Medicaid. But Senate Democrats failed even to propose a budget, and criticism of Democratic inaction prompted President Obama to give a major speech on the budget in late April that essentially repudiated his own FY12 budget and, instead, recommended $4 trillion in cuts over the next twelve years. Going into May 2011 the Senate Democrats still had not formulated a budget alternative to Ryan's proposal. Given all the partisan posturing and political bickering over spending cuts versus tax hikes, perhaps the best hope for a policy breakthrough would be the ongoing negotiations by the bipartisan "Gang of Six" (three Senators and three Representatives) in consultation with Vice President Joe Biden. This group of moderate Democrats and Republicans sought to build on the bipartisan recommendations of the National Commission on Fiscal Responsibility to reduce future deficits and national debt. Thus, only time with tell whether President Obama will take decisive steps to address the sovereign debt crisis, or what his ultimate economic legacy will be.

REFERENCES

Bai, Matt. 2010. "Budget Chief Tilted to Executive Branch." *New York Times*, July 28.

Barro, Robert J. 2009. "Government Spending Is No Free Lunch: Now the Democrats Are Peddling Voodoo Economics." *Wall Street Journal*, January 22.

Bater, Jeff. 2010. "U.S. Posts $150.4 Billion November Budget Deficit." *Wall Street Journal*, December 10.

Blackledge, Brett J., and Matt Apuzzo. 2009. "Obama Repackages Stimulus Plans with Old Promises." *Breitbart*, June 8. http://www.breitbart.com/article.php?id=D98MPHJ80&show_article=1. Accessed June 9, 2009.

Blinder, Alan S., and Mark Zandi. 2010. "How the Great Recession Was Brought to an End." July 27. http://www.economy.com/mark-zandi/documents/End-of-Great-Recession.pdf.

Bowman, Karlyn. 2010. "What the Voters Actually Said on Election Day." *The American Magazine*, November 16.

Calmes, Jackie. 2009. "Obama's Economic Circle Keeps Tensions Simmering." *New York Times*, June 7.

Chan, Sewell, and Jo Craven McGinty. 2010. "In Crisis, Fed Opened Vault Wide For U.S. and World, Data Shows." *New York Times*, December 2.

Chan, Sewell, Sheryl Gay Stolberg, and David E. Sanger. 2010. "Obama's Economic View Is Rejected on World Stage." *New York Times*, November 12.

Clarida, Richard, Jordi Gali, and Mark Gertler. 2000. "Monetary Policy Rules and Macroeconomic Stability: Evidence and Some Theory." *Quarterly Journal of Economics* 115: 147–80.

Congressional Budget Office. 2010. "Federal Debt and the Risk of a Fiscal Crisis." *Economic and Budget Issue Brief*, July 27.

Dennis, Brady, and Lori Montgomery. 2010. "Deficit Plan Wins 11 of 18 Votes; More Than Expected, but Not Enough to Force Action." *Washington Post*, December 3.

Di Leo, Luca, and Tom Barkley. 2010. "Fed to Buy $600 Billion of Treasuries." *Wall Street Journal*, November 3.

Dorning, Mike. 2010. "Obama Considers Chamber Visit, CEO Summit to Counter Anti-Business Image." *Bloomberg*, November 21. http://www.bloomberg.com/news/2010-11-20/obama-prepares-new-overtures-to-business-to-keep-agenda-moving.html. Accessed November 21, 2010.

The Economist. 2010. "False Expectations: The Historic Infrastructure Investment That Wasn't," October 21.

Frendreis, John, and Raymond Tatalovich. 2009. "Riding the Tiger: Bush and the Economy." In *Ambition and Division: Legacies of the George W. Bush Presidency*, edited by Steven E. Schier, 229–37. Pittsburgh: University of Pittsburgh Press.

Gallup Organization. 2009. "Americans Continue to Oppose GM, Chrysler Loans." Poll, March 31.

Gross, Daniel. 2010. "Exclusive: Treasury's TARP, AIG Bailout Costs Fall to $30 Billion." *Yahoo! Finance*, October 1. http://finance.yahoo.com/news/Exclusive-Treasury-TARP-AIG-dg-3890288247.html?x=0. Accessed October 5, 2010.

Heilemann, John. 2009. "Inside Obama's Economic Brain Trust: It's Not Pretty at This Moment." *New York Magazine*, March 22.

Herszenhorn, David M., and Carl Hulse. 2009. "House and Senate in Deal For $789 Billion Stimulus." *New York Times*, February 12.

Hilsenrath, Jon. 2010. "Course of Economy Hinges on Fight Over Stimulus." *Wall Street Journal*, July 26.

Izzo, Phil. 2009. "Obama, Geithner Get Low Grades from Economists." *Wall Street Journal*, March 11.

Kuhn, David Paul. 2010. "None of Your Business: On Obama's Public Sector Cabinet." RealClearPolitics, September 3. http://www.realclearpolitics.com/articles/2010/09/03/none_of_your_business_on_obamas_public_sector_cabinet_107001.html. Accessed September 8, 2010.

Langley, Monica. 2009. "Obama Dials Down Wall Street Criticism." *Wall Street Journal*, March 24.

Lindsey, Lawrence B. 2010. "Did the Stimulus Stimulate?" *Weekly Standard*, August 16.

Lizza, Ryan. 2009. "Inside the Crisis: Larry Summers and the White House Economic Team." *New Yorker*, October 12.

Luhby, Tami. 2010. "Jobless Benefits Cost So Far: $319 Billion." CNNMoney.com. http://money.cnn.com/2010/11/17/news/economy/unemployment_benefits_cost/ index.htm. Accessed November 17, 2010.

Mitchell, Josh. 2010. "Treasury Takes Initial Public Loss on GM Shares." *Wall Street Journal*, November 17.

Mitchell, Josh, and Paul Kiernan. 2010. "Mexico Adds Tariffs in Trucking Dispute." *Wall Street Journal*, August 17.

Modica, Mark, and Hal John. 2010. "Model Corruption." *New York Post*, August 13.

Montgomery, Lori. 2010. "Election-Year Deficit Fears Stall Obama Stimulus Plan." *Washington Post*, June 19.

Ohlemacher, Stephen. 2010. "GOP Lawmakers Take Tough Stand on Bush Tax Cuts." *Yahoo! News*, November 13. http://news.yahoo.com/s/ap/us_tax_cuts/print. Accessed November 17, 2010.

Orol, Ronald D. 2010. "Senate OKs Sweeping Bank-Reform Bill; Sends It to Obama." MarketWatch, July 15. http://www.marketwatch.com/story/senate -defeats-filibuster-threat-on-bank-bill-2010-07-15. Accessed July 20, 2010.

Rasmussen Reports. 2009. "Just 21% Favor GM Bailout Plan, 67% Oppose." May 31.

Samuelson, Robert. 2009. "Obama's Stimulus: A Colossal Waste?" *Washington Post*, February 23.

Shear, Michael D. 2010. "Obama Lesson: 'Shovel Ready' Not So Ready." *New York Times*, October 15.

Tatalovich, Raymond, and John Frendreis. 2000. "Clinton, Class, and Economic Policy." In *The Postmodern Presidency: Bill Clinton's Legacy in U.S. Politics*, edited by Steven E. Schier, 41–59. Pittsburgh: University of Pittsburgh Press.

Taylor, John B. 2009. *Getting Off Track: How Government Actions and Interventions Caused, Prolonged, and Worsened the Financial Crisis*. Washington, DC: Hoover Institution Press.

Wall Street Journal. 2010. "Open Letter to Ben Bernanke," November 15.

The Washington Times. 2010. "Government Motors repayment fraud," April 23.

Whitacre, Ed. 2010. "The GM Bailout: Paid Back in Full." *Wall Street Journal*, April 21.

Yadron, Danny, and Patrick O'Connor. 2010. "The Number: $858 Billion." *Wall Street Journal*, December 10.

Youngman, Sam. 2010. "Rough Road Ahead for Obama, Unions as Compromises Loom." *The Hill*, November 13. http://thehill.com/homenews/administration/129041 -rough-road-ahead-for-obama-unions-as-compromises-loom. Accessed November 15, 2010.

Chapter Eleven

The Obama Presidency

A Foreign Policy of Change?

James M. McCormick

Barack Obama ran for the presidency on a policy of change—change in domestic policy and change in foreign policy. During both the nomination and election campaigns, this focus on change was the overarching theme that he struck at virtually every stop on the campaign trail. In foreign policy, Candidate Obama's emphasis on change focused on an array of issues—ending the Iraq and Afghanistan Wars and bringing American troops home; "resetting" and "restarting" American relations with allies and other major powers throughout the world; engaging with adversaries to address a number of outstanding issues; and dealing with global economic and military issues, most notably nuclear proliferation. The larger aim of this "change" emphasis was to enable the United States to reengage with the world and to move away from the isolated position that America found itself after the seeming unilateralist policies of the Bush administration. In this chapter, we examine the foreign policy approach and policies of the Obama administration and assess how well it has achieved this change.

VALUES AND BELIEFS OF
THE OBAMA ADMINISTRATION

The foreign policy approach that emerged during Obama's presidency was one that appeared to align closely with the liberal internationalist approach to foreign policy (albeit with some realist exceptions). This approach has a substantial heritage in American foreign policy, dating back at least to Woodrow Wilson and Franklin Delano Roosevelt, but it has also found more recent expression in foreign policy elements of the Carter and Clinton administrations.

A LIBERAL INTERNATIONALIST APPROACH

A liberal internationalist approach is one that is grounded in a number of core values and beliefs about the motivations and aims of foreign policy behavior for individual states and for the United States in particular. First of all, key domestic values, such as the promotion of democracies and individual freedoms, are viewed as important ways to create a stable and peaceful international order. In this context, the Obama approach would find appeal among those who see the "democratic peace" theory as the way to global order. Following this tradition, too, the basis of US foreign policy would flow directly from its domestic values as a nation, even as the United States works to promote such values internationally. Second, liberal internationalism calls for promoting international cooperation and interdependence in a variety of ways as a means to knit states and peoples today in a web of interdependence to address common problems and reduce the risk of conflict. In this sense, the United States would promote free trade among nations, but it also would promote cooperative actions across borders by different levels of government and among numerous civil society groups. Third, international law and international institutions are assumed to "have a modernizing and civilizing effect on states" and also fit within this liberal internationalist tradition for enhancing global cooperation and interdependence (on Wilsonianism and this quote, see Ikenberry 2008). In this way, American foreign policy would utilize regional and global organizations, since they, too, are essential in tying states and the international community together. Fourth, and particularly important from this perspective and its Wilsonian roots, the United States would not only stay involved in global affairs, but it would assist in bringing about a stable, liberal order through its cooperative and constructive leadership efforts. Moreover, these actions would not be done in any top-down or directive way; instead, they would be evoked through cooperative actions with states and actors.

In several respects, liberal internationalism stands in considerable contrast to the foreign policy approach of the George W. Bush administration, an approach variously described as a combination of "defensive realism" and "idealism, "revival Wilsonianism," or neoconservatism (McCormick 2010, 212–13). A liberal internationalist approach begins from a more cooperative assumption about foreign policy and global politics than the Bush administration adopted, especially after the events of September 11, when President Bush announced that "either you are with us or you are with the terrorists" (quoted in McCormick 2010, 214). This approach also emphasizes the utility of multilateral means to address foreign policy, an approach that the Bush administration generally viewed skeptically from the outset of its tenure. In this sense, the Obama approach places greater reliance on diplomacy and "soft power" instruments for achieving foreign policy change and thus stands in marked distinction from the Bush administration's seeming reliance on coercive diplomacy and "hard power" instruments.

At least two important similarities in goals, however, exist between Obama's liberal internationalist and Bush's neoconservative approaches. Both approaches favor the fostering of democracies, and both call for American leadership. Yet, they differ substantially on how best to achieve these goals. The Obama approach focuses on building democracy from the bottom up, while the Bush approach sought, at least in practice, to impose it from the top down. Both approaches also favor American leadership, but again, they differ on how to pursue that goal. The Obama approach calls for more cooperative leadership ("partnerships" as the Obama administration continuously describes it), while the Bush administration favored a more assertive American leadership to encourage followership.

THE GLOBAL VISION: A MULTI-PARTNER WORLD

A more precise foreign policy framework for the Obama administration, closely aligned to the campaign themes, emerged during the first year of the administration and took even fuller shape by the middle of the second year in office. In his 2009 inaugural address, for example, President Obama once again alluded to this change in foreign policy from the Bush years with an explicit promotion of American values as the basis of policy and with an appeal for diplomacy toward adversaries: "We reject as false the choice between our safety and our ideals. . . . Those ideals still light the world, and we will not give them up for expedience's sake," and, "To those who cling to power through corruption and deceit and the silencing of dissent, know that you are on the wrong side of history, but we will extend a hand if you are willing to unclench your fist." Yet, he also signaled a continuation of past foreign policy in this way: "We will not apologize for our way of life nor will we waver in its defense. And for those who seek to advance their aims by inducing terror and slaughtering innocents, we say to you now that, 'Our spirit is stronger and cannot be broken. You cannot outlast us, and we will defeat you.'" As Stanley Renshon (2010, 7–8) correctly pointed out for us (and from which we draw), the former set of statements would appeal to liberals (and liberal internationalists in our parlance), while the latter set of statements would appeal to conservatives and political realists. In all, although change was in the air, the degree of change was again mixed with a commitment to continuity in policy.

During the first several months of the administration, President Obama's foreign policy team conducted a policy review. The results of that review were announced through a series of presidential speeches that President Obama gave from April to July 2009 in several world capitals in differing parts of the world (Europe, the Middle East, and Africa). In April 2009 in Prague, the Czech Republic, he extolled the virtues of the changes that have occurred in that country in a few short years and called for cooperation and policy coordination among nations "to renew our prosperity" and "to provide for our common security." He also set out his goal of "a world without nuclear weapons" and outlined a series of steps to move in that direction by completing a new Strategic Arms Reduction Treaty with Russia, strengthening the Nuclear Non-Proliferation Treaty (NPT), and initiating "a new international effort to secure all vulnerable nuclear material around the world within four years." In June 2009 in Cairo, Egypt, President Obama called for "a new beginning between the United States and Muslims; one based on mutual interest and mutual respect" and sought to show the substantial ties between the Muslim world and the United States over the decades and centuries. Importantly, he called for "a sustained effort to listen to each other; to learn from each other; to respect one another; and to seek common ground," and he went on to state that "our problems must be dealt with through partnership; [and] our progress must be shared."

In July 2009, President Obama gave foreign policy speeches in two other capitals—one in Moscow, Russia, the other in Accra, Ghana. In both speeches, he sought to reach out to these differing audiences and to highlight the change in American policy that he wanted to initiate. In Moscow, President Obama called for a "'reset' in relations between the United States and Russia." The aim, he said, would be "a sustained effort among the American and Russian people to identify mutual interests, and expand dialogue and cooperation that can pave the way to progress." Finally, in Accra, President Obama once again struck this theme of international cooperation and partnership: "I see Africa as a fundamental part of our interconnected world—as partners with America on behalf of the future we want for all of our children." In that speech, he particularly focused on issues relating to the needs of Africa and the developing world: the need for democratic governments, development that provides opportunity, governance that strengthens public health, and the peaceful resolution of conflicts. In all these areas, the United States would stand as "partners" with Africa.

At roughly the same time, Secretary of State Hillary Clinton delivered an important foreign policy address at home. In that address, she committed the United States to a leadership position, albeit a particular kind, identified the basic values to inform the Obama administration's foreign policy priorities, outlined how the administration would conduct its foreign policy, and crystallized the view of the kind of international system that the administration wished to create. In particular, she stated that the United States would continue to lead in global affairs, but the nation "need[s] a new mindset about how America will use its power to safeguard our nation, expand shared prosperity, and help more people in more places live up to their God-given potential" (Clinton 2009b).

In particular, she rejected the approaches of the past and committed the administration to working toward "a different global architecture" to address the common challenges and threats in the world today. Importantly, Secretary Clinton said that Americans will

> use our power to convene, our ability to connect countries around the world, and sound foreign policy strategies to create partnerships aimed at solving problems. We'll go beyond states to create opportunities for non-state actors and individuals to contribute to solutions. . . . In short, we will lead by inducing greater cooperation among a greater number of actors and reducing competition, *tilting the balance away from a multi-polar world and toward a multi-partner world.* (Clinton 2009b, emphasis added)

Secretary Clinton also incorporated an important realist exception to her "focus on diplomacy and development" as a basic approach. When the United States is threatened, she said, "We will not hesitate to defend our friends, our interests, and above all, our people vigorously and when necessary with the world's strongest military." In other words, the unilateral option of self-reliance is still very much available.

NATIONAL SECURITY STRATEGY: "A STRATEGY OF ENGAGEMENT"

The national security strategy statement of May 2010 (White House 2010), from which the following discussion is drawn, summarized the foreign policy approach of the Obama administration. Its "strategic approach," the administration declared, was grounded in three fundamental ideas: (1) the need to rebuild the American economy as the basis for strong global leadership, (2) a commitment to living American values at home in order to credibly promote them abroad, and (3) a commitment to reshaping the international system in a way that it will enable the global community to address the challenges of the twenty-first century. To actualize these ideas, the overarching strategy by the United States would be a "strategy of engagement."

Such widespread engagement would be utilized to address four principal goals in order to "achieve the world we seek": (1) achieve and maintain security for the United States, allies, and partners; (2) rebuild and strengthen the American economy through an open international system "that promotes opportunity and prosperity;" (3) promote universal values abroad; and (4) work toward an international order "that can foster collective action to confront common challenges." Each of these four areas requires the United States to address specific issues to realize these principal goals and the national security strategy discussed each in turn.

Security

The first major goal for the United States is to address multiple security threats of the current era. These new threats range from "a loose network of violent extremists," the dangers posed by failing states, and the spread of nuclear weapons. In addition, though, these threats include "asymmetric" ones in which adversaries target outer space and cyberspace as ways to harm and undermine American (and, indeed, global) society.

For each of these threats, the Obama administration outlined its proposed course of actions. For terrorism, the administration called for developing a greater domestic capacity to address emergencies at home, and it remained committed "to disrupt, dismantle, and defeat al-Qaida and its affiliates" abroad in partnership with others. For the threat of nuclear and biological weapons, the administration called for strengthening the NPT, creating a nuclear-free Korean peninsula through the denuclearization of North Korea, and compelling Iran to move away from its pursuit of nuclear weapons. Furthermore, the administration would also seek to secure all "vulnerable nuclear weapons and materials" and counter the potential of biological weapons. For the threat from failing states and unresolved conflicts, the administration called for a "responsible transition" as the United States ended the war in Iraq, endorsed a two-state solution for the Arab-Israel conflict, remained open to offering Iran "a pathway to a better future, provided Iran's leaders are prepared to take it," and offered to aid states transitioning from recent conflicts. Finally, on the threat to cyberspace, the administration vowed to work with the private sector and with other governments "to investigate cyber intrusion and to ensure an organized and unified response to future cyber incidents."

Importantly, the administration was careful to specify its position on the use of force in addressing the terrorist threats. Although the national strategy statement indicates that the use of force "may be necessary to defend our country and allies and to preserve broader peace and security," the administration is careful to specify that it "will exhaust other options before war whenever we can, and carefully weigh the costs and risks of action against costs and risks of inaction." The strategy of the Obama administration is more circumspect in the use of force than the strategy outlined by the Bush administration in its 2002 national security strategy.

Prosperity

The second major goal of the national security strategy is to rebuild and strengthen the American economy as the basis for a continuing leadership role in the world. The statement outlines actions, both domestically and internationally, that must be done to accomplish this goal. Domestically, the administration calls for improvement in the quality of American education from the elementary through the university level. The statement also commits the administration to "support programs that cultivate interest and scholarship in foreign languages and intercultural affairs," and to comprehensive immigration reform as a way to improve America's human capital. Finally, the United States must reduce the nation's deficit, reform the contracting process within the government to reduce waste and inefficiency, and increase the level of transparency, so that the public can more fully follow how the taxpayers' dollars are being spent.

Internationally, the United States must expand the growth of the "integrated, global economy," even as it addresses the "economic imbalances and financial excesses." The national security strategy statement calls on Americans to spend less and save more, double American exports by 2014, and take more actions to open up markets for American products. The Obama administration will also support the G-20 nations' "emergence as the premier forum for international economic cooperation" in the global community, and will provide leadership to that organization, the International Monetary Fund, and the World Bank in making necessary global financial reforms. Finally, the administration called for economic changes in developing economies, although those changes should de done within the context of "long-term development" and "sustainable development."

Values

The third major goal of the national security strategy is the promotion of key fundamental values. These values are the basic fundamental individual freedoms contained in the US constitution that the Obama administration believes are universal and important to promote globally. In order to make the promotion of these values legitimate around the world, they need to be respected at home. In this sense, the United States must prohibit the use of torture against individuals and must adhere to the rule of law in its actions, including in dealing with terrorism. Abroad, the United States will promote democracy and human rights "because governments that respect these values are more just, peaceful, and legitimate." Yet, the United States "will not impose any system of government on another country." Instead, it will support and build the capacity of those states pursuing democratic development. Such assistance will be undertaken both through working directly with other governments and also working through civil society groups to create and expand key democratic institutions. Finally, the Obama administration indicated that its emphasis on global freedom also meant "freedom from want," and that it would promote a new global health initiative, promote greater food security, and continue to respond to global humanitarian crises.

International Order

The final goal outlined in the national security statement is the establishment of "a just and sustainable international order that can foster collective action to confront common challenges." The Obama administration views this component of the national security strategy as crucial to the advancement of the earlier three goals.

To bring about this new order, the national security strategy statement calls on a long litany of American actions and priorities. The United States will sustain its security relations with America's traditional allies in Europe, Asia, and North America; build cooperative relations with those that are the "21st Century Centers of Influence" (e.g., China, India, and Russia); and expand its ties with the G-20 nations (e.g., Indonesia, Brazil, Saudi Arabia, Argentina, South Africa, and South Korea). In addition, the United States will work to strengthen the United Nations, devolve some responsibility for collective action to a variety of international institutions, and invest in strengthening the capacity of regional organizations across the globe as a way to enhance worldwide security.

The ultimate test of this new international order, the national security strategy points out, is the ability to obtain global cooperation to address the current system challenges. Such challenges range from climate change, ethnic and genocidal conflict to global pandemics, transnational criminal syndicates, and issues of the "global commons"—shared seas, air, and space among nations. No one state could adequately address these issues; hence, the administration would work to achieve collective action within the international community.

THE OBAMA WORLDVIEW IN OPERATION

The foreign policy approach of the Obama administration is broad, comprehensive, and ambitious in conception—and considerably at variance with the Bush administration approach. In this sense, the Obama approach represents a dramatic change in foreign policy orientation. The important question, however, is whether this approach has had any impact in the first two years. How much of this approach has been implemented? Has the approach changed the substance of American foreign policy? Has this approach yielded greater foreign policy success than its predecessor in addressing key issues?

IMPROVING AMERICA'S GLOBAL IMAGE

In terms of reengaging the United States with the international community, the Obama approach has surely changed from the Bush administration. President Obama made important foreign policy speeches in key capitals across different continents and regions—Europe, Africa, and the Middle East—in an effort to reach out to the world and improve America's image. He has also engaged key world leaders in bilateral diplomatic summits (e.g., with Russian president Medvedev) and in a variety of multilateral forums (e.g., the G-8, the G-20, APEC). Furthermore, his administration has appointed a large number of special envoys to address a broad range of global issues, whether over Darfur, Afghanistan, North Korea, the Middle East, or elsewhere. Finally, and importantly, the United States has increased its use of regional and international organizations in pursuit of its foreign policy goals. In all, the efforts at global engagement have been substantial and pervasive during the early years of the Obama administration.

Indeed, this engagement, and the president's personal popularity worldwide, has had an effect on America's image abroad. In Pew Research Center polls in 2009 and 2010 across twenty-five and twenty-two countries, respectively, the "US favorability rating" improved considerably in most countries surveyed (Pew Global Attitudes Project 2009, 2010). The greatest improvement occurred in Western European countries (Britain, France, Germany, and Spain), but the view of America was also more positive, particularly in Latin American, African, and Asian nations. On another question in the 2009 survey, which asks whether Obama "will do the right thing in world affairs," large majorities across the respondents in the surveyed countries were now more confident that President Obama would do so as compared to the results for a similar question for President Bush in 2008. The absolute levels for this "do the right thing" question in the 2010 survey continued to show considerable confidence in President Obama for most of the countries surveyed, although the percentages across all the countries were systematically lower than in 2009. In this sense, some confidence in President Obama's actions had begun to erode.

Yet, the global attitudinal change witnessed in numerous countries has not occurred in most Muslim countries. Generally the Muslim countries included in these surveys continued to hold negative views when measured on the US favorability scale or on the "do the right thing" question. In Turkey, Egypt, Jordan, Lebanon, Pakistan, and the Palestinian territories in the 2009 Pew survey, for example, an overwhelming number of respondents continued to have a negative view of the United States, and they expressed low levels of confidence in President Obama "doing the right thing." Such patterns continued for the 2010 survey results and actually eroded for that year.

Keeping these exceptions about Muslim countries in mind and some erosion of confidence in other countries, as well, these results still suggest that President Obama improved the perception of the United States in the global arena. In this sense, this aspect of the global "soft power" quotient of the United States has improved under the Obama administration. But has this improvement in America's soft-power quotient been translated into agreement or accommodation with American foreign policy, either among the global publics or policymakers?

The evidence appears mixed. The 2010 Pew survey results indicate that majorities in about half of the twenty-two countries now support the anti-terrorism policies of Obama, but majorities in many of these same countries continue to oppose the war in Afghanistan. On Obama's policy toward Iran, majorities or pluralities in about half of the surveyed countries oppose it, and on Obama's handling of the Middle East conflict, most of the countries opposed his policy. Yet, on some important global commons issues (e.g., climate change, the world economic crisis, and Obama's overall international performance), the majority or plurality of respondents in fourteen or more of the twenty-two countries voiced their approval (Pew Global Attitudes Project 2010, 4–5). Still, the overall conclusion is that President Obama's popularity among the global publics has not fostered uniform support for his policies.

The same conclusion applies when considering the reaction of policymakers around the globe to his policy efforts. Whether seeking NATO nations to maintain or increase their troops in Afghanistan, urging the European Union nations to stimulate their economies, or seeking to prod greater support from China over North Korean or Iranian nuclear ambitions, Obama's global popularity has not automatically produced policy support from these leaders during the first two years of his administration. Instead, national interests continue to dominate policy choices by these nations and their leaders. Perhaps the greatest series of rebuffs to President Obama's policy efforts occurred during his trip to Asia in November 2010 (Chan, Stolberg, and Sanger 2010). At a meeting just prior to the G-20 summit, the United States and South Korea had hoped to conclude a free-trade agreement that had languished since the Bush administration. Instead, the two sides could not agree and could only insist that they would conclude the pact "in a matter of weeks." (Despite this initial setback, though, they did reach an accord in early December 2010 to eliminate a number of important trade barriers between the two countries [Chan 2010]). Shortly afterward at the G-20 meetings, President Obama failed to get support for his proposal to stimulate global growth before working on deficit reduction from some key trading nations (e.g., China, Britain, Germany, and Brazil). He also failed to get any movement from the Chinese on its overvalued currency. Instead, several countries criticized the decision of the Federal Reserve for weakening the US dollar through pumping an additional $600 billion into circulation (and thus potentially hurting the attractiveness of their exports). Policymakers of other nations pursuing their own interests in foreign policy—and thus disagreeing with American policy at times—is hardly surprising, but their actions suggest the limitation that a change in reputation may have on support for American policy abroad. In short, nations (both publics and their leaders) continue to disagree with American policy, albeit perhaps less vocally than during the Bush years.

INCORPORATING DOMESTIC VALUES IN FOREIGN POLICY: GUANTANAMO BAY AND THE ARAB SPRING

A second area where the Obama approach called for policy change was in the incorporation of domestic values in the conduct of American foreign policy. Indeed, President Obama noted that the United States did not need to compromise its values in carrying out its foreign policy. Rather, he argued, "in the long run we . . . cannot keep this country safe unless we enlist the power of our most fundamental values." His implicit reference, of course, was to the Bush administration's actions toward the treatment of suspected terrorists in seeming violation of domestic and international standards. Hence, one of his first actions as president, just two days after his inauguration, was the issuance of three executive orders to reverse some of these actions. One executive order called for the closing of overseas prisons by the Central Intelligence Agency (CIA) and the elimination of certain interrogation methods in dealing with terrorist suspects; a second directed the closing of the detention camp at Guantanamo Bay within a year's time; and the third set up a special interagency task force "to identify lawful options for the disposition of individuals captured or apprehended in connection with armed conflicts and counterterrorism operations" (see Executive Orders 13491, 13492, and 13493 2009).

Despite these orders, however, the administration has been only partially successful in implementing a change in policy. The interrogation measures, based on only those outlined in the Army Field Manual, have now been adhered to, and the use of water boarding, a practice that had been used over three hundred times during the Bush administration, no longer occurs. The full implementation of the other directives, however, has encountered difficulty, and indeed, not all aspects of the executive orders have been fully brought into effect. To be sure, CIA Director Leon Panetta announced in April 2009 that overseas prisons operated by the organization have been closed (Shane 2009a), but the transfer of prisoners to facilities operated by other countries apparently would continue, although outside "contractors" will not be used to question the suspects ("CIA Claims to Close Secret Prisons" 2009).

The effort to close the Guantanamo Bay prison facility and, in particular, to transfer its prisoners elsewhere has met with considerable resistance. While the administration was able to locate a domestic facility to take these prisoners (an empty maximum security prison in Illinois), the Congress has blocked funding to renovate that facility, fearful of housing suspected terrorists on American soil (Welna 2009). Furthermore, public opposition to the closing of the Guantanamo facility remains significant with 60 percent of the American public in a March 2010 poll supporting keeping it open (Savage 2010). The administration has also had to move back from its original position that it would transfer all detainees at Guantanamo to other prisons or put them on trial. Indeed, as early as May 2009, President Obama acknowledged that his administration would continue to use military commissions to try some prisoners held at Guantanamo, despite earlier opposition to such action, and that he did not have an answer to those "detainees at Guantanamo who cannot be prosecuted yet who pose a clear danger to the American people." In this sense, these latter prisoners are likely to remain at Guantanamo for the foreseeable future. Furthermore, with the thwarted attacks on Christmas Day 2009 and on Times Square in May 2010, the prospects of closing Guantanamo have continued to fade, and it is now "unlikely that President Obama will fulfill his promise to close it before his term ends in 2013" (Savage 2010). Indeed, the status of indefinite detention at Guantanamo and the use of indefinite detentions were confirmed by the Obama administration in March 2011, when the president issued a new executive order confirming these policies—an order that ironically appeared directly at variance with the ones issued after his inauguration in January 2009 (Tapper and Miller 2011). Yet, one official remained upbeat about the current situation and its effect on public (and global) opinion: "Closing Guantanamo is good, but fighting to close Guantanamo is O.K. Admitting you failed would be the worst" (Savage 2010).

In contrast to its seemingly failed efforts to infuse American values into its policy in dealing with Guantanamo Bay, the administration acted much more consistently and decisively with its commitment to promoting American values with the emergence of the "Arab Spring" in early 2011. The Arab Spring referred to a groundswell of popular movements for democratic reform in several Arab countries. The movement began in Tunisia in which the long-serving leader was ultimately forced into exile after several days of popular protests in January 2011. The movement spread to Egypt with days of public protests against the thirty-year autocratic rule of President Hosni Mubarak, an important U.S. ally in the Middle East peace process. The administration thus faced an important crossroads with this uprising: whether to support interests that it wanted to protect or support values that it wanted to promote. Although the administration was a bit indecisive in the opening days of the Egyptian public protests, President Obama ultimately called for the departure of President Mubarak. And indeed by mid-February 2011, Mubarak gave up his post, and an effort at democratic transition was underway in that crucial Middle Eastern country, albeit not without difficulty.

As this Arab Spring swept other states in the Middle East, the Obama administration continued to support these democratic reform efforts—sometimes more pronounced than others. The most dramatic effort by the Obama administration was in Libya and the effort by opposition forces to end the forty-year rule by Moammar Gadhafi. As protests increased and the rebel forces in Libya began to advance, Gadhafi threatened to destroy these forces, with the potential of great loss of innocent lives. President Obama undertook a series of actions to stop these efforts by Gadhafi's forces. He evacuated the American embassy and froze Gadhafi's assets in the United States (NPR 2011). Furthermore, working with allies, the administration succeeded in broadening international sanctions through United Nations Security Council Resolution 1970 (United Nations Security Council 2011a) against the Libyan government and imposing a "no-fly zone" over Libya through United Nations Security Council 1973 (United Nations Security Council 2011b). The latter resolution also included a provision authorizing the member states to "to take all necessary measures" to protect civilians in that country. In large measure, these actions were fully consistent with the "Responsibility to Protect" doctrine endorsed by the global community in 2005 (International Coalition for the Responsibility to Protect 2011). As a result, the administration, as part of a NATO-led coalition, moved to enforce the UN resolution, although the United States had European nations largely take the lead. Some opposition to this administration action was voiced at home, since these analysts were not convinced that American interests were at stake in Libya. Indeed, in outlining his policy actions, President Obama (NPR 2011) argued otherwise: "To brush aside America's responsibility as a leader and—more profoundly—our responsibilities to our fellow human beings under such circumstances would have been a betrayal of who we are." In this sense, President Obama's Libyan policy was carefully legitimized through its adherence to the American domestic values.

ADDRESSING KEY SECURITY ISSUES:
IRAQ, AFGHANISTAN, IRAN, AND NORTH KOREA

The Obama administration inherited several security issues from the Bush administration, and it promised a change policy on them, as well. In dealing with the Iraq War, the administration has surely changed courses, but in addressing the Afghanistan War, it has not. On the nuclear threats from North Korea and Iran, the administration has attempted an engagement approach but with very little success so far. In all, the degree of change in either the substance or the success on the latter three issues has been limited.

Iraq

Perhaps the most important policy change that Candidate Obama promised during his campaign was to end American involvement in Iraq. He has largely succeeded in that effort. Early on, he called for ending all American combat operations by August 31, 2010, with only 50,000 trainers and advisers remaining in Iraq by that date, and he promised the withdrawal of all American forces by the end of 2011. The former goal has been achieved, and the latter seems in sight. One factor that may change these plans is the continued instability of the Iraqi government. Since March 2010 elections, the various Iraqi factions have had difficulty putting together an effective coalition government. If that situation were to continue, it may have some effect on the final drawdown of American forces. The administration, however, has already removed a great deal of American military equipment from Iraq, although the Obama administration's exact plans for American involvement in Iraq after 2011 remain unclear (Myers, Shanker, and Healy 2010, 1, 19). In all, Iraq represents a good example of the Obama approach in action and largely a departure from the Bush approach, although the 2011 withdrawal was originally negotiated by the earlier administration (Myers, Shanker, and Healy 2010, 1).

Afghanistan

If Iraq represents a movement away from the Bush approach by the Obama administration, its policy toward Afghanistan appears to be pursuing a course similar to the Bush administration's in Iraq beginning in 2007. To be sure, Candidate Obama had always said that the real threat from international terrorism was in Afghanistan and that the Bush administration had "taken its eye off the ball" with the Iraq War ("Obama to Couric" 2009). As a result, President Obama quickly committed two additional brigades to Afghanistan, increased the number of American drone attacks against terrorist camps, both in Afghanistan and Pakistan, and appointed a new commander in Afghanistan, General Stanley McChrystal, who was ordered to conduct a review of Afghanistan policy and strategy. General McChrystal completed that review in late summer 2009, and his principal recommendation to the president was the need for a substantial increase in American military forces if there was to be a chance of success.

McChrystal's report became a source of considerable internal debate between Obama and his national security team over the next several months. At the end of this debate—in which the president believed he had only received one real option (i.e., increasing the number of American troops)—the president largely supported the military's position (see Woodward 2010). That is, he ordered thirty thousand more American troops—somewhat less than the forty thousand requested—and opted for pursuing a counterinsurgency option (as the military preferred). In ordering both the size of the troop increase and in adopting the counterinsurgency strategy, the policy choice—a "surge strategy"—seemed closely aligned to what President Bush had chosen in Iraq in early 2007. Indeed, the parallelism became complete a few months later when General McChrystal resigned (over some critical remarks about administration officials in *Rolling Stone* magazine) and was replaced by General David Petraeus, who had carried out the surge strategy in Iraq for the Bush administration. Still, some important differences did exist between the Obama surge strategy and the Bush strategy. In announcing his decision at West Point in 2009, President Obama tied the strategy to a commitment to begin withdrawing American troops from Afghanistan in July 2011. Importantly, though, he conditioned the withdrawal of forces on "taking into account conditions on the grounds." Furthermore, this military approach was linked to a civilian strategy to enhance the effectiveness of the Afghan government and a partnership with Pakistan building on "mutual interest, mutual respect, and mutual trust."

The new military strategy was implemented with some initial success, according to the administration's one-year review (Michaels 2010). The civilian strategy within Afghanistan and the relationship with Pakistan, however, have not improved appreciably in the first year since the president's announcement. Indeed, the stability and effectiveness of the Afghan government has remained an area of concern, as has the continued ties between Pakistani military intelligence and elements supportive of the Taliban and al-Qaida. The Obama administration has now once again adjusted its timetable for American withdrawal from that conflict. The administration remains committed to transferring some security responsibility to the Afghan army during 2011 and 2012, but it will now continue the American combat mission there until 2014.

At the NATO summit in November 2010, the alliance outlined a plan to stay in Afghanistan through 2014, as well. Significantly, the similarity between the strategies in Afghanistan and in Iraq for the two administrations was acknowledged by an anonymous American official in late 2010: "Iraq is a pretty decent blueprint for how to transition in Afghanistan" (Baker and Nordland 2010).

Whether this Afghanistan timetable will be altered as a result of American covert military action in May 2011 that found and killed Osama bin Laden, the head of al-Qaeda and the perpetrator of the September 11, 2001, attacks, remains unclear. In a covert operation that reportedly had been in process since August 2010, American intelligence had seemingly located the head of al-Qaeda (although the bin Laden identity had not been fully determined until the actual attack) in Abbottabad, a Pakistani city with a large military installation and academy that's close to the capital. On May 1, 2011, a contingent of American Navy Seals, supported by other forces, stormed the suspected residence, killed Osama bin Laden, and buried him in the Arabian Sea within hours.

Although this action was hailed as a major anti-terrorism success, it immediately raised doubts about the future direction of policy in Afghanistan and Pakistan. Would this action quicken the Obama administration's departure from Afghanistan because of increased domestic and international pressure? Since Pakistan was not informed of this American covert raid, partly due to suspicion over possible ties between the Pakistan military and intelligence forces with terrorist forces, would this rupture ties with Pakistan? Indeed, the Pakistan government protested vigorously over the intrusion into its nation's sovereignty without its permission. Further, would the discovery of Osama bin Laden in this garrison town within one mile of a Pakistan military base turn the American Congress away from the continued aid packages for Pakistan? In all, and ironically, would the future anti-terrorism policy of the Obama administration become more complicated in the months and years ahead in Afghanistan and Pakistan, despite this killing?

North Korea

In keeping with Candidate Obama's commitment to engage with adversaries rather than to confront them, President Obama followed this course with North Korea and Iran during the first two years of his administration, but he had little success with either regime with this strategy.

The Six-Party Talks (among North Korea, South Korea, China, Russia, Japan, and the United States) were the principal diplomatic vehicle used during the Bush administration to address the nuclear issue with North Korea. These talks went through seven different "rounds" during the Bush years with limited success, as North Korea conducted its first underground nuclear test in October 2006. By 2007, however, an apparent agreement was reached on the eventual dismantlement of the North Korean nuclear facilities in exchange for economic assistance from the United States and others, and for moving toward normalization of North Korean relations with several states, including the United States (McCormick 2010, 230–31; "Six Party Talks" 2010). In 2008, however, the implementation of that agreement became stalled as each side accused the other of not fulfilling its commitment. By early 2009, North Korea announced that it was ending its military and political agreement with South Korea ("North Korea Conducts Nuclear Test" 2009), and the seeming progress on denuclearization of the Korean peninsula was halted.

A new North Korean approach was dramatically evident within the first few months of the Obama administration taking office. On virtually the same day in April 2009 that President Obama was calling for a nuclear-free world in a major foreign policy address in Prague, North Korea conducted a missile test that appeared to be a violation of earlier sanctions. A little more than a month later, North Korea conducted a second nuclear test. That action precipitated the United Nations Security Council to enact new sanctions on North Korea. These sanctions tightened restrictions on imports and exports of military-related hardware to North Korea and called on UN members "to inspect and destroy all banned cargo to and from that country—on the high seas, at seaports and airports—if they have reasonable grounds to suspect a violation" (United Nations Security Council 2009). Such inspections, however, remained voluntary on the part of states (and hence weakened their overall impact), although these sanctions were described as "unprecedented" at the time (MacAskill 2009). Near the end of 2009, the administration's special representative for North Korean policy, Ambassador Stephen Bosworth, traveled to North Korea to try to get that country back to the Six-Party Talks, but his effort did not succeed (United States Department of State 2010).

The administration's efforts at engaging North Korea continued to deteriorate in 2010, and as a result, the administration's approach turned increasingly toward placing more sanctions on that regime. In March, a South Korean warship was sunk, killing some forty-six sailors. After an investigation, it was determined that North Korea was responsible for this action. In July 2010, the United Nations Security Council issued a "Presidential Statement" condemning this attack, although not specifically identifying North Korea as responsible for the incident (United Nations Security Council 2010). A short time after that, the Obama administration announced new unilateral economic sanctions against North Korea as yet another way to "tighten the financial vise" around the North Korean leadership, and Secretary of State Hillary Clinton announced that the United States would not engage in negotiations with

North Korea until it agreed to abandon its nuclear weapons program (Landler and Bumiller 2010). In late November, the situation had deteriorated further with the revelation that North Korea had built a new facility for processing uranium (Sanger 2010) and with the North Korean shelling of a South Korean island, killing both civilian and military personnel (McDonald 2010). In all, the Obama administration's effort at engaging the North Koreans, and using increased bilateral and multilateral sanctions to prod them to return to negotiations, had not succeeded in its first two years as measured by one important indicator: no new rounds of the Six-Party Talks were held in 2009 or 2010. Indeed, the North Koreans have been seeking such a meeting, but the Obama administration, reminiscent of the Bush administration approach, has declined until North Korea's behavior changes (Landler 2010).

Iran

A similar lack of progress has occurred in efforts to engage Iran diplomatically over its nuclear ambitions. Over the past decade, Iran has been subject to numerous critical reports from the International Atomic Energy Agency (IAEA) due to its failure to adhere fully to the safeguards agreement required under the Nuclear Non-Proliferation Treaty. The Bush administration was initially reluctant to engage in direct talks with Iran and instead sought to isolate and sanction the regime (including three rounds of sanctions passed by the United Nations Security Council). By 2006, the Bush administration did participate in the P5+1 (China, France, Germany, Russia, the United States, and the United Kingdom) talks with Iran and offered Iran a series of incentives for cooperating with the IAEA and for forgoing its enrichment and reprocessing activities (Arms Control Association 2010). No breakthrough occurred, however.

Nonetheless, the Obama administration sought to build on this diplomatic start. American officials met with Iran through the P5+1 process in October 2009, albeit without notable success. Similarly, an offer by the United States, France, and Russia to provide a plan for providing nuclear fuel assemblies for its research reactor with international safeguards was not accepted by Iran. Instead, Iran continued its nuclear enrichment activities. As a result, the Obama administration turned to impose additional sanctions on that country in an effort to isolate it internationally.

By the middle of 2010, the Obama administration succeeded in getting several additional sanctions placed on Iran. First, the United Nations Security Council passed a fourth set of sanctions against Iran in early June (MacFarquhar 2010b). These sanctions largely focused on military, trade, and financial actions taken by the Islamic Revolutionary Guards in Iran, since this group plays a key role in the country's nuclear program. Second, the administration also obtained new unilateral American sanctions through congressional legislation later that month (Cornwell 2010). Those sanctions endeavored to restrict foreign banks that deal with Iranian banks or with the Islamic Revolutionary Guards from gaining access to the American financial system and sought to restrict gasoline suppliers from providing much-needed fuel to Iran (despite an abundance of oil, Iran has limited refining capacity). Finally, the European Union in late July 2010 imposed an additional series of economic sanctions on Iran (Castle 2010). Such sanctions were particularly important, since the EU has such a large amount of trade with Iran.

According to the administration's strategy, these sanctions were to alter Iran's "cost-benefit" calculation in pursuing nuclear weapons development. By seeking to engage Iran, promoting a norm of nuclear nonproliferation, and imposing economic sanctions, the administration sought to compel Iran to agree to negotiations over its nuclear weapons ambitions. In late summer of 2010, President Obama insisted that this approach was working (Ambinder 2010), although no immediate negotiations were forthcoming. Near the end of the year, however, some movement appeared as a meeting between the P5+1 and Iran was scheduled for early December. The prospects of a real breakthrough at such a meeting, however, looked dim. The more likely outcome was for continued stalemate between the two sides ("Official: Iran, West Agree on Timing of Nuke Talks" 2010; Dahl 2010). Moreover, the December meeting in Geneva produced exactly that result, although the two sides agreed to meet again in Istanbul, Turkey, in January of 2011 (Erlanger 2010), but the meeting, too, did not produce a breakthrough.

CONFRONTING THE ISRAELI-PALESTINIAN CONFLICT

The administration's engagement efforts in seeking progress to resolve the Israeli-Palestinian conflict has produced a bit more movement than those with North Korea and Iran, but no significant breakthrough has occurred so far. When the Obama administration assumed office, discussions between the two parties had broken off after an Israeli military offensive against Gaza in late 2008 in which at least fourteen hundred people were killed, some five thousand injured, and numerous homes, schools, and other buildings destroyed (UN News Service 2010). As a result, prospects for any direct talks between the two parties were slim, and the new Obama administration decided to pursue a different tack in the short term.

Embracing the Bush administration's Middle East goal of creating a two-state solution to the conflict, the Obama administration's initial strategy was to propose the use of "proximity talks" with the Israelis and Palestinians as a vehicle to restart direct negotiations (Prasher 2010). Under the proximity proposal, the United States, and particularly Senator George Mitchell, the US Middle East envoy, would meet with the Israelis and the Palestinians separately and seek to improve the "atmosphere for negotiations" between the parties as a way of moving back to direct negotiations between the parties (United States Department of State 2009b). Both parties eventually agreed to the American proposal, and proximity talks went on for several months, albeit not without difficulties, especially over Israel building settlements on land seized in the Six-Day War. Nonetheless, the administration's persistence paid off. On September 1, 2010, President Obama was able to announce that direct negotiations between the Israelis and Palestinians would be resumed (Obama 2010). The parties also informed the president that they thought they could complete their negotiations within one year. In these negotiations, the Israelis and Palestinians would have responsibility for them, but the Obama administration would continue to assist them in their discussions.

Even as these negotiations were being launched, though, skepticism remained over the prospect for success. That skepticism increased as the Israeli government announced in early November 2010 that it would build thirteen hundred new housing units in East Jerusalem. This announcement brought condemnation from the United States, and the Palestinian negotiator charged that such action was "destroying the peace process" (Mitnick 2010a). A few days later, the Israeli government announced that it was freezing settlements for three months as part of a bargain for military aid and diplomatic support from the United States (Mitnick 2010b), although that deal was later abandoned by the Obama administration (De Young 2010). Instead, the administration reverted to the use of "indirect talks" between the parties by Middle East Envoy George Mitchell, an approach initially adopted by the administration at the beginning of its term ("U.S. Tries Indirect Peace Tactic" 2010). In this sense, the Middle East peace efforts had come full circle in two years, without notable success.

RESTARTING RELATIONS WITH RUSSIA

One area where the Obama administration achieved foreign policy success was in improving relations with Russia. From the beginning of its term, the administration focused on this relationship, and it has succeeded in advancing both bilateral and multilateral cooperation with Russia. The center of this reset effort was the signing of the New START Treaty in April 2010, but several other cooperative efforts also mark the relationship during the first two years of the Obama administration. In this sense, relations with Russia mark a significant change in policy substance and in policy success as compared to the Bush years.

By the end of the Bush administration, American relations with Russia had deteriorated, in part over the American (and NATO-endorsed) decision on deploying a missile defense system in Poland and the Czech Republic and over the Russian intervention into the South Ossetia region of Georgia in the summer of 2008 ("NATO to Back US Missile Defence" 2008; "Russia's Medvedev Hails 'Comrade' Obama" 2009). The Russians saw the missile defense system aimed at them, rather than at Iran, as argued by the Bush administration, and the Americans saw the Russian actions in Georgia as an effort to undermine the independence of the former Soviet republic. In this wary political environment between these two powers, the Obama administration nevertheless set out to reset relations with Russia.

The first meeting between President Obama and President Dmitry Medvedev occurred at the G-20 meeting in London in April 2009 and produced immediate results. Medvedev characterized Obama as "totally different" from Bush and noted the positive nature of their exchanges. Obama noted "real differences" with Russia on some important issues, but he acknowledged that there was "a broad set of common interests that we can pursue" ("Russia's Medvedev Hails 'Comrade' Obama" 2009). Significantly, both leaders issued a statement that they would begin negotiations on a new agreement "on reducing and limiting strategic offensive arms to replace the START Treaty" (White House, Office of the Press Secretary 2009d), and President Obama agreed to visit Moscow the following July.

At that July summit, Presidents Obama and Medvedev took further steps to improve the relationship. The two leaders announced the creation of a Bilateral Presidential Commission between Russia and the United States. This commission would consist of thirteen different working groups. The initial working groups ranged widely—from ones focused on nuclear energy and nuclear security, arms control and international security, foreign policy and fighting terrorism to others focused on energy and the environment, health, space cooperation, and educational and cultural exchanges. Importantly, too, Obama and Medvedev also announced that Russia and America would work on cooperative efforts to address the issue of defense against the proliferation of ballistic missiles (see White House, Office of the Press Secretary 2009b, 2009c, and the United States Department of State 2009a on the commission and ballistic missile defense).

In mid-September 2009, the Obama administration announced an important change in the Bush administration's European missile defense plan. Under the revised Obama missile plan, the United States would not station radars in the Czech Republic or place ten ballistic missile interceptors in Poland. Instead the administration decided on a ten-year phased deployment of missile defense, beginning with a sea-based deployment and a transportable radar surveillance system. The target of this new missile defense plan would be short- and medium-range missiles, particularly those under development by Iran, with less focus on long-range missiles from that country (White House, Office of the Press Secretary 2009a). This change was seen by some as a concession to Russia, since such a system could be viewed as less threatening to Russia than the Bush plan, although the Russian response was somewhat mixed to this change (see Young 2009).

The cooperative relationship continued over the next year, and by June 2010, on the occasion of President Medvedev's visit to the White House, the Obama administration issued a "reset" fact sheet lauding the extent of cooperation between the two nations (White House, Office of the Press Secretary 2010). And, indeed, there were numerous bilateral and multilateral actions that the United States and Russia had addressed. On bilateral issues, the United States and Russia worked on moving Russia toward accession in the World Trade Organization; collaborated on addressing the global financial crisis; agreed to a new energy initiative; pursued military cooperation (including allowing ground and air transit of forces and supplies bound for Afghanistan through Russian territory); and fostered state-to-state cooperation to promote more open governance, democracy, and human rights. On multilateral issues, the United States and Russia cooperated on passing a new set of sanctions on Iran through the UN Security Council (and, in accord with that resolution, Russia agreed not to ship S-300 missiles to Iran), approving a new sanctioning resolution through the United Nations over North Korea's second nuclear test, pursuing stability and the restoration of democracy in Kyrgyzstan after the violence there in summer 2010, and developing some "confidence building" measures over dealing with Abkhazia and South Ossetia in Georgia.

All of these efforts (including numerous nongovernmental activities) reflect the change in the Russian-American relationship, but none appeared as crucial in reestablishing this relationship as the New START Treaty. This treaty (with its name a play on words to convey the changing ties) would require Russia and the United States to reduce their deployed nuclear delivery vehicles (intercontinental ballistic missiles, submarine-launched missiles, and long-range bombers) by about 50 percent from the previous limit in the 1991 START Treaty (see McCormick 2010, 166) to eight hundred in total, with a maximum of seven hundred such vehicles deployed (New START Treaty 2010). It would also require each side to reduce the number of nuclear warheads to 1,550. Such a total would represent a reduction of about 30 percent from the maximum level allowed under the Strategic Offensive Reduction Treaty (SORT) of 2002 (Arms Control Association 2002). The Obama administration viewed this treaty as not only important in improving the bilateral relationship but also as important in advancing its larger nuclear nonproliferation goal. By the end of 2010, the US Senate had recommended ratification of this treaty, and this centerpiece of Obama's US-Russian and nonproliferation agenda had become a notable foreign policy success for the administration.

INITIATING GLOBAL COMMON ISSUES

In addition to American-Russian relations, global common issues have also been an important area where the Obama administration has moved beyond the agenda of the previous administration with its own initiatives. Nuclear nonproliferation, global financial reform, and climate change represent especially new departures by the Obama administration, but policy success with these initiatives remains elusive so far.

Nonproliferation

Although the New START Treaty represents one aspect of the Obama administration's nonproliferation activities, the administration has a much broader agenda in this area. The administration is pursuing at least three other initiatives to promote nuclear nonproliferation. The first involves the Obama administration's new directives on when nuclear weapons would be used by the United States. Specifically, the administration committed the United States to refraining from using nuclear weapons against those nonnuclear states that are parties to the NPT and those states that are fully in compliance with NPT requirements. If these nonnuclear states were to utilize biological and chemical weapons against the United States, the American response would generally be with conventional weapons (although a slight opening remains for a nuclear response in exceptional cases). Toward nuclear weapons states and those states not in compliance with the NPT, the potential use of nuclear weapons would remain, but such use would occur "only in extreme circumstances to defend the vital interests of the United States, our allies and partners" (*Nuclear Posture Review Report* 2010, ix; Nuclear Posture Review Briefing 2010). In essence, then, the administration was seeking to move toward a more stable nuclear-use policy and encourage other states in this direction as well.

The second initiative was President Obama's decision to convene the Washington Nuclear Security Summit in April 2010 with forty-seven countries in attendance. The goal of that summit was to address how best "to prevent terrorist, criminals, or other unauthorized actors from acquiring nuclear materials" that may be available today. The summit ended with a communiqué, a commitment to meet this goal within four years, a work plan for the future, and an agreement to meet again in 2012 ("Communiqué of the Washington Nuclear Security Summit" 2010). All of these commitments, however, were voluntary, and some potential or existing nuclear states (e.g., Iran and North Korea) and potential proliferators were not invited ("The Nuclear Security Summit" 2010). Still, this initiative is an important first step, and it remains largely a work in progress.

The third initiative focused on a reaffirmation of the world's commitment to nonproliferation at the 2010 Nuclear Non-Proliferation Review Conference. After some four weeks of debate and discussion among the conferees in May 2010, the review meeting did announce two important agreements: the 189 signatories to the NPT reaffirmed their commitment to it, and the parties agreed to a 2012 deadline for a Middle East conference to address unconventional weapons in that part of the world (MacFarquhar 2010a). Although the Middle East conference actually taking place seems doubtful in light of the ongoing conflict in that region, the reaffirmation of the NPT provides important support for the Obama administration's efforts to advance its nuclear nonproliferation agenda.

Financial Reform

Global financial reform was a second global commons initiative advanced by the Obama administration. This initiative was driven in large part by the difficult economic environment that President Obama inherited as he assumed the presidency. The goal of this reform is to create a sounder financial system by standardizing banking regulations and regulating the various investment instruments used worldwide. The principal forum that the Obama administration has been using to make progress on this issue has been the G-20 summits. The American effort actually began with the G-20 Washington Summit in late 2008 at the end of the Bush administration, but it has been continued at the subsequent G-20 summits in London and Pittsburgh in 2009 and in Toronto and Seoul in 2010. A global framework has now been outlined to regulate global banking capital and reserve requirements, as noted at the G-20 Summit in Seoul, but the new framework will only start to be implemented in 2013. Importantly, though, the framework will still need to be incorporated into national law by the states involved. Further, there remain other areas of work, as well, such as developing a common framework on dealing with financial institutions that are "too big to fail" and protecting taxpayers from bearing these costs (see "Complete Text: G-20 Seoul Communiqué" 2010). Finally, differences remain over the regulation of some financial instruments, such as hedge funds, with the European states seeking much greater control of such instruments than the United States (Schneider and Cho 2010).

Climate Change

American policy on climate change under the Obama administration further represents a significant change from the Bush administration. Indeed, the administration came to office with a substantial commitment to lead international environmental change and took a number of initial steps at home to promote that agenda. Early on, Secretary of State Hillary Clinton (2009a) appointed a special envoy for climate change as a way to advance this agenda within the government. The administration also advanced a "green jobs" agenda at home, included some $80 billion in the 2009 stimulus package to address energy issues, and announced new emission standards for new vehicles built for 2017 through 2025 (Stern 2010). Further, the administration was successful in getting the House of Representatives (although not the Senate) to pass a "cap-and-trade" bill, which would have imposed mandatory limits on the emission of greenhouse gases and encouraged the use of cleaner energy sources for the future (Carey 2009).

   With these domestic initiatives in place, the administration seemed well positioned to argue for significant global reform at the United Nations Conference on Climate Change in Copenhagen, Denmark, in December 2009. Yet, this was not to be. President Obama personally attended the meeting of 192 countries, and he worked tirelessly to broker the divide between developed and developing countries on an international accord or even a commitment to a legally binding agreement. What was ultimately achieved was a three-page agreement among China, India, Brazil, and South Africa in which a commitment was made to assist developing countries in adapting to climate change ($30 billion a year through 2012, and a total of $100 billion by 2020). Further, a commitment was also made to limit the increase in the global temperature to below two degrees Celsius. Yet, these commitments were political statements only, and they did not include any means of enforcement. Although President Obama contended that the agreement was a "breakthrough," he also acknowledged that "this progress alone is not enough" (Broder 2009).

   As the Obama administration moved to the next scheduled international conference on climate change in Cancun, Mexico, in late November to mid-December 2010, the prospects for success did not appear bright. The outcome of that meeting was described as "modest," although sufficient to continue the international effort in the year ahead (Broder 2010). Still, environmental legislation is highly unlikely with the new political composition of the US House and Senate, and it appears unlikely that the United States can meet its financial obligations to aid the developing countries in light of the large budget deficits and economic problems at home. Nonetheless, prior to the Cancun meeting, the administration's special envoy for climate change pledged to press forward with its agenda (Eilperin 2010), and afterward, this envoy described Cancun as "a significant step forward that builds on the progress made in Copenhagen" (Broder 2010). In all, though, success with this initiative remains extremely modest.

CONCLUSION

The Obama administration came to office promising foreign policy change, but the degree of change so far has been limited. In outlining a liberal-internationalist foreign policy approach, the Obama administration has surely achieved change from the approach followed by the Bush administration. In seeking to implement that approach—whether evaluated through the changes in the substance of American policy or through the achievements that it has had—the Obama administration has had much less success. In this sense, continuity in several foreign policy arenas remains more prevalent than change during the first two years of the Obama administration.

Indeed, several areas reflect considerable continuity. For instance, the Obama administration made an initial attempt to infuse domestic values into foreign policy with its three executive orders on the treatment of terrorist suspects, but the most visible symbol of the Bush policy—Guantanamo Bay—remains open and military commissions continue, as well. President Obama's personal popularity initially softened America's image abroad as compared to the Bush years, but that new "soft power" has not been translated very easily into support for American foreign policy. Further, on major security issues, with the exception of ending the Iraq War, the Obama administration's policy reflects more continuity than change—whether addressing the Afghanistan War, the Middle East, or the nuclear threats from North Korea and Iran. Indeed, the strategy of engagement with North Korea and Iran has not yielded success; instead, relations with both countries appear to have eroded.

Still, the Obama administration has initiated some substantive foreign policy changes, and in at least one area, it has achieved notable success. The Obama administration has begun to address a number of global common issues with new policy approaches—whether global financial reform, climate change, or nuclear nonproliferation. The degree of success in each of these areas remains unclear, but these policies do represent new departures from the Bush years. Finally, and importantly, Obama's strategy of engagement with Russia has had a substantial effect in improving that relationship and a

New START Treaty is a crucial consequence of the "reset" in relations with that country.

In all, though, these foreign policy results are modest, especially for a "big bang presidency," as Steven Schier characterizes the Obama administration's approach to the office in the introduction to this volume. In this sense, the Obama administration's foreign policy is still largely a "work in progress," as one analysis described it (Pershing 2010), or one with lots of "big ideas" but one short on implementation, as another summarized it (Ignatius 2010). Yet, the Obama administration will find the political landscape over the next two years hardly favorable for implementing its foreign policy approach. With the shift to Republican control of the US House of Representatives and the lessening of Democratic control in the US Senate after the 2010 congressional elections, and with the increasingly threatening international environment—whether from the difficulties in the Afghan War, a more assertive North Korea, or the continuing actions of Iran (or perhaps elsewhere)—the administration will likely find it difficult to continue its liberal internationalist agenda, much as the Clinton administration found after the 1994 congressional elections. In this sense, foreign policy change may be in the air for the Obama administration, but perhaps not in the way that it had originally intended.

REFERENCES

Ambinder, Marc. 2010. "Obama Makes the Case That His Iran Policy Is Working." *The Atlantic*, August 5. http://www.theatlantic.com/politics/archive/2010/08/obama-makes-the-case-that-his-iran-policy-is-working/60967. Accessed November 16, 2010.

Arms Control Association. 2002. Strategic Offensive Reduction Treaty (SORT), May 24. http://www.armscontrol.org/documents/sort. Accessed November 23, 2010.

———. 2010. "History of Official Proposals on the Iranian Nuclear Issue." http://www.armscontrol.org/factsheets/Iran_Nuclear_Proposals. Accessed November 24, 2010.

Baker, Peter, and Rod Nordland. 2010. "U.S. Plan Envisions Path to Ending Afghan Combat." *New York Times*, November 14. http://www.nytimes.com/2010/11/15/world/asia/15prexy.html?_r=1&nl=todaysheadlines&emc=a2&pagewanted=print. Accessed November 14, 2010.

Broder, John M. 2009. "Many Goals Remain Unmet in 5 Nations' Climate Deal." *New York Times*, December 19. http://www.nytimes.com/2009/12/19/science/earth/19climate.html. Accessed November 9, 2010.

———. 2010. "Climate Talks End with Modest Deal on Emissions." *New York Times*, December 11. http://www.nytimes.com/2010/12/12/science/earth/12climate.html. Accessed December 27, 2010.

Carey, John. 2009. "House Passes Carbon Cap-and-Trade Bill." *Bloomberg Businessweek*, June 26. http://www.businessweek.com/blogs/money_politics/archives/2009/06/house_passes_ca.html. Accessed November 23, 2010.

Castle, Stephen. 2010. "Europe Imposes New Sanctions on Iran." *New York Times*, July 26. http://www.nytimes.com/2010/07/27/world/middleeast/27iran.html. Accessed November 16, 2010.

Chan, Sewell. 2010. "South Korea and U.S. Reach Deal on Trade." *New York Times*, December 3. http://www.nytimes.com/2010/12/04/business/global/04trade.html. Accessed on December 6, 2010.

Chan, Sewell, Sheryl Gay Stolberg, and David E. Sanger. 2010. "Obama's Trade Strategy Runs into Stiff Resistance." *New York Times*, November 11. http://www.nytimes.com/2010/11/12/business/global/12group.html?src=me&pagewanted=print. Accessed November 15, 2010.

"CIA Claims to Close Secret Prisons But Promises to Imprison People Somewhere Else and Oppose Prosecuting Past Crimes." 2009. *War Is a Crime*, April 10. http://warisacrime.org/node/41585. Accessed on November 2, 2010.

Clinton, Hillary. 2009a. "Appointment of Special Envoy on Climate Change Todd Stern." January 26. http://www.state.gov/secretary/rm/2009a/01/115409.htm. Accessed November 23, 2010.

———. 2009b. "Secretary Clinton's Speech at the Council on Foreign Relations." July 15. http://www.realclearpolitics.com/articles/2009/07/15/clinton_speech_transcript_council_foreign_relations_97491.html. Accessed on July 4, 2010.

"Communiqué of the Washington Nuclear Security Summit." 2010. Council on Foreign Relation, April 13. http://www.cfr.org/publication/21896/communiqu_of_the_washington_nuclear_security_summit.html. Accessed November 9, 2010.

"Complete Text: G-20 Seoul Communiqué." 2010. *International Business Times*, November 12. http://www.ibtimes.com/articles/81220/20101112/communique.htm. Accessed on November 22, 2010.

Cornwell, Susan. 2010. "Congress OKs Sanctions on Iran's Energy, Banks." *Reuters*, June 25. http://www.reuters.com/article/idUSTRE65N6RZ20100625. Accessed November 16, 2010.

Dahl, Fredrik. 2010. "Analysis: Are Iran Nuclear Talks Doomed to Fail Again?" *Reuters*, November 15. http://www.reuters.com/article/idUSTRE6AE22V20101115. Accessed November 17, 2010.

De Young, Karen. 2010. "U.S. Abandons Push for Renewal of Israeli Settlement Freeze." *Washington Post*, December 8. http://www.washingtonpost.com/wp-dyn/content/article/2010/12/07/AR2010120707310.html?wpisrc=nl_politics. Accessed December 8, 2010.

Eilperin, Juliet. 2010. "U.S. Plays Conflicted Role in Global Climate Debate." *The Washington Post*, November 1. http://www.washingtonpost.com/wp-dyn/content/article/2010/10/31/AR2010103103378.html. Accessed November 1, 2010.

Erlanger, Steven. 2010. "More Nuclear Talks with Iran Are Set." *New York Times*, December 7. http://www.nytimes.com/2010/12/08/world/europe/08iran.html. Accessed December 27, 2010.

Executive Orders 13491, 13492, and 13493. 2009. *Federal Register* 74 (16): 4893–4902. http://www.archives.gov/federal-register/executive-orders/2009-obama.html. Accessed October 29, 2010.

Ignatius, David. 2010. "Obama's Foreign Policy: Big Ideas, Little Implementation." *Washington Post,* October 17. http://www.washingtonpost.com/wp-dyn/content/article/2010/10/14/AR2010101406505.html. Accessed November 29, 2010.

Ikenberry, G. John. 2008. "Introduction: "Woodrow Wilson, the Bush Administration, and the Future of Liberal Internationalism." In *The Crisis of American Foreign Policy: Wilsonianism in the Twenty-first Century,* edited by G. John Ikenberry, Thomas J. Knock, Anne-Marie Slaughter, and Tony Smith, 1–24. Princeton, NJ: Princeton University Press.

International Coalition for the Responsibility to Protect. 2011. http://www.responsibilitytoprotect.org/index.php/about-rtop#world_summit. Accessed May 14, 2011.

Landler, Mark. 2010. "Obama Urges China to Check North Koreans." *New York Times,* December 6. http://www.nytimes.com/2010/12/07/world/asia/07diplo.html?nl=todaysheadlines&emc=a2. Accessed December 7, 2010.

Landler, Mark, and Elisabeth Bumiller. 2010. "U.S. to Add to Sanctions on N. Korea." *New York Times,* July 21. http://www.nytimes.com/2010/07/22/world/asia/22military.html. Accessed November 15, 2006.

MacAskill, Ewen. 2009. "UN Approves 'Unprecedented' Sanctions against North Korea over Nuclear Test." *Guardian,* June 12. http://www.guardian.co.uk/world/2009/jun/12/un-north-korea-nuclear-sanctions. Accessed November 15, 2010.

MacFarquhar, Neil. 2010a. "189 Nations Reaffirm Goal of Ban on Nuclear Weapons." *New York Times,* May 28. http://www.nytimes.com/2010/05/29/world/middleeast/29nuke.html. Accessed November 24, 2010.

———. 2010b. "U.N. Approves New Sanctions to Deter Iran." *New York Times,* June 9. http://www.nytimes.com/2010/06/10/world/middleeast/10sanctions.html. Accessed November 16, 2010.

McCormick, James M. 2010. *American Foreign Policy and Process,* 5th ed. Boston, MA: Wadsworth/Cengage Learning.

McDonald, Mark. 2010. "'Crisis Status' in South Korea After North Shells Island." *New York Times,* November 23. http://www.nytimes.com/2010/11/24/world/asia/24korea.html. Accessed December 6, 2010.

Michaels, Jim. 2010. "Obama Says Afghan Withdrawal on Track." *USA Today,* December 17, 9A.

Mitnick, Joshua. 2010a. "After GOP Victory, Emboldened Israel Declares New Building in East Jerusalem." *Christian Science Monitor,* November 8. http://www.csmonitor.com/World/Middle-East/2010/1108/After-GOP-victory-emboldened-Israel-declares-new-building-in-East-Jerusalem. Accessed November 17, 2010.

———. 2010b. "Netanyahu Strikes a Deal on Israeli Settlements—Could It Freeze Peace, Too? *Christian Science Monitor,* November 15. http://www.csmonitor.com/World/Middle-East/2010/1115/Netanyahu-strikes-a-deal-on-Israeli-settlements-could-it-freeze-peace-too. Accessed November 17, 2010.

Myers, Steven Lee, Thom Shanker, and Jack Healy. 2010. "Iraqi Politics Raises Questions about U.S. Military Presence." *New York Times*, December 19, 1, 19.

"NATO to Back US Missile Defence." 2008. *BBC News*, April 3. http://news bbc .co.uk/2/hi/7328915.htm. Accessed November 19, 2010.

The New START Treaty. 2010. Council on Foreign Relations, April 8. http://www .cfr.org/publication/21851/new_start_treaty.html. Accessed November 23, 2010.

"North Korea Conducts Nuclear Test." 2009. *BBC News*, May 25. http://news.bbc .co.uk/2/hi/8066615.stm. Accessed November 15, 2010.

NPR. 2011. "Obama's Speech on Libya: 'A Responsibility to Act.'" March 28. http:// www.npr.org/2011/03/28/134935452/obamas-speech-on-libya-a-responsibility-to -act. Accessed on May 14, 2011.

Nuclear Posture Review Briefing. 2010. US Department of Defense, April 6. http:// www.defense.gov/npr/docs/10-04-06_NPR%20201%20Briefing%20-%201032 .pdf. Accessed November 24, 2010.

Nuclear Posture Review Report. 2010. US Department of Defense, April. http://www .defense.gov/npr/docs/2010%20nuclear%20posture%20review%20report.pdf. Accessed November 24, 2010.

"The Nuclear Security Summit." 2010. *New York Times*, Editorial, April 12. http:// www.nytimes.com/2010/04/12/opinion/12mon1.html. Accessed November 9, 2010.

Obama, Barack. 2010. "Remarks by the President in the Rose Garden after Bilateral Meetings." The White House, Office of the Press Secretary. September 1 at http:// www.whitehouse.gov/the-press-office/2010/09/01/remarks-president-rose-garden -after-bilateral-meetings. Accessed November 17, 2010.

"Obama to Couric: 'We took our eye off the ball.'" 2009. *POLITICO*, January 14. http://www.politico.com/news/stories/0109/17460.html. Accessed November 23, 2010.

"Official: Iran, West Agree on Timing of Nuke Talks." 2010. *Washington Post*, November 16. http://www.washingtonpost.com/wp-dyn/content/article/2010/11/16/ AR2010111600934.html. Accessed on November 17, 2010.

Pershing, Ben. 2010. "Obama's Foreign Policy a Work in Progress." *Washington Post*, April 14. http://voices.washingtonpost.com/44/2010/04/rundown---041410 .html. Accessed November 29, 2010.

Pew Global Attitudes Project. 2009. "Confidence in Obama Lifts U.S. Image around the World," July 23. http://pewglobal.org/files/pdf/264.pdf. Accessed November 12, 2010.

———. 2010. "Obama More Popular Abroad Than At Home, Global Image of U.S. Continues to Benefit," June 17. http://pewglobal.org/2010/06/17/obama-more -popular-abroad-than-at-home. Accessed November 12, 2010.

Prasher, Ilene R. 2010. "US Pushes Israelis and Palestinians to 'Proximity' Peace Talks." *Christian Science Monitor*, February 9. http://www.csmonitor.com/layout/ set/print/content/view/print/279215. Accessed November 17, 2010.

Renshon, Stanley A. 2010. *National Security in the Obama Administration: Reassessing the Bush Doctrine*. New York and London: Routledge.

"Russia's Medvedev Hails 'Comrade' Obama." 2009. April 2. http://www.google .com/hostednews/afp/article/ALeqM5gEo4B1heuBvO6KK7EiBHKigO1UrA. Accessed November 19, 2010.

Sanger, David E. 2010. "North Koreans Unveil New Plant for Nuclear Use." *New York Times*, November 21. http://www.nytimes.com/2010/11/21/world/asia/21intel .html?_r=1&nl=todaysheadlines&emc=a2. Accessed November 21, 2010.

Savage, Charles. 2010. "Closing Guantanamo Fades as a Priority." *New York Times*, June 25. http://www.nytimes.com/2010/06/26/us/politics/26gitmo.html. Accessed November 1, 2010.

Schneider, Howard, and David Cho. 2010. "U.S., Europe at Odds over Global Financial Reform." *Washington Post*, March 13, A01.

Shane, Scott. 2009a. "C.I.A. to Close Secret Prisons for Terror Suspects." *New York Times*, April 10. http://www.nytimes.com/2009/04/10/world/10detain.html. Accessed October 29, 2010.

———. 2009b. "Obama Orders Secret Prisons and Detention Camps Closed." *New York Times*, January 23. http://www.nytimes.com/2009/01/23/us/politics/ 23GITMOCND.html. Accessed October 29, 2010.

"Six Party Talks." 2010. *Wikipedia*. http://en.wikipedia.org/wiki/Six-party_talks. Accessed November 15, 2010.

Stern, Todd. 2010. "A New Paradigm: Climate Change Negotiations in the Post-Copenhagen Era." Address to the University of Michigan Law School, October 8. http:// www.state.gov/g/oes/rls/remarks/2010/149429.htm. Accessed November 22, 2010.

Tapper, Jake, and Sunlen Miller. 2011 "President Obama Orders Resumption of Military Commission Trials for Accused Detainees at Gitmo." ABC News. March 7. http://blogs.abcnews.com/politicalpunch/2011/03/president-obama-orders -resumption-of-military-commission-trials-for-accused-detainees-at-gitmo.html. Accessed May 14, 2011.

UN News Service. 2010. "Middle East: As Proximity Talks Start, Hopes for Progress Voiced at UN." May 10. http://www.un.org /apps/new/printnewsAR .asp?nid=34643. Accessed November 17, 2010.

United Nations Security Council, Department of Public Information. 2009. United Nations Resolution 1874, "Security Council, Acting Unanimously, Condemns in Strongest Terms Democratic People's Republic of Korea, Nuclear Test, Toughens Sanctions." June 12. http://www.un.org/News/Press/docs/2009/sc9679.doc.htm. Accessed November 16, 2010.

———. 2010. "Security Council Condemns Attack on Republic of Korea Naval Ship 'Cheonan,' Stresses Need to Prevent Further Attacks, Other Hostilities in Region." July 9. http://www.un.org/News/Press/docs/2010/sc9975.doc.htm. Accessed November 16, 2010.

———. 2011a. "Resolution 1970 (2011)." February 26. http://daccess-dds-ny.un.org/ doc/UNDOC/GEN/N11/245/58/PDF/N1124558.pdf?OpenElement. Accessed May 14, 2011.

———. Department of Public Information. 2011b. "Security Council Approves 'No-Fly Zone' Over Libya, Authorizing 'All Necessary Measures' to Protect Civilians, by Vote of 10 in Favour with 5 Abstentions." March 17. http://www.un.org/New/ Press/docs/2011/sc10200.doc.htm. Accessed May 14, 2011.

United States Department of State. 2009a. "Bilateral Presidential Commission Fact Sheet." October 15. http://www.state.gov/p/eur/rls/fs/130616,htm. Accessed November 20, 2010.

———. 2009b. "Briefing by Special Envoy for Middle East Peace George Mitchell." November 25. http://www.state.gov/r/pa/prs/ps/2009/nov/132447.htm. Accessed November 17, 2010.

United States Department of State, Bureau of East Asian and Pacific Affairs. 2010. "Background Note: North Korea." September 29.http://www.state.gov/r/pa/ei/ bgn/2792.htm. Accessed November 16, 2010.

"U.S. Tries Indirect Peace Tactic." 2010. *Milwaukee Journal Sentinel*, December 14, 5A.

Welna, David. 2009. "Democrats Block Funding to Close Guantanamo." May 20. http://www.npr.org/templates/story/story.php?storyId=104334339. Accessed November 2, 2010.

The White House. 2010. *National Security Strategy.* May 27. http://www.whitehouse .gov/sites/default/files/rss_viewer/national_security_strategy.pdf. Accessed November 12, 2010.

The White House, Office of the Press Secretary. 2009a. "Fact Sheet on U.S. Missile Defense Policy, A 'Phased, Adaptive Approach' for Missile Defense in Europe." September 17. http://www.whitehouse.gov/the_press_office/FACT-SHEET-US -Missile-Defense-Policy-A-Phased-Adaptive-Approach-for-Missile-Defense-in -Europe. Accessed on November 18, 2010.

———. 2009b. "Fact Sheet: U.S.-Russia Bilateral Presidential Commission." July 6. http://www.whitehouse.gov/the_press_office/FACT-SHEET-US-Russia-Bilateral -Presidential-Commission. Accessed November 19, 2010.

———. 2009c. "Joint Statement by Dmitry A. Medvedev, President of the Russian Federation, and Barack Obama, President of the United States, on Missile Defense Issues." July 6. http://www.whitehouse.gov/the_press_office/Joint-Statement-by -Dmitry-A-Medvedev-President-of-the-Russian-Federation-and-Barack-Obama -President-of-the-United-States-of-America-on-Missile-Defense-Issues. Accessed on November 19, 2010.

———. 2009d. "Joint Statement by Dmitry A. Medvedev, President of the Russian Federation, and Barack Obama, President of the United States of America, Regarding Negotiations on Further Reductions in Strategic Offensive Arms." April 1. http://www.whitehouse.gov/the_press_office/Joint-Statement-by-Dmitriy-A -Medvedev-and-Barack-Obama. Accessed on November 19, 2010.

———. 2010. "U.S.-Russia Relations: 'Reset' Fact Sheet." June 24. http://www .whitehouse.gov/the-press-office/us-russia-relations-reset-fact-sheet. Accessed on November 19, 2010.

Woodward, Bob. 2010. *Obama's Wars.* New York: Simon & Schuster.

Young, Thomas. 2009. "Issue Brief: The Reconfiguration of European Missile Protection Russia's Response and the Likely Implications." *NTI*, October 9. http:// www.nti.org/e_research/e3_missile_defense.html. Accessed November 18, 2010.

Conclusion

How Transformative a Presidency?

Steven E. Schier

How transformative has Barack Obama's presidency been? We must consider changes in politics and policy already wrought by his actions in the White House, and his future prospects for short- and long-term changes. It's a complicated topic. The authors here bring many differing points of view to it.

ACTUAL AND PROBABLE TRANSFORMATIONS

Some major transformations engendered by Obama have already occurred. Several new policy directions are now in law. Foremost among them is the 2010 health-care reform, which expands health-care coverage to the uninsured, creates health-insurance exchanges to assist health-care consumers, requires all citizens to purchase health insurance, and increases taxes on a variety of medical services and devices. Opponents of the law are challenging its constitutionality in federal court, arguing, for example, that the insurance-purchase mandate goes beyond the power of Congress to "regulate interstate commerce." This issue will probably end up before the Supreme Court. The newly Republican-controlled House voted 245 to 189 along party lines to repeal the law in January 2011. Obama, however, can rely on the power of the veto and a Democratic Senate majority to overcome those efforts.

Several other laws seem more secure. The 2009 stimulus bill, providing $787 billion in federal funds for a wide variety of domestic purposes, is now largely spent, though its impact on the American economy remains much debated. At the end of 2010, a second stimulus passed with contents very different from the 2009 law. It extended the tax cuts of the George W. Bush administration, including the abolition of the estate tax and personal income tax cuts for high-income individuals, much derided by liberal Democrats. Even so, a majority of the 2010 bill involved additional spending through the extension of unemployment benefits and other measures. The bipartisan consensus propelling the bill to passage makes its status in law safe. Richard E. Matland and Andrea L. Walker also note that many changes in social policy regarding women, minorities, and gays, such as repeal of the "Don't Ask, Don't Tell" policy regarding gays in the military, are unlikely to be reversed soon, if ever.

In foreign policy, the major accomplishments are ratification of a new START treaty reducing the nuclear weapons stockpiles of the United States and Russia, the pending ratification of a free-trade agreement with South Korea, and the death of Osama bin Laden. These are components of Obama's broader efforts to bring about an era of cooperation with Russia, expand America's international trade prospects, and triumph over terrorism. As James M. McCormick notes in his chapter, none of these accomplishments amounted to a major transformation in foreign policy.

Certain lasting transformations in American politics promise to boost the Obama presidency. Obama's many social policy changes benefiting women, minorities, and gays, mentioned here by Richard E. Matland and Andrea L. Walker, may enthuse these elements of his electoral base in 2012. John K. White and John J. Coleman note the increasing importance of central elements of Obama's electoral coalition—Latinos, African Americans, and young voters—in American elections. This pro-Democratic trend is likely to persist well into the future. Younger voters will include increasing proportions of Latinos and African Americans, reinforcing the broader trend. Obama's African American support is overwhelming, probably strengthening their identification with the party for the future. The majority of Latinos vote Democratic, and this trend may well persist. Cuban Americans do vote more Republican than other Latinos, but this trends is weakening among younger Cubanos (Marrero 2004). Younger voters persisted in their Democratic voting in 2010. They may remain a disproportionately pro-Democratic group because youthful partisan allegiances tend to persist as individuals age (Sears and Funk 1999). Still, if Latinos and African Americans improve their economic situations, they may become more Republican in their voting, as may younger voters as they acquire spouses, mortgages, and children. At present, though, these demographic changes favor Obama and the Democrats.

Some shorter-term transformations, however, do not augur well for Obama politically. The 2010 census resulted in a shift of six House seats and electoral votes from 2008 Obama states to McCain states (Babington 2010). In the redistricting of all 435 House seats in 2011 by the states, the GOP will totally control the redrawing of 196 seats and Democrats only 49, the largest GOP redistricting advantage since the 1920s (Blake 2010). Transformations of this sort complicate Obama's reelection bid and make continued GOP House control more likely. They also may offset, at least temporarily, the long-term gains for Democrats due to the demographic changes noted above.

POSSIBLE TRANSFORMATIONS

Obama's presidency has produced many possible transformations that hang in the balance as his time in the White House transpires. Several administration policy goals remain achievable, perhaps even by the end of Obama's first term. Our military prospects in Afghanistan, for example, may be changing for the better. In late 2010, reports arrived of gradual success in some aspects of Afghanistan military operations (DeYoung 2010). The demise of Osama bin Laden may augment this trend. Should the trend magnify, it might redound much to Obama's political benefit because public majorities disapproved of our role in Afghanistan by late 2010 (*Washington Post/ABC News* 2010a). The ratification of the START treaty at the end of 2010 may yield diplomatic dividends with Russia that could enable Obama to enlist their assistance in handling difficulties with Iran and North Korea.

Newly ascendant Republicans in Congress may pursue cooperative efforts with Obama on two fronts. First, bipartisan consensus may greet Obama's efforts to encourage teacher-performance pay, charter schools, and other challenges to the preferred positions of teacher unions (Anderson 2010). Second, Obama's willingness to negotiate additional free-trade agreements may garner GOP support, given that party's long-standing support of open international trade (Zengerle and Palmer 2010). Prospects for bipartisan agreement on judicial nominations, Nancy Maveety notes, is less likely. In sum, Obama's successes with Congress will probably involve few "big bang" policy innovations and more incremental changes—"small ball" but without "long game" landmark successes—as Bertram Johnson puts it.

STUBBORN CONTINUITIES

Some changes desired by Obama seem unlikely to occur. As Nicol C. Rae notes, the 2010 elections negate the possibility that 2008 was a realigning election that produced a durable electoral majority and a lasting governing regime for Democrats. Politically crucial Independents had abandoned Obama, with majorities of them voting against Democrats in the 2010 elections and disapproving of his conduct of the presidency (*Huffington Post*

2010). Democrats also received the lowest percentage of the white vote in 2010 in many decades. Obama's reelection may turn on convincing disgruntled Independents and white voters to reelect him, and the prospects for this remain unclear. This may all hinge on yet another uncertainty, that of economic recovery. By early 2011, it seemed that the greatest economic dangers had passed, but as Raymond Tatalovich notes, the pace and prospects for economic recovery are far from certain. The overall fate of the Obama presidency seemingly turns on this. The 2012 electoral uncertainties reflect the frustration of Obama's reconstruction and regime aspirations.

At this writing, Obama is plagued by foreign policy problems that also seem unlikely to be resolved to his liking soon. Chief among these are difficult situations involving Iran, Libya, North Korea, and the Israeli-Palestinian situation. Obama's problems here, as James M. McCormick notes, lie both in the recalcitrance of the nations involved and in the difficulty in building large and effective international coalitions to confront the unruly nations. It may take a major international crisis like 9/11 to empower Obama to overcome such international challenges.

In domestic politics, established lines of conflict in certain policy areas likewise seem resistant to change. Nancy Maveety notes the polarized politics of judicial appointments, now a decades-long pattern, will probably continue. James L. Guth explains how the "culture war" between conservatives and liberals has altered little during recent presidencies, with Obama's being no exception. On these and other fronts, Obama will continue to face the disadvantage of asymmetrical conflict with a "headless" GOP, as described by John J. Pitney Jr. Until, of course, a Republican presidential nominee emerges, at which point the Obama White House will gain strategic ground and have an inviting target.

OBAMA AND 2012

What are Obama's reelection prospects? Polls indicate a mixed picture for him. Some recent trends favor Republicans and conservatives. After lagging for several years, GOP party identification among the public reached parity with that of Democrats in late 2010. Including Independents who "lean to a party," Gallup found that the GOP coalition equals 43 percent of the public and the Democrats' 42 percent (Jones 2010). The number of self-identified conservatives averaged 40 percent through 2010, outnumbering moderates and liberals and equaling the previous high levels of 2003, 2004, and 2009 (Saad 2010). Surveys consistently report that less than a majority of respondents believe Obama deserves reelection (Bloomberg 2010; *Fox News* 2010).

Other poll numbers can give Obama hope. His job approval rating averaged in the high 40s in early 2011. Since job approval numbers often mirror a
president's actual reelection percentage, he remains in a competitive position
for 2012. None of the prominent potential GOP candidates—former Massachusetts governor Mitt Romney, former Arkansas governor Mike Huckabee,
former vice presidential nominee Sarah Palin, or former House speaker Newt
Gingrich—defeat Obama in head-to-head polling matchups (*Washington
Post/ABC News* 2010b; *POLITICO* 2010). Obama's performance against
prospective GOP candidates, however, may be overstated in his favor given
the low public knowledge about several of his rivals (Sarah Palin being an
exception to this). Obama's reelection will be a hard-fought and probably
close battle in which he cannot be deemed a clear favorite.

Obama will coast to reelection if he scores a political "trifecta." First, the
economy must recover enough to cause more Independents and white voters
to support him and to propel his base of African Americans, Latinos, and
young voters to turn out in large numbers as they did in 2008. Second, Obama
needs an absence of foreign policy crises that dominate the public agenda and
raise widespread doubts about his leadership, as did the Iranian hostage crisis
that bested Jimmy Carter in 1979 and 1980. Third, the right sort of opponent
must appear. Ideally, this opponent must be well known and not well liked,
giving the rival a durable disadvantage with the electorate. Sarah Palin may
come closest to fitting this description. For Obama to regain the "big bang"
potential of his presidency, then, much must go right in 2011 and 2012.

Short of a return of the "big bang" are the prospects of either defeat or a
narrow reelection win accompanied by divided government requiring con-
stant negotiation with a powerful congressional GOP. Facing similar frustrations, many of Obama's predecessors fell into the presidential "power trap,"
relying on unilateral powers in the face of entrenched opposition in Congress,
courts, or elsewhere in the executive branch. As I noted in my introduction,
Obama increasingly employs the unilateral tools of the institutional presidency. Their use invites controversy and does not ensure public popularity.
Rather, it emboldens institutional rivals to make Constitutional arguments
against the president and engage in court suits and congressional obstruction
of controversial executive acts. Historically, succumbing to the power trap
means failed reelection or bad second terms. Obama will have to resolve the
tension between his grand ambitions and reduced circumstances after the
2010 elections. How he resolves that tension will set the future course of his
presidency.

Two alternative scenarios, then, emerge for the remainder of Obama's
presidency. Economic recovery could restore his political clout. Successful
management of world tension spots could augment his image as a global

leader. Ongoing demographic change could increase the number of Obama voters. The GOP might nominate a candidate with notable political liabilities. Obama will then have his best chance of fulfilling his transformation dreams.

Or maybe not. Adding up the probabilities of the above scenario makes it a long shot for Obama. It's more likely that Obama's major transformations have already occurred, much as they did for George W. Bush early in his presidency. He will likely continue to face considerable domestic opposition and several intractable international trouble spots. In such a situation, a less directive and more facilitative style, as suggested by John F. Harris and James Hohmann, may suit his presidency best.

We may have seen hints of this in Obama's budget compromises with Republicans in December 2010 and April 2011. The 2011 appointments of Clinton veterans to high White House positions may be another sign of administration moderation. Moderate Democrat William Daley, Clinton's former secretary of commerce, received appointment as White House chief of staff. Bruce Reed, chief domestic policy aide for Clinton, became Vice President Biden's chief of staff. Gene Sperling, chair of Clinton's economic policy council, reassumed that role for Obama.

On Inauguration Day 2009, Barack Obama may have seen FDR in the mirror. For future success, however, that image may need to transform into Bill Clinton—the facilitator—for Obama to have a lengthy and successful presidency.

REFERENCES

Anderson, Nick. 2010. "Obama Could Push Education Reform in Effort to Work with a Divided Congress." *Washington Post*, November 3.

Babington, Charles. 2010. "New Population Count May Complicate Obama 2012 Bid." Associated Press. http://www.timesleader.com/news/Census_may_trip_up_Obama__Dems_in__rsquo_12_12-19-2010.html. Accessed December 20, 2010.

Blake, Aaron. 2010. "GOP Can Draw Nearly Half of New House Districts." *Washington Post*. http://voices.washingtonpost.com/thefix/redistricting/gop-can-draw-nearly-half-of-ne.html. Accessed December 20, 2010.

Bloomberg News. 2010. "Bloomberg News National Poll." December 13. http://media.bloomberg.com/bb/avfile/roCNPdHQmpfc. Accessed December 20, 2010.

DeYoung, Karen. 2010. "Progress in Afghan War Called 'Uneven.'" *Washington Post*, November 23.

Fox News. 2010. "Fox News Poll: Just 29 Percent Think Obama Will Win Reelection." December 16. http://www.foxnews.com/politics/2010/12/16/fox-news-poll-just-percent-voters-think-obama-win-election. Accessed December 20, 2010.

Huffington Post. 2010. "National Job Approval (Independents Only) Pres. Barack Obama." http://www.huffingtonpost.com/2009/03/06/jobapproval-obama-inds _n_726281.html. Accessed December 20, 2010.

Jones, Jeffrey M. 2010. "Obama Approval Slipping among Liberal Democrats." December 16. http://www.gallup.com/poll/145268/Obama-Approval-Slipping -Among-Liberal-Democrats.aspx. Accessed December 20, 2010.

Marrero, Diana. 2004. "Many Younger Cuban-Americans Splitting with Parents on Politics." *Florida Times-Union.* http://www.latinamericanstudies.org/exile/ younger-voters.htm. Accessed December 20, 2010.

POLITICO. 2010. "Power and the People." Poll, November 8–11. http://www.politico .com/static/PPM182_101115_report_nov.html. Accessed December 20, 2010.

Saad, Lydia. 2010. "Conservatives Continue to Outnumber Moderates in 2010." *Gallup.com,* December 16. http://www.gallup.com/poll/145271/conservatives -continue-outnumber-moderates-2010.aspx. Accessed December 20, 2010.

Sears, David O., and Carolyn L. Funk. 1999. "Evidence of the Long-Term Persistence of Adults' Political Predispositions." *Journal of Politics* 61 (1): 1–28.

Washington Post/ABC News. 2010a. "Assessment of Afghanistan War Sours; Six in 10 Say It's 'Not Worth Fighting.'" December 16. http://www.langerresearch.com/ uploads/1119a6%20Afghanistan.pdf. Accessed December 20, 2010.

Washington Post/ABC News. 2010b. "Washington Post-ABC News Poll." December 13. http://www.washingtonpost.com/wp-srv/politics/polls/postpoll_12132010 .html. Accessed December 20, 2010.

Zengerle, Patricia, and Doug Palmer. 2010. "Obama Touts S. Korea Trade Deal, Looks for More." Reuters, December 5. http://www.reuters.com/article/idUSTRE 6B31D220101205. Accessed December 20, 2010.

Index

AAUW. *See* American Association of University Women

abortion: and health-care reform, 34, 89–90; Obama administration and, 86–87, 89; religion and, 80, 82, 84*t*; and women, 193–95

Abramowitz, Alan, 28

academia, and Democratic Party, 125

ACLU. *See* American Civil Liberties Union

administrative positions, federal, women in, 196

Affordable Care Act. *See* health-care reform

Afghanistan, 93, 248–50, 269

African Americans: demographics of, 49; and elections, 52, 53*t*, 81, 82*t*, 189; and family structures, 51; Obama administration and, 201–6; and policy issues, 84*t*; and support for Obama, 94, 95*t*

age: and elections, 52, 53*t*; and party identification, 66

agnostics: and elections of 2008, 81, 82*t*; and policy issues, 84*t*

AIDS, 197–98

Alinsky, Saul, 132–33, 136, 138

Alito, Samuel, 165, 177

al-Qaida, 249

Alter, Jonathan, 3, 128

American Association of University Women (AAUW), 191

American Civil Liberties Union (ACLU), 87

American Recovery and Reinvestment Act, 3. *See also* stimulus package

Americans United, 87

Americans United for Life (AUL), 178

Angle, Sharron, 54

Anglo-Catholics: and elections of 2008, 81, 82*t*; and Obama, 94–95, 95*t*; and policy issues, 84*t*

appointments, presidential, 12; judicial, 163–85; and race, 205–6; religion and, 88–89

Arab Spring, 246–47

Arizona, 203

Asian Americans, and elections, 53*t*

asymmetric warfare: of supporters and opponents of Obama, 121–42; term, 121

atheists: and elections of 2008, 81, 82*t*; and policy issues, 84*t*

AUL. *See* Americans United for Life

auto bailout, 213; and realignment, 25

Axelrod, David, 7, 105, 135

About the Contributors

John J. Coleman is professor and chair of political science at the University of Wisconsin-Madison. His books include *Party Decline in America: Policy, Politics, and the Fiscal State* (Princeton University Press), *The Enduring Debate* (W. W. Norton), and *Understanding American Politics and Government* (Longman). Coleman's research has been published in the *American Political Science Review*, *American Journal of Political Science*, *Journal of Politics*, and other leading political science journals.

James L. Guth is William Rand Kenan Jr. Professor of Political Science at Furman University. His work on religion in American and European politics has appeared in a wide variety of scholarly journals. He is currently conducting research on the role of religion in congressional voting and the influence of religious factors on American public opinion on foreign policy.

John F. Harris is the founder and editor-in-chief of *Politico.com*. He was formerly politics editor of the *Washington Post*, where he received the Aldo Beckman and Gerald R. Ford Presidential Library awards for his White House coverage. His *The Survivor: Bill Clinton in the White House* (Random House 2005) was named a "Notable Book of the Year" by the *New York Times*.

James Hohmann is a national political reporter for *Politico*. Previously he wrote for the *Washington Post, Los Angeles Times'* Washington bureau, the *Dallas Morning News* and the *San Jose Mercury News*. An honors graduate of Stanford University, Hohmann served as editor-in-chief of the *Stanford Daily* and wrote an award-winning thesis about the 1976 Republican primaries and the political ascendancy of Ronald Reagan.

Bertram Johnson is associate professor of political science at Middlebury College. He is co-author (with Paul E. Peterson, Morris Fiorina, and William Mayer) of *The New American Democracy,* 7th edition (Longman 2011). His scholarly articles on intergovernmental relations and campaign finance have been published in such journals as *Urban Affairs Review* and *American Politics Research.*

Richard E. Matland is the Helen Houlahan Rigali Chair in Political Science at Loyola University Chicago. Professor Matland's work crosses several fields, including public policy, comparative politics, and American politics. He has also done work on policy implementation, on school choice programs in the United States, and theories of distributive justice. His work has been published in the *American Journal of Political Science, Journal of Politics, British Journal of Political Science, Comparative Political Studies, Social Science Quarterly,* and *Canadian Journal of Political Science,* as well as many other journals and books.

Nancy Maveety is professor of political science at Tulane University. Her work spans issues in judicial decision making, including the study of concurring behavior on the US Supreme Court. Her 2008 book, *Queen's Court: Judicial Power in the Rehnquist Era* (University of Kansas Press), examined the changing decisional conventions on the contemporary court and traced their legal policy and institutional impact. Her current research continues to address the origin and development of concurring opinion writing and extends this analysis to the decisions of the Roberts Court.

James M. McCormick is professor and chair of the Department of Political Science at Iowa State University. He has authored or edited ten books, including the fifth edition of *American Foreign Policy and Process* (Cengage/ Wadsworth 2010) and the fifth edition of *The Domestic Sources of American Foreign Policy: Insights and Evidence,* co-edited with Eugene R. Wittkopf (Rowman & Littlefield 2008). In addition, he has published more than sixty book chapters and articles in such journals as *World Politics, American Political Science Review, American Journal of Political Science, Journal of Politics, International Studies Quarterly,* and *Legislative Studies Quarterly.*

John J. Pitney Jr. is the Roy P. Crocker Professor of American Politics at Claremont McKenna College. He is the author of *The Art of Political Warfare* (University of Oklahoma Press 2000) and, with Joseph M. Bessette, co-author of *American Government and Politics: Deliberation, Democracy, and Citizenship* (Wadsworth 2011). He teaches courses on Congress, electoral politics, and the mass media, and he has written articles for the *Wall Street Journal, Los Angeles Times,* and the *New York Times* "Room for Debate" blog.

Nicol C. Rae is professor of politics and international relations at Florida International University, Miami, Florida. Rae's research and teaching have focused on Congress, the presidency, and American political parties. His most recent book (co-edited with Timothy Power) is *Exporting Congress: The Influence of the US Congress on World Legislatures* (University of Pittsburgh Press 2006).

Steven E. Schier is Dorothy H. and Edward C. Congdon Professor of Political Science at Carleton College, where he has taught the last thirty years. He is the author or co-author of eight books, the editor of six books, and author of numerous scholarly articles. His books *Panorama of a Presidency: How George W. Bush Acquired and Spent His Political Capital* (M. E. Sharpe 2008) and *The Postmodern President: Bill Clinton's Legacy in U.S. Politics* (Pittsburgh 2000) won "outstanding academic book" awards from *Choice* magazine.

Raymond Tatalovich is professor of political science at Loyola University Chicago. He received his PhD from the University of Chicago, where he studied public policy analysis under Theodore J. Lowi. Among his recent publications is the co-authored volume *The Presidency and Economic Policy* (Rowman & Littlefield 2008).

Andrea L. Walker is a doctoral student in political science at Loyola University Chicago. Her primary interests are American politics, focusing on public policy and urban politics.

John K. White is a professor of politics at the Catholic University of America. He is the author of several books covering political parties and the US presidency. His latest book is titled *Barack Obama's America: How New Conceptions of Race, Family, and Religion Ended the Reagan Era*, published by the University of Michigan Press in 2009.